BICYCLE DIGEST

BY MARK THIFFAULT

DIGEST BOOKS, INC., NORTHFIELD, ILLINOIS

ON THE COVER:
Just a few of the many facets of bicycling are depicted on the cover, compliments of the Schwinn Bicycle Company.

ACKNOWLEDGEMENTS:
The author is indebted to William B. Cordes, owner of Bill's Schwinn Cyclery, 686 N. Tustin Avenue, Orange, California; Steve and Jack Kimble, owners of Newport Cyclery, 2116 Newport Boulevard, Newport Beach, California; American National Red Cross and many others for their assistance in preparation of this book.

CREDITS:
The line drawings in Chapter Eight were reprinted from the American National Red Cross First Aid Textbook, Copyright© 1933, 1937, 1945, 1957, reproduced with permission.

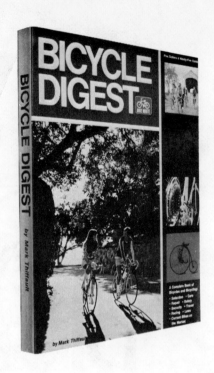

EDITORIAL DIRECTOR:
Jack Lewis

ART DIRECTOR:
Raymond H. Bishop

PHOTO DIRECTOR:
Charles B. Tyler

EDITORIAL ASSISTANT:
Anne S. Tallman

PRODUCTION COORDINATOR:
Judy K. Rader

PUBLISHER:
Sheldon L. Factor

PRODUCED BY:

Charger Productions

ISBN 0-695-80398-0

Library of Congress Catalog Number 72-97510

CONTENTS

INTRODUCTION:

The comeback of the bicycle is a sign of national sanity. In a time when our cities are saturated with automobiles, when noise and air pollution are increasing and the U.S. is running out of petroleum, an upsurge of interest in this best of the self-propelled vehicles is good news for everyone.

In this timely volume Mark Thiffault has marshalled the arguments for a bicycle renaissance in this country. He reminds us that cycling is an exhilarating sport; he and Dr. Paul Dudley White use "jogger's logic" to point out the many health benefits from this form of exercise; he suggests that if we allow the bicycle to perform the full transportation role it is capable of, it can become a vital force in ecological reform and reduce the destructive impact of motor vehicles on our environments; and he gives cyclers many new insights into the contributions these versatile vehicles can make to their lives.

Forty years ago nearly 90 percent of our people walked, bicycled, or rode public transit vehicles to and from their place of work — and only 10 percent commuted in autos. It is tragic that today this ratio is almost exactly reversed. Should there be any wonder, then, that the new bikecology movement is aggressively pointing out what we have lost by our over-reliance on the automobile? It is a well-documented fact that nearly all of our cities are far less livable than they were even a few years ago; and much of the deterioration is attributable to our automania and to the obstacles we have erected to the human-scale movement of people.

At present I am convinced the main impediment to the back-to-the-bicycle movement is the absence of adequate bikeways. If we had safe systems of bikeways and walkways lacking through our cities, I am convinced a majority of our young people would ride bicycles or walk to and from school. Consequently, Mark Thiffault's appeal for better bikeways is a crucial section of this book. We must build thousands of safe and separate bikeways within, around, and between our cities. We must also act to reserve whole streets and parts of streets for bicyclers in every U.S. city. This step (and the providing of adequate parking facilities) would invite millions of school-bound youngsters and work-bound citizens to have fun, keep their bodies healthy, and help combat the rising tide of air and noise pollution. Studies by Denver and other large cities have shown that we could build and set aside such systems of bikeways with as little as 1 or 2 percent of the monies we are spending each year on highways: it is amazing that the leaders of our cities have been so slow to champion such a quiet revolution in "people moving!"

For over a generation, Americans have marched to the suffocating siren song of the combustion engine. We have spent billions to build dangerous, overcrowded highways. Now the energy crisis is trying to tell us that we have pushed our gas-guzzling, stinking combustion machines as far as the limits of our resources will take them. The time has come to turn back to the bicycle, to shank's mare, to clean and convenient modes of public transportation.

Our infatuation with speed and high-horsepower must now be tempered. During the recent debate over the SST aircraft, I made the comment more than once, "It is more important to put the bicycle back in the city than to build the SST." I believe this more today than ever before. If this book makes more Americans "bikecologists" it will serve a vital national purpose — it will help the new generation change its values and its transportation systems and begin once more to put first things first.

March, 1973

Stewart L. Udall
Former Secretary of the Interior

Chapter 1

AMERICA TAKES A GIANT STEP...

IT IS A MOST PECULIAR phenomenon that has occurred in the United States in the last few years. It started merely as a trickle and, not unlike small tributaries rushing together after a pounding summer shower, formed a raging river that has flooded over into nearly every home, whether in a metropolitan suburb or dirt-laned township that progress has, for the most part, left behind. It truly can be termed, in the vernacular of the young, a spontaneous "happening." An American happening.

Most industrial analysts, whose livelihoods are in anticipating and catering to current trends in this country, failed to see the trend. The result, like a Mid-western storm yielding a devastating tornado, was the rebirth of a centuries old mechanical contrivance — the bicycle — interest in which had lain in a state of dormancy for nearly a century.

To glance down any public or private roadway today visibly shows the aftermath of the storm: Streets are choked with spokes, wheels, tires and frames of the latest craze to hit the American shores. People of all ages are feverishly adding more and more bicycles to the same streets. And, at least for the present, the country's prognosis shows no signs of improvement. America is reviving a once-strong love affair with the bicycle.

The conditions that preceded this renewed interest are as varied as the riders who utilize the bicycle. Some, and perhaps the precursors of the current bicycle movement, were college students faced with stiff expenditures that prohibited usage of a car.

Untold snickers and guffaws were directed at this group by other students who firmly believed in the American teenager's dream of saving money enough to buy an automobile. Countless B-rated movies showed, between scenes of kids contorting to popular dance maneuvers of the late Fifties and early Sixties, the star and his clique spending hours tinkering with archaic specimens that later turned into glistening hot rod chariots, about as quickly as Cinderella's pumpkin coach. Bobbie-socked coeds favored the boy with the finest auto, but any auto received immensely more interest for its owner than the kid without one.

This syndrome started to fade when, in the middle Sixties, more emphasis was placed on being individual in lifestyle. While the do-your-own-thing trend was, in itself, a fad that many adopted, it did erase much of the social

persecution aimed at those with odd or eccentric behavior patterns — in this case, the bicyclist. With social acceptance of the young community members, the bicycle continued to grow in popularity.

The environmental issue, which became a source for concern at the turn of the decade, furthered bicycle sales immensely. Individuals received a steady barrage of information on the air and water pollution problems gripping the nation, with the automobile as the armor-hided Public Enemy Number One.

Public outcry reached into legislative chambers, which responded with tougher anti-pollution restrictions for offenders, ranging from the auto to pollution-belching refinery smokestacks. However, by the time implementation of the tougher regulations could be put into effect, lobbyists for the auto and refining industries managed to replace much of the meat with substantial by-products, postponing the measures for a longer period.

Perhaps the crowning blow that jolted many adults into action was notification that many of the national parks — those sanctimonious places where the air is biting and crisp — had air that no longer bit, but stung the eyes and charred the lungs: Pollution had come to the mountain and desert Utopias from the tailpipe of Public Enemy Number One.

More letters to legislators flooded Capitol mailboxes. But the wheels of government often turn frustratingly slowly, with significant progress generally still a long way down the tunnel, not within immediate grasp. This fact alone spurred many to join the swelling ranks of the bicyclist. They wanted to do their part to aid the anti-pollution campaign and it has worked. In mid-1972, reports were filed that graphically showed air pollution levels had decreased in nearly every major United States city. Bicycles no doubt played an important role in this encouraging development.

Industrial psychologists have completed extensive studies of the American workingman, trying to discover some way to increase his productivity and put the United States in a competitive position in the world trade market. They found that many workers felt detached from the overall structure of their employing corporations. The term "plastic" came into being and was attributed to, among other things, the lives these individuals led: Work, sleep, eat, watch the television on Saturday and take the wife and

BACKWARD ....

Defying A Society That Calls For Constant Forward Progression With Nary An Over-The-Shoulder Glance, The Sport Of Bicycling Has Emerged Once Again Into National Prominence.

kids for a stale Sunday drive to complete their existence. It is not hard to feel dissatisfied with this life, to feel removed from all the good things they remembered as kids. There simply had to be more to life than this!

Many looked for a way to get back to nature. Some recognized that, by being encased in their cars on the way to and from work, they couldn't see grass, tree trunks, scampering dogs or smell the flowers.

California collector Jeanne Trepanier poses in costume with solid-iron framed boneshaker, extremely popular after its invention in Paris in 1860. Seat is of iron.

"Why not take the boy's bike to work? It isn't that far to go. What will the neighbors think? What the hell, I'm tired of keeping up with the Joneses; let 'em laugh. Besides, I spend a good hunk of my paycheck for parking, gas and operational expenses, not to mention the time spent bucking traffic and the toll it takes on my outlook." An instant convert to the bicycle fraternity.

America has, for decades, been caught-up in the Sunday Drive Syndrome: Pile the kids in the car on a Sunday afternoon, and spend the day cruising leisurely through the countryside on the outskirts of the city. Stop and have a picnic lunch in an orange grove or on a grassy hillside, play a little ball with the boys and motor back, a new man ready to take on the task of working for another week.

This was a fine idea that recharged the human batteries. Unfortunately, it cannot be done often anymore, for a variety of reasons: The grassy hillsides and sweet-smelling orange groves have almost totally disappeared, plowed and graded to make room for more homesites. The remaining hills almost are totally posted against trespassers by owners tired of cleaning up left-behind waste matter.

Families have to travel farther from their homes in search of such an area, often farther than is realistically possible without defeating the purpose of the drive. The death blow in many cases is that the family has to buck traffic for miles, against cars filled with people that have the same ideas, and it doesn't take much for a harried father to disdain from taking the outing in the future.

So what happens to families on the weekend? Many tend to chores around the house, gardening, or watch the television. To take the kids down to the park for a ball game is an exercise in futility, for the parks are jammed with other families to the extent that running any distance chasing a fly ball would result in trampled sunbathers or sleepers. The seashore, if you're located near the coast, is the same story.

So what can families do together on weekends to conserve the spirit of family unity? More and more of these individuals are rediscovering the bicycle and pedaling for their Sunday drives. It serves to charge the batteries, and put the rider again in contact with his environment. Through family cycling, perhaps there will not be another lost generation, unable to relate to parents that always worked but never played.

Americans have become increasingly more conscious of their physical condition. Many fads arrived, lingered and, for the most part, passed on into oblivion. Diets are a drag and many forms of exercise, such as jogging, often did not win the support or prescription of medical authorities for their patients. And numerous joggers, while initially turned-on by the idea, grew rapidly apathetic about the seemingly little progress made for the amount of effort expended. It took a stout heart or deranged mind to don the sweatsuit atop aching leg muscles and charge off. It also was rather boring, and the jogger never appreciated the area through which he passed, but rather concentrated on plopping one foot in front of the other and getting back to a warm, soaking tub.

Evidently, many physical cultists felt that fun was missing from previous forms of exercise. Many doctors preached the conditioning doctrine of the bicycle and these ex-joggers discovered that cycling mixed the best of both worlds: Plenty of exercise and fun to boot!

It has been the trend since automobiles came on the American market, that they continue to increase in cost with each passing year. Inflation, recession, cost of materials and hourly wage increases in the auto industry have

One of the earliest high wheelers ever made, this is fashioned totally of wood, with exception of leather-covered saddle. Its age is unknown.

caused this price rise. Understanding the cause does not lessen the effect this has on the pocketbook, however, and some individuals began seeking other means of transport to replace the costly second vehicle they could not afford.

In the majority of households, the working male utilizes the car in getting to work, which leaves the housewife without means of zipping around on the errands that occupy a goodly share of her working day. In areas where some form of rapid transit is present, the lack of a second car is no problem. But there are plenty of shopping trips, etc., that don't require the usage of a bus or train, but are too inordinately far to walk and return carrying packages. And shops that offer free delivery are almost gone completely.

The introduction of the bicycle as a means for overcoming the housewife's transportation problem has solved the dilemma in a most admirable manner. Despite the initial outlay for such a vehicle, the only extra expense is for a carrier or basket of some sort, to leave both hands free for steering. Perhaps, for the second time, the bicycle is lending a hand in the liberation of women.

The second time? To uncover the first, one must trace the history of the bicycle, which has had such a profound effect on the world. Looking back, it is found that, like most inventions of permanence, the bicycle's history is clouded in mystery and no little amount of confusion. The first known example of a bicycle, or something similar at least in components, was used in Egypt. Hieroglyphics depict a two-wheeled vehicle, with the wheels joined together much resembling a scooter, which was ridden by Egyptians, but whether for transportation or entertainment is undecided.

While it may be erroneous to classify them as forerunners of the bicycle, two forms of individual mechanical propulsion were invented and used as early as 1640. The creations in question much resembled the modern-day wheelchair. The materials used in the components probably were extremely crude, which could explain why there is but passing mention of them in history books.

Clouds begin to gather over the credibility horizon near the end of the 1700s, as authors dispute the inventor of the bicycle further. Some claim that a Frenchman named de Sivrac produced the closest resemblance to the bicycle we know to date, although it would hardly be recognizable as such today.

The invention, which others claim de Sivrac designed but never built, consisted of a stationary wooden bar that had two equal-sized wooden wheels attached at both ends, with a leather saddle of sorts in the middle. The rider, who actually did more pushing and running than riding, would straddle the bar, place his hands on an immobile handlebar, then push his celerifere, as it came to be known, until sufficient speed had been attained to allow him to lift his feet and coast.

Due to the design of the handlebars, which would not turn in either direction, it can be speculated that the rider never made a great lot of progress in any given direction before having to stop for a course correction. The roads of the day also were used by teams of horses and coaches, and the cyclist most surely had to yield the right of way, which cut his speed and maneuverability down considerably.

Why this crude mechanism captured the interest of the populace of the period is a mystery, as it would appear that better time, with considerably less effort, could be made by pressing ahead on foot. Uphill travel on the celerifere must have been extremely difficult, as any who have endeavored to push a modern bicycle up a hill while straddling the

The Star bicycle had position of the wheels swapped, to reduce the chance of taking headers, with levers rather than pedals for propulsion. It didn't last.

The penny-farthing (below right) dominated the industry until advent of the safety bicycle. Mounting was difficult, facilitated by step-up, as seen below.

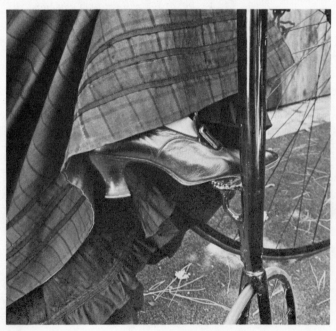

center bar will testify.

Downhill traveling, on the other hand, must have been extremely exciting and possibly similar to a kamikaze raid. Combine the factors of no steering capabilities, no brakes and extremely rutted, rough roads, and the result is a challenge the likes of which is unknown today. Add to these factors the possibility of, upon hitting a deep rut, being jostled into the air, only to alight crotch-first on the wooden support bar, and all the ingredients are present to spur inventors toward rapid refinement of the bicycle!

Impressive and major improvements of the celerifere were quick in coming. A German, Baron Karl Drais von Sauerbronn, combined a light, sturdy frame with the front wheel fitted in a swiveling fork that resulted in the steerable Draisienne or Draisine, in the years between 1816 and 1818. An Englishman named Dennis Johnson realized that further improvements could be made to the Draisine, which included a padded armrest, adjustable and more-padded saddle, and different styled handlebars. Johnson then introduced the Draisine into England, where it became known as the "dandy horse," because young English bachelors, most quite wealthy and known as dandies, utilized the Draisine in riding academies and on the rutted roads. The dandy horse also was termed the "hobby horse" or "pedestrian curricle." By whatever name, it definitely was in vogue in 1818.

There still remained the problem of having to push the dandy horse which, as mentioned previously, was no mean chore up steep hillocks. A young Scot, Kirkpatrick MacMillan of Dumfries, visualized a means of eliminating this physical handicap and, in 1840, introduced a model that was propelled by levers connected with cranks to the back wheel.

The "velocipede" was powered by a cyclist who would push the levers up and down. He included fairly modern handlebars and a more-padded seat, although his efforts did not bring sweeping changes to the biking world. Twenty years later, however, a Frenchman did.

In the Paris velocipede manufactory of Pierre Michaux, either Michaux or an employee, Pierre Lallement, put two pedals on the front axle. As to which Frenchman actually designed the refinement is unknown, but Michaux got the credit in all but a few cases.

Michaux incorporated a heavy wooden frame with rather large, wooden wheels with spokes of the same material. The surface of the wheel that contacted the road was covered with a thin strip of metal. It appears that, through the nickname affixed to the velocipede, the "boneshakers" weren't exactly a joy to ride. Michaux later suspended the seat slightly higher than the frame, which improved performance somewhat. It still was a bear to ride, as the saddle was located behind rather than above the pedals. This resulted in much pulling with the arms to aid the leg work. It was a big seller in the United States and England.

The next step in the progression of the bicycle was completion of a tubular metal frame, invented by an American named Madison in 1867. Perhaps the French could have furthered their contributions to the bicycle industry with the tubular frame, but the Franco-Prussian War began just a couple of years later, and England took over as the inventive leader.

One Englishman, James Starley, made the first attempt at improving the distance-traveled-versus-revolutions-pedaled problem, by altering the frame and affixing a mammoth front wheel. Properly named the Ariel, it commonly was known as the "penny-farthing" after

As seen in these two views, the lever system employed on some penny-farthings was quite complicated, and worked surprisingly well. However, pedals were "in."

The tricycle, much reformed from its early example shown here, is lasting invention from the age of the Ariel.

coinage in use at the time. The English penny was quite large, while the farthing was much smaller.

Starley realized the problem of difficult pedaling and moved the seat on his "high wheeler" more forward, so that the legs actually pushed downward, rather than angling forward. He also included a gearing system that utilized two different speeds, another major breakthrough.

To demonstrate the practicality of the invention, Starley and a partner rode two of the bicycles, later known as "ordinaries," from their shop in Coventry to London, a ninety-six-mile stint, in one day. As modern cyclists will attest, this is quite an accomplishment, even using modern equipment.

Along the route, Starley's partner, William Hillman, became the first of many ordinary riders to "take a header," a problem that would continue to plague the ordinary throughout its existence.

Due to the mammoth front wheel, striking any sizeable obstruction would result in the rider toppling over the handlebars, head-first into the roadway. While no statistics on injuries received while operating this invention are available, it seems safe to assume that scrapes were commonplace, and perhaps even a few fatalities could be attributed

to the ordinary.

Perhaps it was the thrill of the unknown that drew many riders into the ordinary's ranks and the bike dominated the cycling scene for nearly twenty years. Its instability led to the design and construction of other types of bicycles — none of which were particularly successful — like the Star.

This bicycle completely reversed the design of the ordinary, substituting the smaller wheel in place of the high front wheel on the latter, and seating the rider atop the larger rear wheel. Both pedal and lever-propelled models were introduced, but most riders clung tenaciously to their ordinaries.

One major invention that resulted from the instability of the penny-farthing, which remains with us today, is the tricycle. The first models were understandably crude, but the female public adopted them readily. In fact, Queen Victoria ordered one in 1881, but whether she ever used it is a mystery.

In 1876, an Englishman named Lawson and an American named Pope combined talents and designs to produce the first "safety" bicycle, after which current bicycles are patterned. The rider was positioned between wheels of equal size and rotated pedals connected via chain and sprocket to the rear wheel. This invention, patterned in the

Another form of tricycle, propelled by pulling levers toward the operator and steered with the feet, never found much favor with riders. It carried one person.

Origin of the bicycle below is a mystery, as is its inventor. The interesting feature of this model is that, when turned, the center of the bike swivels!

diamond metal frame we have today, overnight made other bicycles obsolete. Mass-production of the Rover safety bike was conducted at the factory owned by James Kemp Starley, nephew of the Ariel builder.

Other refinements came into being in the late 1800s, but one of which was the introduction of tangential spoking. The light metal spokes made the wheels lighter and stronger, a definite plus as far as riders were concerned.

Another was the manufacture of rubber tires. When vulcanization of rubber was perfected accidentally by a down-and-out Charles Goodyear in the late 1830s, upon dropping a blob of India rubber mixed with sulfur on a hot stove, the stage was set for further improvement of the bicycle, although the manufacture of the tire was fifty years later in coming.

A gentleman by the name of Thomson first hit upon the idea of filling a hollow rubber tube with air and affixing it to the rim of a bicycle as early as 1845, but he died without trying his idea. Indeed, the idea was almost forgotten, until John Boyd Dunlop placed a garden hose around the rim of a wheel, sealed the ends and filled it with air. He later made millions, upon perfecting the present-day combination of inner tube and treaded outer casing in 1889.

Another major improvement in the bicycle that ultimately assisted the development of other vehicles was the introduction of ball bearings.

Patented in their original form by a Frenchman named Cardinet in 1802, they underwent further improvements by Lechner in 1898 and then were perfected by Wingquist in 1907. Ball bearings minimized the effort needed to propel the bicycle, and that development has stayed with us up to the present time.

These were the developments that led to the safety

bicycle's widespread use throughout the world, especially in the United States, in the 1890s. Other refinements have appeared over the years, which include different metals for frames and the speed-changing derailleur. But even without these advancements, the bicycle was and is capable of long, practical use.

The impact the bicycle had on the world is staggering. It became a main means for transportation and was the fastest vehicle on the road in the late 1800s. As the numbers of cyclists increased, so did their demands for better roads which, unbeknownst to them, eventually would lead to the decline in popularity of the bicycle in favor of the automobile.

At the time, many cyclists banded together to form cycling clubs, the most famous and still-surviving of which is the League of American Wheelmen. Then, even as now, bicyclists rediscovered the countryside that formerly was bypassed with the arrival of the railroad. They pressured legislators to improve the quality of the country roads, along with homing-in on lodging houses and inns on the routes patronizing only those which met with satisfactory standards.

Tricycles, especially tandem side-by-side models fitted with acetylene or oil lamps for night riding, caused great concern among the populace in the grip of Victorian ethic. Many were the courting couples who would mount the tandem seats for a leisurely roll through the countryside, unchaperoned. Looking at the situation through today's permissive perspective, it seems that the arrangement should have caused no consternation, as both hands of both riders were needed to steer the bicycle, while both pedaled. The closest the couple could get to one another while on

Continued on page 23

13

The frame, handlebars and rims of the bicycle at right were made of hickory, which weathered well. Note the star-shaped frame, pedals.

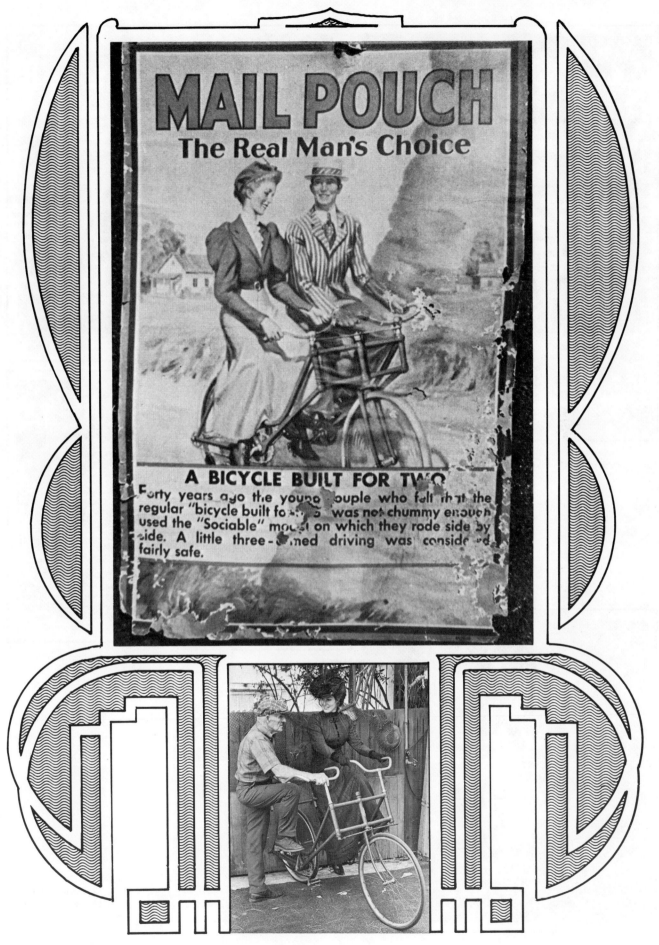

These children's tricycles employed various steering, propulsion systems, none of which worked too well. All are antiques of considerable value.

The cam-driven bicycle at left was valued at $2,500 in 1972. Few were made, but this still works well.

The types of chain used on the safety bicycle models varied greatly, as did the sprockets. However, soon a standard size was established and used on most types.

Braking systems on high wheelers were primitive, simply clamping metal surface atop the wheel.

Traditional tandem, below, saw wide use during Gay Nineties, is similar in design to modern versions.

from the minds of men......

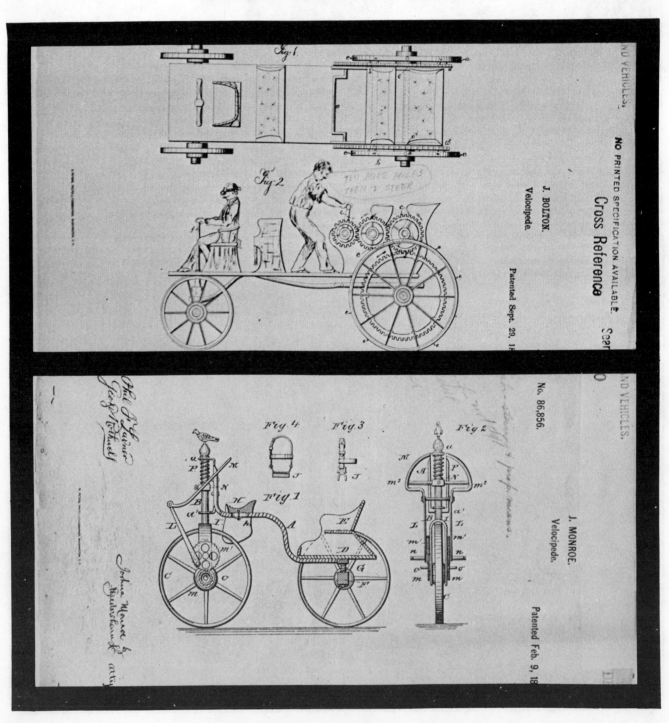

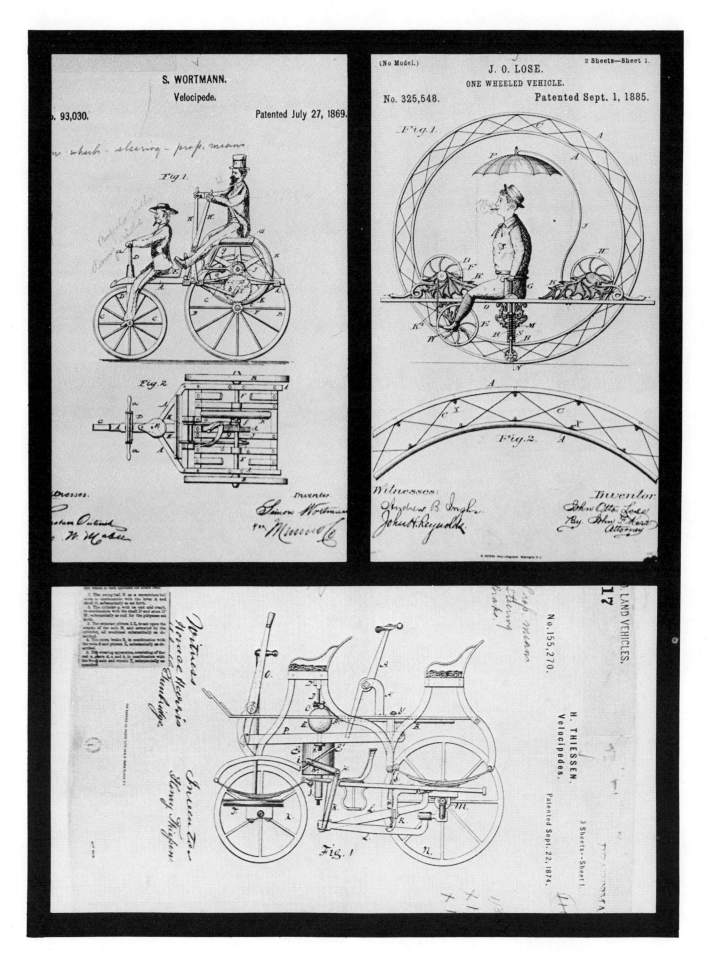

S. WORTMANN.

Velocipede.

No. 93,030.

Patented July 27, 1869.

(No Model.)

J. O. LOSE.

ONE WHEELED VEHICLE.

No. 325,548.

Patented Sept. 1, 1885.

2 Sheets—Sheet 1.

H. THIESSEN.

Velocipedes.

No. 155,270.

Patented Sept. 22, 1874.

3 Sheets—Sheet 1.

LAND VEHICLES.

17

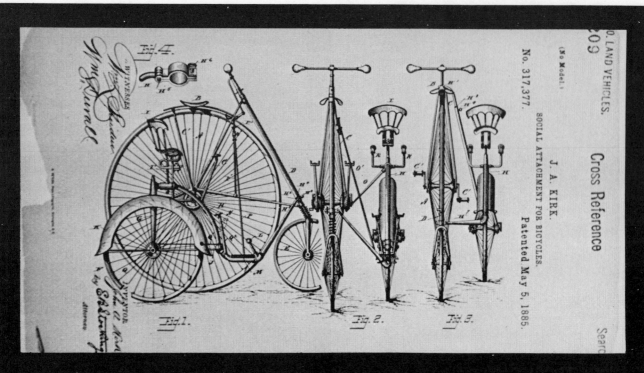

(No Model.)

No. 317,377.

J. A. KIRK.
SOCIAL ATTACHMENT FOR BICYCLES.
Patented May 5, 1885.

Fig.4.

Fig.1.   Fig. 2.   Fig. 3.

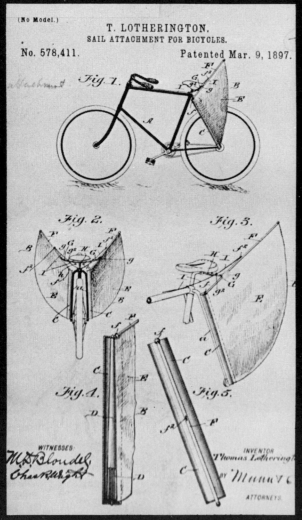

(No Model.)

T. LOTHERINGTON.
SAIL ATTACHMENT FOR BICYCLES.

No. 578,411.   Patented Mar. 9, 1897.

Fig. 1.

Fig. 2.   Fig. 3.

Fig. 4.   Fig. 5.

WITNESSES:

INVENTOR
Thomas Lotherington
BY Munn & Co.
ATTORNEYS.

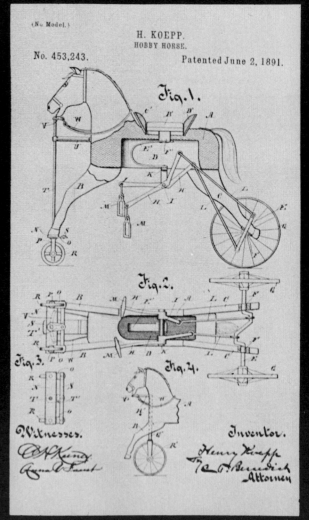

(No Model.)

H. KOEPP.
HOBBY HORSE.

No. 453,243.   Patented June 2, 1891.

Fig. 1.

Fig. 2.

Fig. 3.   Fig. 4.

Witnesses.   Inventor.

Henry Koepp
Attorney.

20

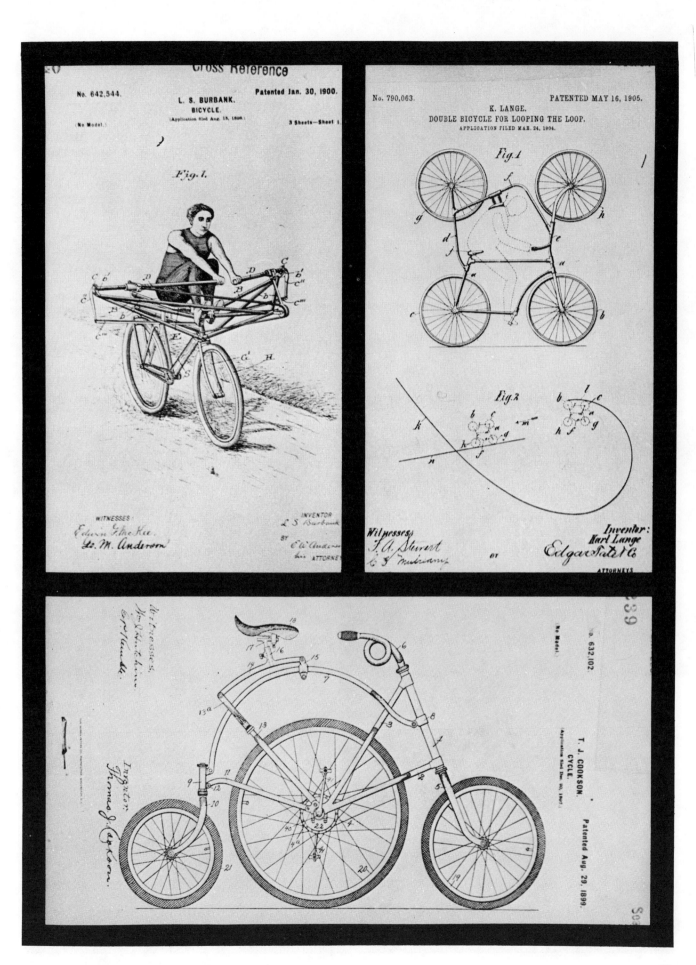

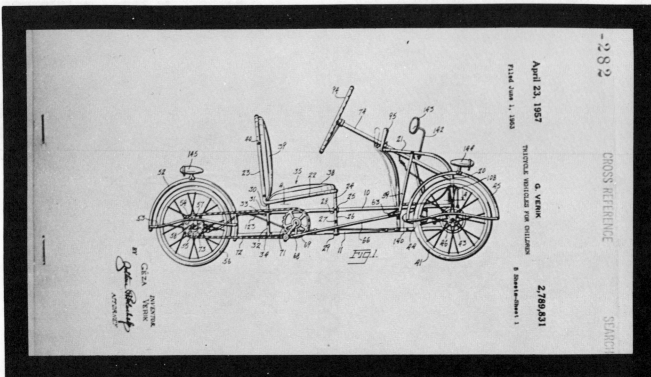

April 23, 1957   G. VERIK   2,789,831

TRICYCLE VEHICLES FOR CHILDREN

Filed June 1, 1963   2 Sheets-Sheet 1

INVENTOR
GÉZA VERIK
BY
ATTORNEY

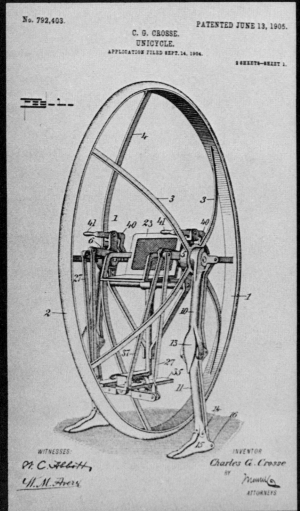

No. 792,403.   PATENTED JUNE 13, 1905.

C. G. CROSSE.
UNICYCLE.
APPLICATION FILED SEPT. 14, 1904.

2 SHEETS-SHEET 1.

WITNESSES:

INVENTOR
Charles G. Crosse
BY
ATTORNEYS

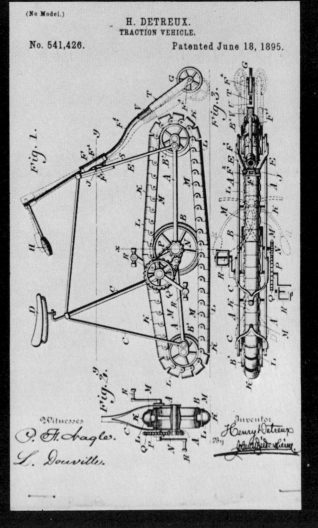

(No Model.)

H. DETREUX.
TRACTION VEHICLE.

No. 541,426.   Patented June 18, 1895.

Fig. 1.

Fig. 3.

Fig. 2.

Witnesses

Inventor
Henry Detreux

Handyman Floyd Yuille, 60, uses standard bicycle with additions in making his rounds, averaging 20 miles per day (right). Ecological impact of the bicycle is seen by numerous "Eco-Plates" available to bike riders.

Continued from page 13

the bicycle was elbow-rubbing distance. If the bike had a flat, though...

As claimed previously, the bicycle was utilized for the liberation or, as was termed in those days, emancipation of the fairer sex near the turn of the century. Women's fashions during this period were dresses of floor-length, tresses and other flesh-concealing apparel, and it was considered quite shocking to expose an ankle to male scrutiny. These fashions conflicted with the attire needed to ride a safety bicycle, which was well suited for female riders; the choice was to be left behind or hike up the skirts and ride along. Judging from current fashions, the outcome, − delightedly then, as now − is blissfully obvious, and the change can be credited to the bicycle's popularity.

One of the best-known advocates of women's rights, an American dressmaker and soap-boxer named Amelia Jenks Bloomer − after whom a well known article of clothing was named − changed the fashion world with her bloomers, a type of loose trousers originally ankle length. It was not long before the length shortened, a benefit girl-watching males of today can attribute to the bicycle.

The bicycle also can be credited with helping other inventions of major worldly importance come into being. Some off-hand examples would be the airplane, which uses ball bearings and rubber tires, as does the automobile. Bicycle gearing was incorporated in theory by automotive manufactuers; the lights on the bicycles lead to the same feature being provided on the auto, although it was refined for the latter − the list could go on and on.

Shortly after the turn of the century, the bicycle began to lose some of its appeal to the newly-created automobile. As affluent Americans purchased the car, the bicycle began collecting rust in the barn or garage, or was delegated to the children. The war years of 1914-18 saw a revival of the bike in Europe but, for all practical purposes, popularity again plunged at its conclusion.

In the heyday of the Roaring Twenties, the bike's popularity remained lost until the stock market crash of 1929. Operation of an automobile was too costly in many instances and the bicycle's popularity was revived. It stayed on as a viable means of transport until economic conditions improved enough to allow resumption of auto operation.

During the Second World War, when all manufacturing outlets were geared toward war production, the bicycle again came out of obscurity. In Europe and England, where bombing had made many roads impassable for vehicular traffic, the bicycle was used with great effect. Many troops, both Axis and Allied, used bicycles when weary legs threatened to give out, and thus it continued until the end of hostilities.

With the surge of returning servicemen at the end of the war, America quickly grew in strength, prosperity and babies, and the bicycle was delegated to the latter. Now, however, those same parents have the leisure time, an interest in human existence and physical fitness, and the bicycle again has rolled into the mainstream of America. The bicycle boom has been going on for several years, which proves that it is not yet another of the many fads for which America is famous.

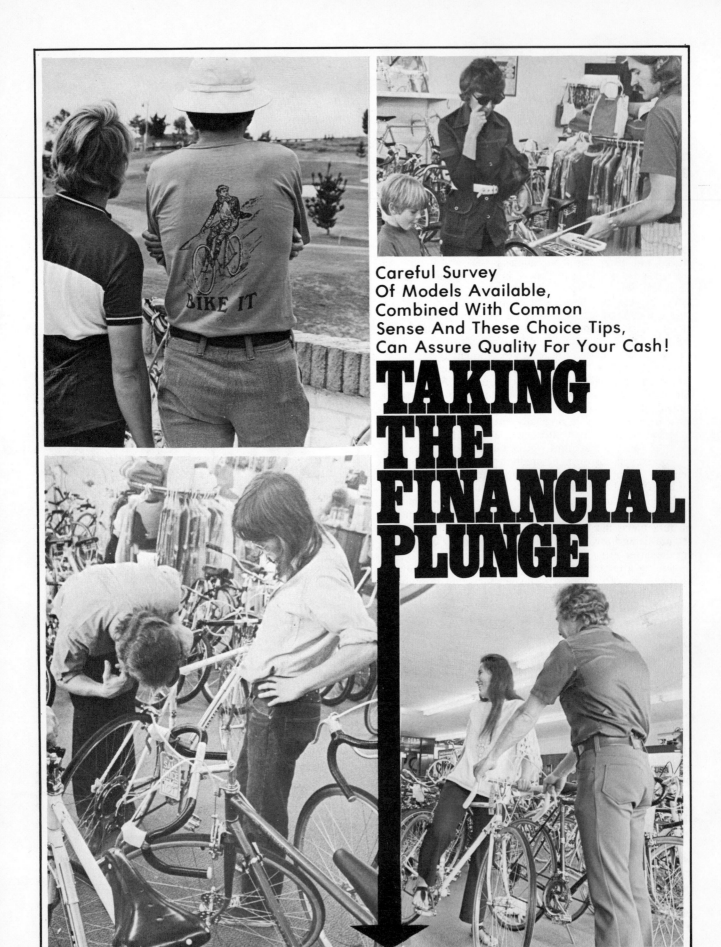

Careful Survey
Of Models Available,
Combined With Common
Sense And These Choice Tips,
Can Assure Quality For Your Cash!

TAKING THE FINANCIAL PLUNGE

N Chapter 2

NOT LONG AGO, I AMBLED into a favorite bicycle dealership in Southern California to examine new models and accessories. The shop was in its usual state, chaotic with frenzied activity: Telephones constantly ringing, prospective customers pushing aside the swinging glass doors to check out models to purchase, and present owners wheeling bikes into the service department for repairs.

The manager and a couple of assistants barely could handle the flow of people. The scene truly was reminiscent of a special sale in a bargain basement, with only the jostling and grabbing absent. It was hard to believe that the bicycle was the cause of all this commotion.

In the course of the visit, a thirtyish gentleman strode in, pointed to a 10-speed bicycle occupying space in the show-

Proper frame fit is one of the most important factors involved in the purchase of a bicycle. With shoes off, top tube should reach within an inch of the groin.

room and claimed that he wanted to take it home that day.

The dealer, after glancing at the man's five-foot, four-inch frame, noticed that the top tube of the bicycle would strike the man considerably higher than it should; enough to be uncomfortable and dangerous to ride. He pointed out the fact that the bicycle was not the customer's size and perhaps he should look at some different models.

The gent piped up and asked, "They come in different sizes? The last bike I had, when I was a kid, came in one size only. I didn't know they came in different sizes."

This graphically illustrates the problems facing dealers — and riders — of the current bicycle generation. Most previously were affiliated solely with the balloon-tired behemoth of one-speed fame and are quite unprepared for the selection available to them upon arrival at any particular bicycle shop. For that reason, a goodly percentage of the ten and a half million American bicycle buyers of 1972 got less than they had bargained for: The fun of cycling forever was to be missing from their riding.

After realizing that, for whatever reason, it simply is impossible to live without a bicycle, there are several factors to keep in mind before charging off to the nearest dealer's and laying down that cold cash. First on the list of soul-searching items is, strangely enough, whether you still can ride a bicycle and live to enjoy it!

It is a sad but true fact that, on the average, the older Americans get, the lazier we get. Age usually is accompanied by affluence, which is followed by a fine spare tire of

fat around the middle.

To make the transition from practially zero physical activity to pedaling a bicycle over even a level course, the rider must be ready for sore, cramped legs, fiery lungs, a beet-red face, and probably a sore posterior. Many an older rider with unquestionable desire has stored his bicycle deep in the dark corner of the garage after only one such ordeal and he's out the money spent for the bicycle.

It is true that a great portion of the over-thirty-five populace is taking to the bicycle for reasons of physical conditioning, which has gained the approval of physicians and even the President's Council on Physical Fitness.

It may be a good idea, however, for riders wishing to rejoin the pedal parade to borrow a bicycle from a friend and take a trial run or two before rushing out and buying their own bicycle. It is not advisable to use a 10-speed for the initial run, for the 10-speed is somewhat different in design and construction than the type utilized some years before. It could result in premature rejection of the sport or possible injury through unfamiliarity.

A solid, ancient balloon tire model will do the trick. It is strongly recommended that the bicycle not be larger than the rider needs, while it may be smaller. By fit, which will be explained in greater detail later, it is meant that the top tube — on a boy's model — should reach to nearly an inch short of the groin with the shoes removed.

As the first rides probably will be shaky, the rider often is inclined to remove both feet from the pedals upon stopping. With a bicycle that's smaller than necessary, this top tube will not come close to contacting the groin area. However, should this be attempted with a too-large bicycle, the top tube definitely will contact the tender location.

Cyclists suffering from this malady often resemble jet pilots ejecting from their stricken aircraft and attitudes toward cycling may again lose favor.

While there are few individuals around these days who never have ridden a bicycle at some point during their lives, even these are showing more than casual interest in the bicycle movement. For this group, a short instruction course is in order, which may include factors long forgotten by cyclists of a previous era.

The proper learning grounds for a prospective cyclist should be free of all traffic and pedestrian hazards, so as to minimize the possibility of accidents and injury. Places such as a shopping center parking lot, deserted schoolyard or infrequently automobile trafficked street are best, provided they have a slight slope present. The slight incline will serve to show different conditions and muscle requirements needed during travel on city or suburban streets.

Upon arriving at the location, put the kickstand down or, if the bicycle has no kickstand, lean it against a light-post or building and take a fast check of its parts and operational procedure. Unlike a car, which affords some protection should a defective part influence its function adversely, the bicycle offers little protection, so it behooves the rider to assure his machine is in proper and safe working condition.

Assuming you have a one-speed, notice first the front tire, which should be in good condition with no exposure-caused cracks. Next, check the rim for roundness by spinning the tire and watching for any wobbles. Check to assure all the spokes are seated and not hanging loosely. Notice the position of the valve stem, which protrudes from the rim and is used to inflate the tube. It should be perpendicular to the rim, not angled in any fashion. To hit a good

Lycia Adams, right, demonstrates the proper way to check wheel alignment, by picking up the bike and spinning the wheel. If it does not spin evenly or wobbles, the rim may be out of round.

When checking the wheels, give the spokes a twang, to check for loose ones. They can be tightened easily.

The valve stem should be exactly perpendicular to the rim, like the one below. If angled, it could be cut, which results in a flat tire.

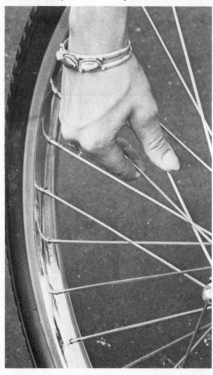

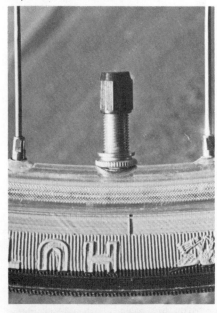

Discover if the cones are loose by trying to wiggle the wheel while holding the bars, as seen below left.

bump could cause a cut in this valve stem if it isn't straight up, resulting in a flat and possible injury.

Checking the front fork, make sure that the axle nuts are tight, as you don't want the wheel falling off while riding. Grabbing the handlebars, try to wiggle the front tire to see if it is loose. If it wiggles at all, the cones that provide alignment for the wheel are loose. It can be fixed but, if you are a newcomer to the bicycle, leave repairs until later.

Next, check the handlebars and make sure they are not loose. Check the frame for obvious cracks — which are extremely unlikely on the bicycle of current manufacture, due to the heavy grade steel used in construction — as you work back to the sprocket and chain.

The chain should be oiled and not rusty, and the sprocket should have no teeth missing. If the bicycle doesn't have a chainguard, either tape your right pants cuff tightly around your ankle or wear bermuda shorts. The chain has a special knack of pulling a loose cuff into the sprocket, which ruins the former and makes further pedaling a weird ordeal.

Should this happen, you will be forced to dismount, lean on the left leg and, hopping as best you can while rolling the bicycle forward, wait until the sprocket revolves and disgorges the cuff — or you can cut if off. Either remedy results in the ruin of a pair of slacks.

Examine the seat and assure that adjustment is tight and it won't slip under your weight. It is advisable to use a softly padded saddle initially — not the hard leather types found on 10-speeds — as this affords more comfort. Besides, it is difficult to learn to ride with your attention focused on a set of screaming buttocks.

Both fenders, if the bicycle has them, should be firm and

Pushing downwards on the handlebars is the best way to check for a loose tube, which could be unsafe (left).

While frame cracks are unlikely on a one-speed bicycle, periodic checks should be held to assure this fact.

To promote both sprocket and chain life, a light coat of oil should be applied to the chain often. Besides preventing rust, which weakens the chain, it cuts noise.

Make sure the fenders on your bike are tight, or the jangling noise will detract from enjoyment of your ride. Tighten all bolts periodically.

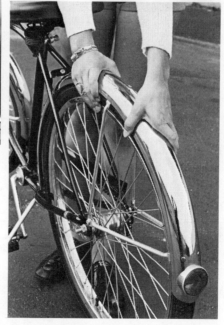

not jangling. Check the rear tire and rim as you did the front, then flip up the kickstand and wheel the bicycle forward slowly. You will note that the pedals, which should be tightly affixed to the sprocket cranks and in good condition, revolve as the wheels turn.

You probably are wondering how to stop this hunk of iron: Most probably, the bicycle is fitted with a coaster brake, which engages the rear tire when backward pressure is applied to the pedals. As with an automobile, the rear brake should not be applied with too strenuous a force, as the bike will skid and result in excessive tire wear. Rather, an even amount of pressure should be applied to the brake, so that the bicycle will stop in a smooth fashion.

Now that you've become familiar with the working

mechanisms of this spoked steed, it's time to climb aboard and explore the mysteries of riding it. As most bicycle riders mount from the left side, as the machine and rider are facing in the same direction, position yourself on the left side of the bicycle. Before endeavoring to pedal, you might try throwing your leg over the frame, sitting on the seat, then coasting for a short distance. This serves to acquaint the novice with the balance necessary to properly ride the bicycle.

Once this has been achieved satisfactorily, the rider should dismount and face the machine from the left side, then roll the bicycle until the right-hand pedal — that on the opposite side — is in its uppermost position.

Then, swinging the right leg up and over the saddle, place the ball of the right foot — the meaty section directly behind your toes — on the right pedal. You naturally will close the distance to the bicycle with your body, as not to would result in physical discomfort — and a leaning bicycle.

With this step completed, push the bike forward with the left foot, almost like pushing a scooter, while changing the body weight to the right foot and pushing the pedal downwards. In the process of pushing off and pumping the pedal down, the body will be drawn up slightly over the top tube. Quickly place the ball of the left foot on the left pedal as it revolves to the top of its stroke; transfer the weight from the right leg to the left, continue pedaling and plunk down on the saddle. This seems complicated, but will occur naturally.

Chances are that the first ride will cover a distance in the vicinity of ten feet, before the bicycle becomes off-balance and the rider is forced to brake and put a foot on the ground to avoid a tumble. This is normal, and the process should be repeated. By grasping the bars and steering, it soon becomes easy to direct the bicycle while pedaling for quite a distance. A note of caution: As the bicycle will be moving slowly, don't endeavor to turn sharply in either direction, as the bike probably will fall over in the chosen direction.

In your enthusiasm, don't overdo it on your maiden voyage. While the consequences won't be apparent immediately, they certainly will make their presence known in the morning, when you try to swing your legs out over the side of the bed, only to discover that someone has cast them in plaster or tied lead weights to your ankles during the night. Muscles that haven't been used for a long period take time to become conditioned to doing such labor. But you'll eventually feel the better for it, regardless of first impressions.

In picking your riding location, especially for the first couple of months, don't include a specific area that has steep hills. While they may be exciting to traverse from a downhill angle, they can be murderous on the return trip. Also, try to avoid areas with shrubs from which ankle-biting dogs erupt: Your leisurely ride could turn out to be a match sprint, with much more at stake than an Olympic Gold Medal!

An important part of riding the bicycle is to ride it properly, so that all parts of the body will be working in cooperation with the others and sharing in the conditioning exercise. In the case of the one-speed bicycle, there isn't a great deal of total conditioning that can be derived from its usage. But in the case of the 10-speed, which is the pride and joy of the current bicycle movement, much can be done to assure total overall conditioning; the model scientifically was designed for this purpose. And, not surprisingly, the 10-speed rider is the one who suffers most from improper cycling position.

A great number of cyclists place the arch of the foot over the pedals while riding and this one factor alone cuts riding time immensely through efficiency loss. This is one of the reasons that steel toe clips and leather straps came into being, and they work exceptionally well.

These clips, affixed to the front part of the pedals, are designed so that only the toes will fit into them, resulting in the ball of the foot being placed directly over the pedal. Some pedals have, in addition to these clips, straps that further secure the feet in place and look much like stirrups on a saddle.

Photo sequence below depicts proper beginner's form: Pushing off and down on right pedal (far left), raising left foot as pedal comes to top of stroke (center), then pushing left pedal downwards. It is deceptively easy.

If the bicycle is equipped with toe clips, the rider probably by now is wondering how he is going to get his feet on the pedals while keeping the machine moving. There is an art to this technique that should be mastered before hitting a stop light in the city and trying to practice with cars zipping past.

The proper way is to revolve the pedals until the right-hand one is uppermost. Get the foot properly into this clip and strap, then push off with the left leg, pumping the right pedal downwards at the same time.

At the bottom of this stroke, hold the pedals in position with the left pedal uppermost and freewheel while pulling yourself upwards with the handlebars. Then, simply affix the left foot in the toe clip, continue pedaling and speed on your way.

It is advisable that, when riding in areas where frequent stops due to signal lights or stop signs are mandatory, only one foot be strapped in. This leaves one foot that, while clipped in, is able to be pulled free to steady the bicycle upon stopping. Simply repeat the foot-mounting procedure upon continuing.

While pedaling, most people tend to apply pressure on the downward strokes, while unconsciously relaxing that leg on the upstroke, when the other leg is applying downward pressure. In itself, this act results in much efficiency loss and riders tend to tire much more rapidly than if they applied pressure on the pedal through its entire revolution. The toe clips aid in this effort, for the rider can exert a force against them and thereby help bring the pedal around.

Improper foot position is shown at top right, with arch of the foot over pedal. The ball of the foot (center) is correct. Toe clips (below right) assure this position.

From a standing start, getting foot in toe clip is hard and should be practiced away from traffic (below). In but a few tries, the cyclist can master the trick.

Derailleur operation is better understood after viewing demonstrator.

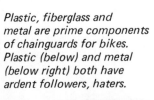

Front changer engaged, the chain begins to slip to the second chainwheel.

Plastic, fiberglass and metal are prime components of chainguards for bikes. Plastic (below) and metal (below right) both have ardent followers, haters.

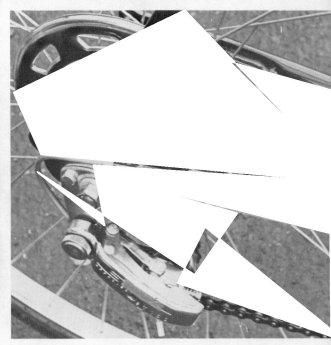

This divides the work equally and smoothly between the legs, and results in enhanced endurance.

Another fault most riders commit is not adopting a rhythm in their cycling. Instead, they will pedal rapidly for a short distance, tire, then resume pedaling ferociously. A cyclist can pedal much faster, easier and longer by keeping a steady pace at all times, shifting to higher or lower gear ratios when this is deemed appropriate.

The gearing mechanisms on a 5, 10 or 15-speed bicycle are complicated appearing at first and truly take some getting used to. Unlike an automobile with a manual shifting stick, there are no specific notches that the shifters engage, which is why shifting takes practice.

In most cases, the right-hand shifter dictates performance of the rear sprockets, while the left-hand shifter affects the front sprockets on the chainwheel. They sometimes are reversed on specific models, whereupon the rider adapts to that system prevalent on his bicycle.

For practice purposes, it again is advisable to adjourn to a deserted location, free of dogs and cars. You'll immediately notice that the bike has two gear shifting levers. Generally, but depending upon the model, moving the right-hand stick forward will engage a higher gear, as will moving the left-hand shifter rearward. Using the same principle, moving the shifters in the opposite directions will engage lower gears for easier pedaling.

Upon making the first shift, the novice rider can expect to hear a curious variety of sounds, all of them signalling that the shift was made incorrectly. When a shift is made correctly, there will be no sound other than the usual tick-tick-tick of the bicycle in operation. However, if a pinging noise is heard, this generally signals that the rear derailleur

is going to shift to a lower gear than you had intended. This is caused by moving the right-hand shifter too far rearward. To correct the problem, simply move the right-hand shifter forward slightly, which will guide the derailleur into the right gear.

Along the same lines, should a whirring sound or loud click be heard frequently upon making a shift, this denotes that the rear derailleur is about to shift to a higher gear than you intended. Simply easing the right-hand shifter rearward slightly should guide the chain into the appropriate gearing ratio.

This same problem can occur when using the front derailleur, signalled by a high-pitched rubbing sound when the outside edge of the changer is touching the chain, whereas a low-toned rubbing sound is caused by the chain hitting the inside edge of the derailleur. In the former case, a simple remedy is to move the left-hand shifter rearward slightly, until the sound disappears. The latter case calls for the reverse operation, that of moving the same shifter ahead slightly. Some bicycles have this gearing system reversed, which will necessitate your reversal of these correcting operations. Be sure to check the pattern on your bicycle.

It should be noted that, on this type of bicycle with a freewheeling capacity, the gears cannot be changed unless the bicycle is moving forward, the chain revolving, without any tension applied. Once speed has been attained and a change is desirable, simply ease off on the pedaling pressure while keeping the chain rotating, then slip into the gear desired. Should you wish to shift to a lower gear while negotiating a hill, you'll have to pedal a little harder to pick up additional speed, then let the pressure off just enough to make the change, and keep pedaling up the incline. It takes

Shifters are found in varying locations on 10-speeds, most placed as these, below. These have plastic wing nuts and covers, which easily loosen and look cheesey.

To change gears, bicycle must be moving with chain under no tension. The shifter then is moved to the desired gear while the rider maintains a steady pedaling rhythm.

a bit of practice to refine the technique, but this will come sooner than imagined. In any case, the rider should be completely familiar with the workings of his machine before ever entering the automobile-dominated traffic roadways.

If you're learning to ride a bicycle with the 10-speed or similar model as your education partner, you will notice a feature that is missing from the one speed type: No coaster brake. It is hoped that this discovery was made before trying to stop the machine while in motion — by applying backward pressure to the pedals — and finding that the pedals merrily revolve counter-clockwise with no slowing effect.

Most individuals, even if they aren't riders, have seen or are familiar with the caliper-type braking mechanisms. By simply squeezing the levers located on the handlebars, the bike slows rapidly and stops. Before testing the brakes while in operation, it is a good idea to discover which lever controls which brake. To overlook this might result in depressing but one lever and, should it be for the front caliper brake, you may find yourself coursing over the handlebars

There are six basic hand positions that can be utilized when riding a 10-speed bike, as shown below. Each is functional and used by riders with different styles. If the arms and shoulders tire, change to another grip.

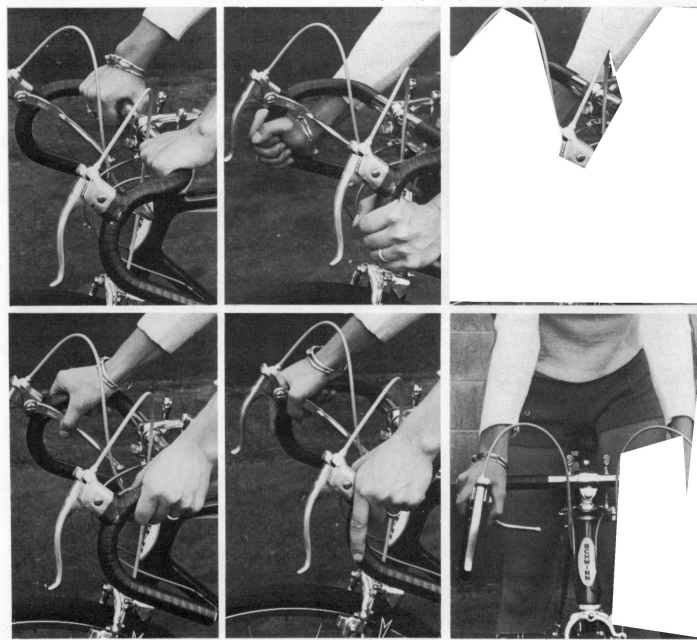

in an admirable but painful flight status.

As with a coaster brake — or an automobile brake, for that matter — no sudden pressure should be applied to the levers unless an unforeseen crash seems imminent. Whenever possible, both levers should be depressed evenly to bring the bicycle to a controlled stop.

Many riders who entertain ideas of touring the country on their bicycles give up the idea rapidly after taking but one or two cruises of any distance; they just don't have the steam to continue and come to feel that touring is out of the question.

Whether touring or pumping down to the park is the objective of the cyclist, one should endeavor to cycle correctly. In the majority of cases discussed in the preceding paragraph, the fault lies not in touring abilities, but in efficiency loss that can be corrected.

Many falter in their cycling, because they do not use all of the body muscles in conjunction with the legs. Consequently, the legs, back or arms tire more quickly when they do the bulk of the work, resulting in frequent rest stops and delays.

The proper manner of cycling on a 10-speed calls for utilization of all muscles working together. While the legs are pumping, the back can be raised and lowered frequently to absorb some of the strain from the legs. There are numerous hand positions on the handlebars that can be used to keep the arms from tiring prematurely. While the neck will tire from keeping the head up, looking forward, turning from side to side — for a quick second or two — will relax tense muscles. Also, upon using the hand position on the top of the bars, the entire body is elevated more and this is the time to twist the neck back and forth.

Like the ten and one-half million Americans who bought bicycles in 1972, you've decided that you can cycle and live to enjoy it, trot on down to the neighborhood bicycle dealership and pick out a bicycle. As mentioned previously, buying a bicycle is a much more complicated matter than what it used to be back prior to the turn of the century, when but few models were available.

The main thing to decide before you push aside the plate glass doors of the showroom floor is for what purpose do you want a bicycle. It currently is fashionable to be seen riding a 10-speed but, in a great lot of cases, the rider could have saved by purchasing a bicycle that fits his wants and needs. Coming away with a 10-speed bicycle to be used strictly for jaunts to the park or shopping trips is like purcashing a hydroplane and putting it in the backyard swimming pool: It never will be used to its full capabilities.

If the purpose of the bicycle will be for grocery shopping or similar short hops, the traditional one-speed — that balloon tire behemoth — is just the ticket. If the bicycle you want is to be used for casual Sunday outings of slightly longer mileage, a 3 to 5-speed is best suited for your needs. For a serious cyclist that intends spending many hours and miles on his bicycle in all types of terrain, get that 15 or 10-speed.

What can you expect to spend for these different types of bikes? Naturally, prices vary according to location, time of year and volume of bicycle sales by an individual dealer, but the average seems to be $10-$50 for a one-speed, $50 to $80 for a 3-speed, and between $80-$300 for the popular 5, 10 and 15 speeds. Especially constructed or custom-made bicycles can run well over the grand mark,

Center pull caliper brakes are found on many bicycles and got their name because even pressure is applied to the rim on both sides when the brake lever is squeezed.

The side pull caliper brake also is used widely, but it exerts a pressing force only on one side of the rim. Both proved to work excellently, when properly aligned.

but aren't common on the streets.

It is the opinion of most dealers that asking someone to recommend a bicycle for your purchase is like having someone select your wife: It's your choice, as you will be stuck with the merchandise.

However, there are many factors to keep in mind that can result in your purchasing a bicycle that you will enjoy for many years. If, that is, you have the gumption to break away from the flock of sheep and truly buy a bicycle that will fit your capabilities and not so much one that happens to be in vogue.

Many bicycle industry executives advocate, upon deciding which model to purchase, buying the most expensive example of that model you possibly can afford. The reason is that quality in the product is directly proportional to

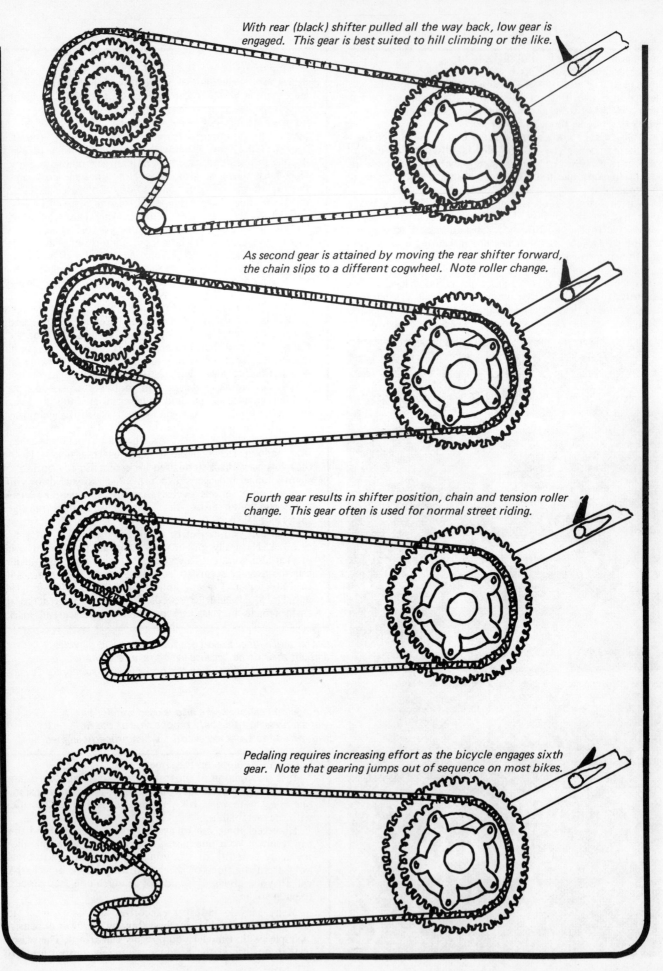

With rear (black) shifter pulled all the way back, low gear is engaged. This gear is best suited to hill climbing or the like.

As second gear is attained by moving the rear shifter forward, the chain slips to a different cogwheel. Note roller change.

Fourth gear results in shifter position, chain and tension roller change. This gear often is used for normal street riding.

Pedaling requires increasing effort as the bicycle engages sixth gear. Note that gearing jumps out of sequence on most bikes.

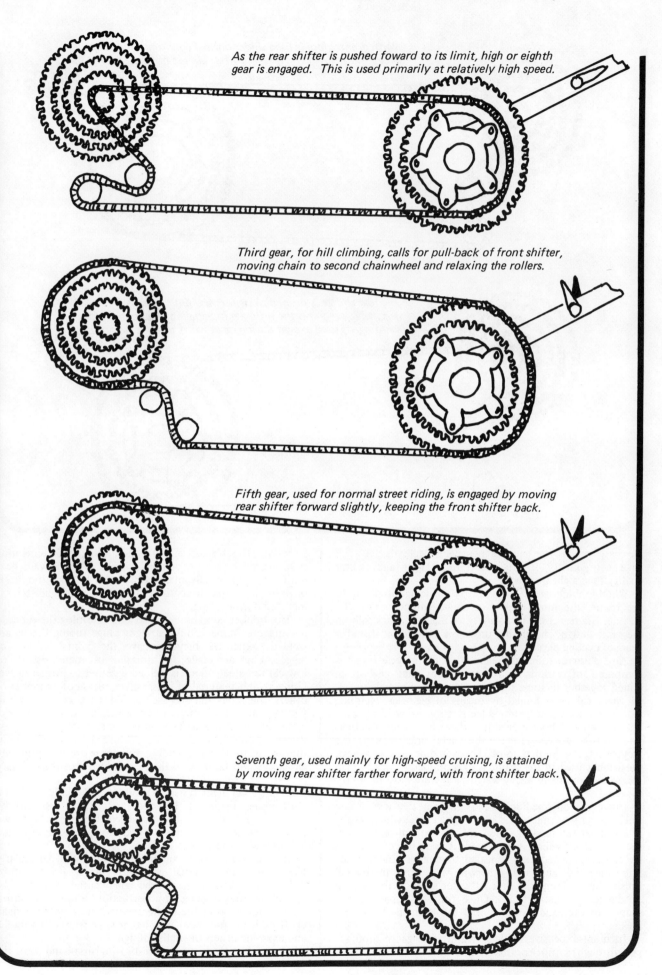

As the rear shifter is pushed foward to its limit, high or eighth gear is engaged. This is used primarily at relatively high speed.

Third gear, for hill climbing, calls for pull-back of front shifter, moving chain to second chainwheel and relaxing the rollers.

Fifth gear, used for normal street riding, is engaged by moving rear shifter forward slightly, keeping the front shifter back.

Seventh gear, used mainly for high-speed cruising, is attained by moving rear shifter farther forward, with front shifter back.

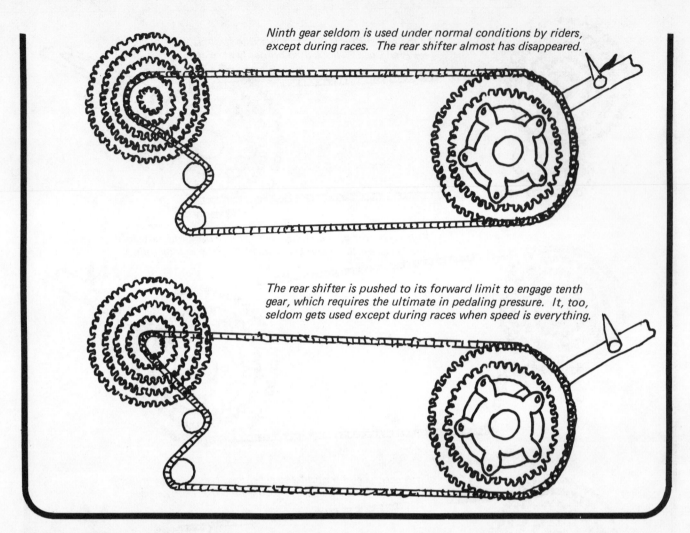

Ninth gear seldom is used under normal conditions by riders, except during races. The rear shifter almost has disappeared.

The rear shifter is pushed to its forward limit to engage tenth gear, which requires the ultimate in pedaling pressure. It, too, seldom gets used except during races when speed is everything.

purchase price. The more expensive bicycle models will have components of much better, stronger and lighter quality than a cheaper model.

When looking over a bicycle, pay particular attention to the frame, the most important single component of the bicycle. Frames come in a variety of metals, all basically in the same design, and should provide a solid foundation for years of cycling pleasure.

Any observer soon will realize that the bicycle frame is composed of various-sized metal tubes that have been joined together in some manner. On a cheap bicycle, seamed, steel tubing is joined by means of electrical welding, which serious bikers abhor. Electrical or arc welding, as it better is known, does indeed fuse the components together, but in the process fatigues the metal and weakens the bicycle's frame at that joint. To overcome this weakness, the tubing used in the frame is exceptionally thick, which means exceptionally heavy weight, a feature most riders try to avoid.

However, on medium-priced models, the low-carbon steel tubing is seamless and of straight gauge, which results in a thinner tubing wall. The term, straight gauge, refers to the process by which it is formed. A solid bar of steel has its center punched out, annealed to remove some of the impurities and faults that otherwise would mar the overall finish, then is immersed in a saltwater solution that aids in producing a smooth finish. Once this is completed, it is shaped to the exact form desired by mechanical pressure means.

In more expensive models, this straight gauge tubing is put through a process that results in double-butted con-

struction. This term means that the tubing, while remaining thin and pliable in the center, has doubly-thick walls near both ends. The advantage of double-butted tubing is obvious: Increased strength at the joints, where all stress is incurred during riding.

The thicker construction also aids in joining the tubes in making the frame. Unlike straight gauge tubing that is arc welded, expensive bicycles have the joints brazed, or lugged. Lugs are made of disjointed soft metal, usually of low carbon steel, which is welded together to form a sleeve. Using a filler material of brass, silver, nickel or a number of others, the tubes and lugs are bonded together securely and strongly at a low temperature which doesn't fatigue the metal nearly as much. This process maintains the lightness desired. Some bicycles even are bonded together without the use of lugs or arc welding, but these are exceptionally expensive and far beyond the reach or want of the ordinary cyclist.

Strong, yet light types of tubing are Reynolds 531 and Columbus, made in England and Italy, respectively. Naturally found on more expensive bicycles, these two types have achieved fine reputations for durability and lightness over the years.

In any event, when examining a model you particularly like, check the manual accompanying it for the tube dimensions, type of steel used and whether it is double-butted or straight gauge in construction. Should this information not be available in the manual, check with the dealer. If he isn't sure, your best bet is to overlook that model and examine others of similar design.

If you like to do some investigating first-hand, lean the

Quick release hub, found usually on racing bikes, enables the rider to change wheels fast. Assure that they remain tight!

By looking down the frame from the front, all tubes should appear as one. If not, the frame is not in proper alignment. Don't buy it!

On expensive bicycles, check to see if the spokes are laced or soldered. Both add strength and aid shock absorbing ability.

bike away from you, grab the handlebars and seat and, putting the ball of one foot on the front sprocket housing, try to push the bike with light pressure. When pressure is released, the bike should spring back towards you noticeably, if the frame is of high quality steel. This isn't a test of strength, and you definitely should not try to make a bend in the frame. If you get carried away, be prepared to buy it!

Next, feel the frame joints for smoothness. The mark of a good factory craftsman is smooth lugged joints, not those rough or bubbled to the touch. If these are found, move on to another bike; if craftsmanship is lacking at this stage, who knows where further discrepancy will be found?

The next logical area of scrutiny is the front fork. It is possible to become bogged-down with technical data in checking such things as angles and the effect they have on performance, but most riders don't take the time or actually have the necessary background to fully appreciate these factors.

Some simple checks that should assure a smooth riding bicycle are, first, to check the length of the front forks. They should be equal in length and only infrequently will they differ. Should they, however, move on to another model.

Check alignment of the forks. They should be equally spaced on either side of the front wheel. By looking head-on at the frame from the front, the prospective buyer should be able to see but one set of tubing, the others being in complete alignment. If not, the frame probably is not sound.

Altogether too many riders choose bicycles that are too large for them in frame size. A quick, yet efficient check is

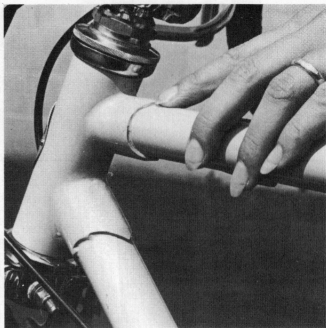

If the bike does have lugs, check for roughness and overall finish. A good craftsman will have smooth lugs with eye-pleasing quality. If not, maybe the frame has other flaws.

Usually, one-speed bikes do not have lugged joints, but are welded and have smooth ones, as seen at left. They are heavy.

to straddle the bicycle. The top tube should reach to within an inch of the crotch, when standing with your shoes off, as mentioned earlier. Don't worry about how the pedals and seat reach; the seat can be raised or lowered to accommodate your specific size. But once that bike is paid for, there is nothing you can do to change the frame size.

Another frame feature to bear in mind, although it may seem minor, is the color. Don't buy a bicycle if the color isn't what you wanted. The dealer can order a specific color of bicycle especially for you. Don't be in a hurry and end up with a bicycle that you won't care much for in a short while.

After thoroughly inspecting the frame, look at the front rim of the bicycle. If it is made of steel, figure that it will be heavier and more shock transmitting than aluminum types currently used on many models. Check the spokes while examining the rim; good, although expensive, types are butted stainless steel, which virtually are rustproof and somewhat stronger than other makes. Check and determine whether the spokes are three or four-crossed, whether woven or soldered. The latter two add strength and absorb some shocks due to road conditions.

Check the wheels for out-of-roundness by lifting up the frame and spinning them. They should revolve at an equal distance from the caliper brakes. While you're at it, check and see if the cones are loose, by setting the bike down,

grabbing the handlebars and trying to wiggle the wheel. If it does, the cones need to be tightened, which doesn't disqualify the bicycle from purchase.

Notice the types of tires that are fitted on the rim. Basically, tires come in two forms, sew-ups and clinchers, the latter otherwise known as tubulars. Sew-ups are of interesting construction, and have the tube sewn directly to the tire casing. This type of tire makes for exceptionally smooth and lively riding, is light of weight, but also is difficult to patch should you have a blow-out on the road.

Clinchers received their name because that is exactly what they do: Clinch the rim. Examining a clincher removed from the rim, it forms a U-shape, with the top of the U fitting into a groove in the rim. They utilize regular tubes, which are much easier to patch, but more difficult to remove from the rim without tire damage. They are heavier and have more tread than the sew-ups, which reduces the chance of a blow-out or puncture. Personal preference is the dictating factor on tires.

While checking the front end, it might be wise to glance at the brake. Generally, brakes for most bicycles now are of the center pull or side pull caliper variety. The significant difference between the two is the manner in which they are manipulated; the side pull type exerting force only on one side of the rim, while the center pull type clamps on the rim evenly from both sides. The coaster brake found on one-speed models still is in existence, although overshadowed by the caliper types. It still is functional on models incorporating its design, and there is no worry about frayed cables breaking.

While testing the pull of the lever-operated brakes, note the distance the lever travels before securely clamping the rubber braking surfaces on the rim. If it is excessive, more

These spokes are seated well above the tube or sew-up surface, and won't cause delaying flats.

If the frame is of good quality steel, it will spring back after pressure is applied, then released. Don't overdo it!

than two to three inches, it needs adjustment. Also, check the bearing surfaces of the rubber brakes on the rim. They also might need attention.

Check the hub on the front wheel. Some cyclists favor a solid aluminum hub, while others claim that the heavier steel does the job well and the weight is nothing major. The machined aluminum types will be found mostly on the more expensive models. Make sure that, if they need grease or oiling, this is not overlooked. Roller bearings don't last long without lubricant.

The pedals found on 10-speeds usually are of steel, even in the expensive models, although some are of aluminum. If possible, try to get the toe clips and leather straps as, mentioned previously, this helps with overall performance. Give them a flip with the toe to assure they revolve smoothly.

The best type of crank — the part to which the pedals are attached — is cotterless, made of aluminum and generally not found on a bicycle of medium price range. However, if you do get lucky and buy a bicycle with the cotterless cranks, assure that you purchase the crank tool before leaving the shop. As the miles fly past, the cranks get loose and the steel axle will gouge the hell out of the soft

aluminum, rendering them useless.

Tighten them whenever you think about it and certainly not less than every twenty miles until a few hundred miles have been logged.

The type of gears your bicycle has should be matched to the type of riding you intend doing. On the typical 10-speed, a good set-up for the average touring rider would be cogwheels with teeth numbering 14-17-20-23-27. The racer interested strictly in getting maximum results for his efforts would choose gearing in the 14-16-18-22-24 tooth category. There are numerous other combinations available and your dealer knows best what you should utilize.

For your chainwheels, a set of 40-50 tooth combo is about the best for the average rider. You can move to a 46-54 or 44-52 set with about the same results. Don't go into odd-ball combinations, however, because your rhythm and timing will be thrown off.

Handlebars come in two basic varieties, the maes and all around. The maes type of bars are found on the 10-speed models, characterized by their underslung appearance. All other types of bars, from the high risers on the young kids' models to the straight grips on parents' 3-speeders, fall into the all around category. For the serious cyclist, none but the maes type will suffice.

Virtually every rider that has envisioned himself on a 10-speed bicycle has said to himself that the seat must be changed, that no one could possibly be comfortable sitting on it. This could be valid when the leather seat is used on a one or 3-speed model where the rider sits more in an upright position, but for 10-speed, where the rider assumes a more forward lean with the body, the seat aids rather than chafes. Years of research have gone into design and construction, and be assured that it is the best around.

Just as you would no more buy a pair of shoes without trying them on, one shouldn't purchase a bicycle without testing it on the road. If the dealer refuses, go to another dealer; this happens infrequently, as they also realize the importance of proper fit and happy customers.

Once out on the road, pedal at different speeds, take some corners fast, try riding with no hands for a short distance — in short, put it through the paces. Note how the cycle reacts to different road conditions, its stability, gearing qualities and overall feel. If for any reason there is something, besides problems that can be alleviated through adjustments, that you dislike, pass the deal up. Keep checking for that one bicycle that turns you on.

Once you have purchased the bicycle of your dreams and have it home, go through and tighten all the nuts and bolts that need it. To do this, you may have to buy some tools from the dealer and make sure they are designed for your machine. Many countries have different systems of measurements for nuts and bolts than the standard accepted in this country and that leaves just about any on-hand tools of American manufacture useless.

In any case, make sure that you have the necessary tools on hand before ever heading out on a road trip of any duration. Even if nothing goes wrong, you still have the sense of security that comes with being prepared.

Up to now, we have been discussing mainly the purchase

The seat found on a 10-speed is scientifically designed for both comfort and function, regardless of how uncomfortable it appears. Some casual riders, however, use padded saddles.

of a spanking-new bicycle from a dealership. It should be duly noted that many a good deal can be made from the used bicycle market, although the bicycle may have a few miles under its chain. By keeping the aforementioned checks in mind when purchasing even a used bike, you stand an exceptional chance of coming away with a most serviceable bicycle, for a lot less money!

Generally, a dealership is the last place you will find any

A wide variety of bike clothing is available to the cyclist, all designed and produced after years of experimentation and research (below left). One item that should accompany the new owner from the shop is a tool kit like the one below. To overlook this accessory can result in no end of headaches.

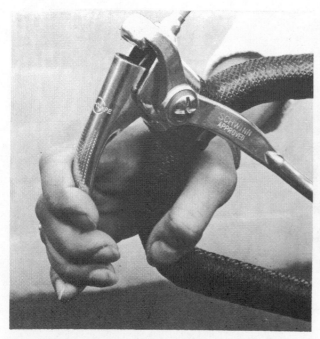

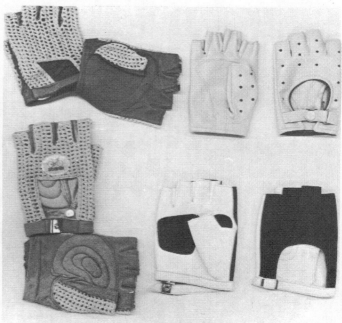

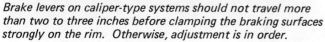
Brake levers on caliper-type systems should not travel more than two to three inches before clamping the braking surfaces strongly on the rim. Otherwise, adjustment is in order.

Many types of gloves currently are marketed for the cyclist, and a serious rider should not overlook a pair. They give much better grip on the handlebars than sweaty hands.

great selection of used bicycles. The classified ads of any newspaper nearly always carry listings of bicycles for sale or trade, and it may behoove you to check these out. Another popular place to find bicycles, albeit old and not the least bit fashionable, is a flea market or swap meet, where a good, functional bicycle can be picked up for under the $10 mark!

Each year, the various police departments around the country have auctions to sell the numerous bicycles that either were lost or stolen. While they may be slightly rusty from hanging in a rack out in the elements, good deals often can be had. It also is a fine place to check for your own bicycle, if you parted company with it sometime in the past, providing you have proof via a registration number, et cetera, to prove it is yours. Once home, that rust melts away under the application of steel wool and elbow grease and, with a new paint job and some oiling, that bicycle is ready for use.

A bicycle today can represent a sizable financial investment, and if you like to keep what rightfully belongs to you, don't overlook a case-hardened chain and lock. If you and your bike are going to be separated for more than ten seconds, chain it up to a sturdy, immobile lightpost or such. At home, keep it in a locked garage, your bedroom or wherever possible to keep the hawk-like eyes of thieves from detecting its presence. Otherwise, you may be able to buy it back at the police auction. Read carefully the chapter on bicycle theft in this book.

A good and oft-times overlooked form of bicycle — that may well be making a comeback among young courting couples of today — is that venerable bicycle built for two. Immortalized in song nearly a century past, it is being seen more and more along the roadways of the nation. For young couples, a couple of friends or the older married folk, this once-popular cycle offers a means of having a memorable date or recapturing fleeting youthful moments.

Whatever type of bicycle you settle on, with proper care, maintenance and perhaps a little love, both you and it can grow old together.

PREPARE FOR PEDALING PERILS

There Are Built-in Dangers In
Every Activity, But Knowing
Them Can Reduce
The Likelihood!

Chapter 3

THE MATTER OF SAFETY IN BICYCLE riding is becoming a major concern on the part of legislators, law enforcement authorities and sane bicyclists alike.

Just as no automobile driver would take to the streets if all but one lug nut were missing from a wheel, no cyclist should ride an unsafe bicycle. Common sense states that an unsafe bicycle increases the chances of accident.

Checking your bicycle prior to each ride is a good habit to form. In addition to assuring a safe vehicle, the rider also will catch any minor faults that could grow into major problems if not taken care of initially.

Check both tires for cracks or excessive wear, which could result in a blowout should a sharp stone or glass sliver be contacted. A blowout at even a casual pace can result in a meeting of skin and pavement. Should the bike go out of control, the rider can find himself squarely in the middle of a traffic lane, surrounded by ironclad predators.

If you have a pencil-type pressure gauge indicator, check the tires for proper air pressure, which usually is listed on the sidewall of the tire. If a pressure gauge is not in the tool kit, make your first stop a service station to check pressure.

Grasp the tires one at a time and try to wiggle them, checking for looseness of the cones. Should this fault be found, correct it before riding out.

Check the axle nuts or quick release hubs on the bicycle for tightness. Should they be loose, there is a goodly chance that the wheel might detach when riding and serious injury, or worse, could result.

Naturally, the handlebars and seat tubes should be in proper adjustment and not loose. The brake levers should be fully operable — if the bike utilizes them — with no excess travel. The brake shoes that clamp onto the rim should do just that, and not be aligned crookedly; if so, adjustment is in order.

The chain should be oiled lightly with a lightweight type, such as the popular 3-IN-1 compound. Care of the roller bearings should be dictated by the type of riding done previously. Should the bike be ridden near or on the beach, sand inevitably will seep into the bearings. This necessitates cleaning and repacking with heavy grease almost immediately. If the bicycle has been used for normal street riding, every six months should be sufficient, but one never can regrease the bearings too often.

Should your riding be done in the late evening or at night, make sure that the lighting mechanisms and reflectors are operable and visible. The problem of lighting a bicycle adequately is a veritable can of worms, with no perfect solution readily at hand or foreseen in the near future.

Most states have regulations that direct any bicycle used at night to have a white light visible from a distance of three hundred feet in front of the bike and a red reflector or red taillight visible from three hundred feet to the rear, when in the headlights of an approaching vehicle. The rear reflector problem has been partially alleviated, as many states now make it mandatory that manufacturers equip any bicycle sold after January 1, 1973, with such devices on the pedals, the frame or both.

Sadly, many cyclist each year are killed at night, even though their bicycles are fitted with regulation reflectors. The pedal reflectors practically are usless at night, when the rider is wearing any type of shoe with heels fitted to the sole. The heel blocks light beams emanating from approaching headlamps.

In view of this problem, it would behoove any night-riding cyclist to take even further precautions to avoid becoming a statistic. A prominent tape manufacturer currently markets rolls of reflective red tape, which can be stuck on the frame of the bicycle for added safety. However, the tape must be placed over the paint, which many riders dislike.

If you decide to sacrifice a little beauty for safety — a wise decision if the bulk of your riding is done after darkness — put chunks of the tape in several locations on the bicycle besides the rear. A strip or two on both sides of the frame, plus the front forks, will make a much more visible picture to a motorist approaching from the side or the front, where he may fail to notice the front light. Every little bit helps.

There are many varieties of front lights, most of which are totally inadequate. Basically, they are broken down into two categories; those that utilize batteries as a power source and those that use a generator activated by continuous rubbing on the tire sidewall.

The battery-type front lights more often than not require the skills of Houdini in order to change the 'D' cells used, and the bankroll of Howard Hughes to meet the demand of the voracious battery-eater.

If left in the rain, the battery housing grows rust so fast it practically can be observed, which further complicates cracking it open for a battery change. To sum up, the battery-operated front beam generally is unsatisfactory.

But the law says that lights must be used, so where does a cyclist turn? The generator lighting system is better than the battery type, but not much.

A small generator, turned by rubbing against the sidewall of either the front or rear tire, provides light for the front and often rear lights. A major problem with this system simply is that, in order to turn the generator, an increased amount of pressure must be exerted against the pedals. Should a cyclist be traveling a good distance, he can be drained of energy by powering the generator.

Also, there is the problem of the light going out whenever the bicycle stops. This often is a necessity in cities with stoplights or stop signs. In essence, the rider becomes a sitting duck for the unattentive motorist or one who happens to have a dirty windshield.

Perhaps the best lighting system available today — which also leaves much to be desired — is the French armband light. It resembles a flashlight that uses one bulb to illuminate a white or yellow front light and red rear. It is affixed to the arm or leg with a cloth band.

While the light uses C cells, at least the housing is easily detachable, making battery insertion more simple. Another plus in the light's favor is that, should a flat or other type of repair be needed, the armband light can be trained

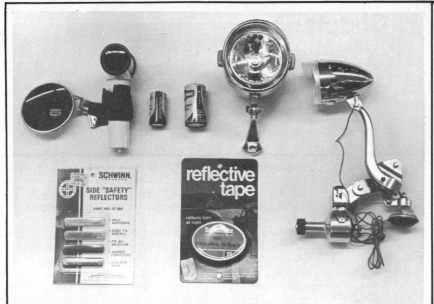

Lights, reflectors, aid in night rides (top left). Riding in the rain or on slick surface is dangerous.(above).

Armband light, powered by two C-cell batteries, shows up well under these headlight-simulating conditions. A bright jacket also helps (left).

The problem with doing wheelies on a bike was illustrated seconds after this photo was taken, as the rider careened into trunk of parked car.

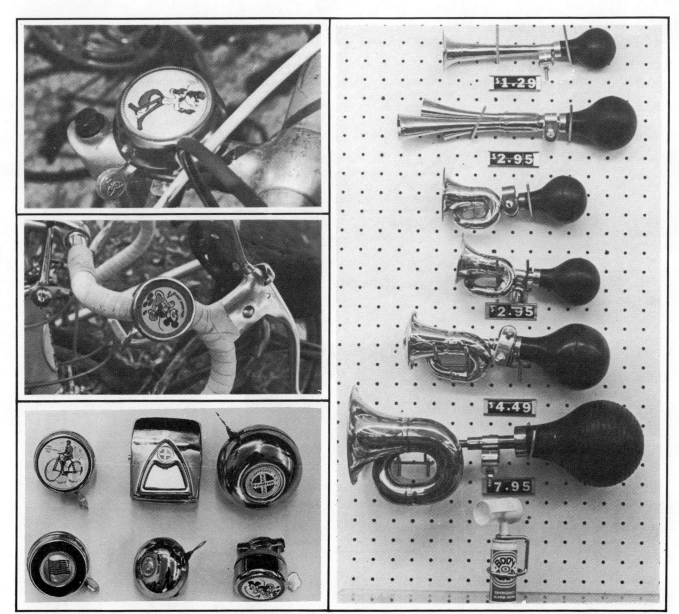

Numerous types of bells are marketed in bicycle stores today, and can aid the rider in being noticed by pedestrians. They will fit on any handlebar set.

Bulb-type horns range from small to gargantuan, and we have not observed a bicycle rider using the bottom type frequently. Kids have a tendency to abuse them.

directly on the affected area, exactly duplicating a flashlight. Its inexpensive cost — in the vicinity $2 — also is a decided plus in its favor, as is the possibility of removal from the bicycle for storage in a dry place.

Some cyclists favor attaching the armband light on the left leg, just below the knee, and this indeed makes for an eyecatching sight, as the light bobs up and down. Others choose to wear it on the left arm, where it is more stationary and aids in spotting chuckholes and the like, but serves about the same purpose as an immobile tail light or reflector when seen from the rear. The light choice and placement is personal preference, but definitely should not be overlooked when riding at night.

A horn or bell also is an added safety factor, and we advise purchasing one. Some riders, especially those who do much night pedaling, sound their horns or bells when approaching any intersection, as a motorist that might not see them should hear them. It also is used for alerting

pedestrians of your pending arrival, and could save much embarrassment, as well as bruises.

There are numerous types of horns and bells currently on the market, and personal preference again is the factor in deciding which to purchase. It should be noted that the bulbous type horns, those which date back many decades, are functional, but every small child who happens upon one when the bicycle is parked is seized by the irresistible urge to give it a try. This constant action does tend to shorten its life-span.

Another type of horn is incorporated in the battery operated light housing, and is activated by depressing a button attached to the handlebars. Its major problem is that, when the battery weakens and the light falters, so does the horn's effectiveness.

Bells have changed little in design since their introduction many years past, and still are as functional as they were years ago. However, the tinkling of a bell often does

45

little to alert motorists, but it definitely is better than nothing in pedestrian traffic.

The safest place to ride a bicycle is where the traffic isn't. There is no future in endeavoring to ride in areas that have a heavy traffic flow, contesting the supremacy of the automobile, as some riders do in such areas as downtown New York City.

If the majority of your riding is done on streets around your home neighborhood, you should know the busy roadways and hopefully avoid them. However, if you plan to ride to another, unfamiliar area, a good plan would be to stop at a service station for a road map that lists city streets. By examining the map, you can plan your route away from or parallel to existing major traffic arteries.

The main cause of accidents is the bike rider himself. Many do not realize that, in most states, a bicycle falls under the same restrictions and regulations as those which

Most states require seats for both riders on one bike, not just one as below. Carrying children in seats on bikes means cautious riding (right).

Riding double (below) is forbidden in most states. Riders should walk their bikes across crosswalk for maximum safety, as seen at bottom.

govern the automobile. Most vehicle code manuals read something like this: "Every person riding a bicycle...has all of the rights and is subject to all of the duties applicable to the driver of a vehicle..." This includes speed limits, traffic signals, stop signs and direction of travel.

Perhaps the singlemost cause of accidents is traveling on the wrong side of the road. Bicyclists are required by law to ride as near the right-hand side of the roadway as possible and practicable, exercising due care when passing standing

vehicles or those proceeding in the same direction.

This route often places the rider between the right-hand flowing traffic lane and parked autos along the curb. Special hazards are found in this lane of travel, and it behooves the bicyclist to constantly watch for them.

Usually, the space between the curb and right lane is occupied by parked automobiles. While pedaling, a rider should be especially watchful for drivers opening their car doors to exit.

Untold riders have had this situation develop, and crashing into the aforementioned door results in his flying over the handlebars. Along the same vein, watch for motorists that pull out from their parking spaces without checking behind for on-coming bicycle traffic.

This problem of visibility is especially acute, for most automobile operators are attuned to watching for vehicles of auto-size, or larger. Motorcycle riders learned early that the safest way they could operate on the streets was to make themselves as visible as possible through the use of bright clothing, constant use of headlamps, and not riding where a motorist is not likely to see them. In these respects, the bicyclist can take note from his motorized cousin.

Some manufacturers now offer riding vests in fluorescent orange or pink colors, which help to make the cyclist more readily apparent to the automobile operator.

While using a headlamp virtually is out of the question for a bicycle rider — its small size and volume of light produced would hardly make a difference, anyway — avoiding blind spots of automobiles definitely should not be overlooked. Most riders know, through familiarization with the automobile, that the right rear and left rear areas are obscured by the roof panels, creating an area in which visibility is nil.

When riding on the proper side of the street, a cyclist need be concerned only with the right-hand blind spot, and avoid pulling into it. A motorist might just ease toward the right side of the roadway when anticipating a right turn, and the cyclist between the driver and parked cars assumes a rather slender shape; like slender enough to slip under a closed door.

Always stay well to the rear of any preceeding auto, and be ready to brake at any moment. Often, the driver may see an approaching hazard at the last minute and, if you happen to be admiring the clouds or flowers at the side of the road, you may dent his trunk. More than likely, it will be your trunk that gets dented!

Motorists often claim, in court, that the child they hit darted suddenly from between parked cars, and that they had no possible way of stopping or of foreseeing the hazard. Just as the motorists, the bicyclist should be especially watchful for children playing on sidewalks, or between parked cars. While a car will lumber on after striking a child, the bicycle more than likely will be thrown off-balance or halted abruptly.

A bicyclist, just like an automobile operator, should obey traffic devices. Altogether too many riders die each year because, upon approaching a stop sign and not seeing any cross traffic, disregard it and sail directly into the path of a vehicle that materialized out of thin air; a great number also are killed each year by making illegal U turns; more are added to the list by running red lights. In short, just about any traffic offense by a motorist is also committed by the bicyclist. But at least the motorist has a fighting chance

Even on paved roads, the rider should be alert for chuckholes and other hazards (above left). Pumping uphill with load on back is safe but tiring (left).

Right turn.

Left turn.

Slowing down or stopping.

when his actions lead to an accident, being thoroughly encased in steel.

The matter of signalling every move prior to making it cannot be emphasized strongly enough. Automobiles use blinkers that are highly visible, even in daylight hours; bicycle blinkers are inconsequential and are seldom noticed. Hand signals are the only way to go for the bicyclists, regardless of how corny or old-fashioned he might think signalling is.

As most riders rely strictly on blinkers in their automobiles, and have for many years, a refresher in the technique of signalling perhaps is in order. The hand signals have not changed in many years and their effectiveness is unparalleled.

In making a right turn, the left arm is extended in an 'L' shape, with the fingers pointed skyward. A left turn is signalled by extending the straight left arm perpendicular to the body. A signal to slow down is given with the arm in a reversed 'L' shape, with the fingers pointed at the ground and the palm rearward. All signals should be given no less than one hundred feet from the spot where the turn will be initiated.

Many police authorities feel that some of the modern smaller bicycles, with what are termed "high riser" handle-bars, account for a sizeable amount of injuries and fatalities yearly, simply because their design encourages dangerous acrobatic maneuvers while riding. These same types of handlebars once were found on motorcycles of years past. Termed "ape hangers," some of the tough-guy lawlessness imparted unto them has prevailed and found favor among youths of this era, those imagining themselves on big choppers rather than on twenty-inch bicycles.

It should be noted that, in most states, a bicycle equipped with handlebars higher than the rider's shoulder level is illegal. No rider can operate a bicycle that has ape hangers or high risers constructed so that the rider must reach above shoulder height to grasp the handgrips.

Some odd-looking bicycle creations have appeared on the scene in the last few years, not all of them legal. In fact, riders who wish to travel back in time to the years and machines of grandfather's time would be smart to do their traveling within the mind's eye: To use a bicycle like the penny-farthing on today's roadways will result in a citation from a police officer. California law, similar in this respect to most others, emphatically states that no bicycle altered or constructed so that the pedal at its lowermost position is more than twelve inches above the ground, shall be used on the road. Should you be lucky enough to get your hands on one of these old machines, save it: It'll probably be worth a great deal of money someday.

It is not unusual to see a bicyclist pedaling unconcernedly down a roadway with neither hand on the handle-bars. This generally is a direct violation of the law, which states that at least one hand be on the bars at all times. This ruling applies when transporting packages, bags and the like. One hand must be on the handlebar, and you'd be wise to make it the hand that reaches for the rear brake.

Better and safer yet, for the rider who often does grocery shopping with the bicycle used to carry parcels, is the addition of some sort of basket or rack. Numerous firms manufacture all manner of racks and baskets, which will carry either school-books or a fair-sized bag choked with groceries, leaving both hands free to operate the bike.

Another law broken by most riders at one time or another is that of riding double, either with the extra rider on the handlebars or on the fender of the rear tire. In both cases, this is strictly illegal and dangerous.

The purpose of this law was demonstrated to me some years ago. A close friend's woodshed one day disgorged two archaic rusty specimens, both balloon tire bombers of uncertain vintage. They were forgotten until, some weeks later, we were faced with being late for school and no other form of transportation was available. Hurriedly mounting up, we respected the low air pressure in the tires and pedaled slowly for the gas station.

Making the trip without incident, I filled the tires of my tired old mount, then moved away to let Jack attend to his.

Meanwhile, one of the station owner's gargantuan German shepards, reputedly of fierce demeanor, mysteriously appeared. His attention focused on protecting his exposed posterior from inviting the toothy critter to attack, Jack forgot about the tire he was inflating until it exploded

Dogs are the cyclist's biggest curse, next to the car, and text explains ways of dealing with them. This youngster is asking for trouble with bare feet (below).

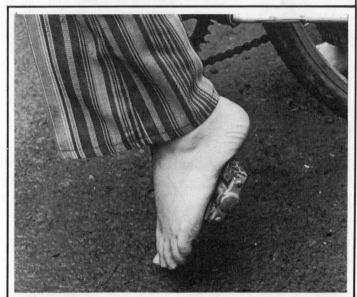

loudly next to his ear. He panicked and raced towards me, now at a safe vantage point across the street. The dog panicked and ran, fortunately in the opposite direction.

Jack picked up the bike and leaned it next to a flower shop. As time was growing ever later, we decided to ride double in hopes of making the school as soon as possible. He was larger, so I hopped on the handlebars, hooked both big toes around the axle nuts, and we were off.

We didn't get far. Upon hitting a grain of sand or other such obstruction on the asphalt, I was shifted off-balance and, as Jack strained to turn the bicycle back onto a straight path, we caught the shoulder of the road. The shoulder dropped off abruptly, and we soon found ourselves tangled in a maze of prickly raspberry bushes at the bottom of the embankment. The bicycle had blown both tires, and was abandoned as we set off on foot, picking the small thorns out of our hides. We didn't ride double anymore.

A notable exception to the passenger rule is the use of a small seat that fits children. These seats are sold by many manufacturers and bolt directly to the frame behind the operator's seat, or on the top tube directly in front of the rider. No seats are designed to be clamped on the handlebars.

The practicality in using an infant seat is subject to much discussion. Dissenters claim that such a set-up is dangerous because, should the operator fall with the bike, the child passenger has no control over what may happen to him. Proponents of the seat claim that safe riding habits more than compensate for the chance occurrence. Either way, it is up to the individual rider.

But if a seat is intended for usage, we can only stress the importance of purchasing a heavily constructed type with good padding on the seat and back, one that bolts to the rear of the seat and frame. All generally come with some type of strap that holds the child securely, and this should be done-up whenever utilized. Ride extraordinarily cautiously when carrying along a child, for the life you save may not be your own.

Countless times has the warning, "don't hitch rides on moving trucks or cars," been depicted in drawings and print. Yet, each year there will be a bunch of riders injured and killed because they failed to obey this law. Most state laws read similar to that of California: "No person riding upon any bicycle, coaster, roller skates, sled or toy vehicle shall attach the same or himself to any streetcar or vehicle on the roadway."

Some states prefer that bicyclists confine their riding to sidewalks rather than the roadways. This is a fine system, when the cyclist and pedestrian who utilize the sidewalk operate compatibly. Unfortunately, often this doesn't happen: The pedestrian with both arms holding bags steps from a shop doorway, unerringly into the path of a cyclist and pow! Oranges roll, glass breaks and one less supporter for the bicycle movement is created.

It is only common sense that the bicycle rider give way to the pedestrian. This action promotes good will and respect for riders, which can count heavily at the ballot box over issues beneficial to riders. Looking at the situation in a different perspective, put yourself in the shoes of the stroller: Would you like to dodge crazed bike riders swerving about you on a sidewalk? Most elderly folks long since abandoned ideas of becoming broken-field runners, and a cyclist's efforts to reinstill this desire could warrant a bop on the noggin with a stout wooden cane!

Any number of back, handlebar and assorted other bags are available to the gear-toting bike rider (left).

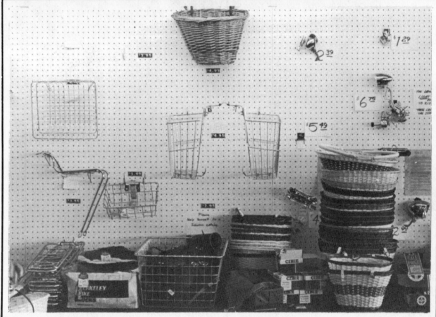

Bicycle carrying racks are well-used by women shoppers, students, etc., who carry many needed items (left).

Besides the automobile and pedestrian hazards encountered on any normal day, the roadway also holds other less noticeable trip-stoppers that are no less formidable. For starters, there is the popular storm drain, a metal grating most often placed parallel to the direction traveled by the bicyclist. If the unwary rider's front wheel slips between the grate's parallel bars, the bicycle abruptly flips foward as the front wheel lodges in the grate and, like the cyclists in the days of the penny-farthings, the rider takes a header.

Chuckholes will produce the same effect on a bicycle and rider, and should be avoided as much as possible. Washboards — those rippled sections of highway caused by the high-speed passage of heavy trucks — also are best detoured, as they tend to jolt and shake the rider almost senseless.

All manner of animals have taken a fancy to the fast-moving bicyclist at one time or another, from massive-shouldered bulls to that ever-present nemesis, the canine. Dogs are more a source of concern than all other types of animals banded together, and there are several types of strategy that can be employed when they are encountered.

First, of course, is the choice of turn-tail and flee from the fanged barker. This seldom is a favorable solution to the courageous cyclist, unless the canine happens to be of a size so sheer that he commands respect on bruising power alone, e.g., Saint Bernard, the bite of which is capable of snapping anklebones as effortlessly as you would break dry pine needles.

Another course is to reverse direction and approach the route from the opposite side of the street. Often, the distance alone will inhibit a restless dog from crossing in pursuit. If it doesn't, you at least have a slight edge in the ensuing race.

Thirdly, there is the possibility of increasing your speed and heading directly towards your adversary, accompanying your strategy with several bellowing war-whoops, of which any beach-hitting Marine would be proud. Often this so acts to confuse the dog, who is unused to cyclists charging him, that he'll put on the binders and head for home. If he strides boldly out to meet your challenge with blood in his

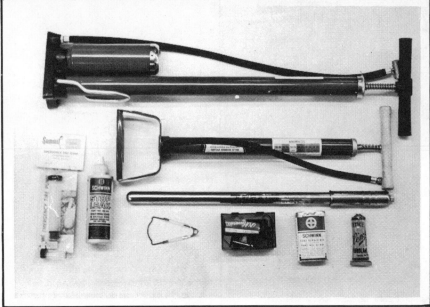

Pumps come in different styles, as do tube repair kits (above).

Once installed, carrier racks and baskets require little or no attention from rider (right).

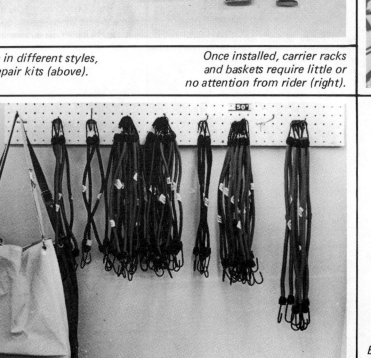

Bunjee cords are used to secure loads firmly on the rack or carrier, and work well. Bags are finding favor with youthful riders as well (left).

eye, employ tactic one.

We know of no companies that carry bicycle insurance per se. Some may have incorporated it into a regular policy, and it would be worth your while to check. If not, perhaps a rider can be tacked onto your present plan, which should cost only a few dollars per year.

Cycling during inclement weather is not the best strategy for the safety-minded rider. In a heavy blanket of fog, for example, the motorist has practically zero visibility. Also, he is not watching for pedaling bicyclists on the side of the road, but is more concerned with staying near the white lines and keeping a sharp lookout for automobiles ahead.

Riding in the rain also can be a pain in the neck, elbow, head and assorted other anatomical spots as well. When any substantial amount of precipitation hits a paved roadway, it tends to lift the oil that has soaked into the surface — deposited by motorized vehicles — which cuts traction to a point similar to roller skating on black ice. Combine the

slick surface with the width of a bicycle tire, and the potential for a hospital visit is almost assured.

There is also the fact that riding in the rain is downright uncomfortable. Many popular 10-speed bicycles aren't equipped with rear or front fenders, so all the excess moisture collected on the tires is spewed onto the rider. If riding correctly on the right side of the road, next to the gutter, the amount of water flipped on the rider can be substantial. It can cause a temporary loss of sight and permanent ruin of riding apparel.

As bicycle tires are not equipped for handling snow chains, nor are there such chains available, riding in the snow should be bypassed. While it may seem exciting or even romantic to pedal off amid swirling snowflakes, remember that those same flakes are sticking to the ground and being packed into a thick, slippery base. Bicycles do not function well when the rear tire is fish-tailing and the powdery snowbanks can be deceptively hard when a rider

Generator lights are fine when the bicycle is moving, but the light fades when the bicycle is stopped. A goodly amount of effort is needed to pump bicycle.

lands in them.

In many areas of the country, county and state department road crews shovel cinders or rock salt on the roads to help break up the pack and yield more traction. As demonstrated by the rotted hulks of near-new automobiles in the East, the salt solution causes rust like nobody's business. It can play havoc with the operating parts of a bike. It also will play havoc with the rider, should his tires flip up a bit of the melted rock salt directly into the eyes. The stinging and burning properties of the salt definitely will cause the eyes to water and close, which makes steering in any one direction quite a task. Should the aforementioned mishap occur with a bit of cinder — chunks of pebble-sized lava rock — in place of the saline solution, permanent eye damage may result.

Even the dry road surface offers hazards traction-wise to the cyclist, one of which is gravel or sand in tight corners. Speeding into such a turn, the rider may find the cycle sliding away from underneath him and contact with terra firma is more than probable. Needless to say, caution should be the primary factor in the prevention of such occurrences.

It's not unusual to find, on country roads of older construction, an unbroken painted line on the right side of the asphalt surface, which denotes the extreme edge of the apron. This paint tends to be slicker than the asphalt, so the bicyclist should ride on either side of it.

It would be impossible to document and record every hazard that can befall the bicyclist, simply because the rider continually finds new ones each day. However, if care and common sense are utilized, chances of riding a bicycle and living to enjoy it are immensely furthered.

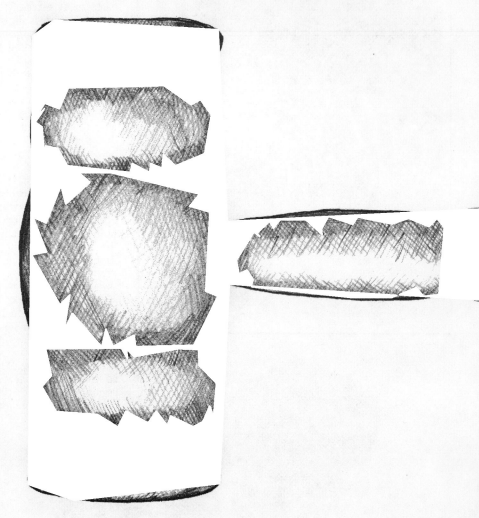

A DAY IN COURT

Police Officials, Recognizing The Problem Of Bicycle Safety, Have In One Community Laid Down The Law For Offenders!

Chapter 4

MOST BICYCLE RIDERS disregard the thought of being stopped — much less cited — for their cycling behavior. In most major cities around the country, this may be fact; police officials generally are exceptionally busy with other matters that demand attention, more serious than traffic regulation-violating bicycle riders.

At least, that's how it used to be. More and more riders now are being stopped by traffic patrolmen for violating laws and, if not cited, are given a thorough talking-to. Sometimes the latter is all that is required to reform bicyclists, especially younger ones. But teenagers, recognizing the fact that handing out citations to bicycle riders would deluge the courtrooms, tend to ignore warnings given by law enforcement authorities.

The City of Concord, a suburb of San Francisco, is breaking all the rules, however, and has its police officers handing out citations whenever they see a violation take place. And what's more, the violators are appearing before duly appointed judges in a special Bicycle Traffic Court!

The program, set up several years ago, is not oriented towards punishing offenders, but rather educating and hopefully thereby reducing the danger to riders.

The make-up of the court is unique, also, as students serve as the judges. Based upon scholastic ability and leadership qualities, the students are selected to serve for a period of one calendar year by faculty and student body representatives. Some of the court officials are carried over to the following calendar year to maintain an experienced staff around which to build an experienced court.

Three students, one Chief Justice and two Associate Justices, preside over the court hearings held every Saturday. A scout from the Police Explorer Post, sponsored by the Concord Police Association, serves as Bailiff. Other officials present include an adult counselor, who is assisted by a police cadet assigned to the bicycle detail that particular day, along with the officer in charge of the bicycle detail or representative of the Traffic Division.

At the beginning of each year, a schedule is developed whereby the student judges are assigned the dates they will preside over court hearings. The position of Chief Justice changes each week, and the students can expect to be tapped for the position four times per year, along with four sessions in which they serve as Associate Judges.

Court convenes each Saturday of the year in the Municipal Court at 10:30 a.m. Citations issued throughout the week are forwarded to the bicycle detail officer and make

Bailiff reads first case to the student judges (right). After being called to order, chief justice details purpose of the Bicycle Traffic Court (below). Police explorer post bailiff shows defendent complaint sheet filed against him (bottom).

Concord police officer taps seal and license number into frame of youngster's bike.

up the calendar for that week.

To keep things legal, each of the judges is given an oath of office by a regular justice. To learn the proper courtroom procedure, they attend sessions, receive a history orientation and are furnished with information sheets to aid in the operation of the bicycle court.

Once all of the defendents are present on a Saturday morning, the Chief Justice calls the court to order and reads the following address:

"Before hearing today's cases I wish to point out to all of you that this court was organized by the Concord Police Department with the approval of the Contra Costa County Juvenile Authorities. The purpose of this court is to impress upon the bicycle riders that they are responsible for the proper operation of their bicycles. We hope that our decisions will help those who appear before us to become better riders and thereby add to the safety of the residents of our city. Any failure to obey the instructions of this court will be referred to the Juvenile Court of the County."

The bailiff then begins calling cases before the justices, and administers an oath to each defendent. To bypass any legal problems, defendents are not required to raise their right hands nor swear in taking the oath: "_____, you have been called before this court on a serious matter. Do you promise to answer all questions truthfully?"

This completed, the bailiff then reads the charges against the defendent to the judges. The Chief Justice then asks if the defendent indeed committed the offense for which he is charged, asks for the defendent's side of the story, and proceeds with his verbal questioning.

The bicycle detail officer had formulated a list of questions from which the Chief Justice may draw, or he may ask others he feels pertinent. They include: "Whose bicycle were you riding? How long have you been riding a bicycle? Did you know what you were doing was wrong before the officer told you? Have you ever appeared in Bicycle Court before?"

Following the questioning and determination of the rider's innocence or guilt, one or more of the following sentences are imposed:

1. Obtain a bicycle license within 15 days. The bicycle must be brought in for licensing.

2. Have a Concord Police Officer check your equipment and return your copy of the citation or some other proof of correction signed by the officer to the Police Department by next Friday.

3. Have your parents deprive you of the use of any bicycle for _____ days.

4. Copy section _____ of the Concord Bicycle Ordinance _____ times and return it to the Police Department by next Friday.

5. Write a composition of not less than _____ words on the subject, _____ and return it to the Police Department by next Friday.

6. Verbal reprimand or suspended sentence as follows: _____ .

The court takes various measures to assure that parents are notified of the proceeding, that their child has been cited, and encourages them to attend. One method is through a letter sent from the Chief of Police's office informing them of the violation and function and purpose of the court. If the child is unable to attend on the date specified on the citation, the parents must inform the bicycle detail officer of the date that the child will appear.

If the parents decline the offer of attending the courtroom proceedings against their child, a copy of the Chief Justice's decision in the case is mailed to them. Parents are encouraged to help enforce the sentence imposed, especially when it requires suspension of biking priviledges.

If authorities discover that the child has failed to carry out the punishment phase of the sentence, the violator is called before the bicycle detail officer to discover the reasoning behind his actions. If after the interview the violator continues to disregard instructions of the court, the parents are called before the bicycle detail officer for an interview. To show that this matter is not to be taken lightly, if this interview of the parents does not result in compliance with the sentence, the case is referred to the county Juvenile Court.

While statistics are not available concerning the effect of the bicycle traffic court in curtailing injuries or fatalities suffered by bicycle riders, it appears safe to assume that those same riders will think twice before violating traffic regulations. This, in itself, will no doubt result in more caution on the riders' part, and perhaps a life saved. If so, the purpose of the court has been well served.

57

Bikeways Can't Be Beat!

Many Communities Are Constructing Bikeways And Finding Them the Ultimate In Safe, Pleasurable Riding. Here's How To Start One In Your City.

IT HAS BEEN SHOWN, through documented figures listed in the preceding chapter, that riding a bicycle — the most popular participation sport in this country — can be dangerous. Everyone from the gentleman in the oval office at 1600 Pennsylvania Avenue in Washington, D.C., down to a rookie policeman on a beat in the smallest rural community have recognized this problem and timely remedies have been presented.

One of the best plans to come out of this crisis is the segregation of the bicyclist from the motorist totally. However, implementation of this domestic isolationist policy resembles the proverbial bear with his paw in the honey tree: Sweet rewards can be attained, but require overcoming stinging obstacles before they can be tasted.

The separatist route has been collared with several names, of which bikeways, bike lanes and bike paths are the most familiar. These, for the most part, consist either of a totally roadway-removed ribbon of pavement or a separate lane on existing roadways in which automobile traffic

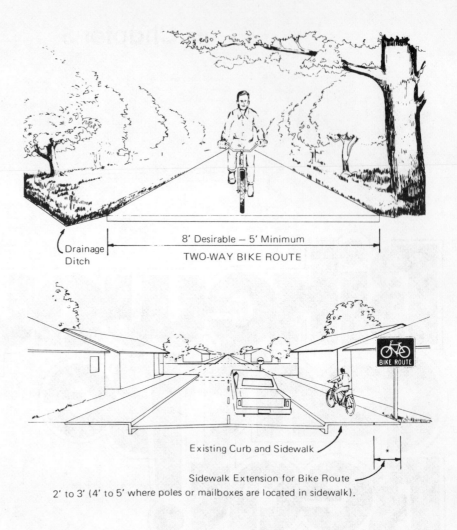

8' Desirable – 5' Minimum

Drainage Ditch

TWO-WAY BIKE ROUTE

Existing Curb and Sidewalk

Sidewalk Extension for Bike Route
2' to 3' (4' to 5' where poles or mailboxes are located in sidewalk).

ONE-WAY BIKE ROUTE EACH SIDE OF STREET

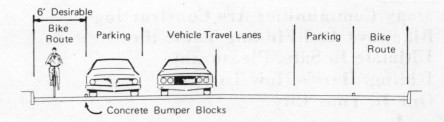

6' Desirable

Bike Route | Parking | Vehicle Travel Lanes | Parking | Bike Route

Concrete Bumper Blocks

strictly is forbidden. Both are functional, perhaps the former being somewhat safer for the rider than an integral highway lane. For the sake of brevity and clarity, all three types of routes will be classified under the term bikeway in this chapter, unless otherwise stipulated.

The vast majority of towns and cities in the United States do not have, or are not in the process of initiating, bikeways. There is plenty of groundwork that, unbeknown to the cyclist, must be completed before any such project can become workable. Many city officials are of the opinion that they have enough work to do without adding more, hence aren't the ones to propose such a program. It also costs the taxpayers money, which is another obstacle to be dealt with, the result being that most officials will let sleeping dogs lie — until ready to bite them in the ballot box.

Surprisingly, the idea of routes designed for bikes especially, despite the current stress placed on this issue, is not of recent vintage. Back near the turn of the century, when Henry M. Flagler built the 2,000-room Royal Poinciana Hotel in Palm Beach, Florida, he included a short bicycle trail adjacent to a golf course. Some thirty-five years later, the city built a three-mile paved strip along Lake Worth specifically for bicyclists. It still is in use today.

However, it was a group of citizens in another Florida town that really sparked the current drive for bikeways. In 1961, Mr. and Mrs. George Fichter formed a bicycle club and, concerned with the problems of mounting traffic and hazardous riding conditions in their town of Homestead, mapped out a maze of secondary roads connecting residential areas with shopping facilities, playgrounds, parks, schools and other much-frequented locales. These secondary roads were termed "bicycle safety routes."

Club members, with the backing of the Homestead Chamber of Commerce, approached city officials with the

program, who also bought the idea. They had the routes recorded by traffic engineers, raised funds to pay for the manufacture and installation of blue and white route signs, then achieved police cooperation in a city-wide orientation of the community with the project.

It wasn't long until the majority of the town was backing the program. Motorists were encouraged to drive more slowly on marked bicycle routes or avoid them entirely, while speed limits were reduced in these areas. In 1962, the bicycle safety routes were dedicated officially.

Quite a few cities adopted the idea of bikeways and more such routes have been established through the years. There currently are in excess of 175 cities with established routes and another, similar number of cities that have scheduled bikeways for their towns. However, this seemingly large number in reality is a scandalously small one, when compared with the crying need for this type of program in virtually every major city and many suburbs as well.

The bikeway provides many more advantages to the using community than simply safety for its residents. The mere presence of a bikeway impels a feeling of a more casual lifestyle, less harried than normal. This feeling is reinforced especially by the slower pace of automobiles on streets marked as bikeways. Everyone slows down a bit, relaxes, and captures a piece of the day.

Bikeways also promote the idea of physical fitness. Almost no one in poor physical condition likes to be reminded of it, by others or his conscience; it is relatively easy to avoid reminders by changing television channels. But when the same individual must traverse a street marked as a bikeway and sees riders pedaling to regain some semblance of physical conditioning, the reminder is awfully hard to suppress.

Also, most riders concerned mainly with physical fitness are not especially choosey about their riding habitat, other than its safety features. It makes no sense to take chances of endangering life in hopes of producing a good physical specimen. The bikeway has proved the perfect argument for individuals who use the latter rationalization, where the threat of danger usually is minimized, if not removed entirely.

As mentioned in Chapter One, many riders take up the sport in hopes of returning to nature, of helping and enjoying their environment. For this, the bikeway is definitely a boon. Most planners of such routes place major stress on assuring that bikeways travel through both flora and fauna-rich areas. Such places as national monuments, historically important sites, lookouts and other viewpoints are included where feasible. They offer the casual rider a chance to scrutinize and enjoy areas he has passed often, but never stopped and really looked at.

In this day of disassociated parents and children, the bikeway actually can aid in building closer family bonds. Now that it no longer is an oddity to find all ages riding bicycles, the bikeway provides a close-to-home pathway for evening or after dinner tours. Sharing an experience with your offspring can and does leave a much more lasting impression than the usual trite conversations of school and work over dinner.

It is not an uncommon occurrence to hear of neighbors who literally build walls around each other, with jealousy, money, education, position and social status the primary building blocks. The introduction of a bikeway often bulldozes these walls, offering closer kinship with neighbors than previously was possible or desirable. It is difficult to ignore a neighbor, out watering his lawn, as you pedal past on your bicycle.

Bikeways, especially those found in the cities, are of special value to small children. With few exceptions, parents in these metropolitan areas sternly prohibit their children riding in the street, or out of view of the house. Primarily, this is for safety reasons, which leave the youngsters only the sidewalk or the driveway on which to ride.

But bikeways in the neighborhood can alleviate the parents' fears for the safety of their children to a great extent. The fact that motorists slow their machines and are constantly on the lookout for riders on the well marked streets drops the chances of accidents. The bikeway also offers a chance for youngsters to see other areas than those specifically within the framework of his neighborhood — a much needed lesson in light of our current transient society.

The bikeway also can help adult riders, more of whom are joining the ranks of the bicyclists each day. With the tight economy in this country, a substantial savings can be accumulated by riding a bicycle on daily errands that previously required a second car.

A compact car's operational expense absorbed by the

owner over a ten-year period amounts to nearly $11,000, according to the Federal Highway Administration. A standard-sized automobile's expense is somewhat higher, roughly $13,500 for the same period. A sub-compact vehicle rests at the other end of the greenback spectrum, costing nearly $9,500 for the ten-year period.

It is worth noting that these figures also are the equivalent of 100,000 miles of operation. They include cost of gasoline, maintenance, parking, tolls and insurance, computed at the present rate, which surely is to rise in coming years. These figures also do not account for the initial purchase price of the auto.

As these figures indicate, a great amount of cash can be saved by either the elimination of the second car entirely, or by limiting its usage. Whereas most housewives formerly were skeptical about using the bicycle for such purposes due to the lack of safety considerations, the bikeways have again opened up such avenues.

The amount of workers that commute to their jobs on bicycles also is on the upsurge, and bikeways can take part of the credit. Once again, the matter of safety hindered cycling prior to the introduction of bikeways. This commuting to work does in fact stimulate the body which seldom gets used in a thinker-type position, where little physical activity is encountered. A healthy body equals a healthy mind.

Despite what the children may say about him, the school principal is concerned about their welfare. Consequently, many favorable responses to bikeways have been forthcoming from these individuals. The installation and use of bikeways tends to remove wrinkles from educators' brows, which then can be replaced by wrinkles for another dozen or so reasons.

One of the largest group of supporters for bikeways is the local police department. To their way of figuring, if more bicycles are used safely instead of automobiles, their workload will diminish considerably. Fewer vehicle code violations will be committed, simply because autos will become fewer in number. The number of accidents will also decrease.

Reaction to bikeways on the part of merchants and retail outlets in any specific community is bristlingly divided. Merchants that favor such bikeways claim that they provide additional access to their stores and drop the need for massive parking lots. Opposing merchants claim that bikeways, if using sidewalk space, make conditions hazardous for pedestrian patrons. Still others feel that their curbside parking, a convenience often utilized by shoppers, will be eliminated with the bikeway boom. Also, the great sums spent in purchasing, paving and painting parking lots would seem largely a wasted investment as fewer spaces would be used.

As far as the individual homeowner is concerned, the bikeway in his neighborhood can readily increase the value of his property, as real estate salesmen are quick to point out. A bikeway means a quieter, less congested neighborhood, and one that is much safer for the children. It also represents an added recreational facility, for which they paid but scant coppers.

If there are all of these advantages to be gained by the bikeways program, why has is it not been applied to all communities throughout the United States? The reason, basically, is that few individuals know how to go about getting such a program initiated in their respective

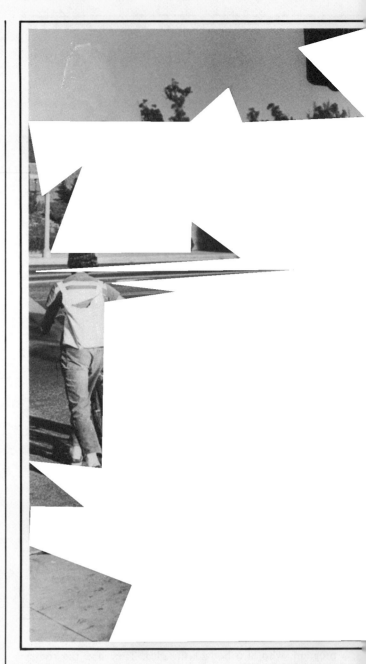

communities.

Looking at requirements and regulations followed by some of the major cities instituting bikeways, one common factor continually shows itself: They all formulated strict plans and stuck to them. All plans are similar in outline and design, they can prove helpful to the individual or club attemtping to start such a program in their own community.

According to others who have formulated bikeways in their cities, there are four basic goals that need be set and attained within the basic framework of the pre-planned course of action. They are: (1) determining bicycling needs and interest; (2) making use of existing facilities suitable for bicycling; (3) establishing a bicycle rental service if feasible, and (4) developing additional bicycle facilities as needs and interest justify.

Oregon, a leading state in bikeways legislation, brokedown the goals even farther. In determining the cycling needs, interest and problems, the planners evaluated the cycling activity within the communities. In this effort, they

approached a number of groups and authorities, notably first were the law enforcement agencies. From this group they received information on conflicts and other problems related to bicycles versus automobiles.

Armed with this information, they then approached local planning commissions and personnel for their feelings on the feasibility of bikeways. Local planning commissions generally are the groups that will work the kinks out of any proposed system, and assure its prompt and adequate implementation.

They next checked with civic organizations and service clubs for their opinions on proposed bikeways. Most of these groups generally will support any proposal that will reduce accidents in their cities or towns. They usually carry quite a bit of weight with city officials.

The Oregon group next checked with bicycling clubs in the immediate towns for their feelings and recommendations. In all but a few extreme cases, bicycle clubs will be more than happy to unify with the proponents of the bikeways, for they stand to benefit most from such a program.

The group then consulted authorities in other cities and states, as well as reviewed state and local outdoor recreation plans. Starting a proposition such as this completely cold can be a frightening experience, and any help offered or ideas secured are much better than nothing. Remember, these folks already have run the gauntlet and are quite aware of things to avoid or encourage. Use their advice. They've played in the ballpark before.

Another group that can be contacted for opinions and support definitely would be sales and rental facilities around the city. Few bicycle dealers will pass up the chance to back a cycling club, for the simple reason that improved riding conditions will increase their bicycle sales. Another reason would be that failure to back such a proposal could understandably put a black mark against their establishments resulting in the loss of customers.

Rental outlets might be inclined to lend financial support or the like, in hopes of making good return arrangements at a later time.

With some basic information in hand at this point, it is time to approach the cyclist directly to discover what he feels is needed, his cycling interests and what problems he feels need be overcome to assure better, safer and happier cycling. The easiest way to accomplish this feat is through the use of a survey — a mimeographed sheet will work — that is distributed where it will reach the optimum number of riders.

The following form, distributed by the City-County Planning Commission of Lexington, Kentucky, is a fine example of the information that should be included on the survey:

As mentioned, this survey form, or one like it that individual committees devise to accommodate varying features in their given area, can be distributed widely. The return address of the unit tabulating the results should appear on the form, along with a filing date to assure expediency.

At the time the survey is distributed, the committee can, through observation, interview or existing records, determine other pertinent factors that will influence the proposed bikeway. Volunteers can assume positions at heavily bicycle-traveled junctions and take counts both of automobiles and bicycles that frequent the area during peak

---

Bicycle Riders, Speak Out! The City of Lexington wants to hear from you.

As a result of the growing needs of a rapidly increasing number of cyclists in the community, the Lexington — Fayette County Planning Commission has undertaken a study of the need for bicycle facilities in the community. We want to hear from adult and child riders, commuters and sports riders, experienced riders as well as those "thinking about it."

This survey has been undertaken as a means of compiling the information necessary to plan for bicycle transportation needs. With your help, we can find out how many people ride bikes in the community and where they ride them.

Additional questionnaires are available through Public Schools, the Planning Commission, the Public Library and bookmobiles, and the Transylvania and University of Kentucky student centers.

1. How many bicycles are in your family?_____(Please count only bikes with a tire size of 20 inches or over.)

2. How old are the bicycle riders in your household? ____ ____ ____ ____

3. Please list the start and finish of the five most important bicycle trips you and your family take in a week:

   From _____   To_____
   From _____   To_____
   From _____   To_____
   From _____   To_____
   From _____   To_____

4. Using 100% as a total, what percent of your household's bicycle riding is done on the days of:

   _____%Sunday   _____%Tuesday   _____%Friday
   _____%Monday   _____%Wednesday   _____% Saturday
                       _____%Thursday

5. Of the bike trips listed, which one is made most often in your family? _____
   Which is the second most frequent bike trip? _____
   Which is the third most frequent bike trip? _____

   a. to work   d. to school   g. to Univ. Of Kentucky
   b. shopping   e. to the park   h. out in the country
   c. around the neighborhood   f. visiting friends

6. By what means (car, bus, bike, walking) does your family presently make trips for these purposes?

   _____ Recreation _____ School
   _____ Work   _____ Shopping

7. If provisions were made for bicycling such as marked or separated routes and parking facilities,

   a. would you use your bicycles more? __Yes __No
   b. would you start using a bike if you don't? __Yes __No

8. Are you in favor of a City operated bicycle registration program to facilitate the return of lost or stolen bikes and to record the number of bikes used in Lexington?

   Yes_____ No____Comments: _____

9. What problems do you often encounter in riding around the community?
   _____

0. If a comprehensive bicycle program is developed for the City of Lexington, what items do you think are important? _____
   _____

Your Name (Optional) _____
Your Address (Optional) _____

periods. These peak periods generally would be approximately an hour before the opening of schools and shops, lunchtimes, termination of school and evening rush hour, when commuters are leaving for home. The traffic counters need not be at the locations all day, but should spend only a couple of hours at each location during each peak period. This gives a representative sampling of the automobile and bicycle traffic in any given area.

If a bicycle rental facility is planned or hoped-for on the bikeway, added investigation should be completed to discover, for example, the current rates of rentals in that area. Most shops that rent bicycles offer either an hourly standard of around fifty cents per hour, or an all-day rate. Like parking lots in downtown areas, most facilities have a cut-off point for the hourly wage, say three dollars. If the bicycle is rented by the hour, the maximum amount that can be levied against the owner if the bicycle was used for more than six hours (at fifty cents per hour) is three dollars. If the bicycle is returned prior to this time, the rider then pays the standard rate of fifty cents per hour.

Most shops that rent bicycles insist on some form of security, most often a driver's license, car keys, billfold or the like. In the case of children's rental, who generally carry none of the above items, parents are required to post the security.

The reason for the security deposit is to prevent theft of the rented item. Many bicycle dealerships also have a requirement along these lines letting a prospective buyer test-ride a cycle. Recalls one dealer, "I never worried about such things as theft some time ago, but when I walked out to check a rider testing a bike and saw him loading it in the back of a van, I knew that something would have to be done.

"Now, I insist they leave their wallets at the counter for security. Those that don't carry wallets don't test-ride bikes unless a salesman is standing right with them."

It would be wise for the bikeways backers to get some definite ideas as to demand for rental bikes and the types most rented. If there has been little demand for rented bikes throughout the city, it might be wise to overlook installing a rental facility on the bikeway; it probably would run in the red. This factor almost would be guaranteed if the bicycle facility stocked only models which weren't necessarily popular with prospective customers. Information as to which type is most rented would generally be available from existing rental facilities.

Just as with any mechanical item, it can be expected that parts will wear and break over a period of time. This failure rate generally will be somewhat higher in the bike rental business, as rentors may be inclined to more rigorously use the bike than were it their own. Therefore, it is in order to learn what methods existing rental agencies use to avoid these break-downs; some may insist upon payment for the repairs, should the damage have been a result of rider negligence. Assure that this fact is clearly stated, both in signs around the facility and verbally upon renting a bike, to avoid any later legal hassle.

Repair costs vary according to the item being repaired, area of the country and current hourly wage for trained mechanics, so the interested group should check and discover the amount involved. A repair facility in the rental shop may either make or break the operation.

It readily can be seen that voluminous paperwork will be compiled before the program can even get off the ground. These facts and figures should be evaluated, along with the survey forms, and put aside for the moment.

The next area that needs attention is evaluation of existing facilities and their possible use as bikeways or bike paths, along with their present usage by bicyclists, satisfactory or otherwise.

The prime individuals to assist in this evaluation are officials of the parks and recreation departments in the city or town. Other investigations should be conducted by individuals to determine the present usage of roads, walks, hiking trails, paved multiple-use areas and parking lots.

Serious consideration should be given to the utilization of the above routes to include bikeways or bike paths where possible, as cost of conversion is slashed considerably. Most are not in constant use and bicyclists may not present a problem in many instances.

Another area that should be scrutinized is not under the jurisdiction of the parks and recreation departments, but may have potential for cycling. This includes side streets, secondary or little-used roads, school grounds, school and college tracks, airports, fairgrounds, parking lots, race tracks and velodromes. Side streets and little-used roads should be carefully examined, as these make up the bulk of bikeways present in the United States. It is much easier to post signs on roads with little automotive traffic than to construct new roads specifically for bicyclists.

It may take some imagination and lots of looking, but there still is another area that could bear fruit. Search for dry canals, dry river beds, abandoned railroad beds, secondary roads paralleling throughways, median strips on highways and existing, little-used pedestrian or riding paths and trails for possible use as bike paths.

It may seem strange to have included the dry canals and dry river beds in this list, for anyone knows that pedaling over sand and rocks is almost impossible, unless the bed happened to be of concrete. Perhaps more interest should be given to the banks of previous waterways. Cattle, fisher-

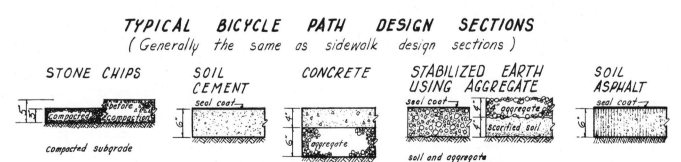

TYPICAL BICYCLE PATH DESIGN SECTIONS
(Generally the same as sidewalk design sections)

STONE CHIPS   SOIL CEMENT   CONCRETE   STABILIZED EARTH USING AGGREGATE   SOIL ASPHALT

NOTE: All of the above types of bicycle paths must be constructed on a well drained subgrade or subbase to prevent settling, or heaving through frost action

men and other forms of livestock have walked along the banks for years, cutting a clear trail through the growing vegetation that is extraordinarily hard-packed. As the bike tire isn't exceptionally wide, this path would be sufficient for riding.

Abandoned railroad beds also are fine areas for cycling — once the ties and rails have been removed. Generally, the passage of the iron horses packed the ground beneath the rails, making passage easy. Provided, of course, the ties were not laid on small rocks for stability, which make bicycle riding impossible.

Abandoned railroad beds are not exactly hard to come by any more. With the merging of railroads by huge conglomerates, the smaller railroads that can't compete go under. When this happens, the ties and rails usually are removed and sold, which leaves the bed open to anyone.

Once these findings are assembled, they should be evaluated in terms of facilities available, and use of the facilities for bicycling.

Before most individuals will be inclined to spend their money on financing bikeways, they want to be informed of their purpose and prospective use. It can only help to have the support of the entire community, and this can be obtained by several programmed events.

The Bicycle Institute of America proposes starting a bicycle safety program in the community, enlisting the aid of the police department, city safety committee, Parent-Teacher Association, school safety patrols and parents at large. This program is a sure bet to win support of practically everyone, as it is impossible not to back an issue that would improve safety for the children.

Another area to venture into is the organization of bike clubs. Children especially are drawn toward joining clubs and, with safety as a first priority feature, clubs should spring up readily.

Receiving the backing of parks and recreation department officials is a decided plus, and should not be especially difficult if the survey results indicate that improved facilities are desired. The main task of the parks and recreation department is to provide recreational facilities desired by the community; bicycling is a form of recreation and rates such consideration.

Civic and service clubs, once notified through talks or speeches at local meetings, seldom hesitate to support the bikeways proposal. They recognize the improved safety such a program provides and, as they are also parents and perhaps riders, generally like to see such facilities available.

Getting on the good side of the press in the community is a desireable goal, as they can provide wide-reaching publicity for the project. By following a story from the ground floor, a reporter is more inclined to become interested personally and go to bat for the project in his news copy.

Planning outings utilizing the bicycle is a good way to involve community dwellers with the bikeways proposal. Be it a casual trip to city hall or a short tour out in the country is no matter. What is, though, is the fact that the bicycle is being used as the form of transportation showing that it, too, deserves consideration as a recreational activity.

Before thoughts of constructing new bikeways should be entertained, give serious consideration to using existing facilities. With a minimum of effort, many of the previously listed locations can be converted for use as bike paths. If necessary, a ribbon of asphalt can be laid on the old railroad beds at minimal cost. Canal banks are almost perfect for bicycling, as they are hard packed and nearly flat.

Canal tow paths, generally found in the Eastern regions of the United States, once were used as walkways for domestic animals pulling barges up the waterways. As this

This bike route was established at little cost, as it uses part of roadway already established for motorists. Signs, paint and labor are much cheaper than paving.

practice is all but eliminated by mechanization, the tow paths are free and open. The canals were laid out with just enough of a grade to keep the water flowing — about one to one-half foot per mile — which makes for perfect cycling. They also are attractive because the waterway provides an interesting atmosphere, with all manner of vegetation and wildlife being found on its banks. In the cases of long-abandoned canals, vegetative overgrowth may have to be cleared before cycling can commence.

As an example of what can be done, the National Park Service, operators and maintainers of the Chesapeake and Ohio Canal in Washington, D.C., have planned hiker/bike paths along the Potomac River every five to eight miles. They plan to include crude camping areas, reachable only by hiking or cycling, with toilets, water and shelters for overnight campers.

In the West, where canals and tow paths are few in number, roads along irrigation ditches can serve the same

While riding a bicycle across a crosswalk may not be illegal everywhere, it is a practice that can have serious repercussions. Walk the bicycle across always.

function. These roads generally have been well traveled, resulting in a hard base that may require only a topping of asphalt.

Some rivers, formerly mighty that now trickle on a concrete bed in most cities, can share the concrete channel with the bicyclist during the summer months. Other cities maintain concrete overflow channels — normally dry — that also can be used for cycling. However, during winter months — or times when flooding can be expected — the routes must be closed to avoid having riders endangered by a wall of water coursing unexpectedly down the channel.

If construction of new bike paths must be undertaken, there are still several factors to consider prior to allocating funds and beginning work. In all, there are four factors that should be examined: Length of the trail, points of interest, aesthetic value and final destination. Before making any decision, the area should be visually examined.

It should be remembered, when examining the area, that the bicyclist is not part mountain goat, and cannot negotiate steep hills. While this will be explored later at greater detail, keep in mind that the path should be as close to level as possible.

The bike path should be appealing to the eye, as cyclists probably are deriving more pleasure from the environment than any motorists. A pleasing landscape enhances the cyclist's enjoyment of the ride, as well as promoting its repeated usage.

Not many individuals would repeatedly ride out across the Kalahari Desert, even if it wasn't hot, because it seemingly has no variety. This factor alone — variety — either can guarantee repeated use or little of the same. If there is a rental bike facility on the bike path, repeated use is of dire importance.

It is relatively easy to include a couple of rolling hills, a bit of forest or other secluded wood, some open road and corners that all add up to variety in the bike path. A stream, pond or large lake, a bridge or two and a meadow add greatly to the path's appeal. If the route passes leafy trees that turn crackly red and gold when autumn nips the air, riders will return again and again to watch nature perform her wonders before winter cuts any riding short.

Appealing to aesthetic virtues, the bike path should be routed past points of interest like historical landmarks, for example. Generally, the caretakers try to keep the location as representative of the period concerned, which lends a unique, heritage-filled atmosphere to the site. Museums, arboretums, exhibits, monuments and nature centers all add greatly to the path, and should be included where possible and practical.

From the use standpoint, it would be wise to construct the path by recreational areas like parks, schools and the like, for this will encourage others to use it. There is no little amount of loyalty given a route designed especially for bicyclists by bicyclists, and you want to get the most usage out of the path. Only then will there be a substantial return for the expenditure of money required.

Consider using parallel roads, canals, river or creek banks, or using a perimeter area of existing roadways for the bike path. This saves time and money, as the surface of the prospective path will not need great preliminary attention.

A bike path should run close to commercial facilities like restrooms, refreshment stands and resting areas. A cyclist is more inclined to stop along his route than an automobile operator, so this should be taken into consideration. These all are factors that can be determined by visual examination of the proposed area.

While checking the proposed site, make a rough sketch of the path's route. Photographs will help reinforce the path's highlights. The route then should be traced on a topographical map, which is available from the U. S. Geographical Survey Office in Washington, D.C.

After the path is laid out completely, return to the area for a check to assure that the geography does not necessitate changes. It then should be staked and measured with surveying equipment so that all the grades are found negotiable. If not, changes are in order.

Grades varying in steepness from one to twenty percent have been incorporated in bike paths over the years, all proving negotiable for the rider. The relative fact is the length of the grade that determines whether it will be ridden or walked. The long climbs are most difficult for riders, even if the incline is relatively small. Type of bicycle utilized also plays a role in the negotiation of a hill.

The average of all maximum grades in bike paths is eight and one-half percent. For comparison, a grade of ten percent is considered the maximum for comfortable walking.

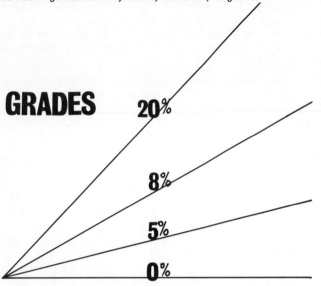

This chart shows what grades can mean to the cyclist. A grade of 8%, while calling for much pedaling effort, can be negotiated. Any more, like 20%, forget it!

GRADES

20%

8%

5%

0%

It is recommended that no grades over this maximum figure be incorporated into a bike path for the average rider.

The modern 10-speed, designed for lightness and featuring the multi-gear capability, is able to handle much more severe grades than a heavier 3-speed model. If the 1-speed bike is going to be the primary user of the facility, keep the grades to a minimum, not to exceed four or five percent. Speaking in figures, this means that for every one hundred feet of path traversed, the rider has climbed either four or five feet. If it is unavoidable that higher grades and longer runs be included, provide a rest stop about half-way up the grade so that cyclists may dismount and rest for a few moments.

The length of the bike path is primarily determined by the individuals that will use it most, and the machines they ride. When someone mentions a distance of five miles for a bike path, this seems like a goodly distance. However, when it is remembered that an average walker can cover between two and one-half and three miles in one hour, the five miles doesn't seem nearly as long.

Most cyclists pedal at an average of ten miles per hour, even faster on popular 10-speed models. This chops the riding time over a five-mile course to something in the neighborhood of twenty-five minutes to a half-hour; not much of a ride, really.

The unfortunate part is that in many cities, the parks and recreation folks simply cannot provide more miles of paths. What has been tried, and has not worked too successfully, is joining paths of short duration together and forming a network of interconnecting paths. One thing is certain: No matter how small, a bicycle path most definitely is safer than street riding.

The width of the path also is a matter that must be taken care of before actual construction of the bike path begins. It has been decided that most users of the bike path ride either in pairs or in groups, and usually two abreast. Consequently, for a two-way path, a width of eight feet is most desirable, leaving four feet for riders passing in each direction. A minimum desired width on a two-way bike path is five feet; any slimmer and cyclists passing one another in opposite directions tend to get edgy.

A good point of the eight-foot distance is that maintenance vehicles, such as a street sweeper, can operate on its

surface. However, should the bike path be designed to accommodate these vehicles upon occasion, a proper base must be installed before the surface apron is applied. This will be discussed later in the chapter.

Another factor that need be considered when installing a bike path, if creeks or streams are included in the overall layout, are bridges. It has been shown in previously-constructed paths that the bridges need be somewhat wider than the minimal five-foot distance required for pedaling over ground, where handlebars and pedals are allowed to extend over the border.

An average of eight feet is about minimal when constructing a bridge, unless it is to be designed solely for one-way traffic. Should this be the case, a four-foot expanse only need be provided.

Surfacing a bridge is an area of dispute, but the main choices are wood, concrete or asphalt. It should be designed so that no bumps are encountered, that could throw the cyclist off-balance and into the drink. The surface also should be kept clean of loose gravel, sand, pebbles and the like, for a loss of traction on a bridge is not desirable.

Bear in mind that most individuals tend to stop and admire a creek or stream upon arriving at the bridge. In order to keep it free of stopped riders, a turn-out could be installed at both ends, and it would be here that cyclists dismount for a closer look at the water.

A bicycle is a highly-maneuverable piece of machinery, but care should be observed when constructing the bike path to assure no sharp curves are included. Bicyclists, like motorcyclists, tend to lean their bikes into the corners, which aids the steering. However, if the tight turn should be located at the bottom of a relatively steep hill, the cyclist may fail to slow enough to negotiate the turn safely, and ruin his whole day. In this instance, make the turn as long and slow as possible.

Once the bugs and kinks have been worked out of the proposed bike path, there is the problem of money, both for construction and, in some cases, for purchasing the land.

There are several avenues open to the planners, among them the chance for Federal assistance. Parks and recreation departments are eligible for direct or indirect support from:

* Housing Act of 1949, as amended, authorizing assistance to urban renewal (administered by the Urban Renewal Administration, Housing and Home Finance Agency, Washington 25, D.C.)

* Housing Act of 1949, as amended, Title VII, providing for an Open-Space Land Program to assist communities, regions, states, in providing necessary open-space land which should not otherwise be provided (administered by the Urban Renewal Administration, Housing and Home Finance Agency, Washington 25, D.C.)

* Land and Water Conservation Fund Act of 1965 for planning, acquiring, and developing state and local outdoor recreation areas (administered by the Bureau of Outdoor Recreation, Department of the Interior, Washington 25, D.C.)

In addition, the Federal Highway Administration has proposed that bicycle paths within existing highway rights-of-way be given serious, favorable consideration, when it is felt that a public need is served where, of course, conditions are appropriate.

The Federal Highway Administration also reports it currently is giving consideration to providing bike paths along routes scheduled for construction in urban and suburban areas, when desirable, especially if they will connect with existing paths in some type of overall system.

The Bicycle Institute of America, 122 East 42nd Street,

New York, New York 10017 can provide planning and counseling to groups interested in establishing bike paths in their communities.

With all factors considered and red tape obstacles worked out, actual construction can begin. This is the area where a team of specialists definitely is required, but individual groups can play an important part in the overall development.

After the path has been staked out, it must be cleared of all brush and debris, a sub-base established, a base prepared and a wearing surface laid atop the base.

While clearing the prospective bicycle path, all dead or diseased trees which could fall across the bike path possibly injuring a rider should be removed. The tree limbs of standing live, healthy trees need be inspected, and any dead or dying limbs pruned away. This will eliminate the chance of one falling.

While the pruning shears are handy, trim any overhanging branches that reach to within seven to ten feet above the ground, directly over the bike path. While its doubtful that a ten-foot-tall bike rider will utilize the bike path, riders of average height need not worry about dipping branches flicking faces during a healthy blow.

Any shrubs adjacent to the bike path should be cleared or cut back at least two feet from its borders so as not to encroach upon the path.

Where ditches or fills are planned for inclusion, clear the brush back at least one foot from both the top and bottom of the slopes. This will prohibit future overgrowth into the bike path.

During the clearing operations of dead trees and stumps from within or the borders of the path, all roots should be removed down a fair distance into the ground. Often, tree roots spread close to or on the surface of the soil and, if not removed, will later buckle the pavement where they cross under its surface. Patching cracks in the surface will be repeated periodically unless taken care of initially.

As the bike path's construction will much resemble normal roadways, steps should be taken to assure proper drainage or you'll have real problems. In addition to preventing the washing out of the path in various sections, proper drainage will prevent its heaving and buckling.

All roads are either crowned or slanted. The former means simply that the road is constructed so that the highest portion of the surface is located directly in the center, so that overflow water will channel down into both gutters along the sides of the road. Slanting of the roadway means exactly what it implies, that the surface is constructed with one high side, from which the water runs downwards to the opposite.

As crowning the road is somewhat more difficult and time-consuming, most bike paths are slanted slightly. This assures that no water will gather into puddles on the surface.

Water also must be removed from underneath the bike path, so that it will not freeze during winter and cause the surface either to buckle or heave, or both. This is accomplished by the usage of catch drains, that remove the water.

Should any portion of the bike path be cut through a hillside, a ditch must be placed on the high side so that any run-off will be caught and channeled away from the bike path instead of slowly — or rapidly, during a flash flood — washing out the surface.

In areas like the Bayou country of Louisiana, or any other area that is exceedingly wet, it's a smart move to install underdrains to channel off sub-surface water. Frost action could cause this water to freeze, thereby buckling or heaving the path.

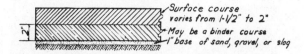

NOTES: Slope 1/4" to 3/8" per foot across surface to insure runoff.
Thickness of paving will depend upon local soil conditions.
Maximum thickness of any course should not exceed 3".
Where two layers are used, the bottom layer can be a binder course to save money.
To achieve longer life for bicycle paths, increase the asphalt content 1 to 2 percent more than called for in road specifications.
Most conventional asphalt spreaders can place widths from 8' to 12'. Where widths less than this are used, the material may have to be spread by hand at an increased cost for a narrower path.

Once the path has been cleared of any obstructions and any sub-surface drainage — where necessary — accomplished, the next logical step is preparation of a sub-base. It positively is a necessity to have a sub-base underneath the final surface, or it will literally go to hell.

It is best to consult a professional, someone like a county, city or state engineer, to dictate exactly which type of sub-base your area requires. In areas that are noted for their dry climate, oftentimes simply compacting the cleared path will suffice for a sub-base. However, in areas that are either wet or unstable, an addition of crushed stone, slag or the like must be applied.

In construction, a bike path is not unlike a driveway, light-duty road or a sidewalk. A base course is applied atop a sub-base, which helps to distribute the weight of vehicles that traverse it, and protect the surface coat. While many would assume that a thin sub- and base coat are all that are necessary, due to the fact that bicycles are of such light weight, it should be remembered that maintenance vehicles and street sweepers probably will glide over this same surface, so a heavy construction indeed is necessary.

Base courses, as well as surfacing materials, vary widely according to area, materials available, construction methods, and cost. Generally, however, a base course is of graded aggregate, crushed stone, slag, soil cement, soil asphalt or concrete. Usage is dictated by the aforementioned factors.

As far as surface usage is concerned, nearly two-thirds of all bike paths currently in operation are of asphalt, according to figures released by the Bicycle Institute of America. Next favored is dirt, then, in order to preference and usage, gravel, concrete, turf, soil cement, blue stone dust and calache.

The leader, asphalt, actually can be broken-down into three separate types: Asphalt cement, hot-mix asphalt concrete and soil asphalt.

Asphalt cement is strong, adhesive, waterproof, durable and it resists the action of most salts, acids and alkalies. It is broken down into four different categories according to hardness, measured by the time lapse taken for a needle to

penetrate vertically into its surface. It is solid at normal temperatures, but liquifies readily when heated, dissolved in petroleum distilates, or emulsified.

Commonly known as paving asphalt, it must be heated before mixing with aggregate or spraying to be workable. It is possible to get bogged-down especially easily by continuing into specific components that make up asphalt, so we suggest that any interested parties contact the Asphalt Institute, College Park, Maryland.

Hot-mix asphalt concrete is commonly used also in paving, and lends itself exceptionally well to bike paths. It generally is made by screening aggregate into various sizes that are then added to the heated asphalt at a plant, and transported to the site. It then is spread to the proper thickness and rolled beneath a steam roller.

For a bike path, the thickness of the asphalt is between one and one-half and two inches, or twice the size of the largest aggregate used, atop a four-inch aggregate base. It costs between twenty and forty cents per square yard per inch thick, which isn't terribly expensive, considering the long life it has. For those interested in more information, write the National Asphalt Pavement Association, 6715 Kenilworth Avenue, Celtic Building, Riverdale, Maryland.

Soil asphalt is somewhat more rigid than the other two types of asphalt previously mentioned, and is made by mixing asphaltic binders with soil. It is extremely complicated to describe, requires the presence of a special traveling mix plant, and should be supervised by an individual thoroughly familiar with its process.

It is a good base and sub-base material, but must be covered with a seal coat to repell moisture that otherwise would seep in, due to the soil mixture in it. A good surface coat is a bituminous seal coat and stone chip. It costs be-

Riding on established routes has been proved much safer than with traffic, if laws are obeyed. Why the rider (below) doesn't utilize bike route is a maddening question.

tween forty and sixty-five cents per square yard, four inches thick.

It is interesting to note that different colors can be mixed with the aggregate used in asphalt concrete to have a colored bike path. The colors, of nearly any shade, are available also by using hot-mix petroleum resins instead of asphalt. These latter colors are more expensive than those simply added to the aggregate, costing nearly twenty cents per square foot per inch. For parties interested in the hot-mix resins, information is available from: Humble Oil and Refining Company. P. O. Box 2180, Houston 1, Texas; Neville Chemical Company, Neville Island, Pittsburgh, Pennsylvania; and the Spray Pave Company, 321 East 12th Street, Oakland 6, California.

Stabilized earth is yet another material that can be used for surfacing the bike path. Its procedure is not quite as complicated as the soil asphalt: All top soil should be removed and at least four inches of aggregate placed on a sub-base at least four inches deep. The topsoil, aggregate and sub-base then should be thoroughly mixed, with the aid of a grader or the like. It then should be graded so that the surface is crowned, then compacted using a roller or other suitable equipment.

In some locations, it may be necessary to haul in another type of soil to aid in binding the top soil, aggregate and sub-base together, something like clay. If aggregate is not used, suitable substitues like crushed rock can be used. To finish off the least expensive type of bicycle path constructable, add some asphalt and stone chip to repel water and make a more durable surface. The asphalt and stone chip can be forgone, however, and the bike path will be perfectly functional.

Another type of surfacing that can be utilized is blue stone chips, although this is somewhat more expensive than the stabilized earth surface.

In preparing the sub-base, all the top soil need be removed and the sub-base compacted through use of mechanized equipment. It is important that the sub-base be low enough so that, when a five-inch layer of the blue stone chips are laid and rolled, the surface is flush with the

ground. This will eliminate any possibility of the surface raveling.

For added protection, the edges of the surface may be held back by strippings of redwood lumber, reinforced with pegs. A suitable substitute for the lumber is metal stripping, but care should be taken to assure that the metal is exactly flush with the surface, as otherwise it might cause tire damage.

Soil cement is another method that can be explored for the bike path. It is a mixture of Portland cement, pulverized soil and water, which is compacted to achieve a high density.

Prior to its application, the sub-base should be cleared of any soil rich in mulch ·with other soil substituted. The soil cement then can be mixed and poured, with the proper ratios of each component previously determined by tests.

The soil cement must remain untouched for seven days to achieve a proper degree of hardness, a process called curing. While drying, it should be covered with a substance like hay or dirt to absorb any moisture from dew or the like.

As soil cement is a mixture of soil and cement, it must receive a seal coat to prevent the eventual soaking-up of

water, causing cracks over a period of time. Various surfacing materials will provide the desired result, such as bituminous sealer with stone chips or, better yet, a one-inch layer of asphaltic concrete. Both should be rolled to achieve a high-density.

This method isn't terribly expensive, costing about fifty cents per yard for materials and nearly one dollar per yard for labor. It is relatively new in application, so more information can be had from The Portland Cement Association, 33 West Grand Avenue, Chicago, Illinois 60610.

The final type of surfacing material available at the time of this writing is concrete. It is used fairly extensively for bike paths throughout the United States, even though it is relatively expensive. Costs run from $14 to $17 per cubic yard, but the ease of pouring and leveling sometimes offsets the price.

Another good point about concrete is that, once poured, it is relatively maintenance-free. However, should any shifting action of the ground take place, the concrete will crack. Other surfacing compounds will not crack as readily, due to built-in lasticity of the materials.

Concrete should be poured over a well-compacted subbase, topped with at least six inches of aggregate. Concrete depth should be nearly four inches, although this figure varies according to area, foundation and soil conditions.

Rather than get a whole squad of bikers with wheelbarrows and shovels out on the path, it might be wise to contract a ready-mix outfit to do the pouring. The bike path requires consistency of materials to be long-lasting, and this feature otherwise might be overlooked. You can cut the cost somewhat, however, by building the forms to

Some riders, like motorists, continue to buck the flow of public safety sentiment, as does this rider (above). He rides on sidewalk instead of in route, where he should.

hold the liquid from spreading all over the countryside. Once it is poured, it must be leveled and left to set until dry. Those parties interested in procuring further information might write to the Portland Cement Association at the previously listed address.

If a bicycle rental facility is planned for the bike path, perhaps the group could explore the possibility of commercial concession, or a parks and recreation department function. The building could be constructed at the time the bike path is being designed, so that all would be in readiness when the facility was opened to the cycling public.

As can readily be seen, constructing a bike path is infinitely more complicated — and expensive — than using existing facilities. Many communities also have come to the conclusion that separate bike lanes and bikeways would be easier to design and faster to put into operation than undertaking the whole construction process. Besides, all the work for a bike path may result only in a relatively short trail.

The city of Boise, Idaho, evidently came to this same conclusion, and introduced a network of bike lanes for its riders. After conducting surveys and consulting traffic and safety engineers, a series of little-trafficked streets were equipped with bike lanes on both sides of the streets.

As they are designed strictly for one-way bike travel, a lane only four and one-half feet wide was needed on one side, and this was added to existing roadways next to the car parking area along the curb. This plan still left twenty feet for two automotive lanes, then a three and one-half foot bike lane traversing the other side of the street.

The committee organizing the bike lanes decided upon installing a bumper curb along the edge of the traffic lane and the bike lane, assuring the segregation of automobiles. This curb was painted yellow for additional safety. Signs denoting the bike lane and parking restrictions were attached to light posts along streets where bike lanes were established.

In Oregon, where one percent of all gasoline tax is earmarked for bikeways, a third type has been established, appropriately termed a bike route. In some instances it is located on existing sidewalks, where both riders and pedestrians share the room. Naturally, the rider should give right-of-way to any pedestrian.

These routes are marked with a combination of posted signs, paint on the sidewalk and lowered speed limits. The signs are of aluminum alloy or other suitable metal, plastic or high-density plywood, painted standard Interstate green and white. They are of .064-inch gauge of metal where metal is used, measuring twenty-four by eighteen inches. It features a white symbol of a bicycle and the words BIKE ROUTE in white on a green background. Where the route will be used extensively at night, they are reflectorized.

At a crossing point, another type of sign is constructed, in the shape of a diamond with a black bike symbol on a yellow background. Underneath is another sign, rectangular in shape, with the words BIKE XING in black on similar yellow background. The diamond measures thirty by thirty inches and is reflectorized.

As these examples indicate, there are many forms of bikeways to be considered for any specific community. They have proved to be effective in reducing the toll of automobile-bicycle related accidents, which make construction more than worth the cost.

There is a crying need for cycling facilities, especially as the number of riders increases steadily each year. With the processes spelled out, all that remains is to organize and develop such program within your community.

BEAT THE BIKE RUSTLER RUSTLER RUSTLER RUSTLER RUSTLER RUSTLER RUSTLER RUSTLER RUSTLER RUSTLER RUSTLER RUSTLER

"h (Chapter 6)

EY MAN, C'MERE," half-shouted the bearded, be-sandaled youth, as I strolled along a beach in Southern California one evening. "I want to show you something."

Curiosity aroused, I ambled across the sand toward the weathered beachfront hot dog stand the man was leaning against. He retreated around the corner of the then-closed facility and returned, grinning broadly, wheeling a glistening 10-speed bicycle.

"Isn't she a beauty?" he inquired reverently, running his gnarled, dirty fingers over the taped, turned-down bars. "One of my buddies found it and let me have it real cheap. I'd keep it, only I got my draft notice and I'm headin' for Canada and can't carry it along. If you want, I could make you a real good deal."

As this incident took place several years before the big bike boom in this country — before the 10-speed models took the industry by storm — I merely looked, confused by the seemingly complicated system of cogwheels and shifters. Shrugging my shoulders, I asked how much he wanted for it. Rubbing his matted beard, he replied, "Well, I paid $25 for it, but I need cash right now, so I'll let you have it for $15. Whaddaya say, is it a deal?"

I was flabbergasted by the offer, as even a novice cyclist like myself could tell that the bicycle cost upwards of the $50 mark. However, ever since I bought a "diamond" wristwatch from a hawker in downtown Los Angeles for $10, which most casually fell apart not ten minutes after the gloater disappeared with my sawbuck, I have been inordinately suspect of "good" deals. I refused the bicycle offer, under the premise that it was stolen, that I would instantly be caught with it by police officers who materialized out of nowhere, and serve a stretch in the hoosegow. I needn't have worried.

Back in the early Sixties, there wasn't much of a problem with bicycle theft, because the demand for bicycles was small, limited mostly to junior-sized machines for the tykes. A thief would have remained lean and hungry had he stuck to hocking bicycles, as the cash value was minimal.

However, during the late Sixties and early Seventies, when the bicycle grew immensely in popularity in every age bracket, the monumental demand for the 10-speed, which dealers were unable to instantly meet, caused a shortage that the bike rustler only was too anxious to fill.

The bicycle black market represents big business today, with millions of dollars changing hands yearly. Looking at statistics from the state of California for 1971, the skyrocketing increase in bike thefts is illustrated graphically: The approximate number of bicycles reported stolen — and a great number never are reported — was a whopping 450,000 for that year. Dollar-wise, this represents nearly $30 million that has ended up in the coffers of the bike crooks!

Thieves find the bicycle an easy target, being light in weight and seldom adequately protected. With the going price of the popular 10-speed at around $100 from a dealer, thieves also are able to turn the bicycle into fast cash, selling them for nearly $75 on the average. The more expensive the original model, the more of a resale value the bicycle has among thrift-minded riders.

But perhaps the singlemost factor that makes the bicycle a potential target is the fact that, even if caught with a bicycle, a thief rarely can be prosecuted for possession of stolen property. Unlike the automobile that is registered

upon purchase with a special department of state governments, the bicycle has no such registration system. When a stolen or abandoned auto is recovered by police officials, it can be traced to its present owner through the registration number; if a bicycle is found, usually there is no way to find its rightful owner.

To compound the problem, counties of the various states that do incorporate such a registration system seldom if ever are united under a state-wide system. Therefore, if a bicycle is stolen in one county, it never will be found or traceable, if recovered in another county of the same state. In some cases, there is a differing system found in two cities just a few miles apart.

Bike thieves have been quick to recognize this fault, and are not above moving to another county to dispose of the goods. But they much prefer traveling simply between two cities, as this cuts the overhead.

In a series of articles published in a major national newspaper, a long look was given to the problem of bicycle theft, the individual that stole bicycles, and methods utilized. Truly, thieves are ingenious when it comes to practicing their trade.

For example, in Davis, California, a college town that hosts a University of California, many students ride bikes. Separate facilities have been established specifically for the

Schoolyards are prime targets for bike thieves, who raid them during class periods with no one around.

pedaling public, and the city is a haven for cycle crooks.

One group of bicycle thieves used this method in Davis: Arriving in the community in a privately owned van late in the evening, as many as seven individuals were dropped at shopping centers, the college campus, elementary schools and other locations where bicycles would be parked without their owners. The thieves, equipped usually with bolt cutters, would snip a lock, climb aboard and pedal off. At a pre-determined time, the thieves again would meet the van at a secluded location, load the stolen bicycles, then motor away to sell the bikes in another town.

In other instances, four or six thieves would ride double through a specific area on either two or three bicycles, then leave the same area, each riding a bicycle. One thief even used a boat to transport his stolen bicycles from the ocean-front theft site to his home!

It is impossible to catalog the methods of stealing bicycles, as ingenious thieves continue perfecting new methods weekly. However, the most popular method simply is snipping the chain or lock with a set of bolt cutters.

The individuals stealing bicycles seldom are hard-core criminal offenders, but more likely the kids down the street who need a few quick bucks. Nearly half of the bicycles stolen are by youths between the age of 14 to 18, usually in the upper middle-class bracket. Some steal for the danger and excitement, some for the improved social status received, and others for a bevy of obscure reasons.

When the narcotics craze was rocking the country and youth sub-cultures were springing up, stealing and reselling bikes became a popular way to get some fast bread needed for buying dope. Addicts, especially those with the heroin monkey firmly enthroned on their backs, found a bicycle could represent nearly a week's supply of nickel bags. Where breaking into a home and stealing merchandise is a felony punishable by imprisonment, copping bicycles re-

A thief likes no sight better than this: bicycle around with no owner in sight. Housing tracts provide prime hunting grounds for bold thieves.

mains a misdemeanor, usually accompanied by probation for the thief. This the addict surely could appreciate!

It is rare to learn of bicycle thieves that are not in cahoots with others during some stage of their operation. The frequency in which bike theft rings are springing up and being discovered by law enforcement officers is on the increase. In some cases, such as a ring that was recently broken-up in Santa Barbara, California, one man masterminded his group of thieves, who netted more than three hundred bikes before the law closed in.

The kingpin, a student working on a master's degree at the University of California in Santa Barbara, took orders concerning size, color and type of bicycle requested from students who realized that he dealt in hot bikes. Through the use of a van, bolt cutters and plenty of guts, he would make off with as many as fifteen bicycles on a good night.

He kept five thieves working for him at all times, and his group stole only Schwinns and Peugeots, expensive and popular 10-speed models. He then stored the bikes in tool sheds in his hometown.

When time came to make a delivery, he would load his van and motor to the Los Angeles campus of the University of California, California State College at Long Beach, University of California at Santa Cruz or California Polytechnic Institute at San Luis Obispo, and deliver the bikes to a contact in that locale. If more bikes were ordered than he personally could deliver in his van, he would ship the bicycles to his contact via a bus line, packed in old bike shipping cartons.

Many of his contacts would place ads in college newspapers, then continue to run the ads until all the bicycles had been sold. Netting nearly $60 per bicycle, the buyers

Some riders go to extremes in protecting their bikes, as did this rider, bringing it inside.

Unlocked bicycles in front of libraries and the like are seldom there when owners return!

These police photos were shot at a Southern California residence raided for suspected stolen bicycles. Untold bicycles had been stripped, reassembled and resold.

never quit calling.

At the same time he would make a drop at another campus, he would steal several bicycles and sell them in his hometown. He claimed he never worried about being apprehended, as he realized theft reports never were circulated in cities outside of the one in which the theft occurred. In fact, not one of the three hundred bikes he stole ever was recovered and returned to its rightful owner.

He never bothered altering the appearance of the stolen bicycles, figuring enough bicycles of that particular model were circulating to eliminate the chance occurrence of someone recognizing his or her bicycle and tracing it back to him. After $30,000 worth of thefts, he was apprehended on another charge and his theft ring discovered. However, as none of the bikes he possessed was registered, no formal charges were levied against him. He agreed to retire and help campus police guard against bicycle thefts.

As another example, one house in Southern California was raided and searched for possible stolen bicycles, and 350 were confiscated. However, only one bicycle was registered and thereby traceable, which left the police with no choice but to return the 349 bicycles and charge him with one count of receiving stolen property. The individual soon was back in business, on probation.

Some theft rings, unlike the one previously mentioned, go to great pains to avoid being caught with traceable merchandise. Police discovered one bicycle that seemed to have been processed at an underground factory. It had been stripped of old paint and professionally repainted, then had the old serial numbers so altered that the police crime lab could not discern them. Another serial number was stamped into the metal in another location.

All types of locks are found on the market, some better than others. It's a safe bet that the ancient model below wouldn't deter the thief! Numerous chains connecting bicycles are insurance against the bike rustler (left).

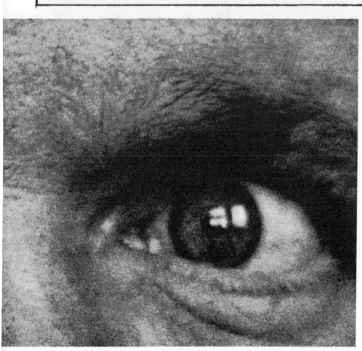

This type of processing, however, is out of the ordinary. Most thieves simply don't worry about altering anything.

Judging by the fantastic statistics of but one of the fifty states, it's easy to see that this problem is not one at which to scoff. Instead of bemoaning the disappearance of the many thousands of bicycles, action should be taken to prevent such loss. The ultimate usage of monies gained from the illegal theft and sale of bicycles probably has been used to finance any number of much worse crimes. As yet, no direct links have been established between mass theft of the bicycles and known underworld operations.

It would seem that most bicycle owners would not object to spending a small stipend for establishment of such programs that could cut theft and resale rates of illegal bicycles. Unfortunately, most cyclists simply don't worry about the theft problem, until it strikes in their own backyard or garage.

For this reason, pitifully little has or is being done, a fault that also can be attributed to a bureaucratic few in high positions of the departments that would be called upon to administer new programs.

For example, again in the state of California, a bicycle-crusading state senator has proposed legislation making the registration of bicycles mandatory at the time of sale. The same bill, if passed, will also provide a piece of the state's Department of Motor Vehicles computer complex for tracing stolen bicycles under a statewide system.

Explained simply, the system works thusly: Whenever a bicycle is purchased from a dealer, it is licensed or registered by that dealer. Local agencies then would handle all of the paperwork, and feed information as to the buyer's name, make and type of bicycle purchased, and its serial number, into a state-operated computerized criminal justice information system.

Whenever a stolen bicycle is reported to the authorities, all of the previously mentioned details from the computer on that particular bike are listed on a hot sheet. If an officer happens upon a bicycle he believes to be stolen, he need only radio its license or registration number to the local dispatcher, who forwards the number by radio to a computer operator. In less than a minute, the verdict is returned via the police radio networks as to whether the bicycle indeed is hot. If so, the police then can await the return of its present owner and make the arrest.

This system is identical to that utilized for automobiles, which proves more than effective in numerous cases.

As expected, the main opposition to these measures has been raised by Department of Motor Vehicles personnel, who don't want the extra work, and some bicycle retailers, who don't want to hassle with all of the paperwork at their level.

The statement, "Write your congressman!" might seem a bit overworked of late, but that is one tack that the seventy-five million bicycle riders in this country could take to better the now-bleak theft picture. With all of the garbage boiled out of the arguments, it appears simply that a few thousand individuals are drowning out the pleas of the cyclists for some type of action to be administered.

Another major problem with this system, that isn't generally spelled out, is the status of a bicycle theft. It remains a misdemeanor, punishable usually by probation for the offender. In other types of criminal cases, where the individual is caught and placed on probation, many again return to their evil ways. Even if caught again, seldom is imprisonment recommended, much to the chagrin of the police officer.

What happens to the minor, that thief under the age of 18, who steals bicycles and is caught? Granted, sometimes

While most chains and locks are lousy,
they at least discourage a thief
in his efforts. He knows another
that is not locked awaits him.

Passed the Senate July 31, 1972

_____

Secretary of the Senate

_____

Passed the Assembly July 27, 1972

_____

Chief Clerk of the Assembly

_____

This bill was received by the Governor this _____

day of_____, 1972, at_____o'clock_____M.

_____

Private Secretary of the Governor

Corrected 8-4-72

CHAPTER _____

An act to add Section 11111 to the Penal Code, and to add Division 16.7 (commencing with Section 39000) to the Vehicle Code, relating to the licensing of bicycles, making an appropriation therefor, and declaring the urgency thereof, to take effect immediately.

LEGISLATIVE COUNSEL'S DIGEST

SB 147, Mills. Licensing of bicycles.

Prohibits, if a county or city has or adopts a bicycle licensing ordinance or resolution, any resident from operating a bicycle on any public street, road, highway, or other public property within the jurisdiction unless the bicycle is licensed in accordance with the provisions of this act.

Requires the Department of Justice to approve licenses and registration forms of issuing agencies.

Authorizes cities and counties to set license fees and requires that proceeds of licensing fees be retained by the licensing city or county and used to implement and improve bicycle registration and safety programs in its jurisdiction or for other purposes for which fees are used on the effective date of act.

Requires the department to maintain records relative to lost and stolen bicycles in the Criminal Justice Information System. Requires the department to impose annual fees on cities and counties which have adopted bicycle licensing ordinances or resolutions to finance the operation and maintenance of that portion of the system devoted to the bicycle records. Requires the fee imposed by the department on a city or a county to be paid by the city or county from the fees collected under its adopted bicycle licensing ordinance or resolution. Limits the fee to 20 cents per bicycle licensed under such ordinance or resolution.

Requires the department to conduct a comparative study of specified bicycle licensing and control plans, and

---

to submit a progress report thereon to the Legislature by February 1, 1974.

Directs the department to make all necessary efforts to obtain federal and private funds for the purposes of carrying out its responsibilities under the act. Authorizes the department, with the approval of the Department of Finance, to receive any grants or gifts for such purposes.

Appropriates up to $150,000 to the department for the purposes of this act. Specifies that any amount expended under the appropriation shall be reimbursed to the extent federal and private grants are, or may become, available for carrying out the purposes of the act.

To take effect immediately, urgency statute.

The people of the State of California do enact as follows:

SECTION 1. Division 16.7 (commencing with Section 39000) is added to the Vehicle Code, to read:

DIVISION 16.7. LICENSING OF BICYCLES

39000. (a) If a city or county has or adopts a bicycle licensing ordinance or resolution, no resident shall operate a bicycle on any street, road, highway, or other public property within the jurisdiction unless such bicycle is licensed in accordance with this division.

(b) Licenses and registration forms shall be approved by the Department of Justice.

39001. Each local authority which licenses bicycles shall provide for the licensing pursuant to this division and any rules and regulations adopted thereunder.

39002. If a city or county has or adopts a bicycle licensing ordinance or resolution, licenses shall be issued by the city or county in which the applicant resides. Cities and counties by ordinance or resolution may set license fees, and shall adopt regulations necessary to enforce this division.

Each licensing agency shall maintain records which shall include: license number; name of licensee; address of licensee; serial number of bicycle; make of bicycle;

---

be reimbursed to the extent that federal and private grants are, or may become, available for carrying out the purposes of this act.

SEC. 5. This act is an urgency statute necessary for the immediate preservation of the public peace, health or safety within the meaning of Article IV of the Constitution and shall go into immediate effect. The facts constituting such necessity are:

There are 1,100 bicycles stolen daily in California, at an annual cost to California families in excess of twenty million dollars ($20,000,000). Further, the incidence of the theft of bicycles is increasing. In order to deter such theft by means of a comprehensive bicycle licensing plan at the earliest possible time, it is necessary that this act take effect immediately.

As this California Senate Bill illustrates, much stress is being placed on the issue of theft and licensing. If licensed, there is at least a chance of recovery.

the simple scare of being arrested by police officials is enough to discourage further thefts. But this is not always the case; what can be done with the young thief picked up repeatedly for similar offenses?

Not long ago, while speaking with a lieutenant of the Los Angeles Police Department, yet another point was brought to light: "Consider this case," suggested this officer. "We have a group of ten kids that run around together, and one of them is a thief. At first, the other nine kids in the group don't want anything to do with the thief, because they claim that he will be caught by the police and sent to jail.

"Sure, we eventually catch this thief, take him downtown and turn him over to juvenile authorities. Almost be-

Bolt cutters in hand, the bike rustler is almost impossible to beat. However, by reading the section dealing with chain and lock testing, you at least can up your chances somewhat!

fore we can return to the area in which the arrest was made, the kid is out on probation, free as a lark.

"Well, the other kids, since they've seen that nothing happened to the one thief, and envy the nice things he possesses, also turn to stealing. So, instead of having but one thief behind bars and nine straight kids, we now have ten thieves to hunt. The cycle is endless and most frustrating for law enforcement officers whose jobs are to catch criminals and put them behind bars."

Should the penalties for bicycle theft be increased? If, instead of probation, a youth was remanded to the custody of a youth institution, would the number of individuals joining the ranks of the bicycle thief be reduced? These are problems best left in the hands of our court system.

Until such time as new programs are devised and operational, it remains up to the individual cyclist to protect his property in the best manner possible. Unfortunately, this seldom is done, or the bicycle theft problem we now experience would be but a vague memory.

I recently drove through a housing tract in Southern California to see if the matter of rider apathy was some-

what exaggerated. In the course of three blocks, I personally counted twelve new high-riser type kids' bicycles and four adult model 10-speeds parked in front of homes with no one in sight. Had I been driving a van and been in the bicycle theft business, I could have compiled a respectable amount of prospective cash in but one hour!

A roving thief likes nothing better than to see this type of situation. Unless the bicycle is an ancient one-speed, showing its age through a nice coat of rust and general disrepair, it should be securely locked to as big an immobile object as possible. Not many thieves will consider stealing a bicycle, if they have to completely refurbish it before bringing a nice profit on resale.

The only sure-fire way to beat the bike rustler when not using your bike is to chain it to your ankle. Otherwise, there is a reasonable chance that it will disappear, despite all precautions taken to avoid this happening.

The next best way to keep a bicycle in your possession is to keep it behind locked doors when not in use. Many riders, safe in the belief their bicycle will be protected when left in the garage, often are surprised when they awake to

83

find it has disappeared. The bicycle thief of today is both cunning and courageous and won't hesitate to raise your garage door late at night if he knews you've got a nice bicycle inside. If you must put the bike in the garage at night, make sure the garage is locked!

As the bicycle generally is used for riding to and from places frequented by the public, it often is necessary to leave the bicycle unattended while conducting business. At such times, the bicycle should be locked securely to at least discourage its removal by the bike rustler.

It truly is staggering, the variety of bicycle chains and locks currently on the American market. Unfortunately, the vast majority will protect the bicycle like a pea-shooter will protect a white hunter from a charging Cape buffalo. A common pair of wire cutters often will bite through the chains, not to mention the bicycle thief's stand-by, bolt cutters.

Not wishing to show a preference for one chain or lock over another, we consulted the Design Division of the Mechanical Engineering Department at Stanford University, Stanford, California, for results of an objective testing of chain and cable locks. During the tests, several sizes of bolt cutters and three types of hand wire cutters were used in attempts to sever the samples. In addition, testing for brittleness of the items, they were placed in a vise and struck with a hammer. The findings of the test, conducted by John O. Dierking, are as follows, listed in order of decreasing effectiveness:

MOST SECURE: (Could not be cut with any of the tools used)

1. Campbell Chain, case-hardened, 7/16-inch diameter oval links with a gray rubber coating. The weight of the six-foot chain is ten pounds without a padlock.

The main drawback with this type of chain, designed mainly for motorcycles, is its weight and massive size. It is most unrealistic to assume that a bicyclist could pack this huge chain around on normal rides. It could be used, however, to chain a bicycle at night in a theft-plagued area.

VERY GOOD: (None could be cut with 18-inch bolt cutters or any of the wire cutters)

2. Campbell "Cam-Alloy" Chain, case-hardened, with 9/32-inch diameter oval links, blue-chrome plate finish, which looks galvanized. It is identifiable by the letters "CA" stamped into the links and spaced intervals. The four-foot chain weighs 2.8 pounds.

This is a more realistic chain for the theft-conscious bike rider, as the weight is not outrageous. This was the only sample of the VERY GOOD chains that could not be cut by 24-inch bolt cutters. A rider who purchases this type of chain, however, also must pick up a rubber sleeve to protect the finish of the bicycle from scratches.

3. Campbell "Cam-Alloy" Chain, same as No. 2, with the exception that it has a polished metal (black) finish. During the testing, it was discovered that the chain could be severed — though with difficulty — by the 24-inch bolt cutters. It also is slightly more brittle than its galvanized brother. Both of these faults could be due to changes in quality control.

4. Hardware store case-hardened chain, manufacturer unknown. Features 1/4-inch diameter twisted links, charcoal gray color. More brittle than Numbers 1-3, but case-hardened as well. It can be snapped with 24-inch bolt cutters. The weight is rather heavy, .55-pound per foot without a padlock.

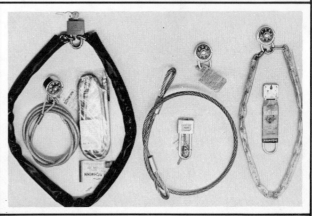

5. Campbell case-hardened chain, 1/4-inch diameter twisted links, black metal finish. It is not quite as hard as Numbers 1-4, nor as brittle. It can be cut with 24-inch bolt cutters, but the link will not snap apart. It held up the best under hammer blows, and weighs the same as No. 4.

GOOD: (Could be cut with difficulty using 18-inch bolt cutters, but not with wire cutters)

6. "Big M" Chain, case-hardened and electro-plated (looks galvanized), with blue vinyl sleeve. It has 5/16-inch twisted links, which can be crushed with bolt cutters. The links are too large for the blades of the wire cutters. It is bulky and heavy, weighing .95-pound per foot without a padlock.

7. "Supertuf Anti-Theft Security Chain," heat-treated alloy with vinyl sleeve. It has 3/16-inch diameter non-welded twisted links. Its weight is a good factor, only .30-pound per foot without padlock.

LESS SECURE: (All could be cut with bolt cutters, and wire cutters with more effort. These are not recommended for expensive bicycles.)

8. "Trelock TOK-Cylinder" stranded steel cable lock. It has 5/16-inch diameter cable with a vinyl sleeve and two keys, made in West Germany. The lock and cable-lock attachments withstand physical abuse and force much better than other the cable locks tested. It is lightweight, weighing only .70-pound.

9. "Abus" stranded steel cable lock, a 5/16-inch diameter cable with a vinyl sleeve and two keys, also made in West Germany. The cable structure is slightly inferior to No. 8, and the cable attachment to the lock can be sheared off easily with a hammer blow. Weight is the same as No. 8.

10. "Schwinn Approved" Chain and Lock Set, part

number 06-650. It has 3/16-inch diameter chain, 36 inches long, case-hardened and tempered with a vinyl sleeve. It comes standard with an American No. 300 combination padlock. The chain is easily cut with 18-inch bolt cutters, and wire cutters can penetrate the hardened case, although won't sever the chain. The shackle on the padlock is not hardened. It is light in weight, only 1.25 pounds including the padlock.

11. "Bike Kable," 1/4-inch diameter stranded steel cable, six feet long, with plastic coating. It has a 4000-pound breaking strength, which does little good as thieves are not inclined to pull the cable apart, but rather use small wire cutters to sever it. It weighs only .5-pound without the padlock.

12. "Bike-Pak," a vinyl coated stranded steel cable with the same characteristics as No. 11.

13. "Ronis," stranded steel cable lock 7/32-inch in diameter with a vinyl sleeve, made in France, with two keys. It has a smaller diameter than the other cables, and thus is easier to cut. The lock-cable attachment also is easily sheared off with a hammer blow. It weighs the same as Numbers 11 and 12.

LEAST SECURE: (All were ridiculously easy to snap with bolt cutters, and relatively easy with wire cutters. These are not recommended for serious theft prevention)

14. "Master" combination chain lock, 1/8-inch diameter unhardened chain. It also has a padlock with an unhardened shackle.

15. "Donner Utility Lock," a 5/32-inch diameter link chain with a flimsy combination lock.

16. "Ski and Sports Lock" a 3/32-inch diameter chain. The lock is cheap and the chain soft and weak.

It is readily apparent, the types of chains and cable locks the bicyclist should shun, if he wants to remain in possession of his bicycle. In addition to this precaution, the rider should have his bicycle registered and licensed where such service is available. If the bike ends up missing, report to the local police all details and the serial number, and your chances of getting your bicycle back are slightly better than otherwise.

Some riders go so far as to make an identifying mark on their bikes in some location that does not detract from its appearance, yet could lead to positive identification if it turns up. Initials are the most popular, and can be scratched into the base metal, not just the paint, on the bottom side of any of the frame tubes.

Many stolen or lost bicycles end up in police graveyards where, if you can prove positive identification, the bicycle will be remanded into your custody. Some also appear at swap meets, so it might be a wise idea to check out such locations. If you do find your bicycle in the possession of a hawker, have someone find one of the security guards or police officers directing traffic on the premises, while you stand back and make sure it doesn't get sold to someone else. Also, don't approach the seller with claims that it is your bicycle, you've called the cops, etc., or he might bolt and escape to steal someone else's bike. Keep back until the police arrive, then present your case.

If a bicycle rustler is downright determined to have your bicycle, he's usually going to get it. But, just as with car thieves, he won't go to great pains usually because he knows that there is another bicycle not far away, much easier to steal. Thieves are lazy; if you aren't, you'll probably keep your bike for years.

THE UNCLUTTERED VACATION

Chapter 7

Camping Out On A Bicycle
Is Not As Wierd As It Sounds, And
Can Be A Memorable Experience!

THE CURRENT AMERICAN LIFESTYLE heretofore has been termed transient. The age of jet transportation is here, and it indeed is rare to encounter an individual or family that has not traveled afar at some time on some mode of transport other than the cramping automobile.

This transitory lifestyle does not encompass just the youth of this country. Actually, the early pacesetters were none other than that much-maligned over-thirty generation. This fact is borne-out by statistics indicating that, in 1960, barely one-third of California's population occupied the same residence as five years previously.

It has been seen, all over the United States, that families are moving from the major cities to suburbia — or even farther out, to little-settled areas — in hopes of escaping some of the ratrace of city living. However, the vast majority of city dwellers are unable to move away, and must be content with vacation-time visits.

Many millions of Americans each year take to the forests, deserts, shorelines and swamps and engage in the tradition-building mode of camping on their vacation. I personally can recall the excitement and anticipation with which I awaited my first camping trip, at the time only knee-high to a bullrush. The bullrush long has been outgrown, as has the thrill associated with the staid, usual type of camping. The feeling of roughing it is pretty hard to swallow when, looking some thirty or forty feet in any direction brings into focus others "roughing it" with the same luxurious equipment, in the same manner, trying to swallow the same gambit.

The choking clouds of blue-gray smoke from innumerable marshmallow toasting fires I could handle. The slow, bumper-to-bumper approach to the park entrance I also could handle, knowing that the cars would dissipate once inside. The gradual lessening in the numbers of animal and avian life I could handle, as it is the American way to sit back and utter, "...yep, I remember when..."

But when the still, mountain softness was raped by the sound of raucous music from the Terrible Transistor, followed by the blare of a television commentator giving a play-by-play report on a portable TV, I knew something would have to be done. Camping in this manner never would hold any excitement or joy for me.

Countless other vacationers have become aware of this syndrome, and some endeavored to find a still-challenging way of spending a vacation. How it was that bicycle camping came into being is unknown, but it proved the tonic that many disillusioned campers and riders needed so desperately. Besides, it's fun and rewarding!

Actually, the previous sentence should read "can be fun and rewarding," if some prior planning and thought are exercised prior to embarking. In fact, probably more prior preparation is required than should you be going on the usual vacation, using modern recreational equipment.

It should be stressed immediately that, when we speak of bike camping, we are not comtemplating just a casual ride to the open lands bordering the city, although this can be both enjoyable and challenging. Rather, we're discussing camping at prime locations like national parks and forests. The idea that a bicycle is meant solely for evening spins throughout the neighborhood has been proven a fallacy — the bicycle is just as mobile, if not more so, than an automobile and should be given serious consideration as a functional recreational type of transporation.

Probably the first question that has come to a reader's mind concerns the problem involved in arriving at these popular areas; they generally are far removed from the city, and the entire vacation could be spent just traveling to them. There are alternatives open, however, which we shall discuss at greater length in this chapter.

But first, there is the more immediate concern of whether such a trip indeed is justifiable for a casual rider entertaining thoughts of using his bicycle as his pack mule. There are details that must be worked-out beforehand, and trial runs to insure the grand performance will be just that.

In planning a bike camping trip, the first area of scrutiny should be the bicycle that you plan to use for such an endeavor. Unfortunately, a 1 or 3-speed hardly would be adequate, which may necessitate purchasing or borrowing a 10 or 15-speed bike. The former two do not have enough gearing range to make for easy cycling, as varying types of terrain undoubtedly will be encountered.

The mountains, we all realize, have steep grades and sometimes unfavorable road conditions. Deserts also have hills, and pedaling up them under a blistering summer sun is sheer idiocy. In other words, the bicycle must be capable of being ridden, not pushed, uphill, if the vacation is to be fun rather than fury.

The bicycle should have the handlebars turned down, like those seen on a majority of 10-speeds. Usually, some distance must be covered upon reaching the campsite, and the forward pitched position assumed by the turned-down bar assures easier, more efficient cycling.

It is of the utmost importance to assure the bicycle has toe clips and straps attached to the pedals. Going any distance without them results in much efficiency loss. Part of the beauty of riding a bicycle on a vacation trip is the closeness of rider to nature, and this would be overlooked if all conscious effort was directed to turning just one more revolution.

A rack or carrier of some sort should be affixed to the rear of the seat. Purchase a good one that bolts securely to the rear axle and seat tube, because this is the foundation for your load.

While not necessary in many cases, it might not be a bad idea to fit the bicycle with fenders, especially if your vacation is to be taken during either late fall or early spring, when some precipitation can be expected. Also, in some areas like the Gulf Coast where swamp or marshland abound , fenders can mean comfortable cycling.

Checking with park or forest authorities upon arrival will avoid regulation violations.

As mentioned in Chapter Three, bicycle tires tend to throw water from the surface of the roadway onto the rider and bicycle frame, which is uncomfortable at best and dangerous at worst. If any cycling is to be done over dirt or gravel roads, expect that small stones lodged in the tire grooves might be hurled up into your face; fenders could prevent this mishap.

Another ingenious little device currently is marketed at most bike stores, which is nothing more than a small piece of hard plastic or thin metal that rubs over the tire pattern as the wheel revolves. This dislodges any trapped stones or the like and, while it may not prevent them from being hurled upward at the rider, it can prevent a flat tire. Pick up a set, whether you have fenders or not.

Probably the most important consideration you should give to the bicycle itself are its feet, otherwise known as tires. These will be doing the bulk of the work for you, and it would behoove the vacationer not to skimp in this area.

Some individuals prefer using touring type clincher tires, while others claim that standard clinchers give them as good, if not better, performance. On standard roads, Michelin "50" tires are good, as are Michelin High Speeds on dirt or gravel roads. Check with your dealer and find what type he feels would be best, then examine your pocketbook and buy what you feel meets your needs.

You can figure on dispensing with a headlight or taillight on this trip, and if your bike presently has them attached, take them off. Lightness is the name of the game in bicycle camping, or touring for that matter, as you must pack extra gear along with you. Also, it is not wise to go riding at night in areas with which you are not intimately familiar.

You may not have realized it, but there actually are two types of darkness: The kind we are familiar with around the city, and the pitch-black, I-can't-see-a-foot-in-front-of-my-face darkness that is encountered away from the cities when the moon hasn't risen. It has been proven that for miles in any direction around a city, the night actually is lighter than in areas far removed from the city's bright lights. When you're on the side of a mountain with not even a small town for fifty miles, and the moon isn't up, it's like the bottom of an India ink bottle. Riding under such conditions can be deadly.

If you have a horn or bell that is separate from the headlight, remove it, also. You'll have no need for one in the forest and they only clutter up the handlebars.

Once you have all of the excess paraphernalia off of your bike and have it into camping trim, go over the entire machine. Tighten every bolt that needs it, replace any fraying cables, oil any points that call for oil and check the

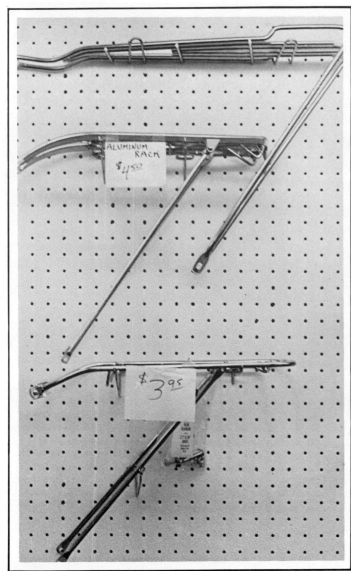

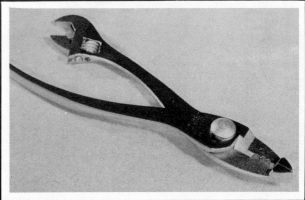

Many types of racks are marketed in bike dealerships today, and are a must for the bicycle camper. It is upon this foundation that the entire load is built.

Combination pliers marketed by L.L. Bean, Inc., serve as pliers, wire cutters, wrench and screwdriver, which can replace the need for carrying along separate tools.

chain. Make sure the derailleur is in perfect condition, that the sprockets are not exceptionally worn and are of the proper size that you require. The important thing to remember here is that should any vital part fail while you're out camping, you have real problems.

Once you have checked the bicycle thoroughly and all systems are "go," start thinking of what you want to take along with you. There are certain musts that should not be overlooked and, if you get the right equipment, you'll have some room left over for things you think you can't possibly do without.

The most important items you must have are tools with which to make repairs on your cycle should it break down. The school of thought as to what should be taken and avoided is varied, but most campers will be wise to pack a screwdriver, small crescent wrench, spoke wrench, free-wheel cluster remover, chain rivet extractor, spare derailleur and rear brake cable, two tire irons if clinchers are used, a tube repair kit, air pump and a spare tubular tire or two, if used. Other items can be taken if desired and there is room, but these definitely should not be forgotten.

Most of these tools are available at your dealer's. One interesting piece of equipment currently marketed by L. L. Bean, Incorporated, Freeport, Maine 04032, is a set of com-

bination pliers. This handy gadget is a screwdriver, crescent wrench, wire cutters and pliers all in one, and weighs only five ounces.

The main thing to remember about packing along tools, spare parts, etc., is not to get carried away. For instance, you should not have any use for a spare chain. When examining your bicycle prior to embarking, if the chain was worn it should have been replaced, as should any other worn equipment that might break during the trip.

Use a little ingenuity: It would be nice to pack along spare braking blocks for the binders, but why? If you checked and adjusted or replaced those presently on your bicycle, there is no reason to assume they may malfunction during the trip. If this does happen on the rear brake, then simply replace the braking blocks with those from the front binder and you're back in business. We all know that the bicycle may take a little longer to stop with only the rear brake operational, but it will stop safely. Should the rear brake blocks malfunction, always replace with the front blocks for your own safety. We know the story of the gent who clamped down suddenly on his front binder without using his rear brake: Instant header.

As space limitations will be your utmost concern, some savings can be realized by placing the extra spokes inside the tire pump. Instead of leaving the tools in their heavy

Keeping the load balanced and low on the frame is the right way of carrying equipment. (Trail Tech Photo)

Bugger bags of Cannondale Corporation are easy to attach to the frame, are light and sturdy. They're popular.

plastic protective covers, try wrapping them in Saran Wrap plastic or the like, as this will save more space.

As you're no-doubt wondering what you're going to pack all of this gear in, the answer is pannier bags or the like. Specifically, pannier bags are those that attach to the carrier and hang on opposite sides of the rear wheel. These are good, and you can expect to pay a pretty penny for the best ones. Most are manufactured in Europe, the recognized leader when it comes to bicycle touring or camping accessories.

A suitable substitute for the expensive pannier bags, once adjusted, are good old Army surplus packs, available at any surplus store for little silver. Any ex-military man will attest to the huge amount of gear that can be packed inside one of the bags, with a little forethought — and jamming.

As they are constructed of canvas, they will need to be supported in some manner to keep the canvas from sagging inwards, and possibly hanging up in the spokes or wearing against the tires. An old cardboard box can be cut and inserted against the four walls of the pack. If you don't want to sacrifice the space taken up by the cardboard on all four sides, you can get away with leaving only one panel on the side flush with the rack. You then can build your load away from this piece of cardboard, yet have the safety feature.

There also are handlebar bags marketed throughout the country. Much readily used gear can be stored in the bag within easy reach, which eliminates the need for stopping to pull it from the pannier bags.

Just about any type of bag will suffice for a handlebar bag. Flight bags, old leather camera bags — you name it —

can be secured to the bars and serve functionally, if not fashionably.

The time of year and area in which you intend camping has much influence on the type of camping and personal gear you should tote along. Naturally, requirements for an outing in mid-December in northern Idaho differ greatly from an August stay in Arizona, for example.

One item should be carried in most cases, regardless of the time of year or area in which you're to camp; a sleeping bag. Not just any sleeping bag, however, but a lightweight one, which is pretty expensive. Their long life more than makes up for the higher initial cost outlay, however.

Through space age technology and the development of new fibers, it is possible now to purchase sleeping bags that weigh as little as two or three pounds. They provide all the comfort found in heavier models of years ago. On the average, such a sleeping bag will run around $70, but if properly taken care of, it will last a lifetime.

The sleeping bag, when rolled-up and placed inside a furnished stuff bag, can be secured either on the rack in the rear of the bike or, if a handlebar bag is not used, on the handlebars. If the bag is placed on the bars, assure that it is snugged down securely and won't influence the handling of the bicycle by swinging in any direction. If the bike has been outfitted with fenders, there is no worry about the bag drooping and rubbing against the tire. If not, make sure it won't.

Some campers who are sure of warm weather in their camping locations — like Arizona in August — prefer to leave the sleeping bag at home and take only a blanket. So-called space blankets, available at most sporting goods stores, are unusual and new. Weighing as little as eleven

ounces and capable of being folded to pocket size, they are lightweight, windproof and waterproof, and will remain flexible up to temperatures reaching sixty degrees below zero. They generally are made of layers of reinforced plastic sheeting with an ultra-thin sheet of aluminum film inside. They will reflect eighty to ninety percent of your body heat, which is enough to keep alive, if not toasty warm.

Some models have a reversible side of fluorescent coloration, which can be used as a signal cloth should you encounter some difficulty or injury. Regardless of these features, we feel the sleeping bag is the only route for a bicycle camper, even if it is heavier.

Should you be vacationing during a period when inclement weather may be encountered, perhaps a tent might be a practical accessory to carry along. Most are designed for two individuals, so if you travel with a partner, the extra weight of the tent can be displaced by transfering some of your gear to your partner. If it rains or snows during your vacation, the tent can be worth the extra weight in gold.

All manner of tents are currently available, but a bike camper should do his hunting in a store that caters to backpackers. These individuals also travel under weight limitations, and manufacturers have designed products with their needs specifically in mind.

Perhaps the most realistic example of a tent that a bike camper should carry is nothing more than a sheet of reinforced plastic or nylon. One such nylon tent tarp, manufactured by L. L. Bean, Incorporated, features tie tabs at the edges for securing with ground stakes. While it weighs only twenty-three ounces, it also costs slightly over $20.

For the thrift-minded, there are other avenues open. One requires the addition of a little work and prior planning, but is somewhat cheaper than the above-mentioned tarp. Most hardware stores have wide sheets of plastic or acetate on huge rolls in stock. It can be pulled to your desired dimensions, then cut and you are left with a big sheet of relatively thick plastic.

Once home, the plastic can be laid out and holes punched in its edges. Ropes can be fastened through the holes and, providing some caution is used, can be tied to a tree to create a lean-to. If the plastic is reinforced, you can figure on using a rope between two trees as a tent main beam to form a tent like the one from Bean's.

If nothing else, the plastic can serve as a groundcloth,

Bugger handlebar bags have snap-on straps for easy attachment. Make sure it doesn't rub on front tire.

Mummy bags like this offered by L.L. Bean for the backpacker are fine for the cycling camper. Lightness is the prime feature.

91

which can do much to make a night's rest more comfortable. Should the ground be damp, a groundcloth is a must.

If you use a tent, it would be wise to practice setting up and striking it a few times in the backyard before heading out on the road. Any quirks or difficulties will be discovered and corrected. It also will heighten your excitement of the upcoming event.

While it may not be practical to dig up your backyard lawn to build a moat around your tent, don't overlook it when out in the sticks. This moat or ditch will channel off any water — providing it's not a flashflood — that might seep toward the tent and make life miserable.

Depending upon the weather, the tent should face in certain directions. If you're camping West of the Rockies, figure on facing your tent either to the East or South, as most of the storms blow in from the North or West. In the Midwest, face the tent again to the South or East. In the Southern regions of the country, the majority of storms blow in off the Gulf of Mexico or the Atlantic, so the tent should face North or East. If camping on the Atlantic Seaboard, face the tent South or West. These are not meant to be hard and fast rulings on wind direction and storm travel during the year and, just like the weatherman, we can't issue long range forecasts. However, these should prove to be the case more often than not.

Some cyclists who do not cotton to the feeling of rocks, twigs and other bits of terra firma beneath their sleeping bags carry along an air mattress or pad of some sort. While the air mattresses undoubtedly are the lightest of all, they are susceptible to punctures from an overlooked rock or sharp broken branch.

Seldom are sleeping pads — even those made of foam rubber — light enough to be realistically used by the bike camper. They also take up precious space, of which the cyclist has none to spare.

If allowable, a bike camper can make a positively heavenly mattress by borrowing a few sprigs from pine branches. Assembling these small, relatively soft boughs the length and width of a sleeping bag, then draping the bag over them, provides a soft, spongy mattress that will hide many of the rocks or other hindrances to a good night's sleep.

Another type of sleeping mattress not often used during this type of camping is the old but functional hammock. Exceptionally light in weight, as is one example marketed by the Quality Shop, Box 5581, Orange, California 92667, and cheap in cost, the hammock is assembled between two trees. It is not a stable creation, and one who is prone to repeated tossing and turning during the night had best find some other bed.

Getting into a hammock with a sleeping bag can be a problem. Probably the best way simply is to climb into the sleeping bag and, holding it up as best you can, position yourself in the hammock. It might be wise to include a couple of straps, if your hammock does not have them, one above the knees and another across the chest. By doing these up over the sleeping bag, even if you roll over you won't splat on the ground. By keeping the straps away from

Backpacker tents are being used with increasing frequency by bike campers, because of light weight and long service life.

the neck, you also won't choke yourself to death if the hammock rolls.

If the outing should take place during a period when mosquitos are likely to be swarming, it might be a nice idea to pack along a mosquito net. In late spring and early summer, mosquitos hatch in enormous quantities near streams and lakes, the same areas in which a camper likes to set-up for the night.

If a hammock is used, the mosquito net can be draped over the entire set-up, providing it is amply long to allow the edges to hit the ground. If the trailing ends do not hit the ground but stay slightly above it, there is the chance that mosquitos will come up into your own den from below. While it is true that the ends will be open, the chance of an odd-ball mosquito flying in and getting within biting range is slim.

If just a sleeping bag is laid on the ground for slumber purposes, a mosquito net still can be used. Simply cut or find a couple of branches that are relatively stout, with a fork on one end. The limb then should be driven into the ground solidly, and perhaps reinforced with stones around its base, at both ends of the sleeping bag. The net then is draped over the two stakes, which measure in the vicinity of thirty inches or so, and you have a mosquito-proof lair for the night.

Individuals who use tents seldom have to worry about the mosquito problem, provided they securely fasten the tent flaps.

If a mosquito net seems to be too much of a problem to worry about, a can of insect repellent should be taken. Many varieties are marketed. They are inexpensive, and can be found in most super markets, drug or sporting goods stores.

While we will delve into first aid more deeply in the following chapter, it is appropriate to mention treatment for mosquito bites, should you be unlucky enough to have provided a meal for the hungry monsters. The best thing you can do is leave them alone. It's a proven fact that, should you scratch them as we all are prone to do, this will spread the tingling properties of the fluid left in the epidermis. We also have found that, should the itching be

Cooking over campfire may be romantic, but is not allowed at many parks or forests due to fire hazard.

L.L. Bean's Hiker Stove and Cooking Unit is light, compact and easy to use. It is advisable to carry unit of some type, in case such gear is not available at site.

93

intolerable, a sound slap on the bite often stops the itching. If you have carried along some first aid cream, this also stops the irritation somewhat, as does dousing the area with cold water.

Mosquitos, especially those found near the southern border of the United States, are carriers of countless diseases. If you have had your innoculations regularly over the years, there is little chance that you will become infected. If you haven't had booster shots for some years, plan to get them before embarking on your camping spree.

The next item on the agenda of necessities you need carry is some type of cooking and eating utensils. In many of the national parks and forests cooking facilities are available; but not always, depending on the fire conditions, etc.

If you do find an area that has a grill or similar facility, you still may need to procure fuel other than wood. If the parks and forests officials allowed each camper to use wood for fires, most of the trees would have disappeared long ago from the areas. Don't try and cheat, either, for a park ranger can smell burning wood smoke on a par with the nationally-recognized bear. Stiff penalties await offenders.

Many cyclists prefer to carry their own stoves and fuel, as this can save the hassle of arriving expecting to find facilities available, which are non-existent. A good example is the white gas-burning Primus stove, which is used by many backpackers, mountaineers and the like. It's light, and can be found in most sporting goods stores. If they don't have it, it can be ordered.

Another example that might be worth checking out is the hiker stove and cooking unit marketed by L. L. Bean, Incorporated. Weighing only 2¼ pounds, the stove burns either white gas or camp stove fuel, is five inches high and 3¾ inches in diameter. Fuel is contained in a refillable fuel bottle that lasts for nearly six hours. The cooking unit is composed of a windscreen for the stove, two cooking pots that can double as a double boiler, a deep skillet type lid and a pot lifter. The price is near $20 for everything.

Some cyclists prefer to have their pots do double-duty as both cookers and servers, eating directly from the pan. Old military mess kits, or even a Cub Scout specimen, work adequately for this purpose. They generally are made of aluminum, capable of being cleaned if even the gooeyest mess is cooked up in them. Most come complete with knife, fork and spoon, and fit together in a compact package. They can be procured from military surplus outlets.

A can opener is an absolute necessity for the camper, and a small yet beautifully working example often is referred to as a "John Wayne" opener. This is nothing more than the type found in cartons of field rations issued to military personnel out on maneuvers, and it will hold a sharp edge for many a moon. While they have been used also as toe and fingernail clippers and cleaners by bush-humping Marines, we recommend that their use be limited to their primary purpose — that of opening cans. One shouldn't cost much more than a dime at a military surplus store.

As drinking out of a saucepan isn't always the most practical or desirable solution to quenching your thirst, a cup of some sort should be taken along, as should a canteen. Once again, the military canteen, complete with insulating cover and canteen cup, fits into a small space or can be clipped onto the bike. The canteen, either of green — what else — plastic or aluminum, holds a quart of liquid. The insulating cover helps to keep the water cool, although it won't equal drinking from a glacial stream.

Some cyclists feel they can get along quite nicely with the water bottles that attach to the frame, like those used by road racing riders. While these work fine out on the road, they seldom hold enough to aid in cooking chores, should the recipe call for water and there isn't any about.

Should you be camping in the desert areas where water sources occasionally dry up, you may be faced with the predicament of needing water, when the nearest waterhole is some great distance away. There is a proven method for procuring water in the desert wastes — if you can wait a few hours — and the already-mentioned gear is all you need to get it.

Dig a fairly large hole about two feet deep in the soil, and set your canteen cup in the center. Cut off a few banjo-shaped leaves from a cactus plant, shred off the tines on one side, and expose the stringy interior. Then, using your plastic groundcloth, lay it over the entire opening with no side left uncovered. With the dirt you removed from the hole, completely seal the borders of plastic sheet. When the border is secured firmly, simply drop a small rock in the center of the sheet, taking care to position it directly above the canteen cup. You can proceed about your business, with full knowledge that, when you return, there will be water waiting.

This arrangement works on the principle of evaporation. As you have dug into the soil and exposed the water-holding cactus leaf interior, along with covering the hole with plastic, the sun will bear down and cause the moisture in the cactus to evaporate. But once the liquid is aerated, it will rise only to the plastic, and cannot escape out the sides. It then will condense back into a liquid upon contacting the plastic and will run towards the low spot created by the rock. It then collects and drips into the canteen.

The water may not taste too hot, so many campers carry mixers like those marketed by Trail Chef. Water is added and shaken, and the liquid is ready to drink. Tasty!

If you're really thirsty and direly need some while waiting for the sun to do its magic in the pit, you might cut open a couple more cactus leaves and suck the moisture from them.

In the northern regions of the country, this is the least of your worries, as water usually is abundant. However, you may be in the same fix as the desert camper without realizing it, as some of the water could be undrinkable in its present state.

Years ago, drinking from a stream never was any problem. However, we all know the results of industrial pollutants pouring into countless streams and rivers across the land, and drinking any of this water can leave a camper sick, if not dead.

Some areas, you can be sure, don't have polluting chemicals in the water supply, like the primitive area outside Grants Pass, Oregon. But if you are unsure as to the water content, the stream beginnings and whether manufacturing outlets are located on its banks, better figure on purifying your water before drinking it. Granted, the idea of having to purfiy water on a vacation does take away some of the overall flavor, both of the trip and the water, but it is a regrettable necessity.

There are numerous ways of ensuring the water you drink is safe; the best known is by boiling. It takes about fifteen to twenty minutes of cooking at a rolling boil before it is safe to drink. This does take some of the sparkle out of the water, but a little can be replaced by pouring the purified liquid back and forth from one container to another for a few moments. Naturally, let it cool in an enclosed space prior to imbibing it.

Purification tablets also are marketed at most sporting goods stores. These are dropped into the canteen and left for an hour or so to completely dissolve. Unfortunately, the resulting taste isn't too sweet but at least it's wet.

Some campers also carry a small bottle of iodine with an eyedropper for purifying water. Usually, just two or three drops need be added to the water and left stand for an hour or so to assure complete safety of the liquid.

It's not a bad idea to include a small compass in your bags, and learn how to use it properly before heading out. It can prove immensely valuable or perhaps even life-saving, so don't leave it behind. They are available at sporting goods stores.

Matches are a definite must, preferably the wooden stick type used to light country stoves. These have a larger head and striking surface and can be scratched against practically anything to light, as opposed to book matches that need the little abrasive strip at the bottom of the book cover. Wrap them in some type of waterproof container or good-sized hunk of Saran Wrap to keep them dry.

Other needed items include a pocket knife with two blades that are sharp, as it will find myriad uses around the camp. Some bike campers also carry along a small hatchet with sheath, but as the vacation is not going to be spent playing lumberjack, we feel this item can be overlooked. In most areas of the national parks and forests, even the firewood is already cut to keep frustrated Paul Bunyons from leveling the hillsides.

Don't overlook an S.O.S. pad or two, plus a dishtowel —

In areas where drinkability of the water is questionable, it is wise to use purification tablets of some type. Usually two tablets will purify a canteenful (one quart).

Once the tablets have been added, shake vigorously for a few minutes before leaving mixture to stand for an hour. If riding, the shaking is automatically done.

Snake bite kits should be taken
in the packs somewhere, just in
case. Learn to use it earlier.

Freeze-dried foods like these from
Armour are light and tasty, take up
little precious room in the packs.

if you don't want to use your personal towel — for dish-
washing duties. The S.O.S. pad, coupled with elbow grease,
can remove even the stubbornest of grime on the cooking
utensils, even in cold water.

As most of the stove fuel will be required for cooking
meals, some of the mess duty chores will need to be done in
cold water. For the novice woodsman or camper, there is a
right way for even washing dishes.

Practically everyone has heard the story of a man scoop-

96

Shaving chores can be accomplished using face soap for cream; don't expect barber-close shave, but it beats none.

ing handfuls of water from a stream and partially drinking his fill, when he happens to see soap bubbles floating atop the water. Glancing upstream, he sees someone taking a bath in the river, and he has just slurped up the dirt.

As no one likes having to make this discovery firsthand, the surest way is to avoid washing dishes or the body in the stream. Instead, when it's clean-up time, take a panful of water and carry it back to the campsite before doing the scrubbing and creating all the soap bubbles. Then, when the pan is clean, dump out the dirty water on the ground or rocks nearby, take another clean container to the waterline and draw a new panful. This water is sloshed over the just-cleaned pan, assuring that no pollutants end up in the stream.

This same principle should be used for washing the body. Many campsites have showers and toilets ready for use, so do all freshening up there — not in what is essentially someone else's coffee pot.

Pack along a bar of soap wrapped in either Saran Wrap or a soap dish, along with your toothbrush and toothpaste. You'll avoid dragon-mouth in the morning and keep your friends. A mirror and comb, along with a razor fitted with a new blade can be put to good use during your outing. Don't worry about shaving cream — most of us can substitute face soap and get a passable, if not super-smooth, shave. A small container of deodorant belongs in the bags somewhere.

A flashlight, even a small one, can be worth its weight in gold when you need something in the middle of the night and can't flick on the nightstand lamp. It also helps to rid your conscious of those spooky sounds in the night.

If you're planning on camping in a national park or forest, the procurement of maps will be no problem when you arrive, or you can check those listed in Chapter Nine. However, you will need a topographical map of the areas and bordering country, to specifically let you know what kind of cycling to expect.

Topographical maps are available, East of the Mississippi, from Distribution Section, U.S. Geological Survey, 1200 South Eads Street, Arlington, Virginia 22202, or in the Western regions from Distribution Section, U.S. Geological Survey, Federal Center, Denver, Colorado 90225. Give

them a detailed description of the areas in which you intend camping, and they'll be more than happy to help you out.

One last item on the equipment list you should not overlook is toilet tissue. While most national parks and forests have restroom facilities available and are well stocked, an emergency situation may develop when you cannot reach one of the said facilities in time.

If this situation occurs while camping, assure that you bury all waste materials and pack the soil on top. This can prevent dysentery, which could easily ruin your vacation.

Rather than packing along an entire roll in your bags, you might try doing this: Strip off three long pieces of the tissue from the roll — preferably in a light or irridescent color — then fold these into compact squares, secured with a rubber band around each. They take up far less space this way than an entire roll.

The reasoning behind selecting either a light or irridescent color for the tissue is that, should you become lost in the brush, draping the light-colored strips on surrounding vegetation presents a much more visible picture to searching aircraft. This situation, however, rarely if ever develops.

A first-aid packet should be carried in the bags, but this will be covered more extensively in the following chapter.

Clothing requirements largely depend upon the location you intend camping, along with the time of year. As a good percentage of your time will be spent astride your bicycle, casually cycling through nature's wonderlands, the bulk of your clothing should be cycling-oriented.

They may be expensive, but in the long run, a couple of pairs of riding shorts can well pay for themselves. A pair of loose, light trousers should be included, and can be worn over the shorts during chilly weather. They also can be used around camp or when exploring afoot, where shorts aren't practical.

Two pairs of socks should be sufficient, as should two riding jerseys or the like. Carry one long-sleeve turtleneck sweater for use over the riding jersey on cool days, or for knocking around camp. Make sure the colors are light, which will help present a more visible picture to motorists you might meet on the roads.

A couple of light windbreakers should accompany you, and can be worn on chilly days. When it gets downright cold, both can be worn over the turtleneck jumper for added warmth.

An extra pair of shoes can be taken, selected by the rider's fancy. Riding shoes with cleats are not especially comfortable for knocking around camp, which is where the extra pair comes in.

A hat of some type — anything from a baseball cap to a camouflage bush hat — should be worn to protect the skin from the sun or keep off the rain.

Along this same line, a good pair of sunglasses should be added to the handlebar bag, for obvious reasons. Don't forget the suntan lotion, and apply it liberally and frequently when cycling in the sunlight. Sunburn is no joking matter, as anyone who has suffered this discomfort will readily attest.

Cycling gloves should not be overlooked, and make sure they have been used prior to this trip. If slightly worn, they will conform much better to the line of the hands, thus preventing hated blisters. If cold weather could possibly be encountered, a set of lined leather gloves can save numb fingers.

The handlebar bag should include a small packet of facial tissues, or a handkerchief. If facial tissues are used on runny noses, take pains not to throw the used bits on the roadway. Save and dispose of them in a trash barrel or by burning.

If there is any chance that rain might be encountered, take along a rain suit or poncho-type rain cape. These are available at most bicycle shops.

Some of this gear can be placed inside the sleeping bag and rolled up to save some space in the pannier bags for food. This area is open to wide discussion, and many variables come into effect. Each rider's taste influences his decision of what food he requires.

Whatever the type of food you desire while camping, keep it light and compact. Many campers decide to wait until arriving at their destinations prior to securing food, and where a grocery store is close by, this indeed works out fine. But in many cases there are no such facilities available, and the hungry cyclist has problems.

For that reason, many carry along the items they need. With the advent of freeze-dried foods, this now is practical. Weighing only scant ounces, enough for a week's ration can be packed along effortlessly.

The military services long have utilized dehydrated or freeze-dried foods, and have some of the best tasting meals going. Marine reconnaissance forces in Vietnam carried and ate, with lip-smacking delight, long range reconnaissance rations, affectionately termed "long rats." If at all possible, pick these up at a military surplus store. Dinners like chicken a la king, beef stroganoff, beef stew and others come prepackaged in aluminum, and require only the addition of hot water. Scrumptious.

It may take some time to assemble all of this gear, so it would behoove the bicycle camper to start a month or two before the projected launch date. When everything is on hand, a trial run or two should be taken to see if the cyclist indeed cares for camping, not just the romantic ideology.

Practice loading and unloading the pannier and handle-bar bags, changing the contents until space in the bags is utilized fully. Once you find the proper arrangement for each bag, bearing in mind to keep the most-used items within easiest reach, run through the attaching and detaching process with the bags and bike. You'll soon find the easiest way to master this, which will save time during the vacation.

As most cyclists will add to the items already mentioned it might be wise to take a couple of practice runs prior to the actual thing. A weekend campout near home can suffice to familiarize the prospective camper with problems that may be encountered later. These trips may not be long or arduous, perhaps to a deserted site near home. Set-up camp like it was the real thing.

As with most cyclists, you will find certain items that you seldom, if ever, use during the camp-outs. When home after the outings, make up a list of items never used, seldom used and used daily. Set aside any that appear under the never used heading, and seriously reevaluate those under the seldom used category. You may find that the dress suit you thought you might need is better left behind.

You will notice immediately, once all the gear is attached to the bicycle, that the steering and handling qualities are severely influenced. This may take some familiarization, better done prior to leaving for the great outdoors.

For instance, you will notice that the bicycle is heavier, so the natural tendency is to stand up and pump to get started. This however, can be a mistake, as the bicycle often leans to either side and, with the additional weight present, could fall. The best way to start is to put the bicycle in the lowest gear possible, then shift to higher gears as speed is gathered.

Once prepared to hit the road, you'll have to decide where to go, and the easiest way to get there. As mentioned

Short familiarization trips can be combined with picnic outings or the like for fun.

earlier, it would be ludicrous for a cyclist even to attempt riding to a national park or forest in most cases, as they generally are many miles from major cities.

There are various means of public conveyance open to the bicycle rider, with more services opening all the time. For instance, it used to be difficult to get a bicycle aboard a passenger airplane; now, several major airlines offer this service to the cyclist for a slight charge. The same is true of the rail services and bus lines.

The best thing a cyclist can do is find which public carrier has a route near the area desired. A cyclist could fly on either Western or United Air Lines, both of which carry bicycles, to the nearest airport, then cycle to the park or forest. He could take a Greyhound bus, if his bicycle is boxed, to a close-by town and do the same thing, or he could take a train.

In 1971, American passenger railways were consolidated into a system called AMTRAC. In talking with an AMTRAC agent, it was discovered that bicycles can be taken along in baggage compartments at minimal charge. Another important factor is that AMTRAC wants the bicycle out of the crate, just as if it was ridden to the station. Rates depend, of course, on the distance traveled.

In the former two types of transport, the cyclist will have to remove the pannier bags and, for airline travel, the pedals must be removed and the handlebars fixed sideways. In bus travel, this already will have been accomplished by fitting the bicycle into a box. Remember to carry along any other specific tools that might be required to put your

Compass like this from L.L. Bean can provide hours of enjoyment and learning, in addition to saving getting lost. Carry one along.

bicycle back together upon reaching your destination.

After you arrive at the town nearest to the national park or forest, simply mount all of your gear on the bicycle and light out for the parkline. According to a spokesman for the National Park Service, United States Department of the Interior, bicycle riders can traverse any of the roads or specified trails utilized by motorized vehicles. Cyclists must pay the standard rate for camping, although pressure is being applied to lower this tariff for cyclists. All rules and regulations that apply to any camper also apply to the bicyclist, and pay heed to them.

Most parks issue campsites on a first-come, first-served basis, so it would be wise to plan on reaching the park in the morning hours. Also, due to the extremely heavy camper traffic, stays will be limited to either a week or fourteen days.

In some national parks, reservations are required for campsites, so check the park directory in Chapter Nine for details. If you are unsure, request a reservation some months before-hand, accompanying the request with a deposit. It will be refunded should you not be able to get away during the requested period.

There usually is no problem in camping in the national forest at any time during the year, but once again, check to make sure. Campsites are sprinkled throughout the forests, and you are required to camp in them in some forests. There also may be limitations as to the use of campfires, due to the hazardous fire conditions in the summer months.

At times of the year when fires are allowed, a campfire permit usually is required and can be obtained from the forest rangers on duty in the areas. Should you light a fire, make sure that it is out before leaving the site; drown it thoroughly with water. Simply covering the fire with dirt is not completely safe, as another camper, small child or wild animal could knock off some of the dirt, exposing a glowing coal. If a forest fire starts as a result of your carelessness, be prepared to pay for the damages and the salaries of the firefighters!

In many of the national parks and a few of the forests, animals such as bear and deer stroll casually and fearlessly through the campgrounds. This indeed does look cute and striking; in fact, they look like giant pets. A few hundred campers each year must be shown, painfully, that these animals are still wild.

Bears are the worst of the bunch, and unheeding campers lose possessions to them each year. It is true that the number of incidents involving bears — or any wild creature in the parks or forests — is extremely small when

Swiss Army knives are functional and find many uses around the camp. Make sure you have some type with you.

United Air Lines transports bikes, good news for the bike camper.

Western Air Lines ferries bikes. Call for advance info.

Respect private property and fire signs, or be subject to arrest. Ask permission to camp in advance.

Rain gear is wise addition to load, as this type by Trail Tech. It can save misery! (Trail Tech Photo)

compared to the overall traffic flow through the areas, but why become one of the statistics? In the case of a bicycle camper, the problem of involvement in an incident is much more serious; you have no automobile to hide in.

Park rangers post signs and issue leaflets ordering that campers refrain from feeding the animals. As a bicycle camper, you shouldn't have any leftover food to hand out, anyway. Rangers also point out that campers should refrain from cooking particularly odious foods, and storing fresh vegetables and meats in ice chests outdoors; if you use freeze-dried foods, you won't have to worry about either of these problems.

Although the animals wander through the campgrounds usually at night, you may meet one on the roadways during your cycling ventures. At all costs, avoid the animal. There is no way to determine what it is thinking, and your kindly actions could be interpreted as unkindly by him; you lose!

Deer in surrounding areas are somewhat more shy than other campground visitors, and you most likely only will meet up with any along the roadways at night. In mountainous areas, where snows falls in the roadways, snowplows often use salt to break up the icy packs that develop. The deer covet this salt and spend hours licking the pavement's edge. A sudden appearance sets them into a panic to flee, and they generally aren't too choosy about

which route they take; over both you and bicycle, for instance. Use caution when approaching them.

While these bicycle camping trips have been described primarily for the visitor to a national park or forest, the same factors can apply to a camping expedition in the country closer to home. Should the latter area be more within your scope, there are a few other matters that must be taken care of to avoid problems.

A big problem is the issue of trespassing. Most land is owned and posted these days, and if you would like to camp on someone's land, ask the owner prior to setting up camp. Most are reasonable people and, should your request be courteous, there is a good chance that you will be granted permission. If the owner refuses, don't argue; simply find another location with more hospitable folks.

Should the owner grant you his hospitality, return the kindness by keeping a clean camp and disposing of all refuse in the proper manner. Don't leave trash strewn about the countryside, and there is a goodly chance of having the hospitality request honored in future years.

By all means, bicycle camping is not for everyone. But for those who have felt something is missing in camping ventures of late, the introduction of the bicycle as a pack mule can produce both a refreshing outlook and a rewarding experience.

(Trail Tech Photo)

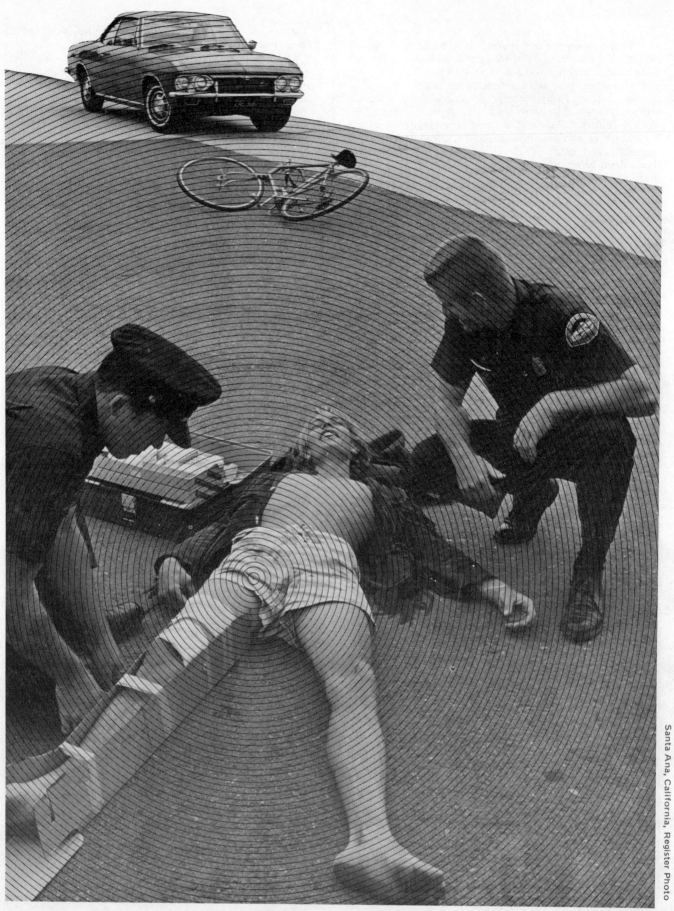

Santa Ana, California, Register Photo

Chapter 8

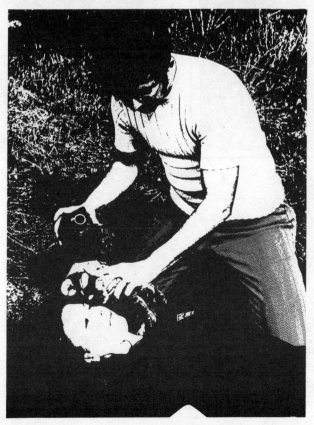

IN CASE OF ACCIDENT OR INJURY...

THE MANY MILLIONS of campers who take to the forests and parks each year rarely, if ever, have need of first aid skills. This will also apply to the bicycle camper. But in isolated cases, the knowledge of first aid will be more than handy – it can save a life.

The manner of first aid, both in concept and application, continually changes as new developments appear in the medical field. Therefore, some of the methods mentioned in this chaper, while they are correct and usable, may be outmoded or outdated when you purchase BICYCLE DIGEST. In such cases, follow the newer practice – providing it comes from a reputable source and has the blessings of such groups as the American National Red Cross.

Basically, first aid means exactly what it says – the first type of aid to be administered to an accident victim until professional help can be obtained. Naturally, in the smaller, more usual cases of insect bites, abrasions and the like, first aid may be all that is required. In the more serious cases, however, trained help should be sought posthaste.

This chapter will not go into a great amount of detail, nor will it cover every facet of first aid training that an individual should possess. Rather, it is recommended that each prospective camper attend a free first aid course offered by local chapters of the American National Red Cross. Students that have completed the course have saved many lives throughout the years.

There are three emergency situations with which everyone, cyclists included, should be familiar: Severe bleeding, cessation of respiration and poisoning. These will be discussed at some length later in this chapter. However, there are a few basic steps that should be taken with any serious or seemingly serious injury.

First, keep the victim lying down to protect him from

unnecessary manipulation and disturbance. Often an injured person will cause further damage by moving about. Heat, in the form of blankets, should be applied only to keep his body temperature from dropping, following investigation for injuries.

Checking for injuries can be difficult. The victim may have some ideas of the extent or location of his injuries, if he is conscious, and they can be added to your findings upon examination. The extent of examination should be determined by the type of accident.

It is easier to note and diagnose external injuries than those affecting internal organs for the simple reason that there often are no visible signs of internal damage, using internal bleeding as an example. You can only speculate, based on the seriousness of the accident.

Many first aiders, upon finding an injury of major proportions, tend to abandon the search for further injuries. This is a mistake as a second serious injury that passes unnoticed can negate all of your efforts on the one initially discovered.

If a person is in a swimsuit, it is much easier to check all anatomical areas than if he is fully dressed. Care must be taken when removing any clothing articles, for the injury may be made worse. Even if there is no visible sign of injury to a specific location, yet you have reason to believe it may have been harmed, avoid bending, twisting and shaking that spot. Don't jackknife the patient.

Naturally, attend to the serious injuries first, but don't overlook those of lesser magnitude. Don't give fluids of any type to an unconscious or semi-conscious victim, for the fluid may enter the windpipe. Don't attempt to rouse an unconscious or semi-conscious individual by shaking, striking, talking or shouting at him. Instead, loosen the clothing around his neck and, if there is no fracture on one side of the body, turn the patient on that side. This allows any secretion to drain freely, preventing drowning. Place a pillow of some sort under his head.

Moving the victim depends largely upon the site of the accident and the seriousness of his injuries. We are not qualified in detailing procedures for moving the victim, and

First aider prepares to administer direct pressure to simulated wound. Kerchief or palm of hand is used.

Often the pressure must be continued for long periods. If the pressure is released and blood flows, reapply.

With the stoppage of blood flow, first aider then should bandage the wound site with the cleanest cloth.

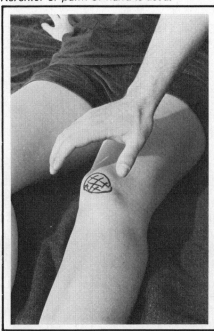
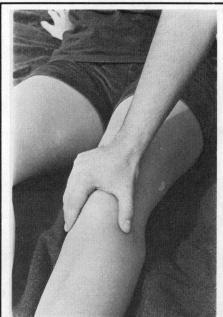
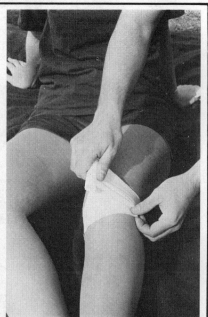

Squeezing the arm between armpit and elbow will lessen blood loss greatly. This cuts flow from supplying vessel.

suggest this be obtained from ANRC. In many cases additional injury has been induced by such action. In no case should an injured person be lifted by grasping his belt, as this often aggravates injuries of the back or internal organs.

If the victim is conscious, reassure him by explaining the first aid steps you are undertaking and their effect. Never insinuate that the person is going to die, or be horrified by his injuries, as this sometimes will send the victim into shock. Don't discuss his condition with bystanders — leave this for a physician. Helpers can be given necessary information, however.

If at all possible, seek medical advice of qualified personnel at the earliest opportunity. Give the doctor a brief description of the situation as you see it and follow the recommendations he makes. If procuring the information by telephone, wait until the doctor hangs up the telephone before leaving the booth, as you may miss part of his instructions. Give complete directions to the physician so that he will not be delayed in reaching the victim.

SEVERE BLEEDING

If the victim is bleeding profusely, there are several techniques that can be used to stop the blood flow. The most effective is the use of direct pressure on the wound. Using either the bare hand or a handkerchief, press firmly on the wound until the flow of blood lessens and stops. This does not happen instantly, so the pressure must be applied until it does.

The second method used for controlling blood flow is by applying pressure to the supply blood vessel. There are only two points on both sides of the body where pressure against the supplying vessel occasionally can be used: On the inner half of the arm, between the elbow and armpit, and just below the groin on the front. In the former, pressure forces the main vessel against the bone and diminishes bleeding below the point of pressure. In the latter, the main vessel is forced against the pelvic bone, diminishing the flow of blood to the lower extremity.

The only other spot where pressure to supplying vessel can be of use is in groin area. Pressure forces veins against pelvic bone, diminishing blood flow to the leg.

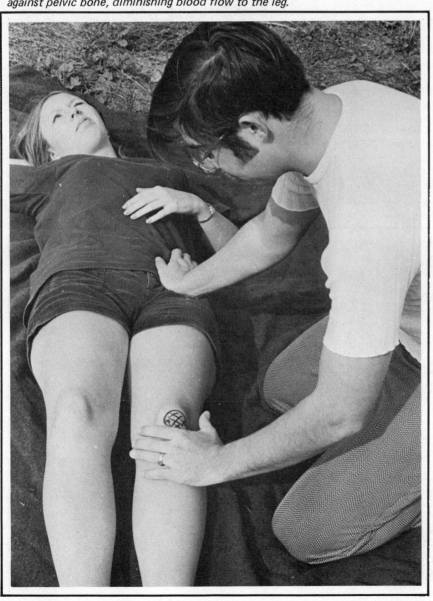

SHOCK

Shock is a depressed condition of many of the bodily functions due to failure of enough blood to circulate through the body following serious injury. If a person develops and remains in shock, death may result even though the injury causing the shock would not be fatal otherwise.

Shock sometimes is difficult to diagnose, as all of the symptoms and signs may not be present. The most important evidence is the victim's weakness coupled with a skin that is pale and moist and cooler than it should be. The eyes often will be vacant and lackluster, with the pupils dilated. Breathing is shallow and irregular, and the pulse is weak or absent. He may be nauseous. His mental reactions may appear normal at first. Later, he may be restless or lose alertness and interest in his surroundings. He may be thirsty.

As it sometimes is difficult to diagnose, all seriously injured individuals should be given first aid for shock, according to the First Aid Textbook of The ANRC. The patient should be kept lying down, preferably on a blanket, and covered only sparingly, according to the outside temperature. On warm days, leave the victim uncovered, as the main objective is not to heat the body, but to prevent a large loss of body heat.

Once down, elevate the feet eight to twelve inches, if the injury is severe or loss of blood a great amount. Do not elevate the feet if there is a head injury, difficulty in breathing increases, or the patient complains of pain when it is attempted. The reason for elevating the feet is so that more blood will flow to the head and chest areas, where it is more needed than in the legs. If there is a head or chest injury or the patient encounters breathing difficulty, elevate the head.

Often a patient in shock will become thirsty, and there is value in the administration of fluids. They must not be

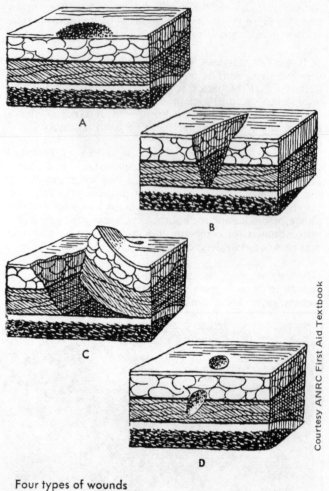

Four types of wounds
A. Abrasion   B. Incised   C. Lacerated   D. Punctured

Courtesy ANRC First Aid Textbook

Unless head or chest injury is present, or unless shock victim has trouble breathing, the feet should be elevated.

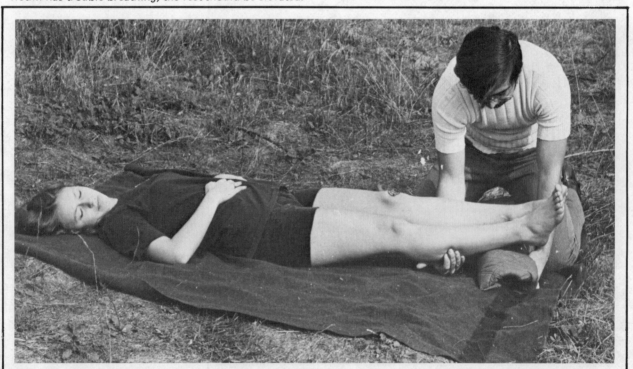

given to individuals suffering from an abdominal wound; a victim who is nauseous; one who faces an early operation; an unconscious or semi-consious victim, or one that can be treated by medical authorities in an hour or less.

As there may be a slight delay with the bicycle camper, it may be advisable to issue small amounts of plain water, neither hot nor cold, initially. If the delay in procuring medical help may be substantial, a half-glass of water mixed with a one-half level teaspoon of salt and the same amount of baking soda may be administered about every fifteen minutes. However, if the victim becomes nauseous, forego any future administrations of water.

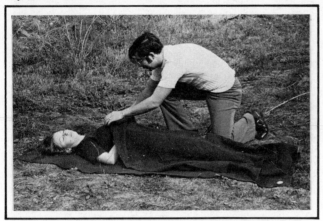

If the outside temperature is low, the shock victim should be covered. The idea is to prevent heat loss.

When giving artificial respiration to children, cover victim's mouth, nose totally with your own. Blow in and let the victim exhale about 20 times per minute.

ARTIFICIAL RESPIRATION

The prompt usage of artificial respiration has saved many lives throughout the years, and the bicycle camper should be informed of the practice. According to the ANRC First Aid Textbook, the objective of artificial respiration is "To maintain an alternating decrease and increase in the expansion of the chest and to maintain an open airway through the mouth and nose."

A person can stop breathing for a variety of reasons. If you were not present when the accident took place but rather came upon the victim shortly after its occurrence, you must take steps that could save the person's life. We'll not discuss the procedures required for removing the cause of the breath stoppage, as the causes are wide and varied.

The first move you should make is to clear the victim's airway of any debris that may be blocking the passage of air. This can be done by sweeping a finger through the mouth and throat area. At the same time, press the tongue forward.

Next, lay the victim on his back and place an object beneath the shoulder blades and neck, which will cause the head to tilt backward, with the lower jaw jutting out. With one hand, pinch the nostrils closed while grabbing the jaw and opening the mouth with the other hand. Now place your mouth completely around the victim's, forming an air-tight seal and blow into the victim's mouth. Remove your mouth and, applying pressure on the chest providing he has no chest injury, let the victim exhale. This should be repeated about sixteen to seventeen times per minute for an adult until he is revived.

If the mouth is damaged or otherwise prohibits the use of artificial respiration through the mouth-to-mouth method, it is possible to use mouth-to-nose resuscitation to

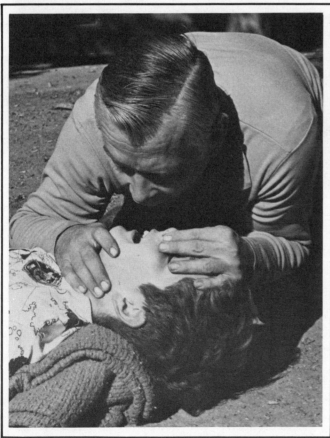

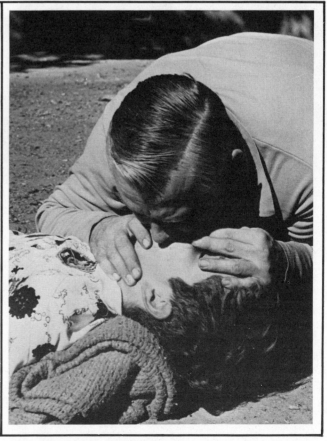

MOUTH-TO-MOUTH METHOD

1. If foreign matter is visible in the mouth, wipe it out quickly with your fingers, wrapped in a cloth, if possible.

2. Tilt the victim's head backward so that his chin is pointing upward. This is accomplished by placing one hand under the victim's neck and lifting, while the other hand is placed on his forehead and pressing. This procedure should provide an open airway by moving the tongue away from the back of the throat.

3. Maintain the backward head-tilt position and, to prevent leakage of air, pinch the victim's nostrils with the fingers of the hand that is pressing on the forehead.

   Open your mouth wide; take a deep breath; and seal your mouth tightly around the victim's mouth with a wide-open circle and blow into his mouth. If the airway is clear, only moderate resistance to the blowing effort is felt.

   If you are not getting air exchange, check to see if there is a foreign body in the back of the mouth obstructing the air passages. Reposition the head and resume the blowing effort.

4. Watch the victim's chest, and when you see it rise, stop inflation, raise your mouth, turn your head to the side, and listen for exhalation. Watch the chest to see that it falls.

   When his exhalation is finished, repeat the blowing cycle. Volume is important. You should start at a high rate and then provide at least one breath every 5 seconds for adults (or 12 per minute).

   When mouth-to-mouth and/or mouth-to-nose resuscitation is administered to small children or infants, the backward head-tilt should not be as extensive as that for adults or large children.

   The mouth and nose of the infant or small child should be sealed by your mouth. Blow into the mouth and/or nose every 3 seconds (or 20 breaths per minute) with less pressure and volume than for adults, the amount determined by the size of the child.

   If vomiting occurs, quickly turn the victim on his side, wipe out the mouth, and then reposition him.

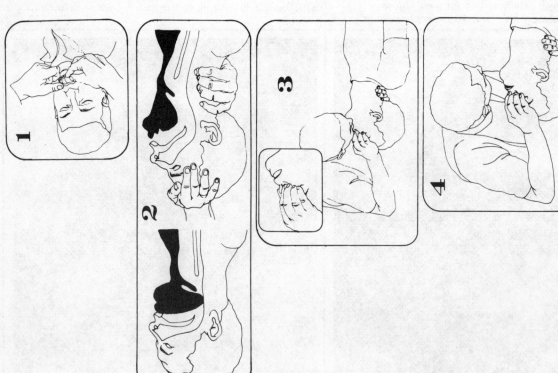

MOUTH-TO-NOSE METHOD

5. For the mouth-to-nose method, maintain the backward head-tilt position by placing the heel of the hand on the forehead. Use the other hand to close the mouth. Blow into the victim's nose. On the exhalation phase, open the victim's mouth to allow air to escape.

RELATED INFORMATION

6. If a foreign body is prohibiting ventilation, as a last resort, turn the victim on his side and administer sharp blows between the shoulder blades to jar the material free.

7. A child may be suspended momentarily by the ankles or turned upside down over one arm and given two or three sharp pats between the shoulder blades. Clear the mouth again, reposition, and repeat the blowing effort.

8. Air may be blown into the victim's stomach, particularly when the air passage is obstructed or the inflation pressure is excessive. Although inflation of the stomach is not dangerous, it may make lung ventilation more difficult and increase the likelihood of vomiting. When the victim's stomach is bulging, always turn the victim's head to one side and be prepared to clear his mouth before pressing your hand briefly over the stomach. This will force air out of the stomach but may cause vomiting.

When a victim is revived, keep him as quiet as possible until he is breathing regularly. Keep him from becoming chilled and otherwise treat him for shock. Continue artificial respiration until the victim begins to breathe for himself or a physician pronounces him dead or he appears to be dead beyond any doubt.

Because respiratory and other disturbances may develop as an aftermath, a doctor's care is necessary during the recovery period.

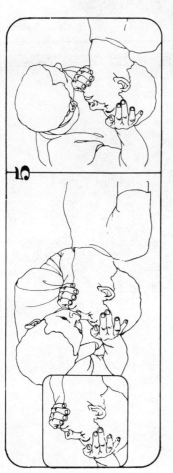

109

revive a victim. With this process, the mouth is closed as tightly as possible and the first aider blows through an airtight seal around the nose. Again, after each breath the chest is allowed to exhale, with help from a pressing hand, providing there is no chest injury.

With children, a combination of the mouth-to-mouth and mouth-to-nose methods is utilized. The resuscitator covers both the nose and mouth of the child victim and goes through the motions described for adults, although repeating the practice some twenty times per minute.

For those individuals who don't hanker to performing mouth-to-mouth, there is a plastic tube marketed and used by many agencies who specialize in saving lives. One end of the tube is placed in the victim's mouth, which then is closed tightly around it, and the first aider blows in another portion of the tube and never contacts the victim's mouth with his own.

The ANRC First Aid Textbook claims that artificial respiration will not help if heart action has ceased completely, because oxygen then is not carried from the lungs to the body cells. However, if the heart is beating and the victim is not breathing, waste no time, for the normal person will die approximately six minutes after cessation of normal breathing. Every second can count.

Plastic tube can be used in artificial respiration, and mouths never touch. Mouth must be closed tight around it.

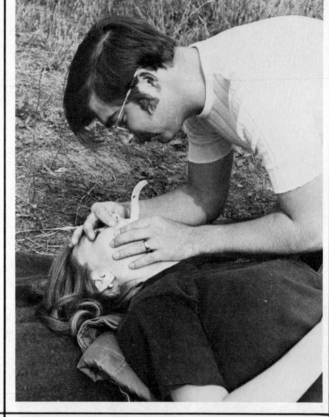

Mouth to nose resuscitation can be used when mouth is damaged. Close mouth tightly, blow air through nose.

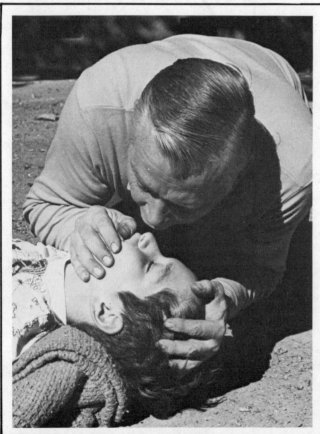

POISONING BY MOUTH

The train of thought associated with poisons and the treatment for victims has undergone serious examination during the last ten years, and some previous theories have been thrown out the window, especially in the area of antidotes.

According to the ANRC First Aid Textbook the first step is to quickly administer fluid in large amounts — four glasses or more with adults. As water will usually be the handiest item, use it.

Sometimes it is important to induce vomiting by inserting a finger or spoon in the mouth. Make sure that the assumed position of the victim is such that he will not re-swallow the poison after it is regurgitated. Then administer commercially-produced universal antidote according to package instructions.

Vomiting should not be induced if the poison taken has strong acids like carbolic acid or alkalis like lye, strychnine, kerosene or when the victim already is in a coma or is exhibiting symptoms.

In the case of acid poisoning, do not induce vomiting, for just as the acid damaged the body going down, so it will on its way back up.

In the case of strychnine poisoning, like that from rat poison, try to keep the victim from moving. The slightest movement could send the victim into convulsions. However, if only a few minutes have passed since the imbibing of the poison, give fluids and induce vomiting. Don't keep it up long, and get medical help quickly.

POISON IVY

POISON OAK

PLANT POISONING

The possibility of contacting a poisonous plant is somewhat more realistic for the bicycle camper than the previously mentioned mishaps. Depending upon the locale of the campsite, there is a goodly chance that a species of poison ivy, poison oak or poison sumac — the most common types in the U.S. — will be growing. There are a few individuals each year that contact and are poisoned by primrose, smartweed, nettle and cowhage, but they are in the minority when compared with the total that brush against the previously mentioned three types.

The active substance that causes the itching and irritation is an oleoresin called urushiol, which is contained in the sap, leaves, fruit, flowers, roots and bark. The plants are sometimes difficult to identify simply because there often is variation of the leaf structure on the same bush. However, most of the poison ivy species can be identified by the fact that they have three leaves per sprout. The upper surface is a glossy, waxy dark green, with the underside being lighter green in color with fine hairs upon occasion.

The poison oak plant derives it name because the leaf structure much resembles that of an oak tree. The western poison oak species may appear as a bundle or clump of plants, with many stems rising from one root system.

Poison sumac is a woody shrub or small tree, never a vine, which is found especially in swampy areas. There are seven to thirteen leaflets, each about three inches long and an inch wide or so. It is bright orange in the spring, changing to dark green in the summer months.

All three species change color in the fall months. Poison ivy and oak changes to orange or red in the fall. The poison sumac turns to orange-red or russet in the fall.

Should you be unlucky enough to brush up against one of them, this is what to expect: Within a few hours to several days afterwards, the skin becomes red and small blisters appear. It itches like hell. The area may increase in size, with marked swelling and numerous large blisters.

POISON SUMAC

Fever may rise and discomfort become great.

About the only thing you can do to rid yourself of the problem is to wash the affected area as quickly as possible with soap and water. Sponge the area next with rubbing alcohol, and follow up with a liberal application of calamine lotion. This will usually relieve the itching and eventually will dispose of the infection. If it doesn't, apply wet compresses of Burow's solution diluted one part to about twenty-five parts of water. This usually will relieve the discomfort and the itching.

BLISTERS

In this instance, we specifically will speak of water blisters, those unwelcome sore spots that develop when the skin continually is chafed or rubbed by ill-fitting clothing, shoes, et al.

The proper way to attend to them follows: The fluid gradually will be absorbed by the body if the source of irritation is removed. If this is impractical, the blister may be punctured. First wash the area thoroughly with soap and water. Then, using a sterilized needle — usually one passed through a flame several times — the blister is punctured at its edge. A sterile bandage should be used to apply pressure on the opposite edge of the blister, to force the water out of the pin-sized hole. It then should be covered with a sterile bandage. If the blister already has burst, simply wash the area thoroughly and apply a sterile dressing.

EYE INJURIES

The ANRC First Aid Textbook separates eye injuries into three categories: Injuries to the soft tissue surrounding the eye or the eyelid, injuries to the surface of the eyeball and injuries beyond the surface of the eyeball.

Naturally, the first is the least serious of the bunch, and a black eye falls into this category. There really isn't much you can do except apply a sterile dressing on the affected part and secure it with a bandage that encircles the head.

The second category of eye injury definitely is serious. When most individuals have something in their eye, they pull the upper lid down over the lower lid to see if this dislodges the foreign matter. Often it will. If the foreign matter is under the lower lid, pull the lid away gently and remove the substance with a handkerchief or the like. If cotton is used, dampen it before attempting to remove the object.

If the object is a chemical like salt from the roadway, the best method of obtaining relief is to flood the eye with water. This may be done with a canteen or at a drinking fountain, from a hose, you name it.

There are important don'ts that the first aider should not attempt, including rubbing the eye, for this drives the matter deeper into the eyeball. Don't check the eye until the hands have been washed, or you may introduce more objects than you initially had. Don't attempt to remove the object with a toothpick, match, pine needle or the like. Make sure that the individual sees a physician if the injury involves an imbedded piece of material in the eyeball.

The third category involves objects imbedded in the eyeball. The first aider should not attempt to remove the foreign matter, as his actions may lead to loss of sight in the eye. Instead, both eyes should be covered and the individual placed in the care of a physician at the earliest possible opportunity. The reason for taping both eyes is simply so the individual will not move his one good eye, which generally is followed in direction by the injured eye, perhaps causing more injury.

SNAKE BITE

In actuality, few individuals ever are bitten by poisonous snakes during the year, but there is the chance that this could happen. There only are four families of poisonous snakes in the U.S., the rattlesnakes, copperhead and water moccasin of the pit viper variety, and the coral snake, in a category by itself.

If bitten by a pit viper, which gets its name from the pits between the eyes and nostrils, this is what to expect: Immediate pain followed by swelling and discoloration. As the poison circulates through the system, the victim becomes weak, short of breath, nauseous with vomiting, weak, rapid pulse and sometimes dimness of vision. He may become unconscious and, if untreated, can die if enough venom has been injected by the snake.

Symptoms of a coral snake bite are identical, except that instead of immediate pain upon being bitten, there generally is only a slight burning sensation and mild swelling at the bite location.

Once determining that the snake was of the poisonous variety, quickly break out the snake bite kit that you should have packed away. Place a constricting band above the bite site, but not too tight. If the two holes are parallel or appear as a : on the skin, then make one incision just

By applying covering over both injured and uninjured eyes, unnecessary movement is prohibited. It can help.

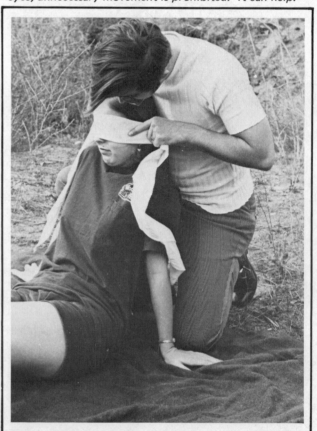

Cottonmouth moccasin

Coral Snake

Copperhead

Rattlesnake

113

under the skin through both marks with a sterile razor blade. If the bite appears .. on the skin, make two top-to-bottom incisions just under the skin, one through each fang mark. No longer are the X cuts prescribed for each fang mark — often this cuts ligaments or blood vessels and causes no end of problems, including getting the poison into the bloodstream faster.

The next move is to apply suction to remove as much of the poison as possible. There are some disputed theories about the usage of mouth suction for this purpose, as some claim that recent tests indicate that the venom will penetrate the lining of the mouth and be induced into the first aider's system. Others claim that it won't hurt the first aider at all, even if it is swallowed.

If suction cups are provided with the kit, as they most generally are, use them. Continue the suction for an hour or so, then get the victim to the care of a physician as soon as possible. The best way is to secure help at the site, thereby eliminating the hazard of speeding the poison's spread through the system by muscular activity.

There is another method of treating snake bite that is used often by the local firemen and police officials, and it is presented here simply for edification, not for projected usage, although it may well be adopted at a later date. It involves simply packing the bitten area in ice and rushing the victim to a physician or hospital. The cold bags slow the spread of poison dramatically.

If bite appears perpendicular to bone structure, twin cuts are made just beneath the skin and poison extracted with suction cup, below. If bite occurs parallel to the bone, single cut is made. Constricting band goes above.

ANIMAL BITES

Should you be bitten while camping, whether by domestic or wild animal, do all you can to restrain the animal and, if necessary, kill it only as a last resort. Both types are susceptible to rabies. If you are bitten and the animal escapes, prepare to undergo a series of excruciatingly painful inoculations in the stomach, the only defense currently known to man for rabies. However, if you can capture or kill the offending animal (do not damage its head!) authorities can determine its rabidity or lack of same and perhaps prevent your ordeal.

Skunks, opossums, coyotes and foxes are the usual carriers you may encounter on your excursion, and it would behoove you to avoid any contact with them. Remember also that squirrels and chipmunks — those cute critters that eat bread from your fingertips, that you're not supposed to feed — sometimes are infected. Leave them alone, no matter how harmless they appear.

While on the subject of skunks, should one have the misfortune to encountering the wrong end of one, about the only thing that will remove the odor from your epidermis is tomato juice. Rub it over the skin, don't drink it. Your clothes will have to either be buried or burned, as there is nothing to remove the odor from them.

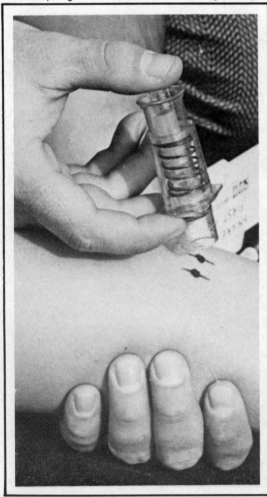

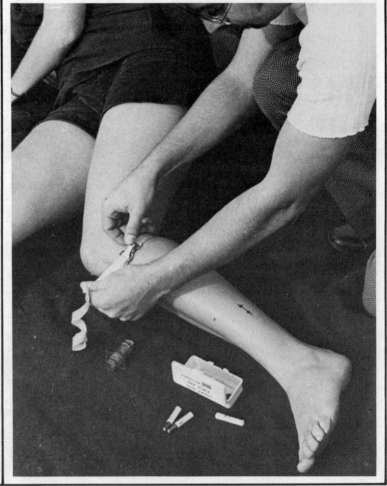

INSECT BITES

The best way to treat insect bites is to avoid them through the use of the many types of commercially-produced repellents. After the bite has taken place, anything that can be done is limited. In most cases, a paste of cold cream and baking soda will relieve the itching, as will calamine lotion. For bee and wasp stings, ice or cold water lessens the pain.

TICK BITES

Ticks are frequently encountered while vacationing, and are pesky critters that cling tenaciously to the skin. They often transmit diseases, including Rocky Mountain Spotted Fever. For this reason, it is best to get the tick out as soon as possible — the longer he remains in place, the greater the chance of contracting the disease.

Although heat from cigarettes frequently has been used to dislodge a tick, the best method is by covering his breathing pores with a coating of heavy oil, be it mineral, salad or motor. This often will have the tick backing out lickety-split. If it doesn't, leave the oil on the skin for about a half-hour, then remove the insect with a pair of tweezers.

Make sure that all of him is removed, for a small chunk left inside may result in an infected camper. Once out, scrub the area with soap and water to remove any disease germs prevalent on the skin.

Animals like skunks and coyotes are susceptible to rabies, and the camper does well to avoid them always.

BLACK WIDOW BITES

Contrary to popular belief, the black widow spider is not found only under stacks of old boards or within the abandoned house suspected of housing eerie residents. Rather, it is quite commonly found in hollow stumps, under rocks or any place that offers some shelter, primarily — but not exclusively — in the southern half of the nation.

It is one of the most easily recognizable spiders of the arachnid family, and the female almost always has a shiny black body with a red hourglass on the underside of the abdomen. The male of the species has a variety of white stripes in addition to the hourglass on the abdomen, a red stripe down the back, and shiny black coloration. The young often have a series of red dots on the back.

If bitten, this is what to expect: Immediate, severe pain, little redness or swelling at the bite site, with the pain spreading rapidly throughout the body. The victim becomes nauseous, sweats profusely and may encounter difficulty in breathing. He may experience painful abdominal cramps or other muscular pains, but in a day or so will usually recover.

If bitten on the finger or toe, put a tight, narrow constricting band near the base of the extremity immediately. If the bite is higher, use a wider band above the bite on the heart side. Remove the band after five minutes.

Next, pack the area in ice for two hours, keeping the site lower than the rest of the body, and cover the victim to keep him warm. If the bite is not on an arm or leg, the only remedy is to apply ice locally. Seek the aid of a physician as soon as possible. If medical attention is some hours away, hot wet applications or hot baths may relieve some of the muscular pains.

TARANTULA BITES

Unfortunately, science fiction movies have portrayed the tarantula, a normally calm, inoffensive creature, as an ogre that spreads death and destruction with his mammoth, powerful jaws. This is the farthest thing from the truth. In actuality, deaths from tarantula bites are extremely rare, and usually occur in the aged or infirm persons who suffer allergic reactions to the injected material.

By and large, the tarantulas that reside in the Southwestern regions of this country are non-poisonous. Their bite feels like nothing more than a pinprick. However, some tarantulas that sneak through customs aboard loads of fruit sometimes are poisonous, and cause marked pain, redness and mild swelling. Few die from these.

Should you be bitten, follow the first aid procedures for a black widow spider bite. Clean the area well with soap and water and apply a sterile dressing.

SCORPION STINGS

The vast majority of scorpions that reside in the American Southwest are not poisonous, and their stings are no worse than a wasp sting or the like. They usually are found in cool, damp places such as under houses, loose banks, in your boots. It is wise to check boots and other likely areas that may house scorpions before sticking either foot or hand into them.

A few scorpions are poisonous, and the sting can cause death, usually in infants, young children and infirm aged. Adults will have a rather uncomfortable time for a spell. In this type of sting, there is usually just a slight burning sensation rather than marked pain and discoloration. If a child is badly poisoned, he becomes restless, nauseous, has cramps in the abdomen and sometimes will go into convulsions.

The treatment procedure in this case is the same as for the black widow spider bite. There is no sense in making cuts similar to snake bite treatment and trying to suck the poison from the area, as the amount of poison is so small.

A. Simple or closed fracture.

FRACTURES

Fractures are breaks in bones and the objective of the first aider is to keep the broken bone ends and adjacent joints immobile.

Fractures are categorized in three varieties: The simple or closed fracture, in which the broken bone is not separated, the compound or open fracture, in which the broken bone extends through the surface of the skin, and the comminuted fracture, in which the bone is broken in several places, separated, and may or may not protrude from the skin.

In the case of a closed or comminuted fracture that doesn't break the skin, there may be some doubt in the diagnosing of the fracture. In this case, it is up to the first aider to use his own judgement, coupled with reports from the victim. Sometimes there may be tenderness, swelling, deformity and pain on motion. If this is observed, generally a fracture is present. If there is a suspected fracture, always treat for one.

The best way to discover the proper method for treating

B. Compound or open fracture.

C. Comminuted fracture.

Courtesy ANRC First Aid Textbook

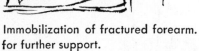

Immobilization of fractured forearm.
for further support.

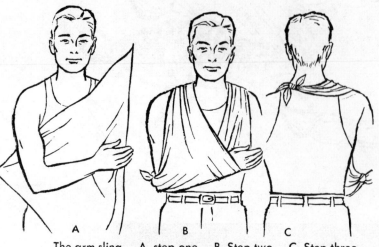

The arm sling.   A. step one.   B. Step two.   C. Step three.

Courtesy ANRC First Aid Textbook

fractures is to take the first aid course offered by the American National Red Cross. It is much easier to visualize the method of splinting, for example, by seeing it done first hand.

A simple splint may be all that is required in many cases. However, in the advent of a suspected neck or spine injury, the victim should not be moved by untrained personnel because such movement may damage the spinal cord, leaving the injured person paralyzed for life.

Improvised splints for broken leg can be wood branches rolled inside towels, sweaters, etc.

Splints then are bound together with cloth, twine, etc., (below left). Cardboard is often used for broken arm splint, (below).

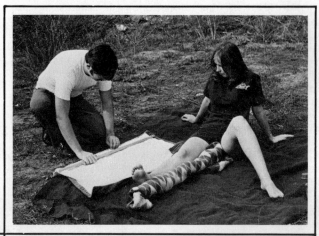

A For arm sling, cloth is folded into a triangle, as shown.

B It then is slipped under arm and one end laid on shoulder.

C Lower corner is brought around opposite side of neck, and the ends tied on the side of the neck, not behind.

D Final step is knotting points located at victim's elbow.

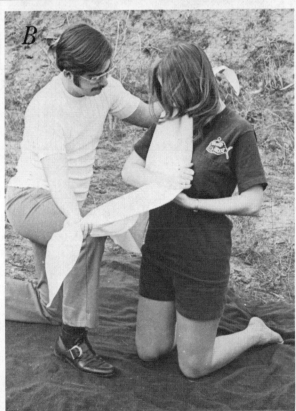

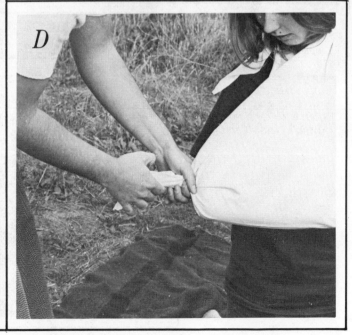

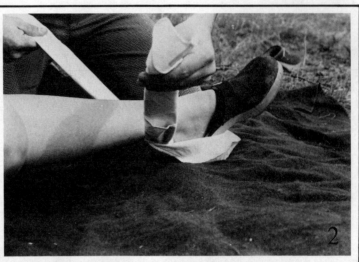

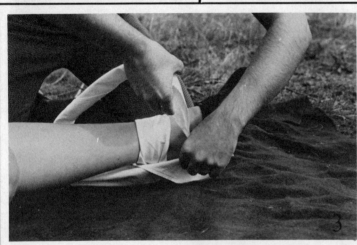

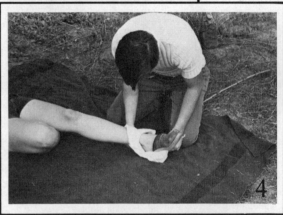

For ankle sprain, cloth is wrapped around shoe heel (1), and crossed behind (2). Points then are crossed over top of shin (3) and pulled through on both sides (4). Pulling both ends (5) tightens bind, which then is tied tight (6).

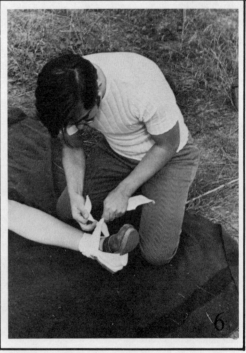

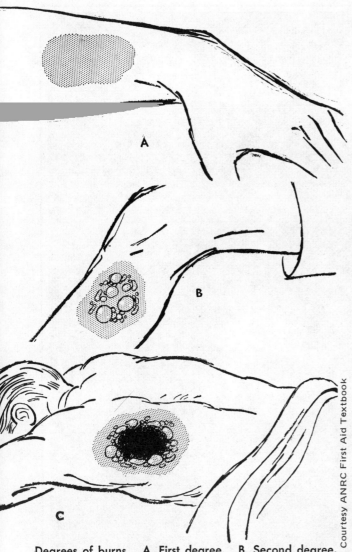

Degrees of burns. A. First degree. B. Second degree.
C. Third degree.

BURNS

Burns are placed in three categories according to depth or degree. First degree burns cause slight reddening of the skin; second degree cause reddening of the skin and blisters develop and third degree, the cells that manufacture new cells below the hair follicle level are destroyed.

Much new research has gone into the area of burn treatment, and the American Medical Association advocates the usage of cool water only for lesser burns. They say that the old methods of applying pastes or greases and wrapping the affected area in gauze only hinders the doctor's efforts when the patient arrives at the hospital. They feel that the grease or pastes can add to the possibility of infection, and that covering with bandages later causes excruciating pain when the doctor has to scrape them off.

They feel that, for minor burns that can be immersed in water — those covering less than ten percent of the body — this should be done immediately. It alledgedly lessens pain and perhaps promotes healing. However, in burns of greater size or seriousness, they feel the time is better spent in getting the victim to a hospital. The best way to treat burns is to avoid situations that result in them.

NOSEBLEEDS

These are common during vacations at high altitudes, or when hot, dry winds pass through for any length of time. There are three ways to stop the bleeding: Assume a sitting position with the head thrown back, or lying with the shoulders elevated; pinching the nostrils together, sometimes after having been stuffed with gauze; and applying cool, wet towels to the face.

HEAT EXHAUSTION

Heat exhaustion is typified in two degrees, mild and severe. In the mild form, the individual is unusually tired, with headache and perhaps nausea. The severe case symptoms are profuse sweating, pale, clammy skin, weakness and he generally has a normal temperature.

The best thing the first aider can do is have the victim lay down and rest, then administer salt solutions of one-half teaspoon salt per half-glass of water every fifteen minutes or so for three or four doses. Get a doctor for the severe cases.

HEAT STROKE

Heat stroke usually strikes the aged, although younger individuals are not exempt. The symptoms are headache, dry skin, rapid pulse, accompanied occasionally by dizziness and nausea. In severe cases, unconsciousness may occur. Temperatures range well above normal, often to 106 or 109 degrees.

Medical attention is extremely important in the case of heat stroke. While awaiting transportation, try to bring the victim's body temperature down to the vicinity of 103 degrees by removing his clothing and sponging the body with alcohol or lukewarm water. If there is no thermometer on hand to check the temperature, count the pulse rate. A rate of 110 beats per minute usually is associated with a tolerable temperature.

Once this stage has been reached, watch the patient carefully. The temperature may continue to drop, or it may start to rise again. If the latter is the case, repeat the sponging procedure. The victim may be given salt solutions if fully conscious.

As mentioned at the beginning of this chapter, the area of first aid constantly is changing. The subject alone can — and has — covered complete volumes and many thousands of printed pages. We have neither the space nor the desire to produce a first aid handbook in this book, and therefore have touched only lightly on the overall subject. For more information on the area of first aid, contact your local chapter of the American National Red Cross.

Chapter 9

National Parks And Forests Are Prime Targets On Which To Focus Your Sights!

SITES FOR YOUR CAMPING SPREE

THE NATIONAL PARKS and forests spread throughout this country could be promised lands for many bicycle campers. They can be captured and savored like never before by those using the uncluttered vacation means.

Each park has its specific rules and regulations that must be obeyed by those camping in any manner. However, there are a few similarities that prevail in most of the parks and forests that well could be mentioned here.

1. Do not disturb or carry away flowers or other vegetation, rocks or any other natural formations, or deface rocks and trees in any manner.

2. The park is a sanctuary for all wildlife; therefore, hunting or trapping usually is not allowed.

3. Be particularly careful while driving after dusk. Drive slowly to avoid striking wild animals.

4. Pets must be leashed at all times. They are not allowed on trails or in public buildings.

5. Be careful with fires. Be sure your campfire is out! Be equally careful with cigarettes; do not throw them from automobiles or horseback. Make sure they are completely out by shredding them between your fingers.

6. Camping is permitted only in the campgrounds.

7. Picnicking is permitted in the campgrounds and in established picnic areas.

Bicycling in the national parks and forests is quite legitimate, providing the cycles stay on roads or trails that can be used by automotive traffic. Conditions of roads vary with each park, so it might be wise for the cyclist to consult a ranger or other official for his feelings on bicycle camping prior to embarking on a cruise. Allow a month for a reply.

Naturally, some parks and forests are not at all designed for the bicyclist, with steep grades, hot or cold temperatures, or high altitudes. However, there is enough variety represented in the following directory of parks and forests that should avail at least one prospective spot to the bicycle camper. Most are accessible by commercial transport.

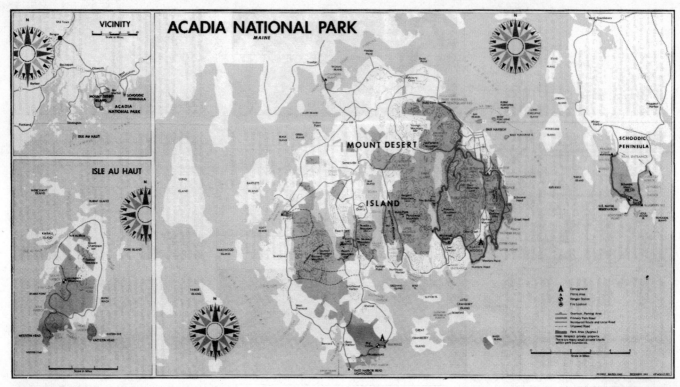

ACADIA NATIONAL PARK, Maine

"Acadia is a remarkable combination of bold granite mountains, coastal headlands, cliffs, lakes, streams, bays, penninsulas, islands and ocean unequaled in topographic variety and scenery along our entire Atlantic shoreline."

Located primarily on Mount Desert Island, the largest island off Maine's coastline, Acadia National Park is ideal for the bike camper. There are many miles of paved and unpaved roads and more than fifty miles of auto-barred carriage roads, perfect for cycling. A bicycle rental facility is located at Bar Harbor on the northeast end of the island.

Camping at Black Woods and Seawall campgrounds is open from May 1 through October 15, with a fourteen-day camping limit. Reservations are not accepted and, during the heavy summer months, plan on arriving before noon for a campsite. There are some hotel and motel facilities on the island.

For further information, write: Superintendent, Acadia National Park, Bar Harbor, ME 04609.

ARCHES NATIONAL MONUMENT, Utah

"...Here there are more natural stone arches, windows, spires, and pinnacles than in any other known section of this country. Nearly 90 arches have been discovered and others are probably hidden away in remote and rugged parts of the area. Spectacular towers, sweeping coves, shapes resembling figures of men and animals, balanced rocks, and other weird forms resulting from the combined action of running water, wind, rain, frost and sun form a setting to which the arches are a majestic culmination."

Under the jurisdiction of Canyonlands National Park some thirty-five miles to the south, perhaps Arches National Monument should be foregone by any but the most dedicated cyclists, as the wind blows frequently and hard in this area.

Camping facilities are available on a first-come, first-served basis. There are no food or commercial lodging facilities available within the monument borders. Fires are allowed in designated areas.

For more information, write: Superintendent, Canyonlands National Park, Moab, UT 84532.

BIG BEND NATIONAL PARK, Texas

"It is more suggestive of northern Mexico than the United States, this huge park that lies within the great curve of the Rio Grande. Expanses of desert sweep away to remote horizons; mountain ranges rise abruptly above arid flatlands; steep-walled canyons and green, ribbonlike stretches of plants define the river course.

"Here you can see well-preserved remains of animals that lived many millions of years ago, smell the aroma of creosote bushes, hear the calls of unusual birds, and sense the lingering echo of a Comanche war whoop. Even so, the real character of this strange country is not immediately apparent. When you visit Big Bend, stay awhile; then you may begin to feel its mood."

This huge park is open throughout the year, although it may be closed during the rainy season in the summer when storms thunder through. Reservations are not accepted for camping in the campgrounds, which have water and comfort stations provided, unless there is a large group of riders making the trip. There are some commercial facilities available, but reservations are required. Food is available in the park.

For further information, write: Superintendent, Big Bend National Park, TX 97834.

BRYCE CANYON NATIONAL PARK, Utah

"Before you and below you, as you stand on the rim of the Paunsaugunt Plateau, lies a city of stone: cathedrals, spires and windowed walls, structures of countless shapes and sizes delicately tinted in shades of pink and red and orange and softened further by grays and whites and creams — all sculptured by the never-lagging forces of erosion. These are the Pink Cliffs of Bryce Canyon."

Altitudes are extremely high — 8,000 to 9,000 feet — which make for pretty rough cycling. Campgrounds are open between May 1 and November 15. No reservations are taken, so if you plan on camping in Bryce Canyon, arrive early in the morning. Stays are limited to two weeks.

For further information, write: Superintendent, Bryce Canyon National Park, Bryce Canyon, UT 84717.

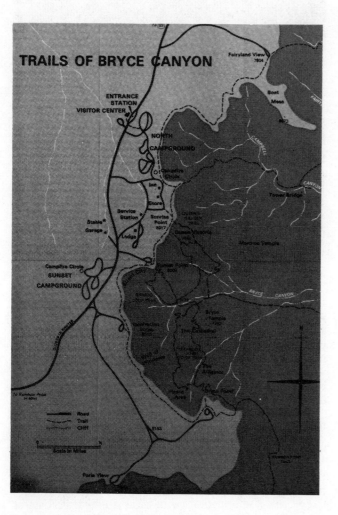

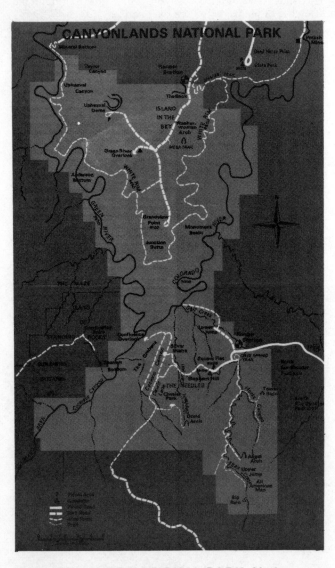

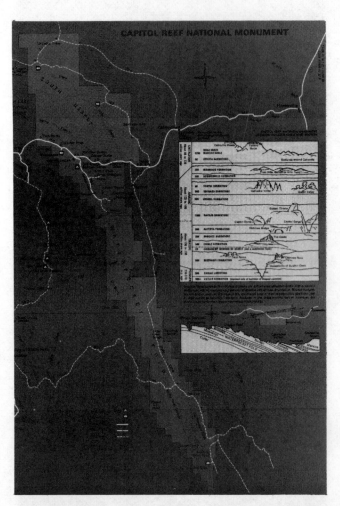

CANYONLANDS NATIONAL PARK, Utah

"First, look at the substance of this great plateau. Sandstone — sands of oceans, winds, floods, and from ground-down mountains — in layer after layer; each with its own past. It is upon this substance that all the forces of nature have worked for about 300 million years to produce the remarkable landscape."

Temperatures in Canyonlands, which is open for camping all year, range from 20 degrees below to 110 degrees above zero. There are periodic thunderstorms during summer months. Water is available in specified locations.

Bicycles must stay on established roads and jeep routes, of which there are many. Campers must bring their own fuel supply for fires as there is none available. Stays are limited to fourteen days, no reservations taken.

For further information, write: Superintendent, Canyonlands National Park, Moab, UT 84532.

CAPITOL REEF NATIONAL MONUMENT, Utah

"Water has been responsible, in one form or another, for the spectacular scenery you see before you. Water, in the form of rivers carrying tremendous loads of stones, pebbles, and grit, ground away at rocks and cliffs to carve the valleys. Water, as glaciers, helped grind the rocks and boulders into soil. Water, as ice, also created the pressures which split rocks to start the processes that made the soil beneath your feet. Water, as rain, softened and eroded the hard marterials and transported them to other areas."

A most remarkable area, Capitol Reef National Monument is located 5,418 feet above sea level. Temperatures during daylight hours in the summer range from the 80s to 90s, although nights are cool.

Only one campground is available, with no reservations taken. No firewood is available, so campers must provide their own fuel.

For more information, write: Superintendent, Capitol Reef National Monument, Torrey, UT 84775.

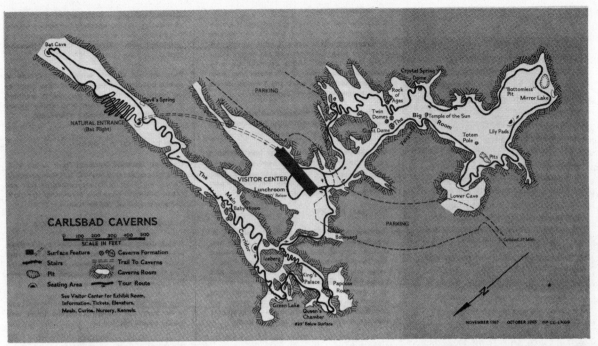

CARLSBAD CAVERNS NATIONAL PARK, New Mexico

"Lying within the dry, rugged foothills of the Guadalupe Mountains of southeastern New Mexico, Carlsbad Caverns National Park offers an experience of unparalleled contrasts. After strolling through the unworldly beauty of the huge underground chambers that are always cool and humid, you are not prepared for the quick return to the harshly contrasting Chihuahuan Desert landscape at the surface."

These breathtaking limestone caverns indeed are quite a sight, and a bicycle camper in the vicinity should not pass it up. However, no camping facilities are available so a rider should not endeavor to stay in the locale.

For further information, write: Superintendent, Carlsbad Caverns National Park, Box 1598, Carlsbad, NM 88220.

CRATER LAKE NATIONAL PARK, Oregon

"Ages ago, Mount Mazama was probably a 12,000-foot volcano in the Cascade Range. Successive flows of molten rock, eruptions of ash, cinder, and pumice gave the mountain its present form."

Crater Lake, the seventh deepest lake in the world, is located near Klamath, at an exceptionally high altitude. It is a beautiful spot with many roads and trails suitable for bicycling, although the thin air may inhibit such efforts and, for that reason, perhaps this park should be scratched from the prospective camping location list.

The campgrounds, issued on a first-come, first-served basis, are open from mid-June through mid-September, depending upon snow conditions. The temperatures always are relatively cool. Food and lodging facilities, commercially operated, are available within the park.

For more information, write: Superintendent, Crater Lake National Park, Crater Lake, OR 97604.

EVERGLADES NATIONAL PARK, Florida

"Everglades National Park was established in 1947 to protect for this and future generations a sprawling sub-tropical wilderness — a complex of unique plant-and-animal communities threatened with destruction. Some of the habitats, such as the everglades themselves, and some of the animals — crocodile, manatee, roseate spoonbill, reddish egret, wood stork, and bald eagle — are rare or unseen elsewhere in the United States. Among other plant and animal inhabitants are the alligator, snook, tarpon, pink shrimp, royal palm, mahogany, and mangroves. This great biological exhibit in an aquatic setting presents a living drama of nature in unspoiled surroundings and gives us the opportunity for an authentic wilderness experience."

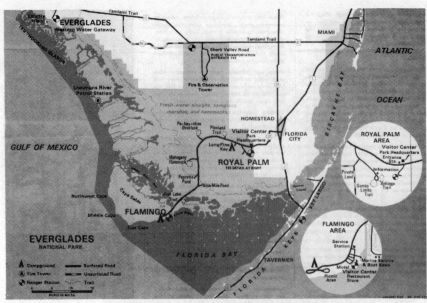

Two campgrounds, Long Pine Key and Flamingo, have drinking fountains, tables, charcoal burners and restrooms. Fees are charged in both and, from December 15 through April 15, stays are limited to two weeks. It is possible to camp, without charge, at designated beach or back country sites, reachable only by foot or boat.

For more information, write: Superintendent, Everglades National Park, Box 279, Homestead, FL 33030.

GLACIER NATIONAL PARK, Montana

"This is a land of sharp, precipitous peaks and knife-edged ridges, girdled with forests. Alpine glaciers lie in the shadow of towering walls at the heads of great ice-carved valleys. Streams flow northward to Hudson Bay, eastward to the Gulf of Mexico, and westward to the Pacific."

Roads in this park are traveling either up or down, grades that prove mighty rough for a bicyclist with camping gear. Also, they are relatively narrow, which could lead to problems with automobiles.

Camping is permitted, with no reservations accepted, and the duration is determined by snow conditions. In the commercial lodges and hotels, however, a reservation is strongly suggested and a deposit required.

For more information, write: Superintendent, Glacier National Park, West Glacier, MT 59936.

NORTH RIM, GRAND CANYON NATIONAL PARK, Arizona

"The high Kaibab Plateau north of Grand Canyon is cool and moist. In contrast with the desert at its base. Fifty miles long and 35 miles wide, it is covered by a forest of ponderosa pine, spruce and aspen, broken here and there by grassy mountain meadows. The road to the North Rim leads through this virgin forest, a drive as memorable as the canyon scenery at its southern end."

The Grand Canyon might be a nice place to visit by car, but it is virtually out of the question for the bicycle camper. Elevations on the North Rim range from 7,800 to 8,800, which means a long climb.

Camping is permitted, limited to seven days near the North Rim Inn. Commercial facilities are available only in summer. Reservations are required at the Grand Canyon Lodge and North Rim Inn.

For more information, write: Superintendent, Grand Canyon National Park, Grand Canyon, AZ 86023.

SOUTH RIM, GRAND CANYON NATIONAL PARK, Arizona

"On the northern part of the Coconino Plateau, some 7,000 feet above sea level, the pine-forested South Rim looks across the mile-deep, 217-mile-long canyon to the higher North Rim — 9 miles across by line of sight and 214 miles by road."

The South Rim has basically the same qualities as the North Rim, including exceptional heat and rugged conditions. Camping again is limited to seven days. Food and other essentials are available from concessionaires.

For more information, write: Superintendent, Grand Canyon National Park, Grand Canyon, AZ 86023.

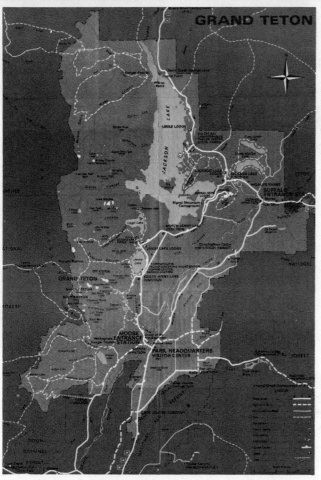

GRAND TETON NATIONAL PARK, Wyoming

"The lofty peaks of the Grand Tetons — blue-gray pyramids of 2½-billion-year-old rock, glacier-carved and still glacier-spotted — their canyons and forested lower slopes, and the basin called Jackson Hole are all encompassed in Grand Teton National Park."

Scenery in Grand Teton is superb, although the elevation is quite high for strenuous physical activity. There is a large network of trails and roads suitable for cycling, for the in-shape riders. Camping is funished at numerous campgrounds, and most are full by noon. Camping season runs from May through October.

For more information, write: Superintendent, Grand Teton National Park, Moose, WY 83012.

GREAT SMOKY MOUNTAINS NATIONAL PARK, North Carolina and Tennessee

"The Great Smoky Mountains, which form the boundary between North Carolina and Tennessee, are a majestic climax to the Appalachian Highlands. With outlines softened by a dense forest mantle, the mountains stretch in sweeping troughs and mighty billows to the horizon. The name Great Smokies is derived from the smoke-like haze that envelops these mountains."

One of the most beautiful parks in the nation, much care must be exercised by cyclists riding on the narrow paved and unpaved roads that crisscross the site. Camping is available in seven developed and four primitive areas, on a first-come, first-served basis. From June 1 through Labor Day, camping is limited to seven days.

For more information, write: Superintendent, Great Smoky Mountains National Park, Gatlinburg, TN 37738.

HALEAKALA NATIONAL PARK, Hawaii

"Maui, the demigod, the son of Hina, went to the great mountain which the sun passed over each day and, as the sun's rays crept over the mountain, Maui snared them and held them fast with his ropes. 'Give me my life,' pleaded the sun. 'I will give you your life,' said Maui, 'if you promise to go more slowly across the sky.' And to this day, the sun is careful to go slowly across the heavens; and the great mountain is known as HALEAKALA – 'The House of the Sun'."

Haleakala crater has no roads within its cone, but rather an extensive network of trails and the like. A campground is located at Hosmer Grove, within the park boundaries, at an elevation of near 7,000 feet. Reservations are not accepted.

Travel information can be had from the Hawaii Visitors Bureau, which has an office at 3440 Wilshire Boulevard, Los Angeles, CA 90005. Further information on the park is available from: Superintendent, Haleakala National Park, Box 456, Kahului, Maui, HI 96732.

HAWAII VOLCANOES NATIONAL PARK, Hawaii

"A smell of sulphur...a sound of crackling as if the surface of the earth were being torn apart...the sight of fire ebbing and exploding in the dark night...above me the snow-covered tip of the most massive single mountain in the world...around me the density of a tropical jungle with exotic trees and lovely flowers..." – James A. Michener.

This park is nestled in one of the world's most beautiful locations, and the bicycle camper can really enjoy the scenery. Many miles of roads and trails, although at a relatively high altitude, are suitable for cycling.

Camping is permitted in several authorized campgrounds, some with

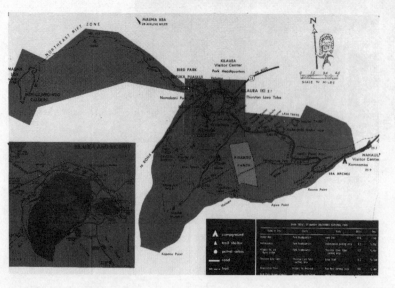

water and fuel. The park is open to campers throughout the year, although summer is somewhat less rainy. Reservations are not accepted.

For information on transportation to the islands, contact the Hawaii Bureau, 3440 Wilshire Boulevard, Los Angeles, CA 90005. For more information on the park, write: Superintendent, Hawaii Volcanoes National Park, HI 96718.

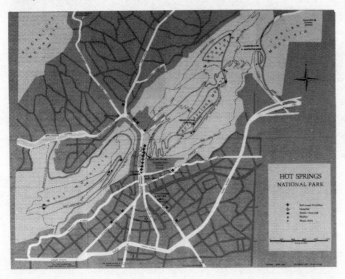

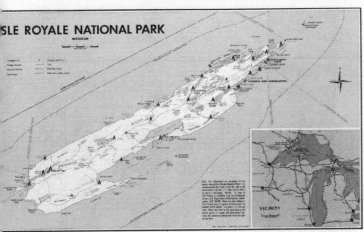

HOT SPRINGS NATIONAL PARK, Arkansas

"Long before the first Europeans came to these shores, Indians already had discovered the wonders of the hot springs of Arkansas. Tradition says this was hallowed ground; here warriors laid aside their arms and, regardless of tribe or tongue, bathed in peace."

Located almost smack-dab in the center of the city of Hot Springs, this location is ideal for bicycle campers. The elevation is low, cycling easy and countryside beautiful. While bicycles are not allowed on the multitude of foot trails, there are enough roads through the surrounding countryside to make the visit a memorable occasion.

Camping is limited to two weeks during the summer months, thirty days during the rest of the year. There is only one campground, and campers must register at the campground office before setting up. There are many other accommodations in the city of Hot Springs, just two miles from the park.

For more information, write: Superintendent, Hot Springs National Park, Box 1219, Hot Springs, AR 71901.

ISLE ROYALE NATIONAL PARK, Michigan

"A wilderness archipelago in Lake Superior, a roadless land of wild creatures and unspoiled forest, of lakes and scenic shores, accessible only by boat or floatplane — this is Isle Royale National Park. Here you are close to nature, whether camping, hiking, fishing, canoeing, or studying by sight or by camera the flowers and trees, the mammals, birds, and insects." There are paths suitable for bikes.

Camping on the island, reached only by floatplane or boat, is open from May 15 to October 20. Commercial or National Park Service transportation is available; information from the Superintendent, Isle Royale National Park, 87 North Ripley Street, Houghton, MI 49931.

LASSEN VOLCANIC NATIONAL PARK, California

"A 100,000-acre expanse of coniferous forest, with 50 wilderness lakes and almost as many mountains, is dominated by the grandeur of Lassen Peak. This plug-dome volcano of 10,457 feet sleeps at the southern tip of the Cascades. The great mass of Lassen Peak began as stiff, pasty lava forced from a vent on the north slope of a larger extinct volcano known as Tehama. The lava was squeezed up to form a rough, dome-shaped mass, plugging the vent from which it came. After this plug dome was formed, Lassen Peak was calm for a long period. Beginning on May 30, 1914, eruptions occurred intermittently for more than 7 years. Other evidences of volcanism are the beautifully symmetrical Cinder Cone and the active hot springs, steaming fumaroles, and sulfurous vents."

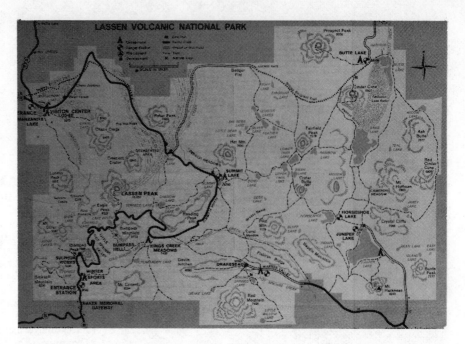

A most beautiful yet demanding setting, many of the roads are well suited to cycling. The temperature is mild during the summer months, the only time bicycle campers would be in the area. Heavy snows close most of the park's roads during the winter months.

Camping is available in numerous locations throughout the park system, again on a first-come, first-served basis. As much of the scenery is glimpsed from the roadways, cyclists to this park should be ready to spend the vast majority of their time astride the saddle.

For more information, write: Superintendent, Lassen Volcanic National Park, Mineral, CA 96063.

MAMMOTH CAVE NATIONAL PARK, Kentucky

"As you stroll through the huge rooms, over yawning pits, past the leaching vats of the saltpeter miners, past the preserved body of an ancient Indian, and under cascading decorations of stone, you will sense man's long association with Mammoth Cave."

While the park offers little to the bicycle camper, there is nice scenery in surrounding areas that lend to a relaxing atmosphere. Camping facilities are available. Commercial concessions also are present, with reservations required at the latter.

For more information, write: Superintendent, Mammoth Cave National Park, Mammoth Cave, KY 42259.

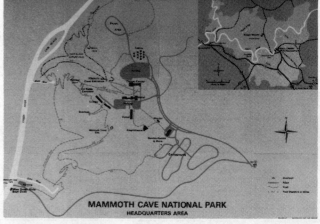

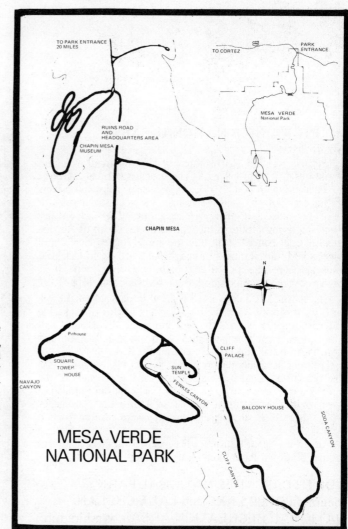

MESA VERDE
NATIONAL PARK

MESA VERDE NATIONAL PARK, Colorado

"For approximately 1,300 years, beginning about the time of the birth of Christ, Indians lived in this region, farming, fashioning tools and household utensils, and trading with other Indian groups. Their culture evolved over the centuries, until about 700 years ago, when they abandoned their homes and moved to the south and east."

The restored cliff dwellings make for a fascinating vacation subject. Camping is permitted from about May 1 through October 15, and is limited to seven days. Reservations are not possible, so it is advisable to reach the site in the morning.

Concessions selling both food and fuel are close by, and fires must be attended at all time in their specified locations.

For more information, write: Superintendent, Mesa Verde National Park, CO 81330.

MOUNT MCKINLEY NATIONAL PARK, Alaska

"Mount McKinley dominates an immense wild area of Alaska. Within the 3,030 square miles of the national park are towering mountains, alpine glaciers, and gentle, rolling lowlands crossed by wide rivers. In the valleys and along the foothills, wildlife is a part of the balanced natural system. Grizzly bear, caribou, Dall sheep, wolves, and moose roam its tundra. The park is also a place for man, a place for him to understand and to enjoy."

This park is not recommended for the bicycle camper, at least from my viewpoint. The summers are cool, wet and windy and, using a tent, there is no guarantee that the rider will remain warm and dry. In addition, there only is about thirteen miles of paved roads traversible by private vehicles.

For more information, write: Superintendent, Mount McKinley National Park, Box 9, McKinley Park, AK 99755.

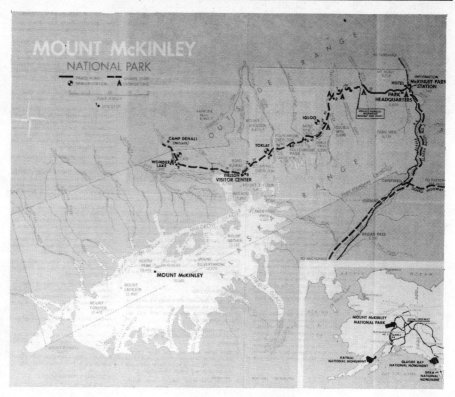

MOUNT RAINIER NATIONAL PARK,
Washington

"Mount Rainier, a towering, ice-clad dormant volcano, dominates this national park. The most superb landmark of the Pacific Northwest, it rises 14,410 feet a few miles west of the crest of the Cascade Range. Its gleaming mantle of ice is composed of many glaciers, more than are on any other single mountain in the United States south of Alaska. This mantle conceals all but the most rugged peaks and ridges of Mount Rainier. In delightful contrast to this bold landscape are the parklike subalpine forests with their flower-covered meadows and dense forests downslope."

The altitude is relatively low in this park, with the exception of Mount Rainier proper, and make for nice cycling and camping. However, the weather generally is cool and rain can be expected periodically throughout the summer months, so riders should be prepared for it.

Camping is available on a first-come, first-served basis, Visitors are advised to bring their own fuel as most of the wood in the area is wet or "green." The campgrounds are open for the period from about June 1 through October, or until snow closes the roads, and stays are limited to two weeks.

For more information, write: Superintendent, Mount Rainier National Park, Longmire, WA 98397.

NORTH CASCADES NATIONAL PARK,
including ROSS LAKE and LAKE CHELAN
NATIONAL RECREATION AREAS, Washington

"The section of the Cascade Range encompassed by North Cascades National Park and the two National Recreation Areas has an array of alpine scenery unmatched in the conterminous 48 states: deep glaciated canyons, more than 150 active glaciers, hundreds of jagged peaks, mountain lakes and streams, and plant communities."

A rugged park with little appeal to the bicycle camper, due mainly to the absence of suitable roads and trails. The weather usually is fairly cool, and rain can be expected throughout the summer season.

Both developed and primitive campsites are available during the summer, with no reservations accepted. The primitive sites are accessible only on foot over hiking trails.

For more information, write: Superintendent, North Cascades National Park, Sedro Woolley, WA 98284.

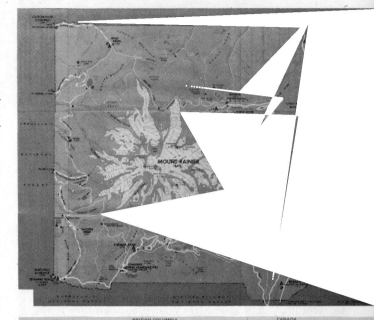

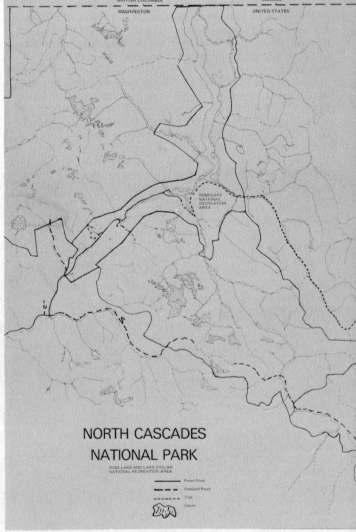

NORTH CASCADES NATIONAL PARK

ROSS LAKE AND LAKE CHELAN
NATIONAL RECREATION AREA

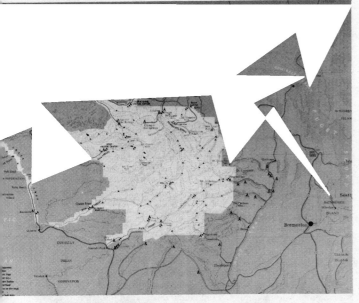

OLYMPIC NATIONAL PARK, Washington

"Olympic National Park is a 1,400-square-mile expanse of wild, forest-clad and glacier-studded mountains, with — at lower elevations — coniferous rain forests, lakes, streams, a 50-mile seacoast with rocky headlands and beaches, and a thriving wildlife population."

This strange mixture of territory is sure to appeal to some cyclists, offering just about any set of conditions desired. It should be noted that, east of Mount Olympus, average yearly rainfall is nearly 140 inches, while west of the peak is one of the driest sections of the Pacific Coast region.

Camping is permitted in a number of locations throughout the park, with no reservations accepted.

For more information, write: Superintendent, Olympic National Park, 600 East Park Avenue, Port Angeles, WA 98362.

PETRIFIED FOREST NATIONAL PARK, Arizona

"The Painted Desert of northern Arizona is a strange landscape of curious shapes and colors in patterns to excite the eye. Here, in the weirdly eroded badlands, are found these mysteries of nature, the trees that have turned to stone. Thousands of great logs, brilliant with jasper and agate, lie scattered about; here and there the ground is paved with broken sections and chips, many of which preserve the smallest details of the original wood. Petrified Forest National Park was created to protect some of the largest of these deposits for the enjoyment of present and future generations.

An extraordinary sight, a visit to this park could be combined with a tour of the Southwest, or if camping in another locale. There is a reason for this: Camping is not permitted in the park. It is open during the daylight hours every day of the year.

For more information, write: Superintendent, Petrified Forest National Park, Holbrook, AZ 86025.

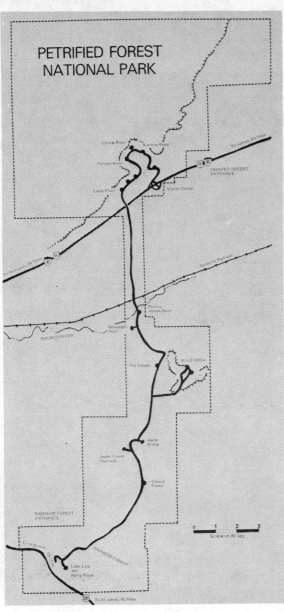

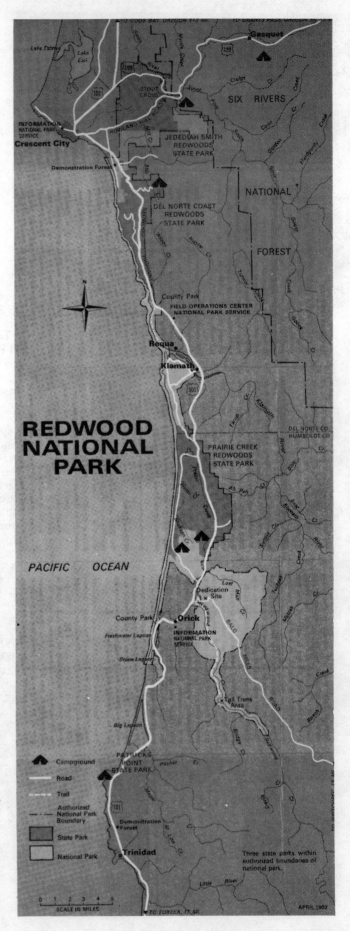

REDWOOD NATIONAL PARK, California

"In a sense, this park is dedicated to the memory of the Oligocene epoch of earth's history. For it was then, over 30 million years ago, that the coast redwood evolved and grew in great forests along the California coast. Here we are preserving a remnant of that forest. It is not enough that you walk beneath giants that sprouted 20 centuries ago. You are present in a forest that existed before the human species evolved upon the earth."

Located near the coast, the park is ideal for the bicycle camper with traveling on his mind. It is possible to mix the giant trees with ocean vistas, bird-watching or perusing migrating whales and sea lions.

Camping is permitted in both the state and national parks, by reservation before June 30 of the year you intend camping, in both systems. If reservations are not filled, campers are accommodated on a first-come, first-served basis. Don't count on many no-shows, however — the parks are extremely popular with the natives.

For more information, write: California State Park Office, Hiouchi, CA 95531.

PLATT NATIONAL PARK and ARBUCKLE RECREATION AREA, Oklahoma

"Platt National Park and Arbuckle Recreation Area provide activities for the vacationer or nature lover. Platt National Park is a refreshing sweep of woodlands, and Arbuckle Recreation Area provides water-oriented sports in the Oklahoma prairie."

Camping is permitted in both areas. During the summer months, however, stays are limited to fourteen days in the park, thirty days during other seasons; Arbuckle retains the two-week limit throughout the year.

The distance between the park and the recreation area is easily traveled by bicycle, opening another facet of vacation to the bike camper. Reservations are not accepted at either spot, so arrive early in the day.

For more information, write: Superintendent, Platt National Park and Arbuckle Recreation Area, Box 201, Sulphur, OK 73086.

ROCKY MOUNTAIN NATIONAL PARK, Colorado

"Rocky Mountain National Park, embracing 410 square miles of the Front Range of the Rockies in north-central Colorado, is one of the most spectacular yet most easily accessible high-mountain areas in North America. With elevations ranging from 8,000 feet at park headquarters to 14,256 at the summit of Longs Peak, it has glacier-sculptured valleys, rugged gorges, alpine lakes, and vast areas of alpine tundra."

Better take along an oxygen — puff, puff — mask — puff, puff — if you plan to cycle in this park! Camping is permitted, stays limited to seven days, on a first-come, first-served basis. They usually are filled by early morning.

For more information, write: Superintendent, Rocky Mountain National Park, Estes Park, CO 80517.

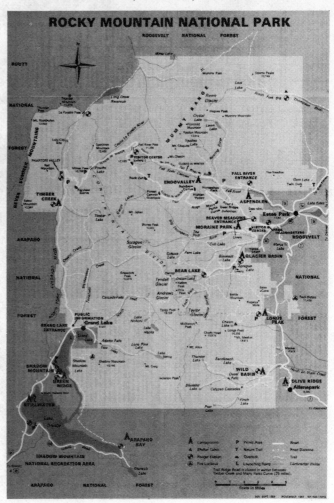

137

SEQUOIA and KINGS CANYON NATIONAL PARKS, California

"The giant sequoias are survivors of an ancient lineage of huge trees that grew over much of the earth millions of years ago and persisted in places that escaped the last ice age. Today, these trees grow nowhere else except in the scattered groves on the western slope of the Sierra Nevada. They have thrived here because of a particular combination of physical characteristics, climate, growth habits, and fire."

Two of the most popular parks throughout the nation, there is plenty to do and see in both. There are numerous roads and trails suitable for bicycle riding, the climate is temperate, although there are many steep slopes and uphill grades.

Campgrounds, none of which may be reserved, open about June 1 and continue only until snow forces closure. Stays are limited to fourteen days only.

For more information, write: Superintendent, Sequoia and Kings Canyon National Parks, Three Rivers, CA 93271.

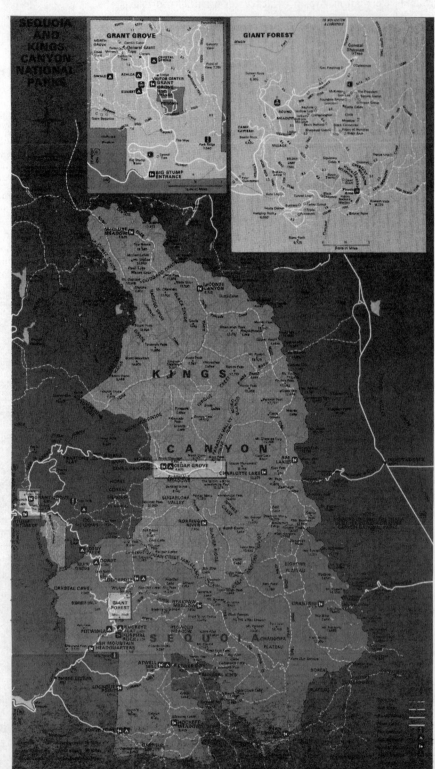

138

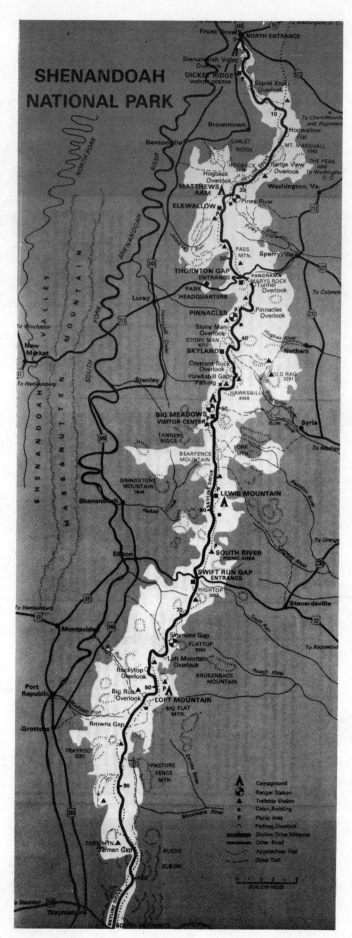

SHENANDOAH NATIONAL PARK, Virginia

"To know Shenandoah National Park, to discover its secrets, take time to stop, look, listen, and explore. For adventure, leave your car at one of the overlooks or visitor-use areas, and hike or ride horseback along the trail. Between Skyline Drive and Shenandoah's boundaries are miles of ridges and valleys, and hills and hollows, laced with sparkling streams and waterfalls. Trout lurk in shadowed pools, and wild gardens of rock, vines, shrubs, and wildflowers nestle only a short walk from the busy roadway."

Skyline Drive, a 105-mile stretch of highway cutting through the park, is of great interest to bicycle campers. It can leisurely be ridden during the daytime, with stops at campgrounds along the route at night, or vice versa; grab a campsite early, then spend the day on the trails afoot. Bicycles are not permitted on the trails.

Camping is available on park grounds or on those operated by concessionaries. No reservation in the former is accepted, and stays are limited to two weeks between the periods of June 1 through October 31. Camping is permitted all year.

For more information, write: Superintendent, Shenandoah National Park, Luray, VA 22835.

VIRGIN ISLANDS
NATIONAL PARK

"St. John is the smallest and least populated of the American Virgin Islands. Nearly two-thirds of the island and most of the colorful offshore waters are set aside as our only national park in the West Indies. In this park, you will experience a change of pace — from woodland hikes to a marine adventure on an underwater nature trail. And you will see forbidding rocky coastlines, seascapes, and crescent-shaped bays where gleaming white beaches contrast with blue skies and changing blue-green seas against a background of lush hills."

This national park offers virtually nothing to the bicycle camper. The roads aren't necessarily long, which limits the amount of cycling. Couple this fact with the operation of a bike on the opposite side of the roadway and all factors are present to make the ride a short one — to the hospital.

Camping is continuous throughout the year, with a limit of two weeks per calendar year. Equipment can be rented, should you fail to take your own. Reservations must be made not more than one year in advance; send notices to the Concessioner, Cinnamon Bay Campground, St. John, VI 00830.

For more information, write: Superintendent, Virgin Islands National Park, P. O. Box 806, St. Thomas, VI 00801.

WIND CAVE NATIONAL PARK, South Dakota

"On the Southeastern flank of South Dakota's Black Hills, Wind Cave National Park preserves, in relatively unspoiled condition, part of the original prairie grassland. Preserved here also is a distinctly different type of limestone cavern — a series of subterranean passages and rooms, some lined with colorful calcite crystal formations. The strong currents of air that blow alternately in and out of the cave suggested the park's name. This strange phenomenon is believed to be caused by changes in atmospheric pressure. When outside pressure drops below that of the cave's interior, the wind blows outward; when it rises, the wind blows into the cave.

The rolling landscape is perfect for cycling, and facilities are present for the bicycle camper. Take care, however, as a herd of bison roam the park often near the roads, and could interpret your presence as that of a challenging bull, or whatever.

The campground is operated on a first-come, first-served basis. There are concessionaire facilities such as grocery and lunchroom locations present in the park.

For more information, write: Superintendent, Wind Cave National Park, Hot Springs, SD 57747.

Underground Caverns, Wind Cave National Park, South Dakota

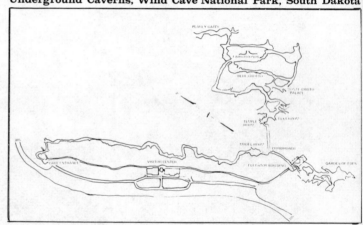

CITY OF REFUGE NATIONAL
HISTORICAL PARK, Hawaii

"Defeated warriors, noncombatants, and taboo breakers escaped death if they reached the sacred land of Honaunau ahead of their pursuers."

This historically-rich area of Hawaii can well be programmed into camping excursions at other national parks on the island. No overnight camping at

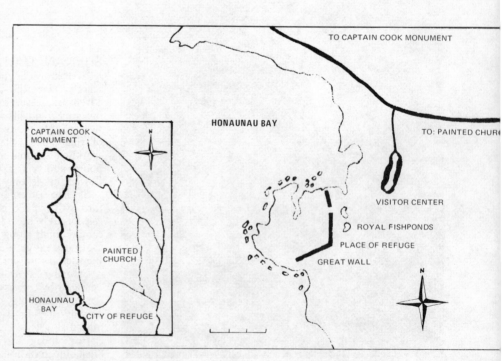

the City of Refuge is permitted.

Information on transportation to the islands is available from the Hawaii Visitors Bureau, 209 Post Street, San Francisco, CA 94108. For more information on the park, write: Superintendent, City of Refuge National Historical Park, Honaunau, Kona, HI 96726.

YELLOWSTONE NATIONAL PARK, Wyoming, Montana, Idaho

"The world's first national park, Yellowstone is a wonderland of geysers, hot springs, mud volcanos, canyons, and a wildlife display unsurpassed in the United States. The park was established on March 1, 1872, and now contains about 3,400 square miles in the northwest corner of Wyoming, overlapping into Montana on the north and west and Idaho on the west and south."

Yellowstone has over 500 miles of public roads, a real mecca for the bicycle camper. Unfortunately, during the summertime competition for camping spaces is nothing short of fierce, and they are awarded on a first-come, first-served basis. Needless to say, get to the park early!

For more information, write: Superintendent, Yellowstone National Park, WY 82190.

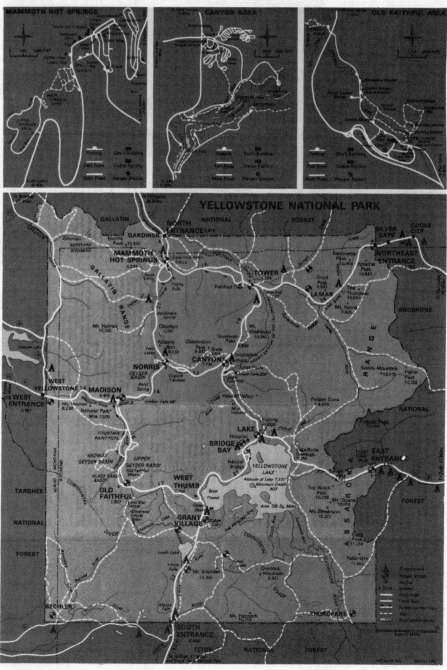

YOSEMITE NATIONAL PARK, California

"This is Yosemite National Park — a 1,189-square-mile scenic wonderland with sculptured peaks and domes; waterfalls tumbling from hanging valleys down the faces of shining granite cliffs, groves of giant sequoias and extensive forests of pine, fir and oak; wildflowers in alpine meadows; hundreds of species of birds and mammals; and scenic drives and trails to areas of high-country grandeur with sparkling glacial lakes."

Yosemite, like Yellowstone, is great for the bicyclist. More than 200 miles of public roads crisscross the park through the scenic country. Camping competition again is fierce, but can be had by the early birds.

From June 1 to September 15, camping is limited to seven days in Yosemite Valley and fourteen in the rest of the park; from September 16 to May 30, it is limited to thirty days throughout the park.

For more information, write: Superintendent, Yosemite National Park, CA 95389.

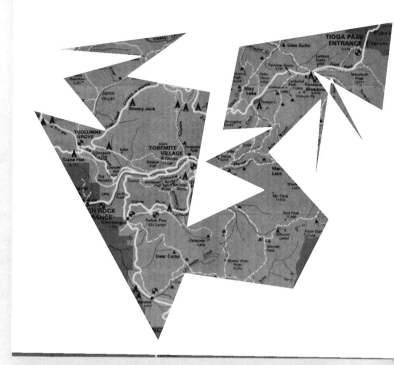

ZION NATIONAL PARK, Utah

"Nothing can exceed the wonderful beauty of Zion...in the nobility and beauty of the sculptures there is no comparison....There is an eloquence to their forms which stirs the imagination with a singular power, and kindles the mind a glowing response." — Clarence E. Dutton, geologist, 1882.

This park features only a 12-mile route that can be taken by the bicyclist, as he is forbidden to use his vehicle on the numerous trails that cut into the major points of interest.

Camping is limited to fourteen days in both the South Campground, which is open all year, and the Watchman Campground, open from May through September. Food is available within the park borders.

For more information, write: Superintendent, Zion National Park, Springdale, UT 84767.

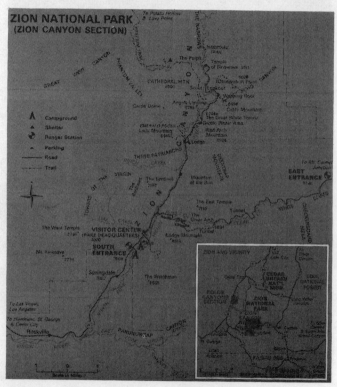

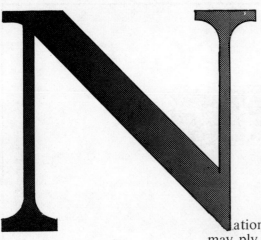

ational Forests are other areas in which the bike camping enthusiast may ply his trade. They have rules and regulations not unlike the national parks, so it would be wise for the camper to check with forest ranger either beforehand or immediately upon arrival for specific regulations to follow.

Unfortunately, space limitations prohibit listing the national forests of every state in BICYCLE DIGEST. If you plan to camp or tour in the national forests, it is recommended that you consult the League of American Wheelmen, 5118 Foster Avenue, Chicago, Illinois 60630, or the Bicycle Institute of America, 122 E. 42nd Street, New York City, New York 10022.

USDI PHOTO

TOURING

Chapter 10

For The Sightseeing Cyclist That Doesn't Care To Unduly Rough It, Tours Are The Ticket!

BICYCLE CAMPING IS A natural off-shoot of touring. It originated in Europe probably as early as the first bicycle and has expanded since that time.

In all probability, Europeans did not embark on tours in the early days using the bicycle per se. They more than likely traveled between two points on some matter of business. Stopping at roadside inns or hotels along the way, the stage was set for future developments when the business was left behind.

It is only natural that the bicycle should be called upon to substitute for the automobile in Europe as, by and large, the ratio of European families owning and operating motor vehicles is far lower than that in this country; astronomical cost primarily is responsible for this. The high cost level exists because of a lack of natural resources, specifically crude oil deposits from which petroleum by-products are refined.

Italy and France, for example, often market gasoline alone in excess of 90 cents U.S. per gallon. As most European working class members earn far less than their American counterparts, it's not hard to understand why many families abstain from purchasing an auto.

The lack of an automobile is not necessarily regarded as a big problem in Europe. The slower pace of life — noontime siesta in Spain, for example — is indicative of the differences between the continents.

The European continent, historically rich, lends itself more to sightseeing by bicycle than much of this country. The relative smallness of the countries and lack of natural boundaries; excluding the Soviet Union and Swiss Alps, make border crossing possible in little time. The lure of another country is a strong motivating factor for the bicyclist.

Being bordered by only two countries, the U.S. doesn't have these advantages. The many natural boundaries of desert, mountains and plains inhibit the scope of travel. It is almost impossible for the touring cyclist from Minnesota to cross the border into Mexico under normal circumstances — he'd never make it that far in a couple of weeks.

Most touring cyclists prefer to ride around their home areas. Many, however, are taking commercial transport to far-off locations and touring areas they may not have seen before. Some are even winging to Europe, taking advantage of reduced air fares, seeing the Continent on a more earthy level. The following is one cyclist's view of European touring:

"*The April dusk had turned Florence its typical pinkish-orange as we walked our bicycles through the campground near the Piazzale Michelangelo overlooking the Arno and the Renaissance city.*

"*'Don't see many of you anymore,' we heard someone say over our shoulders. We nodded to an Englishman, who was lounging around his camping-equipped Mini Morris.*

"*'Where are you coming from?' he asked.*

"*'Well, most recently from Rome,' we answered. 'But I*

suppose you could say we've been all over. We've had quite some time.'

"'*Yes, it's a good way to travel, but people just aren't cycling much today,' he concluded in an almost disappointed voice.*

"*After more than a year on the road in Europe, we feel that there may be more people turning to bicycles for cross-country transportation, both in Europe and the United States. There are a number of reasons, not the least of which include the negative aspects of other forms of travel.*

"*Flying from one city to another gives the traveler a sense of one large urbanized environment. There is no sense of land or surroundings while sitting in a jetliner 30,000 feet above the earth.*

"*Trains and buses are better suited for touring, but one still is confined by having a preconceived destination before getting on board. And that prohibits people from stopping at an interesting place which they previously might not have known existed.*

"*Of course, the most popular form of travel is via auto, but anyone can do that. In an age when many people are striving to do things differently in a creative fashion, a bicycle trip can result in a meaningful experience simply because it is not an accepted form of travel. A challenge is involved.*

"*At least, this type of philosophy may introduce someone to cycling, and that can lead the cyclist to realize the true beauty of traveling on a two-wheeler.*

"*Upon returning to the United States, we reread the letters we had written our friends and relatives, who were kind enough to save them for us. A description, written by my wife, while cycling through France, best states the theme of cross-country bicycling. She wrote, '...the physical part is very hard, but somehow it feels so good to really make your bodies go up those hills. Then the wind takes you down, and you feel like you're flying.'*

"*Possibly not even the finest writer or poet could really tell the story of being out on a bicycle day after day, seeing things which you always knew were there but were never aware of until now. So many parts of nature are truly seen for the first time. Things like green meadows, birds, the sun and wind. Man's senses come alive as never before.*

"*Our adventure took us through 14 countries and over 6,200 miles of roads. However, the quality, not the quantity, is most important. The reason for stating numbers is to show that even great distances can be navigated on a bicycle. And people don't have to be professional cyclists to undertake a cross-country venture. Nor do they need more than a few days to get a taste of what cycling does for the mind and body.*

"*Don't get the idea that cross-country cycling is all pleasure. While an individual surely can feel a strong bond with nature, he also may have to deal with the environment under adverse conditions. Wind, rain and cold all spell* trouble for the cyclist unless he prepares himself before going out on the road.

"However, ugly weather also helps us with our knowledge of nature. We are accustomed to escaping indoors as soon as rain falls, winds blow, or temperatures drop. So most of us never know the joy — yes, joy — of being thoroughly soaked in a summer storm. Throughout history people have learned to live with nature. At least that was true until the past few decades when technology has made it simple to · get away from the bad side of nature. But seeing and feeling what our ancestors endured is part of the education afforded by bicycling.

"While in Europe, we decided to cross the Swiss Alps with our bikes, and one day will always stand out in my mind. We had 25 miles to travel to reach the top of a 7,100-foot pass. And we wound up walking 15 of those miles, pushing our bicycles up the inclines. The skies snowed on us, as the temperature dropped into the twenties. But we kept forging ahead and finally reached the summit eight hours after we began. The lush, green valley of Valais stretched out for miles below us and, as we sped down the other side, we soon were back in the warm climate of summer. To think of where we came from and how we had done it was as much a spiritual experience as a physical one.

"And that, to me, is what cycling is all about." – Roger Wallenstein

In most cases, the touring cyclist does not encumber himself with a vast amount of gear. Instead, he will stop at motels along his pre-planned route — not unlike cyclists of old in Europe — taking his meals in commercial facilities. He cycles through the countryside at a leisurely pace, drinking in the natural beauty and tranquility of the land.

Some cyclists don't have the kind of money required for this type of touring, however, and must take along cooking utensils and sleeping gear not unlike that used by the bicycle camper. Others research the route they intend to take carefully, endeavoring to find motels with the cheapest rates and restaurants that can save them a buck or two. Much of this information is available from Chamber of Commerce organizations in the many towns along his propsective route.

Others have found that facilities manned by volunteers of the American Youth Hostels offer the entire package they wish. The rates are extremely low for sleeping and most hostels have cooking facilities available, stocked with everything but the grub. A closer look will be given to the AYH movement, both in this country and abroad, later in the chapter.

In most respects, the bicycle tourist plans as carefully as his camping counterpart. A prospective tour location is designed, then many letters are written, opinions garnered and results evaluated before final preparations.

When selecting a tour route, insure there is a variety of terrain available, as nothing is more monotonous than the same scenery for miles; the Iowa corn belt, for example. Rolling past corn stalks often higher than the head for a couple of weeks would, at least, turn him off of corn for awhile.

It's a good bet that, if a national park or forest is in the area, the terrain will be varied. Consult the Chamber of Commerce for this information, as well as any other items within the specific area that you might take interest in, like historical monuments which abound throughout the nation.

In planning your route, it is wise to consider the amount of ground you tend to cover in one cycling day. If you average sixty miles, your overnight stops should be programmed for smaller intervals. The reason is that, during a ride through new country, most cyclists are inclined to stop periodically and examine what the area has to offer, or explore small side roads off the main tour route. By programming stops at somewhat less than the cyclist's average daily distance, frantic dashes to the motel holding your reservation will be avoided.

In your letters, solicit opinions as to the best cheap motels in villages on your route. Once you have the names of several motels, write and ask for a price schedule, and for a brochure if they have such available. You then can compare for the one that best suits your tastes — and your wallet. Forward a letter to the motel or hotel of your choice, giving them the exact date you anticipate being in the town, and send a check as a deposit.

Most motels and hotels will inform you that they hold reservations only until about five in the evening and, if you haven't shown by that time, they will rent to the first taker. If you don't arrive at the location prior to the time indicated, your money will be refunded in all but the shadiest of cases.

If you decide to stay in the dormitories of the American Youth Hostels, prepare to arrive only between the hours of five and seven in the evening, as the hostel is closed during the remainder of the day. Also, the hostel management requires that you furnish your own sleeping sack, which keeps the mattresses and blankets clean for future tenants, or a sleeping bag. The sleeping sacks can be purchased from AYH or made at home of old sheets.

You can obtain other valuable information from bicycle groups or clubs that are centered around the area you intend touring. If this fails, ask around for other cyclists in your home area who might have ridden through the area at an earlier date. These individuals will offer more sound advice; experience is the best educator.

If there is a national park or forest in the vicinity, consult the directory in the preceding chapter for the address of the superintendent or supervisor and write him a letter. They will send maps and information about commercial facilities available near the park for the individual that doesn't camp. Again, allow a month for a reply.

After a prospective tour route has been chosen, a rider must decide how he plans to arrive at the starting point, if the tour is not around his home area. Most areas of the country are accessible by air transport or commercial bus lines, and the cyclist should evaluate his time factor and on-hand cash. Airlines naturally are more expensive than a bus or train, but take less time.

The bicycle usually will have to be crated in an old bicycle shipping carton before baggage handlers will allow it on board the aircraft, so some time will have to be spent upon arrival at the jumping-off spot reassembling the bike. Trains accept the bicycle in riding condition, which does save time. There is a chance that it can be damaged in the baggage compartment, so ask the handler if he can hang it on a wall or the like. If traveling by bus line with the bicycle in a carton, for your own sake have a block of wood or thick cardboard placed between the forks in the front. Baggage handlers are notorious for their disregard of fragile items and this precaution can save bent or twisted forks.

The tourist can ferry his bike to the jumping-off spot via the auto, take his tour, then return via his auto at the end. This is a fine system, provided there is some type of parking facility available which can at least guarantee that the auto will be there when you return, without having lost some of its parts.

If you find that such facilities are not available at your starting point, write to the sheriff's department in the town where you will leave your auto. If they cannot harbor your

שדה בוקר
SEDE BOKER
קרן היסוד
KEREN HAYESOD

מחנה דלק

Touring outfits, bicycles and routes vary greatly, as shown by this group of Israeli bikers photographed in their homeland. Rocky routes call for good tires!

vehicle on their grounds, they might at least mention the name of a notable and trustworthy citizen who might look after it for a few bucks.

There are many schools of thought regarding touring Europe on a bicycle, the gear to take and equipment to leave behind. According to the International Bicycle Touring Society, 846 Prospect Street, La Jolla, California 92037, the rider should take his bike on the plane with him. They allege that rental bicycles generally are not satisfactory and that purchasing a new bicycle is an unnecessary expense.

Others, however, claim that rental bicycles are satisfactory on the Continent and negate the possibilities of having

a U.S. bike damaged in handling. Bicycles can be purchased new from the factory in Europe at lesser cost, which should be considered.

Getting a bicycle aboard a European-bound jetliner is not the problem that it once was, although some hassle still may be encountered at the check-in counter. IBTS, in a free handout entitled "Hints On Cycling In Europe," says, "Don't call up beforehand. Simply go to the check-in counter at flight time and say that you have a bicycle. Usually, the clerk offers no objection. If he does, tell him that you will sign a release from damage claims. If he starts quoting the regulations, tell him that, at this late date, all you can do is to remove the pedals, swivel the handlebar, and steady the front wheel with a strap. Don't enter into an argument. These people will help you, if you give them a chance."

According to information solicited from airline carriers,

YOUTH HOSTELS IN U.S.A.

There are more than 100 Youth Hostels including supplementary accommodations extending across the U.S. Regular hostels offer accommodations for between $1 and $2 a night. Supplementary accommodations are available to hostellers at somewhat higher fees.

*open all year   S.A. supplementary accommodations

EASTERN REGION

CONNECTICUT
1. Sugar House, Canton
2. Bantam Lake, Lakeside *

MAINE
3. Bear Mountain Village, South Waterford *

MARYLAND
4. North Branch, Cumberland *
5. Kiwanis, Sandy Hook *
6. Old Stonehouse, Seneca

MASSACHUSETTS
7. Strathmore House, Brookline S.A.
8. Christ Church, Boston
9. Lingham Home, Framingham
10. Old Lilacs, Granville *
11. Hy-Land, Hyannis, Cape Cod
12. La Salette, Ipswich S.A.
13. Friendly Crossways, Littleton *
14. Star of the Sea, Nantucket
15. Midcape, Orleans
16. Camp Karu, Pittsfield S.A.
17. Mount Everett, Sheffield
18. Springfield College Camp, Springfield
19. Little Meadow, Sunderland
20. Little America, Truro, Cape Cod
21. Lillian Manter Memorial, West Tisbury, Martha's Vineyard

NEW HAMPSHIRE
22. Green Tops, Alton
23. E. Charles Goodwin Community Center, Claremont S.A.
24. Ragged Edge, Danbury *
25. Gray Ledges, Grantham *

NEW HAMPSHIRE (Cont.)
26. North Conway Community Center S.A.
27. The Lime Kilns, North Haverhill
28. Cotton's, Warren

NEW JERSEY
29. Old Mine Road, Hainesville*

NEW YORK
30. N.Y. Student Center, Hotel McAlpin S.A.*
31. Sloane House "Y" S.A.*
32. Niagara Falls Y.M.C.A. S.A.*
33. Downing, Syracuse *

PENNSYLVANIA
34. Bowmansville
35. Cannon Hill, Brickerville
36. Rising Waters, Bushkill
37. Denver
38. Ridley Park, Media
39. Shirey's, Geigertown
40. La Anna *
41. Chamounix Mansion, W. Fairmount Park, Philadelphia *
42. Weisel Park *

VERMONT
43. Sterling School, Craftsbury Common *
44. Lowell *
45. Putney School, Putney *
46. School House, Rochester *
47. Old Homestead, Warren *
48. Ski Hostel Lodge, Waterbury Center *

WEST VIRGINIA
49. Chestnut Ridge Camp, Morgantown *

DISTRICT OF COLUMBIA
50. Washington International *

SOUTHERN REGION

GEORGIA
51. Dixie Rest Motel, Bainbridge S.A.*

NORTH CAROLINA
52. Camp Carmel, Linville

MID-WEST REGION

ILLINOIS
53. SIU Little Grassy, Carbondale *
54. Y.M.C.A. Hotel, Chicago S.A.*
55. Galena *
56. Palos Park *

INDIANA
57. Dunes Lakeshore, Chesterton

IOWA
58. Oneota, Decorah
59. Andy Mountain, Harper's Ferry S.A.
60. Wesley House, Iowa City S.A.

MICHIGAN
61. Bessemer-Indianhead, Bessemer
62. Friedenswald, Cassopolis *
63. Y.M.C.A./Y.W.C.A., Detroit S.A.*
64. Blue Lake, Kalkaska *
65. Foote, Milford *

MINNESOTA
66. Cliff Wold's Canoe, Ely
67. Gunflint Canoe, Grand Marais
68. Crow Wing Trails, Sebeka
69. Twin Cities, St. Paul *

MISSOURI
70. Epworth Among the Hills, Arcadia *
71. Shannondale Community Center, Gladden *
72. Lewis & Clark, Kansas City *

NEBRASKA
74. Ponda Rosa, Buffalo City
75. Wesley House, Lincoln S.A.*

OHIO
76. Myeerah, Bellefontaine *
77. Wintergarden Community Lodge, Bowling Green *
79. Community Camp, New Plymouth
80. Huston's, Toledo *

WISCONSIN
80A. Rock River, Beloit
81. Ches Perry, Cable
82. Deepwood Ski Lodge, Colfax
83. The Red Barn, Greendale
84. Friendship Farm, Kansasville
85. The Farmhouse, Tomah
86. Two Rivers *

WESTERN REGION

ALASKA
87. Juneau Methodist, Juneau

ARIZONA
88. Aspen Lodge, Alpine
89. Bisbee YWCA *
90. Congregational Church, Flagstaff *
91. Arizona Rancho Motor Lodge, Holbrook *
92. The Outfit, Tucson

CALIFORNIA
93. Mountain Home Ranch, Calistoga
94. Meadowlark Farm, Hemet *
95. Armed Services YMCA, Long Beach S.A.*
96. Hidden Villa Ranch, Los Altos *
97. Laguna Beach Ranch, Pt. Reyes *
98. Cal-Expo, Sacramento *
98.A San Diego *

COLORADO
99. Boulder S.A.*
100. Rocky Mt. Camp, Divide
101. Rockwood Ranch, Durango

HAWAII
102. Hale Aloha, Honolulu *

MONTANA
102A. Alpine Lodge, Bozeman S.A.*

UTAH
103. Alpine Prospector's Lodge, Park City
104. Venice, Venice *

WASHINGTON
105. The Lodge, Ashford *
106. North Branch YMCA, Spokane *

WYOMING
107. The Hostel, Jackson Hole S.A.*

YOUTH HOSTELS IN CANADA

In Canada there are at present over 50 regular youth hostels which have been graded A, B or C, and for which the following overnight fees are charged:

	Junior	Senior
A	$2.00	$2.50
B	$1.50	$2.00
C	$0.75	$1.00

☀ open all year   S.A. supplementary accommodation

A number of summer hostels are also available as supplementary accommodations, please check with the Regional Offices for locations.

MARITIME REGION

3. Wentworth, Cumberland Co., N.S. A*
4. Antigonish, N.S. C
5. Bramley Gardens, Middleton, Annapolis Co., N.S. S.A.
6. Eldridge Homestead, Yarmouth S., N.S. S.A.
7A. Frankaleen Hostel, Bras d'Or, Cape Breton Co., N.S. B
7B. Gardiner Centre, Cape Breton Co., N.S. S.A.
7C. Emmanuel House, St. John's, Nfld. S.A.

ST. LAWRENCE

8. Montreal, P.Q. A*
8A. Ottawa, Ont. S.A.
9. Shirley's Bay, Ont. C
10. Auberge de Carillon, P.Q. A*
11. Auberge de Neuville, P.Q.
12. Sutton, P.Q. C*
12A. Rockburn, nr Athelstan, P.Q. C*
13. Dunkin, nr Mansonville, P.Q. C*
14. Bolton Glen, nr Knowlton, P.Q. A*
14A. Richford, Vermont, U.S. A

GREAT LAKES REGION

1. Gananoque, Ont. A*
2. Toronto, Ont. S.A.
15. Niagara, Ont. A*
16. Collingwood, Ont. A*
17. Cedardale, Galt, Ont. C*
18. Northern Eagle, Minden, Ont. A
18A. Nepanee, Ont. S.A.

PRAIRIE REGION

19. Karianne, Robsart Saskatchewan C
19B. Lynx Enterprises, Saskatoon, Sask. S.A.*

MOUNTAIN REGION

20. Ribbon Creek, Alta. C*
21. Spray River, Alta. C
22. Mount Eisenhower, Alta. C*
23. Corral Creek, Alta. C
24. Takakkaw Falls, B.C. C
25. Mosquito Creek, Alta. C*
26. Totem Creek, Alta. C
27. Ramparts Creek, Alta. C*
28. Hilda Creek, Alta. C*

NORTH WEST REGION

29. Beauty Creek, Alta. C
30. Athabasca Falls, Alta. C*
31. Mount Edith Cavell, Alta. C
32. Maligne Canyon, Alta. C*
33. Jasper, Alta. S.A.
34. Elk Island National Park, Alta. C
35. Nordegg, Alta. C

PACIFIC REGION

36. Secret Cove, Halfmoon Bay, B.C. C
37. Vernon, B.C. C
38. Gray Creek, B.C. C*
39. Vancouver, B.C. A*
40. Kamloops, B.C. S.A.

YUKON

41. Yukon Wilderness Unlimited, McCabe Creek, Yukon S.A.*

the simple bicycle carton can save all of this hassle. Carriers are more inclined to welcome a box than a uncrated bike. Remember to reinforce the front fork with wood or cardboard. This requires a slight time loss upon arrival at your foreign port, as you must reassemble the bike.

One thing is agreed upon by all agencies that offer touring information: All feel that a regular touring bike with fenders, carrier, clincher tires and low gearing is best. Sometimes they will be equipped with a light or a bell, but not always.

If you wish to purchase bicycles from Old World manufacturers, IBTS lists several outlets as offering fine examples of touring types:

* Ron Kitching, Hookstone Park, Harrogate, Yorks, England (in the northern part of England)
* Jack Taylor, Church Road, Stockton-on-Tees, Durham, England (in the northern part of England)
* Witcomb, Tanners Hill, Deptford Broadway, London, S.E. 8, England
* C.N.C., 112 boulevard de la Chapelle, Paris 18, France
* Cyclo-Louvre, 44 rue Etienne Marcel, Paris 2, France
* Oscar Egg, 57 avenue de la Grande Armes, Paris 8, France

Should you have any questions, the French factories will answer letters written in English, but replies often take quite a while.

If you desire a custom built bicycle, be prepared to part with a goodly sum. Prices start at around $200 and the ceiling is the limit, depending upon your desires. Usually, the price range for the average cyclist who doesn't want his machine gold-plated, runs between $200 and $500, to which another hundred or so is tacked for shipping costs. This latter figure can be eliminated if you pick up the bicycle yourself.

IBTS reports that usual procedure is one-third of the total amount down upon placement of your order, the balance collected when the bicycle arrives COD. Filling the order naturally depends on the status of work in the shop, and the average time from placement of order to delivery is around six months. The shops are least busy during the winter months.

Again, letters written in English to the builder will be answered, but as there are no English-speaking employees in the plants, phone calls will be a waste of time and money, unless you happen to speak French. If you plan on picking up your bike from the maker, hire an interpreter to go with you. Of course, get a firm commitment, if you can, from the manufacturer as to when the bike will be ready before arriving in Paris with your pannier bags.

The number of custom makers gradually is declining in Europe. However, IBTS lists several makers still building custom bicycles:

* Rene Herse, 12 rue du President-Wilson, 92 Levallois Perret, France (Levallois Perret is a suburb of Paris)
* Rene Andre, 20 rue Jean-Maridor, Paris 15, France
* Alex Singer, 53 rue Victor-Hugo, 92 Levallois, France
* Jo Routens, 8 course Berriot, Grenoble, France

The following specification list was compiled by IBTS for individuals ordering custom-made bikes from French makers. The name of the individual components are given both in English and French:

DEFINITION OF COMPONENTS

FRENCH	ENGLISH	REMARKS
Cadre	Frame	Measure from center of bottom bracket to the point where the seatpost enters the frame. Give in centimeters (1cm = .39 inch, 2.54cm = 1 inch)
Email	Paint	Specify color. Chrome adds $50
Plateau	Chainwheel	Specify number of teeth and size. Recommended: 30-46 or 30-40-50
Moyeux	Hubs	Recommended: ATOM NORMANDIE. CAMPAGNOLO not necessary.
Rayons	Spokes	Stainless steel. (Inoxidable in French)
Jantes	Rims	Recommended: SUPER CHAMPION
Blocages	Wheel lock	Recommended: CAMPAGNOLO quick-release
Pneus	Tires	MICHELIN 700-C or WOLBER Super Sport
Roue libre	Freewheel	Specify number of teeth. Possible sizes: 14-16-19-23-28; 14-16-20-24-30; other
Derailleur	Rear derailleur	HURET, CAMPAGNOLO, SIMPLEX, etc.
Derailleur pedalier	Front derailleur	Same as rear derailleur
Pedales	Pedals	ATOM 700 or other. Three widths
Freins	Brakes	MAFAC best, WEINMANN acceptable
Cale-pieds	Toe clips	CHRISTOPHE, short, medium or long
Garde-boue	Fenders	Plastic or alloy. If plastic, give color
Tige de selle	Seatpost	CAMPAGNOLO, SIMPLEX, UNICA-NITOR
Selle	Saddle	BROOKS or IDEALE
Guidon	Handlebar	Recommended: RANDONNEUR
Potence	Gooseneck	Specify length, measured center to center
Porte-bagages	Carriers	Specify front, rear or both. (Special bracket to hold handlebar bag away from bars is called protege-mains)
Eclairage	Lights	Recommended: SOUBITEZ

Many bike tourists carry their machines to the start of the tour route on an automobile, train, plane or bus. If the automobile is used, the tourist has the advantage of saving some cash in transportation both ways, but loses some time. Also, the car must be left unattended in most cases, and conceivably could be stolen or stripped of parts. Check the text for ways to avoid this mishap while using the automobile.

Naturally, the individual can exercise his own opinion and specify the types of components he wishes on his bicycle. However, comfort is the most important commodity and, while it may be impressive — and ghastly expensive — to outfit the bike totally with Campagnolo components, they may not improve the comfort in the least.

Whether cycling in Europe or in this country, bicycle bags are the next areas of scrutiny. Just as with the bike camper, the tourist should endeavor to keep the load as light as possible, hung low on the bike and centered as much as possible.

Bike bags are broken-down into three categories: Handlebar, pannier, and saddlebags. They are made of all manner of materials, from canvas to woven nylon to leather. The best bags are made in Europe, but some American manufacturers now have bags that are extremely functional.

Handlebar bags are fairly self-explanatory, are used for carrying much-used small items, and are attached to the handlebars; pannier bags hang on both sides of the rear, and sometimes front, carriers. These carry the bulk of the cyclist's load; saddlebags actually are deceiving, as a novice cyclist will have visions of the type of leather bags used by cowboys of a by-gone era. In actuality, they are small bags that are strapped to the rear of the seat, generally used for carrying tools and spare parts.

Most cyclists can get by with two pannier bags, a handlebar bag and a saddlebag. If you start outfitting the bike with a front carrier and additional pannier bags, figure on expending much more pedaling effort or cutting daily mileage considerably.

Equipment should be kept to an absolute minimum, as should personal effects. Although each cyclist will take items different from another cyclist, the following guide may help some riders with the gear choice. This list, prepared by IBTS, applies for both U.S. and foreign tours:

Clothing and Grooming
2 riding jerseys, dark
2 pair of riding shorts or
1 pair of shorts + 1 knickers
2 sets of underwear
2 pair of knee-length hose
1 pair of shoes
1 pair of slippers
1 windbreaker, unlined
1 hat
1 raincape, plastic
1 shoeshine kit
4 hankies
  toilet articles
1 pajama (optional)
1 plastic leggings (optional)
1 sunglasses (optional)
2 inflatable hangers (optional)

Valuables
1 passport
  travelers checks
  camera and film

For Men Only
1 sport jacket, dacron, or
1 dressy sweater
1 pair of slacks
1 shirt
1 tie

For Women Only
1 dress or
1 suit or
1 blouse and skirt
1 pair of nylon hose
1 sewing kit

For The Bicycle
1 tire repair kit
3 spanners
1 spare tube (or 2 sew-ups)
1 pair of gloves
1 lock, small
1 pump
2 elastic straps
1 strap-on flashlight

When you get the pannier bags together with all of this gear, it appears as though it never will fit. Determine which items you will want within easy reach, which items will go in what bags. Load and unload all of the gear into the bags a few times, discovering the proper placement of the items for best balance. This way you won't be mailing home gear that won't fit into the bags.

The bicycle will handle quite differently when loaded with equipment, so take a trial run before taking off, even a few small tours around your home area on the weekends to familiarize yourself with problems encountered while touring.

In the U.S., securing maps of different areas is relatively simple. On many, though, only major traffic arteries are depicted, as the maps are geared for the motorist. By inquiring of local officials in the towns you intend passing through, alternate routes can be determined.

In Europe, maps are a must as the country is not strictly a series of small roads suitable for cycling. Even where such roads are accessible, the cyclist first must discover them.

When you have chosen the areas in which you intend touring in Europe, get detail maps of the same from bookstores. If your tour is in England, get the Bartholomew series; in France and the low countries, Michelin maps; in Germany, the Shell Generalkarte; and Holland, special maps from the Dutch Touring Club, 5 Museumplein, Amsterdam.

If you would like to visit Europe various clubs will be of help. In this country, check with IBTS at the address given earlier; the Cyclists Touring Club, 69 Meadrow, Godalming, Surrey, England; Federation Francaise de Cyclotourisme, 66 rue Rene-Boulanger, Paris 10, France; Chambre Syndicale du Cycle, 7 Karl Marx Boulevard, St. Etienne, France; Alliance Internationale de Tourisme, 9 rue Pierre Fatio, Geneva, Switzerland; and Societe Polonaise de Tourisme, Senatorska 11, Warsaw 5, Poland; the League of American Wheelmen, 5118 Foster Avenue, Chicago, Illinois 60630, and the Bicycle Institute of America, 122 E. 42nd Street, New York City, New York 10022.

Many of these groups have regular itineraries of upcoming tours, with previous arrangements as to sleeping and eating. If you don't go as part of this group, it is up to you to figure your own way.

As mentioned earlier, it is pretty rough to survive for under $10 a day while touring in this country. In Europe, lodging rates are cheaper by and large and food can be had for fewer coppers.

There are four sleeping choices available to the bike tourist in Europe: tent, hostel, pension or hotel, in order of least expense. The tent is free, but it calls for lost time in setting up and striking camp, and carrying it on the bike means something else must be left behind, because of the weight factor. A hostel costs only one dollar for overnight lodging, but sleeping quarters consist of a big dormitory. In Germany or Switzerland, riders over the age of twenty-five cannot stay overnight in the hostels. A pension, the equivalent of a tourist's home, is available for about two dollars per night. A hotel runs around three to four dollars per night, but often this includes breakfast.

There are enough International Youth Hostel facilities throughout Europe that a tourist can find one almost each night. In this country, though, the hostels are not as widespread and a touring cyclist should not expect to find them with Europe's frequency. The cost is around three dollars per night.

The Youth Hostel movement was initiated by a German schoolteacher named Richard Schirrmann in 1909. He took his students hiking throughout the countryside, but the idea of shelter was a problem. His school was the first hostel established in the world.

The following year, he was appointed administrator of a museum in a 12th Century castle, and obtained permission for some rooms to be used as dormitories. The idea spread and, by 1932, an International Hosteling Conference was held in Holland. Criteria was established whereby members could stay in hostels of any country, regardless of age, sex, race, religion or national origin. Standards of health, sanitation, safety and operation were adopted; the importance of suitable wardens or houseparents was stressed, and the use of sheet sleeping sacks by each hosteler was made mandatory; alcoholic beverages were forbidden in hostels, and smoking was restricted to the recreation or common room which each hostel provided.

Two years after this meeting, a pair of married school teachers, Isabel and Monroe Smith, established the first American Youth Hostel in Northfield, Massachusetts. It has spread much more slowly though this country, and there still are many states that have no hostels. There is a total of 107 hostels in this country, and an additional fifty in

Touring in foreign countries gives the cyclist an opportunity to study the language and culture, but learning to pronounce words like those on the sign can be difficult! Note the touring bicycle used.

Canada. Forty-seven countries now have them, with a world-wide hostel total of 4,241. More than 22 million individuals claim membership in the Youth Hostel organization.

Of interest is the fact that the Youth Hostel organization is not limited to bicycle riders. In the U.S., a car, motorcycle, scooter, bus, plane or train can be used to reach the first hostel on a trip, or to cover the long stretches between hostels. In England, Algeria, Ireland, Germany, Japan, the Netherlands, New Zealand and North Belguim, cars are not permitted. Motorcycles are not permitted in Australia, Wales or England.

Membership fees are $5 for a junior pass, for individuals under 18 years of age; $10 for a senior pass, for 18-year-olds and older; $12 for a family membership; $15 for an organization pass; $2 each for special individual youth pass; $50 for life membership; and $100 for a family life membership.

In the family membership, children must be accompanied by the parents when in Canada, although they may be unescorted in this country. It includes children up to 18 years.

The organization pass is intended solely for American or Canadian non-profit groups of not more than twenty-five individuals, including the leader. AYH recommends two leaders with this group.

The special individual youth pass is available through schools, churches, Y's, Scouts, Settlement Houses, Boys Clubs, for those under eighteen, in groups of ten or more. The leader, teacher or official must make the application on organization stationery, giving full names, addresses and birthdates of each youth. It is valid in the United States only.

The family life membership includes children under 18, and is good in U.S. and Canadian hostels only.

For groups or individuals desiring further information, there are pamphlets, books and movies available for sale or rent from AYH. These include "The AYH Hostel Guide & Handbook," $1.25; "Family Hosteling Manual," $.75; "The International Youth Hostels Handbook, Volume I (Europe and North America)," $2.80; "International Youth Hostels Handbook, Volume II (Asia, Australasia, Africa and the Americas)," $2.65; "Europe Camping & Caravaning International Guide," $4 (plus $.75 postage East of the Mississippi, $1.25 West of same); "Canada Handbook: Hostel Locations," $.75; "The AYH North American Bike Atlas," $1.50 to members, $1.95 to non-members.

The whole idea behind staying at one of the youth hostels is of everyone pulling his weight. Cleaning chores are shared by visitors, so each naturally takes pains to avoid making a mess.

For additional information about AYH or brochures available, address your inquiries to AYH National Campus, Delaplaine, Virginia 22025. They will reply promptly.

The AYH sponsors trips abroad and in this country, using bikes, Volkswagon buses, train, plane or commercial buses, or by hiking. The trips are of varying duration, and more information can be obtained from the AYH councils located throughout the country. The councils resemble chapters of clubs incorporated into the overall system. The councils established are listed below:

ARIZONA: Arizona State Council, 4634 E. Lewis, Phoenix, AZ 85008

CALIFORNIA: Golden Gate Council, 625 Polk Street, San Francisco, CA 94102; Los Angeles Council, 318 N. La Brea Avenue, Los Angeles, CA 90036; Northern California Council, P. O. Box 15649, Sacramento, CA 95813; San Diego Council, 7445 Grand Avenue, La Jolla, CA 92037; San Gabriel Valley Council, 215 W. 1st Street, Claremont, CA 91711

CONNECTICUT: Fairfield County Council, P. O. Box 173, Southport, CT 06490; Hartford Area Council, YMCA, 315 Pearl Street, Hartford, CT 06103; New Haven Council, 48 Howe Street, New Haven, CT 06511

DISTRICT OF COLUMBIA: Potomac Area Council, 1501 16th Street N.W., Washington, D.C. 20036

ILLINOIS: Metropolitan Chicago Council, 3712 N. Clark, Chicago, IL 60613

IOWA: Northeast Iowa Council, Box 96, Postville, IA 52162

MASSACHUSETTS: Greater Boston Council, 251 Harvard Street, Brookline, MA 02146

MINNESOTA: Minnesota Council, P. O. Box 9511, Minneapolis, MN 55440

MISSOURI: Lewis & Clark Council, 12201 Blue River Road, Kansas City, MO 64146; Ozark Area Council, 2605 South Big Bend, St. Louis, MO 63143

NEBRASKA: Nebraskaland Council, 3357 Holdrege Avenue, Lincoln, NE 65803

NEW YORK: Metropolitan New York Council, 535 West End Avenue, New York, NY 10024; Syracuse Council, 735 S. Beech Street, Syracuse, NY 13210

OHIO: Columbus Council, P.O. Box 3165, Columbus, OH 43210; Lake Erie Council, 2000 Terminal Tower, Cleveland, OH 44113; Lima Council, Box 173, Lima, OH 45802; Toledo Area Council, 5320 Fern Drive, Toledo, OH 43613

PENNSYLVANIA: Delaware Valley Council, 4714 Old York Road, Philadelphia, PA 19141; Pittsburgh Council, 6300 Fifth Avenue, Pittsburgh, PA 15232

WISCONSIN: Wisconsin Council, P. O. Box 233, Hales Corners, WI 53130

CANADIAN COUNCILS

NATIONAL OFFICE: Canadian Youth Hostels Association, Sports & Recreation Center, 333 River Road, Vanier City, Ottawa, Ontario K1L 8B9, Canada

MARITIME: 6260 Quinpool Road, Halifax, Nova Scotia

ST. LAWRENCE: 1324 Sherbrooke Street West, Montreal 109, Province of Quebec, Canada; National Capital Division, 270 MacLaren Street, Ottawa, Ontario K2P 0M3, Canada

GREAT LAKES: 86 Scollard Street, Toronto 185, Ontario, Canada

WINNIPEG: Prairie Area Office, P. O. Box 135, Postal Station C, Winnipeg, R3M 3S7, Manitoba, Canada

MOUNTAIN: 455 – 12th Street N.W., Calgary 41, Alberta, Canada

NORTH WEST: 10918 – 88th Avenue, Edmonton 61, Alberta, Canada

PACIFIC: 1406 West Broadway, Vancouver 9, British Columbia, Canada; Vancouver Island Division, Room 106, 1951 Cook Street, Victoria, British Columbia, Canada

With this information locked away inside the old brain housing, about the only remaining task the bike tourist must perform is to pick a site and escape! How else can you get so much for so little?

Chapter 11

by
Dr. Paul Dudley White

(DR. PAUL DUDLEY WHITE is recognized as one of the world's most respected cardiologists, especially in the area of diseases of the heart. Born June 6, 1886, to Dr. Herbert Warren and Elizabeth A. Dudley White in Roxbury, Massachusetts, Dr. White received his preparatory education at Roxbury Latin School before attending Harvard University. He was graduated with an A.B. degree in 1908 and M.D. degree in 1911, He served internship at Massachusetts General Hospital prior to completing graduate work as a Harvard University traveling fellow in London in 1914, engaged in research, practice and teaching, especially in the field of heart disease. He then returned to the U.S. and assumed a Resident in Medicine position with Massachusetts General Hospital.

(In 1916, Dr. White was commissioned Medical Officer of Base Hospital No. 22 with the British Expeditionary Force in France. From 1917-19, he had the same position with the American Expeditionary Force in France. Following cessation of hostilities, he assumed a position of Medical Officer with the American Red Cross in Greece. He has since traveled extensively giving lectures and with teaching missions to Czechoslovakia, Australia, South Africa, People's Republic of China, Canada, Brazil, Poland, Italy, Pakistan, India, Israel, the Soviet Union, Mexico, Chile, Belgium, Argentina and others.

(He has served as chairman of a National Red Cross committee on cardiovascular disease; executive director of the National Advisory Heart Council; is a member of the American Academy of Arts and Sciences, American Medical Association; past president of the American Heart Association. He is a member of the Royal Society of Medicine (England), Royal College of Physicians (London, Ireland), is founder and past president of the International Society of Cardiology. He is a member of the National Academy of Medicine of France, cardiac societies of France, Mexico, Czechoslovakia, Brazil, Chile, South Africa, Australia, Italy, Belgium and Argentina. He is a member of the Soviet Academy of Medical Sciences, Association of American Physicians and many more.

(Dr. White has been honored with Czechoslovakian and Cuban decorations, France's Legion d'Honneur, Finland's Order of Lion, U.S.A.'s Freedom Medal — the highest award this country gives to civilians. In 1964, Dr. White was honored with the Lasker award for distinguished achievement in the field of cardiovascular diseases.

(He has authored several books, including "Heart Disease," "Heart Disease In General Practice," "Electrocardiography In Practice," "Coronary Heart Disease In Young Adults," "Clues In The Diagnosis And Treatment of Heart Disease," "Fitness Of The Whole Family," "Hearts: Their Long Follow-Up," and "My Life And Medicine."

(He currently resides and practices in Boston. It indeed is a pleasure to feature his comments.)

I HAVE WELCOMED the invitation to prepare a chapter for this book on the subject of the effect of bicycling on the health of the cyclist. I must begin, however, with the warning that everyone should insist that the bicycling must be safe and preferably done on special paths and trails. A decade or more ago a few of us in metropolitan Boston incorporated a Committee for Safe Bicycling and during the years that have passed have helped to establish safe paths, usually for both cyclist and pedestrian together since as a rule they can use the same path if it is wide enough, not only in Massachusetts but in many other parts of the USA.

Accidents, which usually involve motor car and cyclist, have often not been the fault of the motor car driver. In many cases they have been due to the carelessness and illegal action of the cyclist him-or-herself. I have seen much reckless cycling by individuals of all ages riding against the traffic, or too fast, ignoring the traffic signals, failing to signal on turns, and not being equipped with adequate lights or horns or bells. I believe that the great majority of the bicyclists of today do obey the rules, but the minority — and they are too many — are the offenders and they bring discredit on the others. I hope that this book will have a very wide circulation so that it will be read by the careless as well as by the careful.

And now to turn to the more pleasant and interesting effect of cycling on the health, both general and special. First, the physiology of the process: I find that relatively few individuals have ever been told about the wonderful pumping mechanisms with which nature has endowed us, to

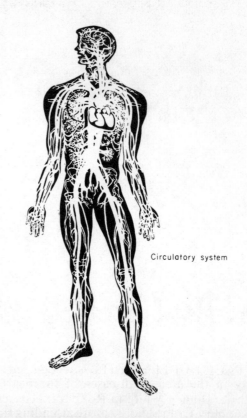

Circulatory system

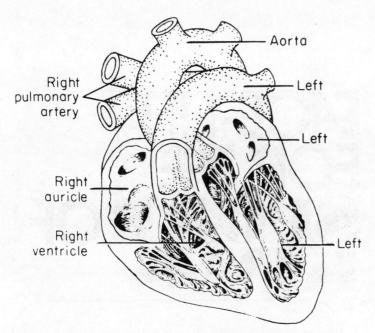

Right pulmonary artery

Aorta

Left

Left

Right auricle

Right ventricle

Left

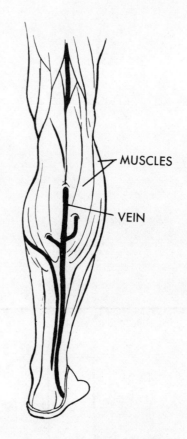

MUSCLES

VEIN

aid the heart in maintaining a proper circulation of blood to our brain, our lungs, our heart itself, and to the muscles. Over four hundred years ago in Italy anatomists and physiologists discovered that the veins of the arms and legs have been supplied by nature with valves which prevent the blood from accumulating by gravity in the lower part of the body. William Harvey of England, who had studied in Padua, Italy, from 1599 to 1603, had been shown these valves and after his return to London used their function to complete one of the greatest discoveries of all time, namely the circulation of the blood, which he presented in a small book in 1628.

When the leg muscles of the thighs and of the calves contract as in simple walking, running, bicycling, swimming, tennis, golf, or other sports, they squeeze the deep veins within them and, because of the presence of valves in the veins, the blood is pumped up towards the heart and thence to the brain by the heart. Thus the heart is not the only pump in the body. It has been estimated that this muscular action of the legs relieves the heart of about one-third of its work by the simple exercise of walking, and the same should be true of bicycling.

A third pumping mechanism in the body is dependent on the muscle of the diaphragm in making the cavity of the thorax into a suction pump by causing a negative pressure therein during deep inspiration. This suction action not only brings air into our lungs but also helps to bring blood up from below. This vital action of the diaphragm should not be impeded by obesity in the abdomen, emphysema or other diseases of the lungs, or by generally poor physical fitness. Moreover, the pollution of the inspired air with tobacco smoke results in the contamination of the oxygen by carbon monoxide gas which, as it enters the blood, drives out the oxygen from the hemoglobin in the red blood corpuscles. This lowered oxygen content in the blood can have catastrophic results if the coronary or other cardiac reserve happens to be low. Thus the physiology of the circulation of blood enters into the physical exercise of bicycling in a major way and needs clear understanding.

Having discussed the physical benefit of cycling, I would like now strongly to emphasize the mental or psychological benefits. The best antidote for emotional stress or fatigue is the physical exercise of the legs in walking or running or cycling a few miles. If it cannot be done safely outdoors,

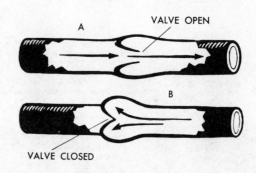

A

VALVE OPEN

B

VALVE CLOSED

one may use an exercise bicycle or a treadmill indoors: It is better than a tranquilizer drug in most cases unless the mental fatigue is profound. One psychological advantage that the cyclist has over the pedestrain is the exhilaration of going further in a short time and in exploring more of the countryside. But of course it is possible to go too far and to become physically exhausted. Much common sense is needed in this recommendation.

Another beneficial effect of bicycling on the psyche is the satisfaction of using the legs in transportation, thereby saving money, not polluting the air, and simultaneously aiding one's health. It is not necessary to be a champion racer or to have a ten-geared bicycle — it is possible to maintain one's health by riding an old-fashioned single or three-speed bicycle and one can get plenty of benefit in riding slowly as one can in walking slowly. Still another nice custom of camaraderie associated with group riding as in bicycle tours in this country or abroad has been established by the Youth Hostels and other organizations with which I have been associated. This adds also to international friendship, a goal of world peace which we all seek.

FACE-LIFT FOR THE SPORT OF KINGS

Chapter 12

Here's Polo Sans Horse
And With A Set Of
Cycle-Oriented Rules!

rAPID, MUFFLED HOOFBEATS, the dull *chunks* of wooden mallets smacking wooden balls, the wheezing of lathered, spent horses and the grunts of colliding horsemen are sounds that for centuries have been synonymous with the Sport of Kings.

Today, however, another variety of sounds — whirring chains, nerve-grating squeaks, jangling metal, lusty cuss-words — join the sounds of mallet meeting ball in a Twentieth Century version of this sport of polo; specifically, bicycle polo.

Borrowing from history, the horse variety of polo, termed Chaugan, originated in Persia during the Eighth Century B.C. When the Turks were ravaging and conquering points East, they took Chaugan for recreation. Some 1,100 years later, long after the Turks had been repulsed, the game was discovered by British cavalrymen in the Himalayan area of northern India. Returning Britishers introduced the sport to Europe, changing the name to polo, a bastardization of the Himalayan term, "pulu."

It was the Persian poet, Firdausi, who, some thousand years ago, produced the much-recognized description of polo: "The sport of kings and the king of sports." In his day and for centuries thereafter — well into the mid-1900s — the sport of polo indeed was reserved for kings or other members of the elite upper class who lived like kings, and for good reason: Who else could afford it?

Perhaps the biggest expense incurred in this sport, in which riders attempt to knock a wooden ball through goal posts on a grass turf, lies in the procurement and training of polo ponies. Horses used in this sport must have clean lines, intelligence, courage and stamina, all qualities in-bred over a period of centuries. It is not unusual to find an excellent mount that has sold from $10,000 to $30,000. When it is considered that a single player uses at a minimum around six horses per match, it is easy to see how costly this sport actually is. To stable an entire team, the cost was — and is — astronomical.

Horse polo has declined as a sport mainly for this reason. Not many interested parties could afford to get involved or, once involved, continue to participate to a large degree. The love of the game spurred the ingenuity of several individuals to seek a more financially-practical means for playing. The result was the birth of bicycle polo.

Bicycle polo, though relatively unknown, has been played with varying frequency for nearly a century. An Irishman named Richard Mecredy introduced the bicycle version of polo in 1891, to his Ohne Haste cycling club in Dublin. The first game was played at the Scalp in County Wicklow in October of that year.

This was not an especially advantageous time to introduce such a sport into America, for it was short years afterward that interest in the invention of Henry Ford virtually wiped out the bicycle boom. The Big War of 1914-18 didn't help matters much and the Milton Bicycle Polo Club, established in Hamilton, Massachusetts, in 1897, became almost a memory.

However, the Aiken Preparatory School in Aiken, South Carolina, adopted the game and kept it alive through the years. Just when bicycle polo again was gathering membership and growing in popularity, another war began and interest in the sport degenerated to near nil.

One gentleman — R. Bennet Forbes — refused to let the sport die and in 1942 founded the United States Bicycle Polo Association. The Aiken Preparatory School, Forbes' staunchest supporter, continued sustaining the sport during the war years.

It wasn't until the late 1960s, however, that any noticeable amount of public interest again was generated toward the sport. A group of students at the University of Pennsylvania thought that the game might be fun, and staged practices and tournaments on the campus. Upon graduation, several found themselves employed in the New York City area and decided to pursue Forbes' original concept of the sport. Through this group, the USBPA has been strengthened and expanded, with the help of the U.S. Polo Association. The game now is being played all over the U.S., with more teams springing up yearly.

The game is both insane and hilarious to watch. It is played, both by ladies and gents, on either a grass or paved surface about the overall size of a football field. The maximum size the surface can measure is 110 by 80 yards, with a minimum size of 90 by 60 yards. When played on a surface of asphalt or concrete, the field dimensions are doubled. However, most of the matches are conducted on the grass fields, usually at high schools on weekends when the areas are not in use.

Most football fields have yardage lines already marked at a distance of every ten yards. The rules state that the playing surface should have two quarter lines and one half-way line, so in most cases the fifty-yard stripe acts as the center line, with either the twenty or thirty-yard stripes as quarter lines. However, if the field specifically is used for bicycle polo, then the lines should be measured and marked accordingly.

The sidelines of the football field serve also as sidelines for the polo games, and the end-zone markers act as goal lines. A goal twelve feet wide is set up at both ends of the field. They are six feet high, and will collapse if a rider collides with them. Bamboo poles often are used for the goal posts.

The rules state that the entire playing field should have at least a five-yard border to act as a safety zone. Players charging hard after a ball near the sidelines often will continue off the playing surface upon hitting the ball, so this safety zone is desirable.

Equipment-wise, it is up to the player to furnish his own, including spares. Basically, all that is needed is a ball, a mallet, a bicycle and a helmet.

The ball used is a regulation horse polo ball, made either of bamboo root or willow wood, and is exceptionally hard.

Mallet rests against favorite mount, Raleigh Twenty (below). Hit by rider second from right, ball zips past No. 53 after nearside backhand (below right). A gaggle of riders scramble for loose ball (bottom right).

It can measure no greater than 3¼ inches in diameter — about the size of a grapefruit — and must weight between 4¼ to 4¾ ounces. Its light weight and wood construction make it capable of breaking ribs, once knocked at a high speed by a mallet.

The mallets can have a shaft length not greater than thirty-five inches, excluding a wrist strap on the end of the handle. The head of the mallet, which cannot weight more than twelve ounces, may be fashioned in any shape. Most, however, resemble traditional polo mallets used in the horse-type games. Metal insertions and additions — which would turn the mallet into a veritable fungo baseball bat — are prohibited.

Any type of bicycle may be used in the game, but the favorite seems to be the Raleigh "Twenty" model, stripped of its multi-gear capacity. This small bike is easily maneuverable, and the seat tube extends high enough to accommodate large riders. They retail in the neighborhood of $80, which is why some riders continue using older, on-hand types.

Helmets are mandatory in hopes of saving head injury,

Offside backhand results in goal-scoring shot by No. 82 in tournament play (below). Referee in black shirt views fine offside backhand by center rider. It is one of four types of shots employed during matches (bottom).

should the noggin encounter a high-flying ball. They are of the design used in field hockey competition, and aren't exceptionally expensive. Made of plastic, they are capable of deflecting or absorbing a great quantity of shock upon being hit.

Four players from each team are fielded at the start of a game, with two substitutes allowed on the sidelines. The latter only may enter during a playing period if a regular is sidelined through either accident or injury and is unable to continue.

Playing periods, called chukkas, are of 7½-minute duration, with six chukkas per game. A time-out lasting three minutes is called at the end of each chukka, with a five-minute halt at half-time. Players may be substituted between playing periods.

Play is continuous during each chukka, unless the referee calls for a time-out because of accident or injury. When the time runs out, the referee stops the match when the ball goes out-of-bounds or is in a position not favoring either team. Teams change sides following each chukka.

The only other times the clock is stopped during a chukka is when the ball is knocked from the playing surface. Should it roll over a sideline, the referee then bowls the ball in from that point. If it rolls over an end-line, a safety is called and the defending team puts the ball into play from that point. When a goal is scored, the ball is rolled in on the center line.

There are four basic shots a player uses during the majority of each match, being the offside backhand and forehand, and the nearside forehand and backhand. The nearside describes the left or mounting side of the bicycle, while the offside is the right side of the bicycle. Left-handed riders are not allowed to use their favored hand in bicycle polo, as this would give them an advantage in many cases.

Normally, there is but one referee during polo matches, unless the game is of particular importance, in which two goal line referees are appointed, along with two sideline refs. A timekeeper/scorer is present at all games.

There are a variety of penalties for infractions that stop the time clock. Like horse polo, a penalty is meted-out for hitting the ball with any part of the body other than the mallet. It is possible, however, to block the ball when hit by an opponent, with any part of the bicycle or body with no infraction called. If the ball lodges in such a manner that it cannot immediately be dropped, the play then is blown dead by the referee, who throws the ball in from the side-lines.

An important rule set by the USBPA concerns the "right of way." Adverse to horse polo, where a rider charges or attempts to "ride off" an opponent and gain possession of the ball by plowing his horse into the opponent's, such action results in a penalty in bicycle polo. The reasoning behind the ruling is simple: Horses are resilient and tend to bounce back from a collision. A bike, however, will more than likely become damaged should collision occur, resulting in delay of the game and added expense. As this sport was devised to save money for competitors, allowing such "riding off" would defeat its entire purpose.

Explained simply, right of way means that any rider with the narrowest angle of approach to the ball is the only person able to hit it. For example, if two riders are approaching the ball from the left in a side-by-side position, the rider on the extreme left cannot endeavor to hit the ball. To do so, he would have to crash into the rider to his right, possibly causing injury either to the rider or mount.

If two riders are approaching the ball from exactly opposite directions, they both must endeavor to hit the ball from their offsides.

There are other infractions intimately connected with the sport, which give an aura of ice hockey. Hooking is a prime example. The rules state that "no player may hook an opponent's mallet, unless he is on the same side of an opponent's bicycle as the ball, or in a direct line behind. The mallet may not be hooked or struck unless an adversary is in the act of striking at the ball."

Furthermore, all hooking must be done below the waist, and cannot be accomplished by leaning over or across any

Nearside forehand isn't a power shot (left). Right of way is demonstrated above, with No. 84 closest to ball. A casualty of play (below) rests on the sidelines.

part of the opponent's bicycle. Naturally, no contact between the opponent's body and an adversary's mallet is allowed.

Perhaps the most interesting facet of the penalty situation is that the referee decides the seriousness of the infraction, and awards the opposing team accordingly. For instance, if a player commits a serious offense to save a goal from being scored against his team, the opposing team is awarded a free hit from the thirty-yard line. The offending team must assume positions behind the endline, not between the goal posts, and stay there until the ball is hit. In essence, this almost guarantees a goal for the opposing team.

To complicate matters even further for the offending team, should they make any violation during the free hit — like coming from between the goal posts — the goal is awarded by the referee without further ado.

Other penalties against an opposing team include free hits from forty yards out, or from where the infraction occurred. With a well coordinated team, a break like this usually means a quick score.

There are three ways to start a match after the two teams have been fielded. They are The Forbes Rule, The Corey Rule and The British Rule. In The Forbes Rule, both teams assume parallel positions on their respective sides of the center line, facing the referee. He then bowls the ball, underhand and hard, into the space separating the two teams and the game begins.

The Corey Rule often is employed, and is distinguished by the positions of the teams. On opposite sides of the center stripe, the teams begin pedaling in two circles at least twenty yards from the referee. Counting down from five, the game is started when the referee hits zero and bowls the ball down the half-way stripe.

In The British Rule, both teams assume positions on opposite sides of the center stripe, and the referee places the ball on a center spot between the teams. At a given signal, one member of each team sprints for the ball, while all others remain behind their respective quarter lines. Once possession has been established, the fun and games are on.

Naturally, the object of the game is to score more goals than the opposing team. Based on individual members' abilities, handicaps are given, the total of which is added to their team score. Just as in golf, this tends to equalize the competition somewhat, as no player likes to be on a team with zero chance of winning any matches.

The basic type of play, while maintaining firm position within the framework of the rules, differs in locations throughout the country. It has been said that West Coast teams are somewhat more aggressive than their East Coast counterparts, but this has yet to be proven. The East Coast teams allegedly demonstrate more finesse and ball handling ability than West Coast players, another unsubstantiated fact that we're going to neither confirm nor deny.

The game stresses teamwork, and the rules have been written around this attitude. It is prohibited for one player to strike the ball more than three times in succession, and the third hit must be a pass. Therefore, if a player is driving toward the goal and has hit the ball twice, he cannot score with his third hit, but must pass it to a teammate who,

Collisions are infrequent, but do happen (below). The result is broken spoke or flat tire, as seen below right. No. 53 rider scores easy goal after awarded a free hit.

hopefully, will finish the drive.

Some teams prefer to play with two attacking riders and two who remain behind the center line for defensive purposes. Others prefer to leave but one man back to act as a goalie, with three others attacking. Still others feel that they have sufficient speed to attack all four riders, who then can retreat behind their center stripe should the opposing players threaten with a goal.

Whatever the strategy employed, the game is a fine way for arm-chair Sunday football television executives to get some usually much-needed exercise, that doesn't seem like work. The forty-five minutes of all-out playing does much to recharge those human batteries.

The United States Bicycle Polo Association, P. O. Box 565, F.D.R. Station, New York, New York 10022, is available to help in any manner, including furnishing equipment to interested parties at a discount rate. All it takes is eight players to form two teams, and it's safe to say that bicycle polo will have found another community in which to expand and grow.

While organization of the sport isn't the best, due to small groups that make up leagues in specific areas of the country, the USBPA has attempted to upgrade competition by hosting both national tournaments and the Cartier Challenge Trophy Tournament. In the former, teams vie for the Forbes Memorial Trophy. The latter, sponsored by the world-famed jeweler, has as top prize a gold and silver trophy for the winning team.

While the idea behind the national tournaments is good, the location for such competition virtually rules out inclusion of teams West of the Appalachians.

While this is sound logic at present — most of the teams are located East of the Mississippi — soon the USBPA will have to consider more centrally-located sites, as bicycle polo enthusiasts West of the muddy river refine their skills and ready for the contest.

While it's true that the sport never will compete realistically with major professional sports for either bucks or spectators — or maybe even Little League baseball, for that matter — it won't again be relegated to obscurity as it has for most of its history. It simply is too much fun to forego!

Chapter 13

An Olympic Gold
Medal Is The Holy Grail Of
A Small But Growing Group
Of American Bicycle Racers,
And Is Nearly Within Reach!

POWER PEDALING FOR GRECIAN GOLD

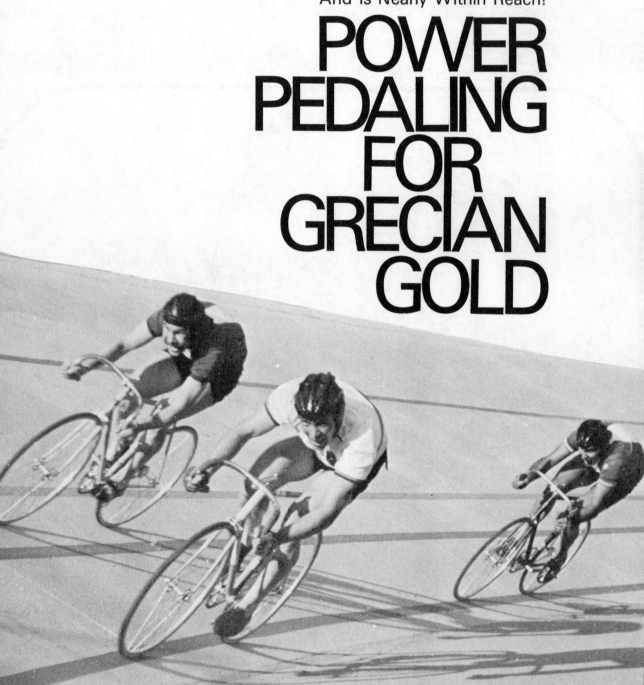

UNTIL JUST A FEW YEARS AGO, bicycle racing was a sport that attracted spectators and competitors on a par with a desert jackass derby — practically zero here in the United States.

In other parts of the world, specifically Europe and now Asia, bicycle racing is presented in quite another light. Thousands of spectators jam the stands around the oval tracks to watch their respective favorites pedal furiously toward victory, nationwide acclaim and rich rewards.

Ever so gradually, the sport of bicycle racing in the United States is making the transition from anonymity to national recognition. More and more people are discovering that races are being held here and that it is one of the most exciting forms of competition they are likely to witness at a reasonable rate.

Reasons for this expansion of interest probably are hundredfold: Many citizens, conscious of their physical condition — or lack of same — have turned to the bicycle as a means of getting in shape in a much more enjoyable man-

ner than donning sweatsuit and sneakers for a seemingly fruitless jogging jaunt through their neighborhoods; ecologists concerned with the worldly state contributed to the bicycle's rise in popularity, shunning the exhaust-emitting auto for the pollution-free bike; others, particularly students with limited finances, have discovered the bike to be a viable means of transportation with bare minimum expense; families tired of clamoring into their autos for dull, typical Sunday drives found the bicycle to be a fun escape from the tedious mien; and, of course, there was the inevitable crowd who jumped on the pedaling bandwagon because everyone else seemed to be.

But in the purchase of this bicycle, Americans recognized that not just any old bike would do for these purposes. It must be something socially acceptable, easy to operate and not too cheap. The perfect supply for the booming demand was the ten-speed bicycle. Virtually overnight, dealers carrying this model, made in numerous countries throughout the world, found on-hand stocks wiped out. Rush orders to manufacturers soon were filled and again snapped up by a feverish public, often in less than a week. Both dealers and makers were delirious with joy, their feverish production efforts matched and overtaken by customers hot to pay their price, usually near the $75 mark.

After a year, it was recognized that this trend was not just another fad that would pass quickly, with everything returning to the dismal norm as the shops remained choked with the multi-gear machines. The more ten-speeds the manufacturers pumped into the already bulging flow, the quicker they disappeared from dealers' showcases. Stockholders in bicycle manufacturing outfits had exceptional dividends, their just reward for many lean, hungry years.

As people took to the open roads on their new machines, their interest naturally was directed toward a sport that utilized their new love. Grand Prix bicycle racing skyrocketed into the limelight as a result of this new-found popularity, exploding finally into a new sport on the

Coming out of the first turn, racers are packed in closely. One fall could wipe out the whole group. Spectators (bottom left) also are nice to watch!

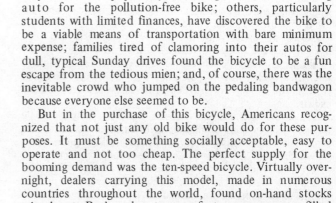

Riders and teammates prepare for the start of a long race. Prior to the gun, all bikes will be lined up behind the start/finish line for obvious reasons.

national athletic horizon.

A new sport? Hardly. It has been around, in its anonymity, for many long years. A handful of factors contributed to its slow growth in the United States, one of which was its lack of qualified, dedicated competitors. Realistically, who wanted to ride a bicycle before few spectators, when all the acclaim was being given to football, basketball and baseball players?

Along the same vein, the number of cyclists was kept low by the lack of cycling clubs in the United States. Where could an interested cyclist go for information and training? Even if a cyclist did find a club, it was doubtful if he could furnish the money for traveling to world-wide competitive events.

However, perhaps the biggest obstacle facing bicycle racers was the lack of racing facilities. Grand Prix racing requires an especially-surfaced, banked, oval-designed track, of which there are pitifully few, due mainly to the expense of construction. Few city officials would attempt to get the funds for construction of a track especially with the present public apathy unless he wished to be the target of much criticism and ridicule.

There are other factors, of course, but much of this has changed now. With public interest comes the factor most important to all competitors: Greenbacks. This money enables organizations like the Amateur Bicycle League of America to build better racing facilities, interest more competitors and spectators and cover travel expenses. Much of the money goes to help fund Olympic hopefuls during games every four years.

Perhaps the best oval track in the United States is located on the West Coast, in the small community of Encino, California, near heavily populated Los Angeles. To the first-timer, the track reminds one of the tracks utilized for roller games competition, except that it has a myriad of multi-colored lines running parallel over its nearly one-sixth-mile surface. The track has played host to the 1963 Pan-American team trials, 1968 National Championships and Olympic team trials, and in early 1972, to the Grand Prix of the United States.

Dubbed the Encino Velodrome, which means "a banked bicycle racing track" in – naturally – French, it was constructed in 1961. It was resurfaced with concrete in 1963. The spacious infield is carpeted with grass and beds of petunias and has several bike racks for storage of bicycles not in use during any particular race. During competition, a stand is set inside the grass border, where cold liquids are dispensed to riders requesting them, free of charge.

Outside the chain-link fence that borders the top of the track to restrain anxious or unwary spectators, are numerous wooden bleachers. Around the fence proper are many flagpoles, from which fly the flags of the countries represented by racers.

The multi-colored lines around and across the track have various purposes and meanings. As expected, one set of parallel black lines across the track from the outside edge to the asphalt strip that borders the infield are for start/finish purposes in all but three races. The start/finish lines for the 4000-kilometer individual and 4000-meter team pursuits bisect the track equidistantly on each side. The final line crossing the track is almost three-quarters of the way through the first banked turn, and distance to this point measures two hundred meters from the regular start/finish line.

Painted on the surface of the track, from the infield to the outside edge, are five lines that much resemble lanes that separate racers during track and field events. Closest to the infield strip of protective asphalt is the bottom black line, the shortest official distance around the track. During the pursuit and kilometer races, the riders must not drop more than six inches below this line or suffer disqualifica-

Receiving a push from teammates or coaches, a handful of racers put some leg into their work. Top finishers in this semi-final heat will move into the finals.

tion.

The next line up the track is termed the top black line, which denotes the limit of the pole line. The term "pole" frequently is used in racing circles and denotes the most favorable, shortest distance around the track. In the interest of safety, regulations require that any rider within the confines of the pole line with two hundred meters or less to travel in any race may not go above the top black line. To do so might cause collision and possible serious injury.

Scant inches above the top black line is a yellow stripe termed the relief line. This line is used in team races when riders are changing partners. To drop below it before being touched by a partner results in disqualification.

The remaining line before the outside edge or top of the track is the safety line. Red in color, this line denotes the area that slowly riding cyclists must remain above.

The top line, or outside edge of the track, is bordered by a chain link fence. It naturally indicates the extreme edge of the surface, an area often sought during match sprints.

There are many different types of individual races conducted during Grand Prix races, most of which look confusing to the beginner or spectator. Make no mistake — it is complicated!

It should be pointed out that different types of strategy, all learned basically through experience, are utilized during each different race and it would be extremely time and page consuming to delve extensively into them here. It is best understood by watching the competition.

Many first-time viewers come to the track expecting to see riders streak off fast and pedal full-blown until they cross the finish line. However, using the aforementioned strategy, many two-lap races have taken up to thirty minutes to complete, with riders actually astride their cycles at a standstill! There is a lot more to this sport than just climbing aboard and pedalling — brainpower often defeats brawnpower.

At almost every event, the first race the spectator sees is one in which just two riders race for a specified number of laps, usually two. There are sprints or, as often they are termed, match races or match sprints. They are time consuming but necessary for establishing the field of riders.

These are matchings of wits along with matchings of strength. At the starter's gun, after being pushed-off by a team member or coach, both riders head for the top of the track at a snail's pace, each trying to maneuver the other into taking the lead. When this happens, the following rider will pedal up close behind the leader and slipstream, quite content to remain behind — initially.

This seems strange to anyone that has previously viewed competitive sports, wherein the spectator sees everyone charge for the lead and endeavor to hold that position throughout the race. However, there is a definite advantage to this strategy: The preceding rider actually parts the air with his body and must expend more effort than his follower, who realizes an energy savings of up to fifteen percent. He is shielded from the air when he tucks-in behind

During miss-and-out race, a Mexican cyclist leads out of the first turn (top), then slips to fourth place one lap later (bottom). Two are cut from pack each lap.

the leader.

When the riders are entering the last corner prior to starting their last lap, an official clangs a large bell, which informs the riders that they have but one lap remaining. Usually instantaneous with the bell's clanging, the riders abandon all sense of strategy and rely strictly on pedal power. Here is where the spectator gets what he expected — and more!

Coming out of the back turn, the riders add momentum descending from their positions near the outside edge of the track, to the pole position. At speeds clocking near fifty miles per hour, the following rider retains his position until coming out of the first turn of the last lap, when he starts his move around the leader. All down the back stretch he attempts to inch forward until he is pedalling alongside the leader.

Into the last turn he is forced back slightly because of his position, but he gains additional speed coming down the home stretch and, if he's got the power to pour on the coal, he will overtake the leader and pass him shortly before crossing the finish line. As in any other sport with variables, often this doesn't happen and the leader wins.

These match sprints can be compared with heat races in other sports and serve the same purpose. The winner of that particular heat or sprint, plus winners of other sprints held subsequent to the event, are put into a semi-final race. Perhaps the four or five fastest finishers then vie against the top four or five racers from another semi-final event of the same distance in a final, such as the Nishiki 1000 Meters, often held at races. The top three finishers then are awarded medals for their performances: Gold for first place, silver for second and bronze for third. And what important event would dispense with the victory bouquet? With flowers in hand, the winner takes a victory lap around the track and, more often than not, ends up tossing the bouquet to an attractive female spectator.

Another race that encompasses the use of more cycles and riders has been termed a mass start. As its name implies, a large number of riders — decided by either size of track or official discretion — are started at once from the start/finish line. The winner is the racer who first crosses the finish line after pumping the pre-determined distance. Racers do not have to race against a clock in this event.

A potentially gruelling race is the miss-and-out. A large number of riders are push-started from the start/finish stripe and begin riding around the track. At the official signal, beginning with that lap, the last rider or two in the pack are cut from the race. This continues until there are just a handful of riders left, who then sprint for the finish line. The first rider across the finish line wins, no small accomplishment after sometimes circling that one-sixth-mile track twenty or twenty-five times.

To the first-time viewer, a handicap race seems to be grossly unfair. Racers are positioned at various intervals from the start/finish line, through the first turn. At the starter's gun, the riders are pushed-off by officials and the first racer to complete the specified number of laps and cross the finish line wins the event. It appears that the man positioned at the start/finish stripe doesn't have a chance, as he's already behind and this is sometimes the case. But this is the strongest racer, the one who has the least number of handicap points based on performance and ability, so he

Between races, riders change sprockets or tires on the infield (below). At top speed, racers (right) appear softly blurred and yet graceful. A maze of spokes and forks are nearly all to be seen (below right).

is expected to overtake and beat the other riders, if everything goes as planned. The race is generally short, hardly more than four laps around the track.

A tough event relished by few competitors is the point race. A distance for the race is pre-set, with sprints at ordered locations. Points are then given to the first five racers to complete the sprint distance, usually on a scale of 7, 5, 3, 2, 1. The racer who finishes the event with the most points wins.

One of the most — if not the most — gruelling races pits a racer against the unforgiving stopwatch. In the 1000 meters time trial, he is started without a push and races for the best time. A sprint from start to finish, this race takes its toll on riders most often in the last lap when endurance fades and racers are pumping on sheer will-power alone.

Individual pursuit is an interesting race that plies two cyclists against one another in a warped game of tag. The riders are started from a standstill on opposite sides of the track, the object being to either catch and pass the other rider or beat him to the finish line. If the one rider is caught, the other is the winner. This seldom happens, however, and the race goes the distance of 5000 meters for professionals, 4000 for amateurs and 3000 for women.

Combining the features of multi-bike racing and a game of tag is the team pursuit. Similar in basic principle to the individual pursuit, the object again is that one four-man team overtake the other or beat them to the finish line. The teams change their riders' positions on just about every lap, with the former leader peeling off up the track and into the slipstream created by his teamates while another takes the lead. The distances are the same as for the individual pursuit, and this event generally goes the distance, unless one team has riders that suffer mechanical difficulties.

In keeping with the international flavor of Grand Prix racing, an Australian pursuit is included in possible events staged. Similar in name, principle and distance only, this pursuit is not for out-of-shape riders.

Three, four or more riders are equally spaced around the track, position determined by prior draw. To win the race, one rider has to catch and pass all other riders, or first complete the specified distance for the event.

Another similar event is the Italian pursuit. Two teams

Most racers prefer to do their own tire work, as in this case a competitor pumps air into a sew-up. These tires are held to rim by glue and high air pressure.

The infield of the velodrome generally resembles a bike junkyard, with components strewn about at random. Here the riders relax or work on machines for later races.

start the race on opposite sides of the track, but only one rider races at a time. After one lap, the rider heads for the infield, his work done. This continues until only one member from each team remains on the track, and the first across the finish line wins the event for his team.

The Madison-style team race features two-man teams in competition. Both racers are on the track simultaneously, although only one is in the race at a given time, competing against another couple. One member of each team, after pedalling full-blown for a number of laps will tap his partner, thereby changing positions. The weary racer will then pedal slowly around the track until his time again comes to take the lead. The first team to complete the

It is especially important that the quick release hubs be tight before taking to the track (below). Color is no distinction in the symphony of speed (bottom).

specified distance is declared the winner.

Roller races are actually a departure from the track racing, in a sense. Special rollers, consisting of three cylinders, two close together and another apart, are connected by means of a rubber or leather belt. The rear wheel of the bicycle then is placed between the rollers. Then, by assuming the proper position with balance, riders can attain speeds in excess of sixty miles per hour in a stationary position.

Road races and criterium events are not staged on the oval track, and require different skills and equipment. The latter event is staged on a closed course — the four streets around several city blocks, for example — which affords spectators not generally exposed to the sport the opportunity to view the international cyclists in action.

A road race, on the other hand, is not an attendance-drawing event, as the course often is over city and rural routes and varies from about twenty to 125 miles. Riders utilize regular ten-speed bicycles with various added accoutrements. These are both physically demanding endurance races, the winner being the first to cross the distant finish line.

There are, of course, variations to the races that are decided by the hosting officals. The preceding list does, however, prove to be the most common form of the events held anywhere in the world. The choice of which races will be run at Grand Prix events usually is determined prior to the race date, so individuals can prepare more strenuously for them.

As expected, spectators viewing a road race see the ten-speed bicycle they've come to know and love being used. But when watching track racing for the first time, viewers oftentimes are shocked by the departure from the ten-speed bike they ride. It looks similar — sort of — but most of the gadgets that cost so much are missing.

For starters, the bike has a somewhat different front end than the cycle purchased off the dealer's floor. Instead of having a fork that gracefully sweeps forward, the track or sprint bicycle has little curvature of the fork. The bike has a shorter wheelbase than the normal ten-speed, which is caused by a shortened frame. The frame itself is different also, being lighter and made of special alloy metals for stronger construction.

Probably the singlemost feature spectators notice miss-

ing first are the levers on the handlebars that operate the braking mechanisms found on the front and rear wheels. The reason for their non-appearance is simple: The bike has no brakes! The next logical question, then, is how do the racers stop the bike after the race or keep from crashing into a rider who slows down abruptly in front of him during a race?

Due to the lack of free-wheeling, the bike can be slowed by applying slight backward pressure on the pedals. This can be accomplished by lifting up slightly with the feet while pedaling rather than pressing down. As the bike slows more and the rider prepares to depart from the track, one of his coaches or handlers appears to catch the bicycle, thereby bringing it to a halt from which the cyclist can disembark.

During the race itself, if the cyclist has to slow suddenly for any reason, the results can be catastrophic. As it often takes several laps of slight backward pressure on the pedals to slow the bike enough to facilitate complete stoppage, the

There even are classes for younger cyclists and women, although notoriety comes with age in this sport (right).

For the winners there are smiles, medals and a bouquet; for the losers, a chance to try again tomorrow (below).

rider relies more on speed and quickness to maneuver his machine from the path of danger. If this is impossible, because of being boxed-in on all sides or the like, get the first-aid kit ready because there are going to be a whole bunch of abrasions to treat!

A sharp reader probably has noticed that it is impossible to lift the feet to slow down the bike, while keeping the feet on the pedals. The same reader might have questioned why, if a collision is inevitable, why the rider wouldn't abandon his mount for the somewhat softer infield? The reason the rider can in the former and can't in the latter, is that his feet are strapped to the pedals. The straps yield more secure footing to assure that a foot won't slip off

while coming down the back stretch toward victory, or throwing the cycle off-balance and causing possible injury to the rider.

In trying to make the bicycle as light as possible, which thereby cuts wind resistance and lends to quickness, tires weighing between three and eight ounces propel the machine. These are especially-sewn-up tires that are affixed to the light alloy rims by a combination of glue and super-high air pressure, often approaching the 150-pounds-per-square-inch mark. They have no tread pattern.

It's not unusual to see riders changing tires frequently during the course of an afternoon's racing, and this no doubt aids the individual psychologically. The exchanged tires then are placed in cloth wrappings to keep them dirt and oil-free. The riders cannot afford to have any substance cut-down their traction during a race, especially when it could cost them serious injury.

The bicycles use spoked rims that are held on the frame by quick-release hubs. Prior to each race, the cyclists will attack the spokes with a spoke-tightener, as a loose spoke during a race can cause injury to the rider or bicycle. The quick-release hubs allow the racers to change rims and tires much quicker than affixing a tire on the rim and blowing it up with a handpump.

The road bicycle, that which is used in road races and

As spectators watch, one class of cyclists begins a
one-lap race in Southern California. While prizes are
usually minimal, the interest generated helps cycling.

often in criteriums, is somewhat more like the conventional
ten-speed. It retains the multi-gear feature, plus the free-
wheeling capability that accompanies the former. By free-
wheeling down hills, the rider conserves much energy during an exceptionally long race, enough that could spell the
difference between first and fortieth place.

Other needed and included accessories on the road
bicycle are handbrakes, a tire pump, water bottle and a
spare tire, which is folded neatly and tucked behind the
seat. The water bottle is clamped to the frame, as is the tire
pump, the latter on the frame directly below the seat.

Quick-release hubs are a necessity, as are treaded tires
for best road life and holding capabilities. The treaded tires
actually channel oil and water into the grooves in the tire
surface, resulting in better traction during wet conditions.

The pedals once again are stirrup-like, with straps to
hold the feet. The wheelbase is longer, the forks more
curved. In short, this bike has more creature-comfort
features, as dictated by the length of time that must be
spent on it during a road race.

As for the athletes themselves, there is a definite difference from the sporting idols Americans have been known to
worship and dedicate bubble gum cards to in the past. For
the most part, they are of average height, weight and build:
Not at all the gigantic jock-strappers from the gridiron with
shoulders as wide as railroad ties, legs like oak stumps and
the hands of King Kong.

These characteristics are not needed in cycling, for it's
not how big you are, but how fast you pump a bicycle; in
fact, smallness of size and stature often are definite

advantages, for the lighter the weight, the more the quickness. Small riders have proven this time and time again, as
they beat larger men, that size doesn't mean a great deal in
bicycle racing. That, in itself, should endear the sport to the
masses, who can now associate someone of their size with a
professional competitive sport.

Like competitive swimmers, cyclists have come to understand that anything capable of slowing them down must be
removed. And, like swimmers, this means the hair on the
legs and forearms. The fractions of a second difference
could be all that is required between a silver or gold medal.

Hair length varies from super-short to quite long, but
doesn't make much difference in times as it is held down by
a protective helmet each competitor is required to wear on
racetracks. This is not a helmet in the usual sense of the
word, as it is expected that all but the face will be covered.
Rather, it is formed in the shape of strips running from
forehead to the back of the skull, with open spaces in between the strips. Helmets are made of leather or other suitable substitutes, and secured by a chin strap. It is designed
in such a manner to provide security against head injury in
the advent of a high-speed accident.

Riders wear a variety of multi-colored, tight-fitting
jerseys that are tucked into a set of racing shorts. Almost
without exception, the jersey reflect the colors of the
rider's homeland, and make each race a veritable whirling
kaleidoscope. The jerseys are lightweight, usually made of
nylon, without pockets on track models, whereas road racing jerseys have pockets both front and rear for the packing
of foodstuffs and other provisions direly needed during the
long hours of a road race.

Riding shorts are made of two different types of
materials, predominately wool or strong helenca. They
stretch slightly to conform to body configuration and reach

The many moods of bicycle racing, along with assorted types of equipment utilized, are depicted in this group of photographs. Each is demanding, yet rewarding.

from mid-thigh to lower abdomen in length. They are fitted with thick chamois pads to absorb the inevitable perspiration and prevent chafing.

All riders use gloves, not unlike a baseball player's batting glove in appearance. They are padded in the palm area, fingerless and provide a better grip on the handlebars than sweaty hands. They also are used to clean tires or slow down the bicycle by being placed on the tire when returning to the infield after a race or warm-up exercises.

Their padded shoes are exceptionally light, often constructed of kangaroo skin, and have a cleat embedded in the sole. The cleat fits into a groove in the pedal and, with the strap affixed over the shoe, provide a non-slip feature. Socks are not often worn.

Most of these items are not terribly expensive and can be purchased at a dealer specializing in racing attire, or from individual weavers and jobbers who will custom-craft them to the riders' specifications. Many companies now are offering these items in their regular line of goods.

It's doubtful that bicycle racing will capture the hearts and minds of the sporting American public completely in the near future, but it has come a mighty long way from its humble, anonymous beginnings. More and better competitors are turning up with increasing frequency, thus improving the U.S. Olympic team's chances of bringing home some metal from the quadrennial games.

MACHINES OF THE MIDDLE EAST

Chapter 14

Still In Its Infancy When Compared To Giant American Bicycle Makers, This Outfit Has Come A Long Way In Just Over Fifty Years!

Israeli bicycle industry founder Menachem Goldberg, as he appeared in an undated photo earlier in the 1900s (below). HOC factory worker inspects spoke ends as they roll down production line in plant (bottom right).

WﾠITH THE EMIGRATION of the late Menachem Goldberg from Latvia to Israel in 1921, the country gained more than a refugee: It also welcomed its entire bicycle industry.

Settling in the suburbs of Tel Aviv when it was still considered a hick town located somewhere near Jafa, Goldberg's enterprises did not consist of the manufacture of bicycles. Rather, he was in the business of importing and distributing bicycles of foreign manufacture all over the British mandate districts, Palestine (Eretz Israel) on the west bank of the Jordan River, and the eastern Trans-Jordanian Palestine.

He built up quite a trade, selling Phillips models of England, Michelins of France and Sachs of Germany, from 1921 until the War of Liberation in 1948. After its conclusion, Goldberg found he could not secure any of the country's limited on-hand currency to continue the importation of bicycles for resale. Even after his long years of dealing with the foreign makers, they could not feel

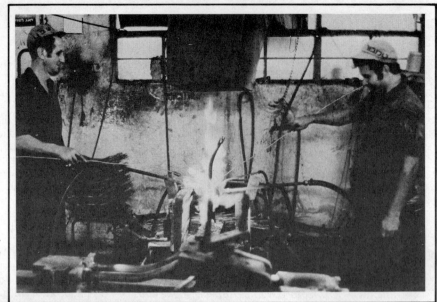

Arab and Israeli workmen labor together brazing front forks for HOC roadster bicycles, only one made.

After frames have cooled, subassembly begins. Here workman attaches axle and components in bottom bracket.

This complicated system results in manufacture of bike rims; it rolls and shapes them automatically.

Bicycles completed and partially wrapped in protective plastic, they are stored prior to distribution for sale.

Sparks shoot in all directions as rims are buttwelded. Automation is supplemented by manpower during production.

justified in unloading the bicycles on a credit basis, understandable in times of turmoil.

This was the situation that led to the establishment of his plant, Harash Ofan Cycle Works, Limited, in 1950. During the first tough years Goldberg, assisted by his son, the late Ben Zion, managed to produce an average of 1,000 bicycles per year. His countrymen were skeptical of his bicycles, preferring those of European brand name quality, which were imported by immigrating refugees who realized the potential market and capitalized upon it.

It took over a decade — indeed, until after the conclusion of the Six Day War — before Goldberg was able to overcome this stumbling block and increase production to its present level of nearly 6,000 per year. The population of the occupied territory produced the demand which led to the sales increase.

Standard in the HOC bicycle line is the Roadster model, which resembles a conventional, multi-geared touring bicycle in this country. They have not engaged in the manufacture of racing bicycles, but may in the foreseeable future. They have sponsored several races in Israel.

Today, the company is managed by a third generation to the founder of the firm, along with myriad young executives. Of particular interest is the employment of both Arab and Jew craftsmen, who work side-by-side in the manufacture of bicycles "as if to demonstrate that peace might come to this part of the world riding on a bicycle, rather than on the wings of a dove."

Chapter 15

BANDS FOR BICYCLISTS

Strength In Numbers Has Been Justified In Political Arenas, So Why Not For The Cyclist?

Something for your body, your mind and others

AT LAST COUNT, there were five hundred or so bike clubs and organizations in this country. Many are independent, while others are included on the rolls of a few larger organizations.

Most independent clubs consist of a few members in a specific community, organized primarily for fellowship and secondly for betterment of cycling conditions throughout their areas.

The major organizations have rearranged the priorities slightly. As an example, the League of American Wheelmen and Friends For Bikecology, while maintaining the fellowship principle, are more concerned with bettering cycling conditions and making environmental contributions; Friends For Bikecology is more geared toward the environmental angle.

A large organization of cyclists carries much more weight with state and Federal officials, those responsible for implementing changes in both cycling routes and the environment, than does a small club. For this reason, I encourage individuals throughout the country to affiliate with major groups; their goals are for the good of cycling, and there is strength in numbers!

While not meaning to slight any cycling group, the following is a look at two of the better known organizations present in this country. Others no doubt perform the same functions, and cyclists in their areas of influence might be wise to affiliate with them.

FRIENDS FOR BIKECOLOGY
1035 E. De La Guerra Street
Santa Barbara, California 93103

182

Friends For Bikecology is a non-profit, special interest, nation-wide group attempting to "identify and solve social, economic and environmental problems relating to bike systems." The term, Bikecology, as the group interpretes it, is ecology through bicycling. They feel that bicycling causes minimal stress on the earth's ecological systems, since it requires few natural resources to function and at the same time creates little disruption.

Their symbol is an abstraction of man's international vehicle — the bicycle — and an adaptation of the Greek letter Theta, the ecology symbol seen so often these days. Together the symbols mean Bikecology — ecology through bicycling.

The organization, located at 1035 E. De La Guerra Street in Santa Barbara, California 93103, defines as its goals the following:

* To promote cycling as a legitimate form of transportation with equal rights of the road.

* Work for more and safer bikeways and the development of a bikeway network in urban, suburban and rural areas composed of recreational bikepaths and everyday transportation routes with commuter lanes — the backbone of a bikeway system — exclusively set aside; encourage communities to develop and begin to implement a comprehensive bikeway master plan, calling for bikeways developed with the cyclist in mind, not just the motorist; with routes designed for physical and psychological separation of bike from car, including commuter routes. Individuals responsible for implementing cycling facilities are encouraged to reject "car culture" influences.

* Encourage the reduction of "autopia" — man's surrender to the automobile; conserve space in communities through the use of the bicycle so that existing parking lots, gas stations, car washes and the like may be restored as green parks, and busy auto traveled streets in the downtown areas can be converted to pedestrian malls.

* Promote and support laws creating and sustaining truly balanced transportation, starting with the release of highway trust funds, state gas tax funds, and local general funds to develop bikeways and mass transit facilities; give people a wide choice of transportation modes that are energy efficient and create minimal air, noise and space pollution. Encourage people to rely upon alternate forms of transportation as a way of life, with greater reliance on bicycling, walking, riding the train or bus, joining a car pool or combinations thereof, which will result in less dependence upon the automobile.

* Develop and promote programs to help reduce bicycle theft and improve methods for returning stolen bicycles.

* Urge bicycle manufacturers and retailers to advertise their product as a serious form of transporation, rather than just a toy. Support legislation benefiting bicyclists, including clean air legislation.

* Advocate the development of bicycle communities, in which most residents depend upon the bicycle for transportation rather than a car, and outnumbered motorists are actively aware of the cyclist's presence.

* Promote rigorous instruction in bicycle safety, especially in the schools at primary levels.

* Encourage cyclists to get together for fun and recreation, such as bicycle tours and overnight rides; urge cycle groups to join with other environmental organizations, as a coalition, in order to correct our deteriorating environment, resulting in part from our unbalanced transporation system.

Grade school children are demonstrating amazing awareness of pollution problem, as indicated by these posters which won honors in Friends For Bikecology-sponsored contest.

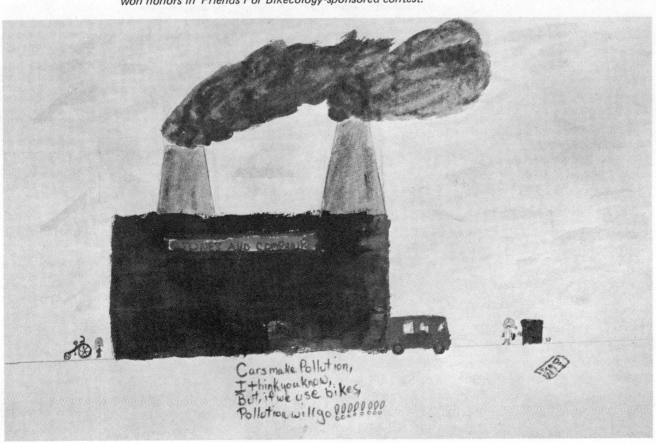

Cyclists should work not only for recognition of bicycling, but also for all types of good environmental policies and legislation.

* Encourage families and individuals to save their earnings by relying upon a more modest means of transportation – the bicycle.

* Encourage bike enthusiasts to become better organized and more militant in their insistence for more and safer bikeways.

The last goal of Friends For Bikecology might present them in the public view as a small group of radicals; the term, militant, seems to have been tagged on extremist political or racial groups. However, this is not the case, as evidenced by their National Advisory Committee members: Stewart L. Udall, former Secretary of the Interior; Dr. Paul Dudley White, renowned heart authority; Congressmen Edward I. Koch, Seymour Halpern and Jerome R. Waldie; U.S. Senators Gaylord Nelson and Alan Cranston; California State Senator James R. Mills; Oregon Representative Donald L. Stathos, and many more.

The stance of this group has the support – whether it likes it or not – of the Federal government. The United States is faced currently with an energy crisis, which simply means that we cannot continue to expend the natural resources the American people are demanding in the form of electricity, petroleum for combustion engines, coal for heating and natural gas like propane and butane for cooking, to name but a few. Some solution must be forthcoming soon.

Dramatic examples of this problem have surfaced in recent years. The power blackout of the New England states during the sweltering summer of 1971 and numerous brownouts in which the demand had to be sharply curtailed are indicative of the problem. Much of the nation was placed on a rationing system in the near-zero winter of 1973, because of a coal shortage, resulting in closure of schools and factories. The Environmental Protection Agency advocated the curbing of automotive traffic in freeway-choked Southern California by eighty percent during peak smog months of May through October; the list goes on and on.

If America continues at its frenetic pace, what lies in store? Simply, natural resources will have to be imported from foreign countries, not all of which are allied politically to this country; the Arab nations and their vast supply of oil, for example.

Oil is stalwart in the American business industry. Importing it from the Arab nations, whose political loyalties – and ultimately, their oil rights – have been known to shift with changes in government, could be disastrous for an American economy dependent upon such supply.

Even if the oil could come from the Arab nations without such occurrence, it would have to be loaded aboard oil tankers. This no doubt would increase the accidental spillage, because more tankers would be steaming atop the oceans of the world. We already have seen the devastation to marine and avian life caused by floating oil, not to mention the effect on the land or the vast sums of money required to clean the resulting goo. It is feasible to assume that staunch resistence from environmental groups throughout the world would be encountered.

An example of the effect ecology-minded groups can have on governmental planning was demonstrated not long ago in North America. The oil-rich areas of Alaska were to be tapped via a pipeline across Canada and into Washington state, where the crude oil was to be refined. Recognizing the immediate danger to the Alaskan tundra – which could be destroyed even without an oil leak – and the Canadian

Graphic proof of automania appears in this photo, which could have been taken in any major city. The wasted land used for parking for autos could be better used!

lands the pipe would traverse, Canadian and American environmentalists fought the action until the plan was scrapped; even then it was more the result of Canadian government reluctance to avail their lands for the project.

While it is doubtful that Americans will take to the bicycle as a plausible substitute for the automobile — which, incidentally, will have $900-plus tacked on the sticker price for pollution control devices by 1976 — it can be expected to be used with increasing frequency as a secondary mode of transportation.

A big drawing card for new members into the Friends For Bikecology group is the organization's stand on bikeways. Through pressure on legislators and support of candidates that support the bicycle movement, Friends For Bikecology has played an important role in the construction of bikeways in several states.

The problems regarding bicycles and bikeways, as the group sees them, are seven-fold:

1. The general attitude that the bicycle is more of a toy than a legitimate form of transportation tends to negate any attempts to establish bicycling as a major constituent in the transportation system.

2. Due to "autopia" (man's surrender to the automobile) there is very little space left in the city for the bicyclist. Most large cities have devoted 50-65 percent of their land to the automobile. Besides roads and parking facilities, there is a great abundance of 'car culture' architecture: drive-in banks, drive-in theaters, drive-in restaurants, drive-in car washes, etc. These so-called conveniences add up to great sums of land being devoted to a machine rather than to people. Cities are becoming devoid of "people spaces" and this includes places where people can freely circulate as pedestrians or as bicyclists. In addition to people, 'autopia' has severely affected our ecological systems.

3. Bicyclists are plagued by thieves, insulted by motorists, bedeviled by dogs and must operate in hazardous traffic conditions. The bicycle philosophy appears to be contrary to the car culture. Whereas the bicyclist is concerned about his immediate environment — the "here and now" — the motorist is concerned with getting from one point to the next as quickly as possible. Obviously, when cars and bikes are placed in the same circulation corridors, conflict arises. Bicycling under these conditions is like growing corn on a bowling alley!

4. Developing legitimate recreational bikeways has been difficult in the past. For this reason, bicyclists are generally forced to use roads built for the automobile, thus promoting unfair competition between bicyclist and motorist. All too often, "left over spaces" (land that is left over after development because of its unusable size, shape or location) are developed for recreational uses, including bicycling, while the choice land is developed for non-recreational purposes.

5. Planners tend to imitate the automobile in designing bike systems. In many cases, their own car culture influences coupled with a lean understanding of the essence of bicycling appears to be a primary factor. Even then, if an honest concept is devised, the reality of developing such a concept becomes impaired due to fatalistic attitudes.

6. "Road Gang" lobbies (auto clubs, oil companies, concrete and asphalt companies) have a strong hold on the transportation budgets. Since the bicycle industry is so small compared to other transportation industries, bicycle lobbyists cannot effectively compete. Also, if it should happen that legislators propose financial aid for bikeways, by the time programs are ready to be implemented, funds are usually cut or diverted because of a financial crisis. Recreation programs are generally considered the first to be eliminated because people reflect upon recreation as a luxury and not as a necessity.

Insight of youngsters is catching on with adults and, ultimately, legislators. One child's idea of what cycling has to offer is shown in the poster (below).

7. In general, Americans have been conditioned to accept austere recreation programs. As a result, it becomes difficult for them to make value judgments on the worth of recreation either from a social or economic aspect. National priorities rarely reflect human resource priorities.

Friends For Bikecology has devised countermeasures that individuals, city, state, and Federal governments and the bicycle industry can take to offset these problems and put bicycling in its proper perspective.

INDIVIDUAL ACTION

The group states that the individual should use his automobile only when necessary, and supplement its use with the bicycle. They advocate locating the residence as close to the place of business as possible, thereby permitting bicycle use in a commuter sense. Both of these solutions will make the individual less dependent upon the automobile.

Also, they feel that the individual would do well to purchase only one automobile, and continually fix it rather than trade it in on a new model. With the money saved on interest alone, bikes can be purchased for the entire family. Also along the purchase vein, the group feels that the purchase of a television set can be foregone, and this money used for bicycles. "The comfort of television is very much like the automobile in that both are isolating," claims their Bikecology Overview pamphlet.

Other individual action is to discontinue membership in automobile clubs, which lobby for more highway construction, and join bicycle-oriented organizations; namely, Friends For Bikecology.

The group suggests that individuals refrain from purchasing any of the dozen or so auto magazines on the newsstands, and subscribe instead to a bicycle magazine and encourage its editorial staff to enlarge its scope into reporting the social and environmental aspects of cycling.

Friends For Bikecology discourages the purchase of toys and games that imitate the automobile, and encourage manufacturers to develop bicycling games instead. They also encourage the formation of car pools with neighbors and bicycle exchanges between same.

And lastly, they encourage individuals to vote for politicians who are sympathetic to the desires of bicyclists, ecologists and conservationists.

CITY & STATE ACTION

Friends For Bikecology feels that laws should be developed and enforced to eliminate hazards to cyclists, which would prescribe a course of action in bicycle-car and bicycle-pedestrian situations. They feel that each state Department of Motor Vehicles should establish a bicycling element in driver education programs and into motor vehicle codes, and implement questions on tests for driver's licenses about bicycling. This would acquaint automobile drivers with laws applicable to bicycle riders and car operators and conceivably reduce car-bike accidents.

Programs could be established in schools and other locales whereby individuals can be instructed in riding techniques, laws, safety and defensive riding, in addition to maintenance, planning bike systems, physical fitness and the social effects cycling has. Along the same vein, school administrators could encourage use of the bicycle by students and possibly include cycling in existing physical fitness programs at the school, either during periods specifically set aside for physical training or at recesses, lunch breaks or after school. Theoretically, this would lower the injury and fatality rate suffered by children by making them aware of current regulations concerning bicycle operation.

Much cycling hazard could be reduced by Public Works Departments of the cities through the introduction of a new system of sewer grates, unlike those with metal slats through which bicycle tires can slip. Also, cleaning natural obstacles like overhanging limbs and brush from bikeways could make them safer.

Where applicable and feasible, bicycles could be allowed to share sidewalk space with pedestrians, thereby availing routes to shops and stores to the bicyclist. Bicycle parking spaces could be devised by simply transforming a single auto parking space into one for bikes at locations like theaters, museums, parks, schools, public service buildings and others. Parks in the planning stage could have bikeways included where compatible with natural design elements.

Friends For Bikecology encourages that states and cities devote proportionate financial support to development of bike systems relative to other modes of transportation and recreation.

"Since the public subsidizes oil and gas companies, fuel taxes should go not just for highways, but could also be applied to the needs of persons involved in all types of transportation," they claim. "For those who do not have transportation facilities or who cannot afford them, a subsidy at federal, state or city levels should be available to help provide some means of transportation such as bicycles. Cities that currently have transportation subsidies for bus transit districts should be required to provide a subsidy for development of bike networks as well. Transportation is an urban necessity and should be financed through taxes just as police and fire departments, schools and parks."

The organization also feels that "bike-hike" sites, where hitch-hiking bike riders can solicit rides to another locale, should be established at various points throughout the city. They also feel that major people-movers like trains, planes and buses could upgrade their facilities for handling bicycles as viable cargo. Buses, for instance, could be modified so that pegs are placed in their outer shells for holding bicycles, as has been done in Europe.

They also feel that a "recreation train" system can be adopted whereby railroads can transport campers, cyclists or hikers to recreation areas like parks, beaches or historical centers, thus providing an exciting method of reaching such areas without depending upon the automobile. Such a program would help disadvantaged individuals because they would be able to afford the low-cost transportation, and the railroads generally are found in every inner city.

A bicycle junkyard facility for recycling old bike parts could be established in most communities where the socially and economically deprived individuals could pick up used bike parts free and assemble them into a workable form of transportation.

Just as the early Spaniards established missions in California approximately a day's ride by horse apart, like facilities could be built or converted from existing structures for the biker. The group thinks that they should be spaced about thirty to forty miles apart, the reasonable distance a bike rider can cover in one day.

A take-off on the White Car system used in France is the proposed White Bike system, whereby cycles so painted are considered free bikes and used for spontaneous transportation from one location to another over established routes. Whether this idea would work naturally depends on the theft status of the city.

One that could work feasibly, however, is the establishment of bike rental concessions in parks, housing and tourist areas, central business districts, or any location in which automobile usage is not desirable or practical.

When purchasing or developing new roads, the city officials should program corridors exclusively for bikers, and state highway departments and city road, park and recreation departments could be geared to handle such a program, feels Friends For Bikecology.

FEDERAL ACTION

The group advocates the year 'round usage of daylight savings time. They feel that standard time creates a situation which forces an individual to use a car in place of the bicycle, as nightfall comes earlier in fall and winter.

In addition, they feel the government should re-evaluate the Department of Transportation's road standards in relationship to multi-transportation uses; provide subsidies so cities can develop mass transit systems as well as bike systems, and the Postal Service could issue a bicycle or Bikecology stamp.

BUSINESS AND BICYCLE INDUSTRY ACTION

While many businesses will scoff at such an idea, Friends For Bikecology recommends that they could encourage car pools and bicycling among employees by offering special benefits such as shorter working hours to those utilizing such a system. These hours could be made up, however, by less sick leave as the workers would be in better physical condition. Parking problems would be minimized, as would lateness due to prevailing traffic conditions.

"The bicycle industry could become more sensitive and responsive to the needs of bicyclists by gaining a more complete understanding of the social ramifications of the bicycle experience," states a spokesman. "The industry could recognize its own maturity by promoting bicycles as a pure and honest activity rather than an imitation of something (auto names like Fastback on bikes) which it is not. In advertising, the bicycle should be presented as a partial solution to environmental problems, which adults as well as children can use and enjoy.

"In the design and manufacture of bicycles, better safety features such as illuminating and reflective bike parts for night use must be developed. In all cases, safety features should be an integral part of the bicycle. Features that need to be developed are better child carriers, bicycles or tricycles for the handicapped and aged, and features that prevent theft."

Friends For Bikecology takes a scathing look at advertising in their pamphlet, and points out many factors Americans rarely see. "The automobile (and bicycle) industry is pushing Americans toward mass consumerism by way of advertising. The American industry tells us to buy the 'style object.' Cars are sold as 'dated models' rather than on merits of quality. To be 'where it's at,' the public is manipulated into purchasing the new model. To a limited extent, the U.S. bicycle industry has begun to follow suit by selling the bike as an imitative toy; a 'stick shift fast-back' could be a car or a bicycle! Unless advertising is challenged, consumerism will continue to spiral and the earth's natural resources will continue to be depleted. Goods must be sold on their own merits of quality rather than fashion or style."

Many of these goals will not be attained in short order, but at least the problems have been brought to the public attention.

Friends For Bikecology is staffed by volunteers of all political, racial, educational and religious backgrounds. If you would care to join their rolls, student memberships are $3 per year; sustaining memberships, $5 per year; contributing memberships, $10 per year; supporting memberships, $50 per year and patron memberships, $100 or more per year. All members will receive a Bikecology button and periodic newsletters. Supporting and patron members receive, in addition to these items, a Bikecology lapel pin.

To sum-up the Friends For Bikecology philosophy, the following is quoted directly from their Overview pamphlet: "The entire problem comes down to one fact: Each individual must accept responsibility for the world in which he lives, and accept his responsibility for changing it. If we can inspire a general understanding of man and his (our!) environment, his personal values will change. This in turn should lead to a general shift in values on the part of the entire culture toward greater concern for an intelligent stewardship of natural resources. If we desire to change the world we live in, let's find the magnet which draws man to the land, in contact with its forces — the bicycle."

LEAGUE OF AMERICAN WHEELMEN

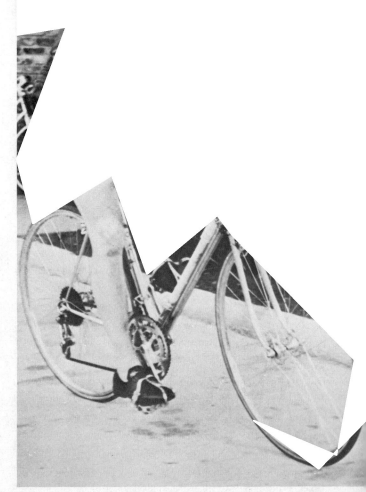

Keith Kingbay, a top official in LAW organization, practices what he preaches by riding as often as possible. He has cycled across the U.S. in the past.

This group of cyclists first banded together at a meeting in Rhode Island May 31, 1880, at a time when the bicycle was a mainstay in the American lifestyle. Indeed, it was the fastest form of transportation on the rutted, dirt roads.

Almost from its outset, LAW has pushed for better roads for the cyclist. This almost led to the dissolution of the group, as the automobile benefited most from the better roads and almost put the bicycle into oblivion. What is really ironic is that LAW is the parent organization of the American Automobile Association and the American Highway Society.

LAW has had its ups and downs, ranging from nearly 100,000 members in the 1890s to around one hundred in the 1930s. It has grown somewhat from those days, and membership roles again run into the thousands.

LAW first demonstrated its strength in numbers nearly a century ago, testing a ruling prohibiting bicyclists from using the Haddenfield, New Jersey, Turnpike. The Pike Company refused to allow bicycles on the pike and, when LAW backed the Philadelphia Club in starting suit, the Pike Company backed down and revoked its anti-cycling policy.

In 1879, the New York Board of Commissioners ruled that no bicycles were to be allowed in New York's Central Park. LAW took the case to court, where it was fought for eight years before Governor Hill signed the "Liberty Bill" ending discrimination against bicycles on parkways, streets or highways in that state.

Today, LAW has the same aims and goals as it did when it began nearly a century ago, with a few adopted during the changing times. They are:

* To promote bicycling for people of all ages
* To encourage favorable legislation for bicyclists

Friends For Bikecology strongly believes in the establishment of bicycle communities, where most people ride rather than drive.

* To acquaint bicyclists with their neighbors who share similar interests in the joys of bicycling

* To distribute information about bicycling to interested parties and organizations

* To assist in the planning and conducting of cycling programs; rodeos, bicycle trains, century runs, etc.

* Inform the bicyclist regarding correct riding techniques for greater enjoyment of their bicycles.

LAW avails its facilities to anyone who requires them. They are currently filling several needs of bicycle riders, including:

* Publicizing bicycling through all news media

* Assisting in the formation of bicycling activities

* Distributing a nationwide roster of LAW members to assist bicyclist in obtaining bicycling information about their and other areas

* Answering individual inquiries, concerning bicycling or bicycling problems

* Publicizing and distributing bicycle literature

* Aiding in the establishment of bicycling facilities

* Teaching the art of bicycling to newcomers in the sport

LAW sponsors several rides each year, which reinforces their goal of acquainting bikers with their neighbors. Often, riders partipate from all over the nation, which much stresses the fellowship of cycling that LAW deems so important. Their membership continues to climb each year, which means that others regard the goals as similar to their own.

Both of these groups have overlapping goals, although their methods of fulfilling them may differ somewhat, as does the arrangement of priorities. In any event, both exist for the benefit of the bicyclist and, when so many are lined up against bicycling, your support is needed. You surely have nothing to lose!

Chapter 16

As with any mechanical contrivance, parts can break or wear out. Here are righteous repairs the penny-pincher can perform!

MACHINE MAINTENANCE

An OLD PROVERB states, "Anything that possibly can go wrong will and anything that can't possibly go wrong also will!" The damnable truth of this proverb is usually proved to the bicycle rider when he is umpteen miles from nowhere and his machine kaputs.

If the rider is like the vast majority who own bicycles, he will say a few harsh words, then start pushing his steel steed toward the nearest town.

Naturally, there are bike riders that have taken the time to become intimately familiar with their machines, and have learned to fix everything but the most serious maladies; a cracked frame, for example.

But the novice or less dedicated bike rider may benefit from the information contained herewith. Broken-down into individual categories, repairs of specific components are documented. While you may never require some of the repair criteria, you at least will have some idea of how to resolve the problem should you need it.

TOOLS

As with any specialized piece of equipment, there are specific tools needed for repair operations on the bicycle. This is especially true on bicycles of foreign manufacture, as the standard measurement size is not the inch and fractions thereof, but the metric system. If you have a European-made bike, American tools won't fit.

Most bicycle manufacturers market tools specifically designed for their line of machines, and these are the tools that you should procure, with the exception of a few all-purpose types available in the home. It is impossible to dictate exactly which tools should be packed away in the saddle or pannier bags, as each individual differs in thought in this area. Therefore, the following list is more a guide than a mandate; use your own judgment as to your needs.

* Pliers — If a pair is lying around the house, it will suffice for bike repair needs. If you have to purchase a pair, don't necessarily expend great sums of cash on a hardened,

Good tools are a must for the home repairman, and the text includes ideas on this subject, like combination wrenches and crescent wrench pictured below. Good tools are costly.

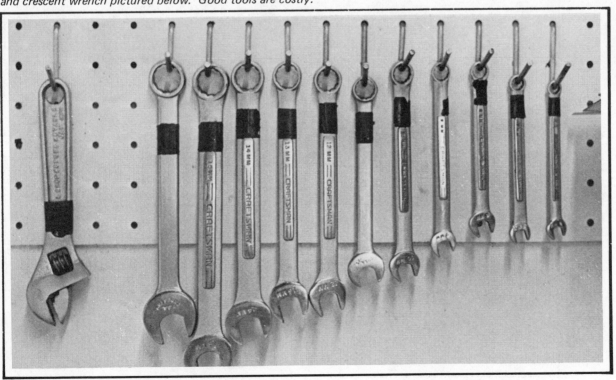

drop forged type. A cheap pair usually will work fine.

* Crescent wrench — A small one no larger than six inches probably is the most useful. A cheap model will work fine, providing the lower jaw doesn't wiggle inordinately when apart slightly. If this occurs, the wrench will have the nasty habit of stripping heads off bolts.

Some cyclists prefer a spanner to wrenches, which is a thin, metal blade with various-sized notches and holes machined into it. These often fit different bolt and nut heads.

* Screwdrivers — Make sure that the screwdriver or screwdrivers you purchase are of top quality, with forged shanks. Try to get at least two with varying blade widths, preferably thin and medium, and use the screwdriver with the blade that best fills the screwhead slot. If the blade is much thinner than the width of the slot, the screwdriver can slip around and burr the head or strip the slot.

If the blades and shanks are not forged they may break or chip when being turned in the slot, resulting in a less than effective screwdriver.

* Cone wrenches or hub spanners — A set of thin metal open end wrenches, these are used for removal of hubs or for adjustment of cones.

* Hammer — A household variety usually is too heavy and, if it has been used much, the surface may not be level. A hammer can be used to assist in tapping out bearings and the like but, if you're an emotional person, keep it in the kitchen drawer; if you get mad at some component, it just may end up smashed: Great for the frustrations but hell on the pocketbook.

* Box end wrenches — These can save rounding-off the head of a hex nut or the like, as they completely surround the head. Some riders like the dumbbell wrench arrange-

On derailleur-equipped bicycles, some type of chain tool is required to separate the thin links present.

Open end wrenches can be used to good effect for at-home repairs.

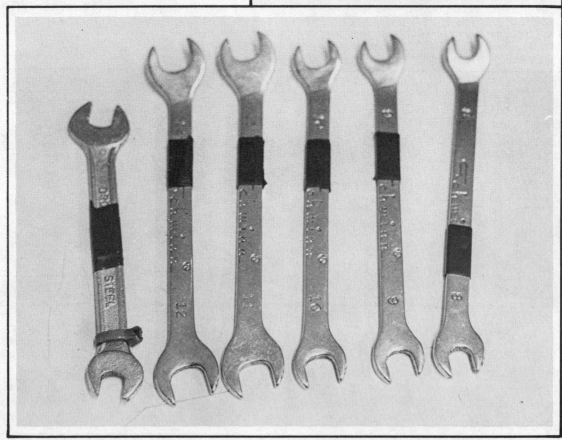

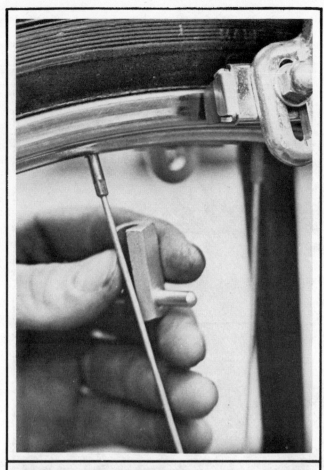

A properly used spoke wrench can save a rim and keep the wheel running smooth. Used improperly, disaster!

ment better. This wrench resembles weightlifting dumbbells with different size holes cut in the bulbous round ends.

* Combination wrenches — These are a compromise between open end and box end wrenches, having closed and open ends on the same tool. They tend to get heavy.

* Wire cutters or cable clippers — The latter make short work of snipping cables that have frayed, leaving clean edges. Wire cutters will do the job, but tend to leave the ends mashed which makes for rough threading through cable housings.

* Vise grip or adjustable offset pliers — These will find use in various repairs at home, but generally are too heavy to tote along on a tour. If you can afford both, get the vise grips with jaws at least five-eighths-inch wide and pliers that will open to at least two inches. Both items are capable of enormous destruction, so take care when using either.

* Chain rivet extracting/inserting tool — This little item is needed for any chain less than one-eighth-inch in diameter, as are most on bicycles using the derailleur, which does not have a master link. The master link is found on bicycles like one-speed bombers, and the chain can be detached simply by removing this link with pliers. If the rivet tool comes with a spare twisting tip, take pains to hang onto it — the tips have a habit of disappearing.

* Freewheel remover — This items comes in two varieties, either splined or two-pronged. Each is used for a specific type of freewheel, so determine which your 5 or 10-speed bike needs before purchasing either.

* Spoke wrench — The spoke wrench, in the hands of the inexperienced, can completely ruin a hub. Know what to do with it before tightening the spokes.

* Tube or tire repair kit — A necessity for any bike rider at any time, this kit should be carried whenever the bike is used.

Most bike shops have equipment similar to that at left. An out-of-round rim touches metal jaws upon revolving, and technician adjusts spokes.

Adjusting the height of the seat is a simple matter, as only one binder bolt must be loosened on the tube.

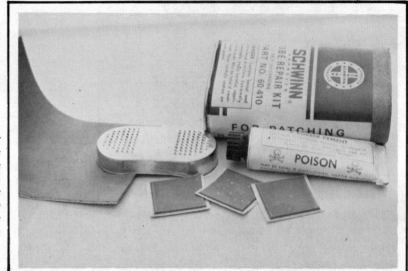

A tube patching kit (right) is a must for riders that use tube tires, and is easy to use. Many types of lubricants (below) are marketed and work well. A bike needs lubrication for smoothness of operation. A pencil-type pressure gauge (bottom) saves trips to the gas station for checking air pressure.

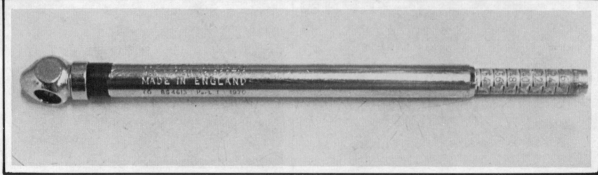

* Tire pump — Can save trips to the garage before outings to replenish lost air in the tires, as well as keeping a cyclist going after a flat on the highway. Most are capable of being affixed to the bicycle, usually on the seat or down tube.

* Tire pressure pencil gauge — With this pocket-size, clip-on gauge, pressure can be checked accurately and quickly before or during any ride. Most air pumps at service stations have this gauge built-in. Proper handling and tire performance rests upon proper inflation.

* Lubricants — Light oil and light grease keep the wheels turning, giving life to bearings. A can of 3-In-1 oil lasts a long time, is light on the pocketbook and cheap insurance against time and greenback-consuming repairs. Light grease like Lubriplate, used to keep countless machine guns and semi-automatic rifles operating in Vietnam, is fine for the bearings. Gold Medal or many others will substitute admirably.

* Tire irons — Two, three or more of these can save tire or tube damage, if used properly. In the past, screwdrivers were used to facilitate removal of the tire casing from the rim, so that the tube could be removed. Many ruined tire casings and pinched tubes later, someone invented these goodies. Unless you like patching two holes rather than one, and dramatically reducing the life of your tires, use them.

* Rags, cans and solvent — While these don't fall into the tool category, they go hand-in-hand with repair procedures. Be especially careful when using solvents — kerosene seems favored over gasoline — and do not store left-over kerosene in the garage or workshop, especially near the rag pile. These combustibles have been known to ignite spontaneously.

TIRE & TUBE REPAIR

Most bicycle riders at least know the rudiments of fixing flat tires, just as most automobile operators know the tire changing sequence for their cars. Times have changed, however, and the near-indestructible balloon tire is not used with the frequency it once was, the narrow gum-walls being substituted. Many riders often do more damage than good, when attempting the repair of gum-wall tires.

Clincher tires — those with the rib or bead that fits into a groove on the rim and that utilize tubes — are much easier to repair than sew-up tires, which are cemented on the rim with a combination of glue and high air pressure. The latter has the tube sewn to the inner casing of the tire.

Before removing the tire from the rim, in the event of a slow leak, check to assure that the valve core is not the culprit causing the problems. Sometimes, if the core is not seated all the way, it will lose air. Drop a bit of soapy water

Adjusting the tension of brake cables, or replacing same does not require removing the brake assembly.

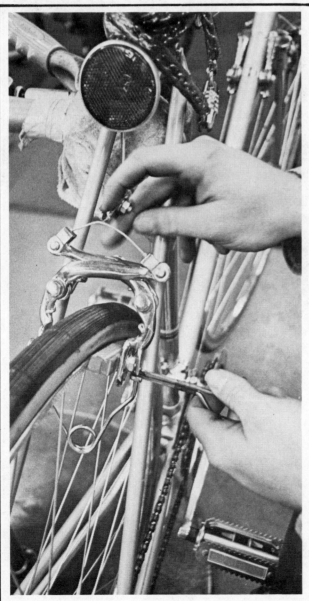

Respoking an entire rim is a chore best left to proper repair personnel, as the procedure is quite complicated.

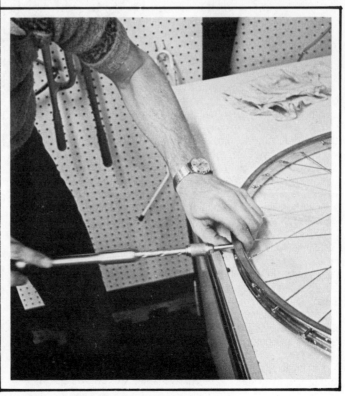

or saliva into the core and, if it's the problem source, bubbles will form. In this case, try tightening the valve core with the valve cap that should be used to cover the stem. Again apply the liquid. If it still leaks, replace the valve core unit. If that isn't the problem, proceed with the repair critieria listed below.

The first step in repairing the clincher tube that sustains a flat is to remove the wheel from the frame, using the proper tools. Next, remove the tire casing, or at least one side of it, from the rim. This often can be accomplished simply by applying force away from the rim with the hands — trying to fold the casing up enough to insert a finger as a pry bar.

If this is not possible, break out the tire irons, insert one and lift the casing slightly. The casing will give due to its rubber construction and another iron is placed slightly farther along around the rim. Sometimes the combined lift and pull of the two irons will allow the casing to slip off of the rim on the near side, and the repairman then can proceed with this step around the rim's entirety.

If this cannot be accomplished by using just two irons, another may have to be inserted farther around the casing.

If tire irons are unavailable when a flat occurs, screwdrivers may be substituted. Much caution need be taken when using them, for the casing can be torn, punctured or the tube pinched. While they might be used on the clincher-type tire, they never should be used on sew-ups. The casing is thinner and damage is almost sure to occur.

Once the casing has been loosened over the entire circumference of the rim, the tube can be removed with little fuss or bother. Just make sure, when removing the valve stem, that you don't pinch or cut it.

When it is separated from the rim, inflate the tube slightly with the bike pump you hopefully have with you. If a water source is available, be it hose or horse trough, immerse the tube and the bubbling of air will make the puncture site readily apparent. Remove, dry and deflate the tube after marking the hole with a piece of chalk, crayon, or with the scuffer furnished with your repair kit.

Once the surface of the tube is perfectly dry, take the scuffer, usually found on the lid of the repair kit, and buff the area around the puncture site until it is fairly rough. Don't get carried away and sand a hole in the tube! The reason for scuffing the surface is that the patch tends to bond better if the surface is slightly roughened.

Apply a liberal coating of cement furnished with the kit to the site, and either leave it alone or blow on it until it becomes tacky to the touch.

The patch kits usually come with a couple of pre-cut rubber patches, accompanied by a much larger strip of patching material. If the hole is small enough to warrant using one of the pre-cut patches, simply peel the backing off of the sticky patch and center it over the hole. The surfaces then should be pressed together — if the can containing the repair goodies is round, roll it over the patch site a few times — to ensure a firm bonding.

Before reinserting the tube inside the tire casing, see if the cause of the flat is still present. Then proceed, taking pains to get the valve stem exactly perpendicular to the rim. Then, with the wheel lying on a bench or the ground, force the lip of the casing back inside the rim with hand pressure. If this is difficult, apply a little soapy water to the casing if there is some around. Inflate the tube to about ten pounds pressure and determine that it isn't leaking and that the casing is properly seated. If so, continue inflation to the proper level.

For in-the-field repairs, many of these facilities — water source, soapy water — are not available. Should you sustain

The wheel pictured below has more problems than just being bent. Valve stem is tilted, and spokes are gone.

After patching the tube, the valve stem is inserted back into the rim. Make sure that it is straight (below).

The tire casing is the pushed into the retaining beads of the rim (bottom left). Progress around rim (bottom right).

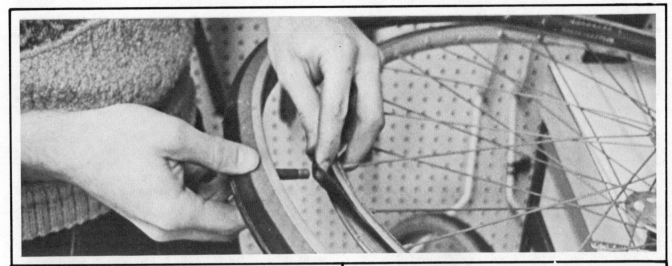

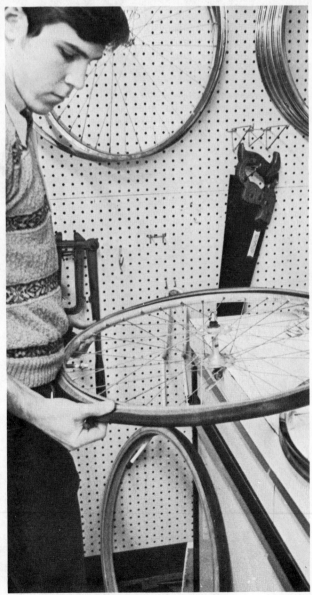

a flat, here are a couple of tried and true methods that can give passable results.

Follow the procedure already outlined for removing the tube from the tire casing. Inflate the tube and search visually for the leak. If it doesn't immediately become apparent, hold the tube close to the face and continue moving it in a circle until the stream of air on the skin pinpoints the leak. To double-check, expel a judicious drop of saliva on the suspected leak site. If it is the spot, the moisture will bubble furiously. Repair the hole as already discussed and run through the procedure again in the event there may be still another hole in the tube.

The patching method outlined thus far is termed cold patching. A hot patch method is slightly more sophisticated, takes a little more time, but is great for assuring firm bonding through vulcanization. Equipment for hot patching rarely is carried on the road.

After locating the hole, the hot patch applicator, with a self-contained patch, is clamped onto the tube at the puncture site. The applicator is replenished with a flammable fuel, which is ignited with a match. The applicator gets quite hot and can't be touched for some time. When it has cooled sufficiently for handling, remove it and you will see that the patch has been blended with the rubber of the tube.

The repair of sew-up tires is much more complicated than its distant cousin and, before attempting the procedure yourself, it may be wise to watch another individual with experience do it.

Remove the wheel from the frame and strip the tire off of the rim after deflating it completely. Once off, you will note that the tube is covered by a strip of tape, which later will have to be pulled up at the puncture site.

Inflate the tire slightly with air and immerse it in water. You will immediately note that bubbles rise from around the valve stem: This is characteristic of the tire design, and the problem may not be at that location.

Finding the leak is time consuming if it isn't readily apparent by bubbles slipping from under the tape. Once discovered, you will have to lift the tape from above the site — about a four-inch strip will do. The tube must be pulled away from the casing and a patch installed.

Take care when clipping the thread that holds the tube to the casing or you may wind up cutting a hole in the tube. With the thread cut, gently lift the tube and expose the puncture site, and check for the cause of the flat. The site then must be buffed with the scuffer, cement applied, then the patch affixed. Talcum powder should be dusted onto the patch site and inside the casing to prevent the tube from bonding with the casing.

This accomplished, the tube must be resewn to the casing. Use the old holes and an overhand stitching method rather than attempting to make new holes. With this done, the tape should be reapplied. Coat the rim with cement and affix the tire to it.

Inflate the tire to around ten pounds of pressure, then check to see if the leak still is present. If not, deflate completely then reinflate to the proper pressure listed on the

Tires come in a variety of sizes and styles, not all of which can be substituted on different makes of bikes.

accompanying chart and leave it stand overnight. This will assure proper bonding and drying of the cement. If all looks good the following morning, remove the tire from the rim and use it as a spare.

If the tube sustains a long, jagged cut or is old, replace rather than repair it.

While in the area of tube repair, the often vexing problem of high pressure leaks comes to light. Simply stated, this is a leak that occurs when the bicycle tire is inflated to its proper level but, when the tube is removed from the casing, a puncture site cannot be found.

The reason for this problem is because when the tube is removed from the casing, it tends to rapidly expand when filled with just five or ten pounds of air pressure. This is not enough to force the air to escape from the usually pinprick-sized hole. Rather than attempting to put fifty pounds of pressure in the tube separated from the tire, which probably would cause it to disintegrate in your face, dispose of the tube. It's much cheaper to replace than an eye.

Should your tire suffer damage enough to make usage a questionable matter, dispose of it. Make sure, however, that you replace that tire with another with exactly the same nomenclature, the same digits. For example, a 20x1.75-inch tire would appear to be equal in all shape and form as a 20x1-3/4. It doesn't take a math major to discover that 1-3/4 is equal to 1.75, in number at least. But try to substitute the two and you'll find worlds of difference. Get the right tire size for your bike.

SPOKE TIGHTENING

Loose spokes — or those that are overly tight — can cause complications for a bike rider, not the least of which is ruination of the rim. They can cause uneven travel between the forks, which makes braking a problem.

To determine the uniformity of spoke tightness, turn the bicycle upside-down, resting on the seat and handlebars. Spin the wheels one at a time and angle a light sliver of wood in the path of the spokes as they revolve. Striking the

RECOMMENDED TIRE PRESSURES

SIZE (INCHES)	PRESSURE (POUNDS)	SIZE (INCHES)	PRESSURE (POUNDS)
16x2.125	40-45	24x1-3/4	40-45
16x1.75	40-45	24x1-3/8	55-60
12x1-3/4	40-45	26x2.125	25-35
20x2.125	25-35	26x1.75	40-45
20x1.75	40-45	26x1-3/4	40-45
20x1-3/4	40-45	26x1.375	55-60
20x1-3/8	55-60	26x1-3/8	55-60
24x2.125	25-35	27x1-1/4	70-75
24x1.75	40-45		

Using inflation chart at left, it is simple matter to prolong tire life.

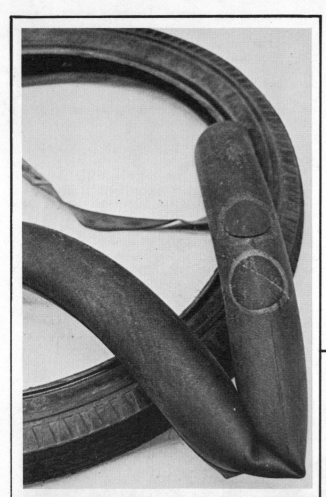

small wooden stick results in a pinging noise, which should be of the same pitch for each spoke. If not, they are not uniform.

If the sound is duller than the others, chances are that the specific spoke is looser. Check the other spokes and count the number of threads that are visible as the spoke disappears into the nipple flush with the rim. Adjust this to match. If the sound is more high-pitched for a spoke, it probably is much tighter and should be loosened appropriately with the spoke wrench. With all of the spokes sounding similar, the chance of having a rim wobbling is reduced.

Should you have this wobble in your wheel — in which the rim does not revolve equidistantly between the fork legs through one revolution — the problem becomes more complicated and sometimes baffling. If the wheel wobbles to the left, the objective is to move it toward the right. This is done — unless the nipples are frozen in place — by loosening the spokes that attach to the right half of the rim, and tightening those that feed into the left half of the rim.

Adjust only a few of each to see what effect this has on the performance of the wheel. Sometimes it will compound

Tubes patched frequently (left) should be discarded. Sometimes muscle is needed to force lip of casing over rim edge (below left). Once on bike, align the wheel.

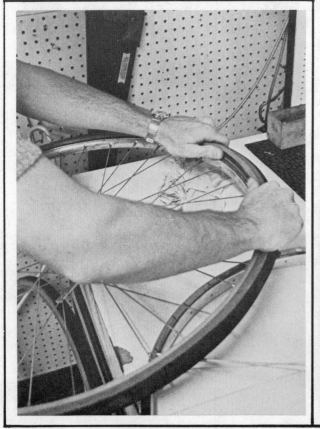

the problem and, instead of having one noticeable wobble, you end up with a couple or more of lesser magnitude. Not all rims are perfectly balanced and will not always spin true.

The system does not work on the rear wheel, because those spokes are adjusted differently to account for the derailleur gearing mechanism on 5 and 10-speed models. Rather than fool around with these, take the rim to the bike shop.

Spokes can get broken for a number of reasons, like hitting curbs or sticking feet or sticks into the revolving wheel. If broken spokes are your malady, first determine whether the entire rim is worth saving.

Take the tire off of the rim, just as you must take the wheel off the frame. Then remove the broken or bent spoke from its housing in the hub and rim and take it to the bike shop. Get new spokes that exactly match those removed from the bicycle, preferably of the same thickness. Try to match the nipples.

Once home, feed the new spoke through the hole in the hub that accommodates it, from the side opposite that in which it will attach. Notice the pattern established by the remaining spokes that were factory installed, and follow the pattern as best you can.

As the spoke is fed through the hub, it may not point to the hole that it should fit. Again, follow the pattern and check the overall length of the spoke once it is fitted in the spoke hole against others already in place. If it fits, twist on the nipple. Do this for all of the spokes that need installation, matching the pitch of the remaining ones and test it for wobble. If it wobbles, use the procedure previously outlined.

FRONT HUB

The front hub is a complex bit of engineering. It contains bearings, races, an axle, numerous washers, nuts and, on occasion, a disc brake.

Spoke ends must be seated flush with the interior surface of the rim, to avoid causing flat tires.

Just as with an automobile, the bearings must be lubricated with light grease occasionally if they are to continue rolling smoothly. The bearings on the front hub should be recoated with grease every six months, or as previous riding dictates. For example, if the bicycle was used to go plowing through the surf at the beach, regreasing in six months would not be necessary — an entire set of bearings would have to be installed far before this time period is up. The combination of salt and sand will play havoc with them, causing rust and finally freezing them in position.

Disassembling the front hub starts with removal of the entire wheel from the forks. Once free, the axle nuts need be unscrewed completely from the axle. The same is done with the cones, using the proper tools. With the cones out

When replacing spokes, try to maintain pattern visible with remaining spokes. Make sure they are same size.

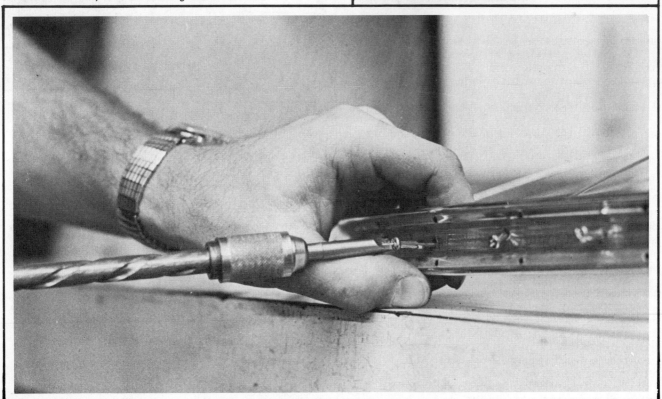

Just a few of the many components of coaster brake hub are visible with nuts and dust caps removed from axle.

A light coating of grease should be applied to the bearings before reinserting them in the housing. It will keep bearings turning smooth.

and, providing the hub has loose ball bearings rather than those in cages, a dust cover will be visible.

Take care when removing the dust cap, for the bearings are loose inside a cap below and are just waiting to fall out and roll under the two-ton freezer in the garage.

With all of the components removed from the hub and separated from the axle, it is easy to clean them in kerosene or a commercial solvent. After a thorough scrubbing, the parts are dried and inspected. If the bearings are pitted, worn or have signs of rust, replace them with an exact set from the bicycle shop.

With a light grease, coat the loose bearings after placing them in the bearing cup and work them around with a finger to assure all surfaces coated. Clean the inside of the hub if needed, then put everything back together, remount the wheel and you're ready for more riding. Naturally, if a component is worn or shows visible signs of abuse during reassembly, replace it; the time spent repairing isn't worth the slight cost at the outset.

If the bicycle is fitted with bearings housed in cages — permanently installed inside a metal ring — the job is made somewhat easier. It is a simple matter to clean and regrease these without worrying about one becoming lost. Repeat the reassembly procedure already outlined.

Many times, after hitting a curb or chuckhole with the front wheel, it will acquire a most disconcerting wobble, often rubbing against one of the brake blocks. The cause might be cones loosened by the shock, and tightening them may be all that is required to true the wheel.

For this operation, loosen the axle nuts and, after determining the direction of the rub, tighten the cone on the opposite side and loosen the one on the side where the rub occurs. Then tighten the axle nuts and give the wheel a spin.

If the rub isn't cured, loosen the axle nuts again and try tightening both cones equally, but not to the degree that free spinning of the wheel is hindered. If the rub still is present or more pronounced, repeat the tightening/loosening procedure until a cure is effected.

FRONT FORK/HEADSET

Ninety percent of all bicycles taken into repair shops that belong to grade school children suffer from one malady: The headset needs adjustment. Children are notorious in their disregard of such minor obstacles as curbs and delight in bouncing over them.

Each time the front fork encounters such a hindrance to smooth running, it takes a terrific amount of shock. As with anything that continually encounters such hammer-like force, it tends to become loose. Coupling this looseness

With the locknut once again tight, the headset is ready for more curb-jumping and other tortures.

A loose headset, common malady on youngster's bikes, is easily remedied. Locknut (raised at left) is tightened.

— not a major problem in itself — with the bicycle being left out in the rain, it's only a matter of time until rust invades the steering tube, rendering the bearings useless.

If the loose headset is discovered prior to rusting, it usually can be cured by simply unscrewing the locknut at the top of the steering tube, then tightening the threaded top race until the entire assembly is firm. The locknut then is retightened and the headset is ready for more curb-jumping.

If the headset is loose and the chrome badly rusted, or difficulty and excess noise are encountered when turning the handlebars, the bearings probably need replacement. This is a major repair that can be accomplished by the individual owner with time and patience.

The first step is to remove the front wheel and raise the frame so it is off the ground and in easy work-reach. If the bike has caliper brakes, remove the front assembly by loosening the hex bolt that engages the horizontal cable at the rear.

Next to go is the handlebar and stem assembly. Loosen the expander bolt at the top of the handlebar stem and, using a block of wood over the bolt, tap it with a hammer to free the stem inside the fork tube. Pull on the handlebars and the entire assembly should come away from the headset.

Next, loosen the locknut at the top of the head tube and remove it from the assembly. If there is a washer present in the headset, it should appear next; remove it and place it with the locknut and other components yet to come where they won't get lost or kicked.

Lay the bike on its side, after placing an old sheet or something similar on the ground that will prevent the bearings that are next to be removed from becoming lost. With this done, loosen the threaded top race which will disengage the forks and expose the bearings; they may fall out if not contained in cages, so watch where they land on the sheet. Once they are out, if loose, count their number and place them with the other components, the number of which was increased by addition of the threaded top race.

Many times removal of the threaded top race will not result in all of the bearings falling out; some may slip down inside the head tube as the fork becomes loose. Therefore, when removing the fork assembly, watch for any bearings that might have remained inside.

As the fork is withdrawn, a second set of bearings will become visible and have a tendency to fall all over, which is why this part of the procedure is done over the old sheet. These bearings rest on the top of the fork crown race and fit inside the bottom head race. If they are caged, as are many of American and some European designs, you needn't worry about them becoming lost. If loose, check closely and count the exact number that belong here.

With all of the components off the bicycle, clean them thoroughly with solvent or a petroleum distillate then inspect them for cracks, pits or the like. If noted, the part should be replaced. If not, simply pack the bearings lightly with grease and reassemble the headset by reversing the procedure outlined above.

HANDLEBAR/STEM ADJUSTMENT

If you have ever encountered a bicycle that has its handlebars angled rather than pointing straight ahead in the direction the bike is heading, you have seen a bike that needed a stem adjustment. This is a relatively easy repair to complete, and the only tool needed is a wrench.

Walk to the front of the bicycle and straddle the front wheel with your legs. Grab the bars and try to turn them until they are straight. If this is possible, simply tighten the expander bolt at the top of the stem and you're in business. The bolt should not be tightened to the degree that it stops the bars from moving under severe pressure, because if you have an accident and contact immobile bars, you will suffer more serious injuries than if the bars would give and move.

Should you not be able to straighten the bars with hand pressure alone, simply loosen the binder bolt a couple of turns with a wrench. See if the bars will move now; if not, tap the top of the binder bolt as explained in the process for removing the headset. Once free, the bars should turn easily to the desired position. Then simply tighten the expander bolt until it is relatively tight.

If you should encounter difficulty in trying to tighten the expander bolt, pull on the bolt as high as it will go and begin turning the bolt in the tightening direction, usually clockwise. If this doesn't tighten the bolt, remove it from the stem and pull the handlebar and stem assembly from the headset, flip the bike over and retrieve the small wedge nut that will come rolling out.

The design of this wedge nut is such that when the bolt is threaded into it, the wedge nut expands against the interior of the stem tube, which keeps the bars and stem in position. After it is retrieved, stick the bolt through the hole in the stem and screw the wedge nut on the bolt. The entire stem and handlebar assembly should then be inserted into the headset and tightened as before.

The stem should extend from the top of the headset only about 2½ inches, remaining below the height of the seat at all times. If the rider is uncomfortable in the down position, he should not be riding a bicycle that uses such design. If the bicycle does not incorporate the design currently referred to as the 10-speed look, then the problem of stem height is not so great. As anyone who has seen a high-rise specimen will attest, the stem — in this case termed a gooseneck — extends much more than 2½ inches from the headset. These may be adjusted either up or down to suit the rider's height requirements. With a 10-speed, however, the bicycle is matched to the rider by frame size and such adjustments are much more limited.

Handlebars can slip slip and change position, which necessitates that the rider change them to the spot most adapted to his riding style.

There is a small binder bolt that can be adjusted at the center of the bars. With a small wrench loosen the bolt, position the bars, then retighten. Take care that you don't exert the strength of King Kong on the small bolt, as it strips rather handily.

One problem that occasionally crops up with riders of 10-speed bicycles, or any model that utilizes the taped, down-slung handlebars, is fraying of the tape at some point.

Stripped of all paraphernalia, this is appearance of handlebar stem separated from the bicycle frame.

This sometimes is caused by a spill, and retaping is relatively easy to accomplish.

The first thing that must be done is to remove the handlebar plugs from the ends of the bars. On some models they will be held in place by a screw that must be loosened, but more than likely they will be simply inserted tightly in the ends. Pull them free from the bars, then remove all of the old tape.

Most of the tapes available today either are cloth or a stretchy plastic. Some will have a gummed backing that will adhere to the bars, but if not don't fret.

Start wrapping the tape about three inches from the center of the bars and wrap it around the starting spot a couple of times to completely cover the end. Then start angling the tape toward the end of the bar, making sure the tape is overlapped on the previous layer a bit. Continue until the end of the bar, then make a complete revolution with the tape overhanging the end about half-way, tucking the cut end of the tape up inside the hole. Reinsert the plug gently or the tape will tear and you'll end up repeating the taping procedure.

Should the bar have been bent while taking the fall that resulted in tape replacement, it should be straightened or, preferably, replaced; it is weakened and never will be the same.

If the bars are still attached to the bike, lay it on its side being careful not to break the braking lever. If the bars are aluminum, there is a chance that, while standing on the good end, you can straighten the bent bar partially by exerting upward force. If the bars are of steel, the process can result in a double hernia; replace.

FRAME

The second chapter of this book went into a goodly amount of detail of the qualities synonymous with a good frame. If you skipped that part, go back and read it now, or some of this information may not make sense.

If you used discretion and good sense in picking out a bicycle, thoroughly examining the frame for rough lugs, butted tubing and metal of which the tubes are constructed, then you realize just how much wear and tear the frame can take. The lugs, which take the stress of road jolts, are brazed or soldered to the frame at an exceptionally low temperature, necessitated by the carbon content of the tubing. It is for this reason that any cracks or breaks in the tubing cannot be repaired by the home handyman.

About the only thing a rider can do with this frame, other than keep it clean, is to replace the paint. This is quite a chore as every item must be removed from the bicycle, leaving the frame bare.

For those who wish to repaint their machines, it first should be stressed that the paint on the frame, if the bicycle is of decent quality, is good and long-lasting. Try to leave it on the bike as long as possible.

If repainting, completely strip the bicycle of all components. The old paint must be removed completely, which can be accomplished through the aid of a liquid paint remover and plenty of rags. In attacking the frame with steel wool or the like, you'll end up putting fine scratches in the metal or, if using excess elbow grease, thinning the metal. The tubes are a uniform thickness throughout, with the exception of the ends, and such action may cause the frame to be severely weakened and perhaps broken.

With the old paint completely removed from the frame, it should be dry and dust-free; spray on the first of two or three primer coats. These must be sprayed evenly and lightly to avoid paint drip spots or the like. Before each coat of primer is sprayed on the frame, make sure that the previous coat has dried completely.

In spraying on the first coat of the color you have selected, again make the coat light and even, with no paint runs visible. After it has dried, apply more coats — as many as

you wish. When the entire frame is in A-1 condition, reattach all the goodies that you removed earlier, using plenty of patience and time; you don't want to scratch the beautiful paint that you just applied!

This process is difficult, and some riders may wish to have a bicycle shop do this for them. If you take the bike in with all equipment intact, the price will be somewhat higher than if the bike were stripped as it takes time for the shop repairmen to remove the stuff. But, if you don't know how to accomplish this, leave it to them and consider it money well-spent. You don't want to end up with excess nuts and bolts lying all over the garage.

PEDALS, CRANKS & BOTTOM BRACKET

Hardly any part of a bicycle suffers more abuse or general wear and tear than do the pedals, especially on children's bikes. They get bent through collisions or from simply laying the bicycle on its side and, unfortunately, on the pedal.

Whether the pedals are damaged or not, they should be relubricated at least once a year, as they pick up all manner of dirt and moisture from the roadway. As with anything else, they will rust badly if not lubed.

The pedal either has rubber blocks or a metal platform, held to the pedal by bolts and a main shaft. On the metal or rattrap pedals, frequently there is a cover that obstructs view of the main shaft or spindle bolt head. On rubber

With a screwdriver inserted in the slot of the crank cone, and tapping its handle with a hammer, a loose crank can be tightened.

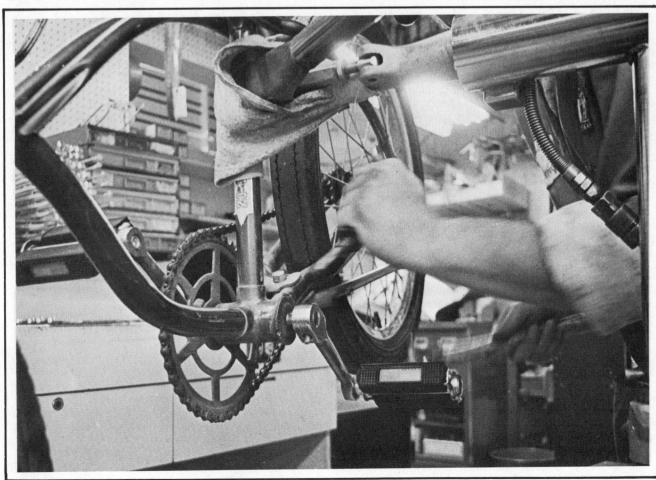

205

pedal block assemblies, this cover usually is missing and there appears no way to free the blocks.

As anyone removing the left pedal from the bike will discover, it is made with left-hand threading, which means that it must be turned to the right — clockwise — to loosen it.

The rubber block assembly has long bolts that run through the rubber and into an end plate secured there by nuts. To remove the rubber block assembly, loosen the nuts and the entire shebang will come away from the main spindle, usually covered completely by a metal barrel. The spindle is connected via a locknut which is unscrewed and placed where it won't get lost. This is followed by a washer, if the bike is outfitted with one, and the adjusting cone. Hold the pedal over a sheet when removing the cone, to catch the bearings.

The barrel covering the spindle can be loosened, which will cause the bearings on the other end of the spindle to fall out. As with all bearings, count them so one won't be left out when reassembling.

The spindle now can be unscrewed from the end plate. All parts should be cleaned and examined, and any with excess wear visible should be replaced. Pack the bearings in light grease and reassemble the components. The pedal now is like brand new. If replacing the platform or rubber blocks, assure they are fitted with reflectors.

In rattrap type pedals, which don't have rubber pedal blocks and their long bolts connected to the end plate, the process is no less difficult. A dust cap covers the end of the spindle, which sometimes has threads for easy removal. If so, simply remove the dustcap, locknut and adjusting cone and the platform will come free. Watch for the bearings to drop out from both ends. Clean or replace components and reassemble.

If the dustcap is not the type with threads, it must be pried loose gently with a screwdriver or other flat-bladed instrument to expose the locknut. Follow the disassembly procedure already outlined.

Cranks are the long metal arms that connect to the pedals and axle housed within the bottom bracket and revolve when pressure is applied to move the bicycle. Through vigorous use the cranks can become loose, which is characterized by squeaking or slippage of the pedals at some point during each revolution. This problem should be corrected as soon as detected, for the axle and bearings are at stake.

The crank is connected to the axle in either one of two ways: By the use of a cotter pins or a bolt, which are termed cottered or cotterless cranks respectively. Some bicycles of American manufacture have the cranks and axle as one solid piece of metal.

To fix a loose cotterless crank, you must pick up a special and inexpensive crank tool at the bike shop. Remove the chainguard and chain, then the dustcap by unscrewing it with the tool you purchased, a screwdriver if the cap has a notch cut into it, or an Allen wrench if the cap calls for it. With this done, place the socket found on the installer portion of the crank tool atop the bolt head and tighten with reasonable force. Take care not to overdo it, for the crank generally is made of a relatively soft alloy that cannot stand up to such pressure. It's also expensive to replace.

Fixing a loose cottered crank is infinitely more difficult and calls for much patience. Often this looseness is caused by a cotter pin that is not seated completely in its hole in the crank, or because the nut that tightens the bond of the crank and axle is not tight enough.

Unfortunately, tightening the small nut is a tough job,

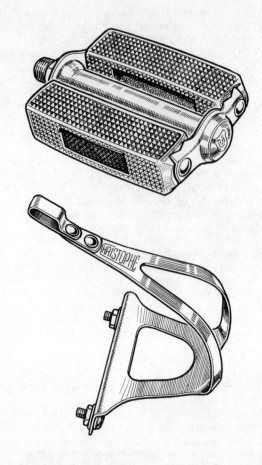

because if the cotter pin is not seated, it tends to resist all efforts to move it closer to the axle. You are tempted to smash the pin with a hammer to move it through the crank farther and expose more of the nut; this is a no-no, for hitting the pin with any force will damage the bearings just inside by causing flat spots on them.

If there is no other way, like a bike shop with good service facilities close by, tap the pin lightly with a small hammer, then try to tighten the nut. If it can be tightened slightly, continue the process, for the pin now is seating properly. If tapping does not do the trick, take the bike to a shop and have them do it.

On a bike with the crank and axle of one piece of metal, this process used for the cottered or cotterless cranks is not necessary. However, the crank still can become loose, and adjustment is made by tightening a cone located on the left side of the bike. After unscrewing the lock ring that is on the outside of the cone, the cone is adjusted by inserting a screwdriver blade in one of its two slots and tapping with a hammer. The lock ring then is tightened and you're ready to roll.

That should take care of the looseness. However, if you've come this far and haven't lubricated the axle and bearings for a few months, why not simply continue with disassembly and make a thorough job of it?

The process is not extremely difficult with the assembly described above. Remove the chainguard and chain, then the left pedal, remembering that it is loosened by turning clockwise.

Take out the lock ring and other components down to the bearings, counting the bearings inside the housing if not of the caged variety. Then simply remove the assembly from the right side of the bottom bracket, clean in solvent or the like, regrease the bearings and put the assembly back together reversing the aforementioned steps.

Lubricating the components in the bottom bracket of a bike with cotterless cranks is somewhat more involved. Again, remove the chainguard and chain and, using the extracting/installing tool purchased to tighten the cranks, remove them from the axle. Now, loosen the locking ring on the left side of the bicycle. Next to come out are the bearing cup and ball bearings; watch where they fall if not caged.

This done, pull the axle out of the bottom bracket from the left side, and collect all bearings. Check inside the bottom bracket for remaining bearings. Don't turn the bike upside down or the bearings will course down the open tube channels connected to the bottom bracket and in all probability, will stick inside. Not only does this mean replacing the bearing, but there will be a clatter whenever a bump is encountered.

With the components out, clean them thoroughly, dry them and apply fresh grease where needed. Assemble the components and you're in business.

Lubrication is more complicated still when the cranks are cottered, and care must be taken. Again, remove the chainguard and the chain from the bike. In removing the cotter pins from the crank, much discretion must be used here or the pin, its threads or the crank itself can be damaged.

After the nut is removed from the end of the cotter pin, there are a couple of ways of removing the pin without damaging it. One is to use a C-clamp or the like, which can slowly be tightened to force the pin gradually from its housing. Another way is to try tapping the pin gently with a hammer. Perhaps the best way is to use a center punch like those used by carpenters to pound nail heads below wood surface, and tap it lightly with a hammer against the center of the pin.

To reinforce the crank, thereby preventing its bending while tapping out the pin, place a block of soft wood against the opposite side of the crank, that has a deep 'V' notch cut into it. The cotter pin will be driven into the 'V' notch deep enough for the repairman to grasp its head and pull it free.

Once the cranks have been removed from the axle, follow the procedure outlined for lubrication of cotterless cranks.

After lubrication of components of any of these three assemblies, don't overlook the bottom bracket for cleaning prior to reinserting the goodies. If there is all sorts of gunk present inside, your thorough cleaning of the parts may be for naught.

One other problem that frequently crops up in bicycles made for youngsters is a bent crank, which ends up scraping on the chainguard with each revolution. Most kids simply grab dad's hammer and give the offending crank a solid whack or two; this is a no-no. Instead, the bike must be taken to a bike shop and they will perform the repairs using equipment designed specifically for that purpose. Hammer blows will cause more damage than good; this may result in ruined bearings, for instance.

FRONT SPROCKET/CHAINWHEEL

On virtually all 1 and 3-speed bikes, the front sprocket is permanently attached to the crank/axle assembly. On 5 or 10-speed models, however, they are connected via a system of either three or five bolts.

Chainwheels or front sprockets get bent for any number of reasons and they do not function well in such a condition; this precipitates chain wear and, upon occasion, the chain coming off. It also can generate a variety of weird and disconcerting sounds that are not associated with the pleasant tick-tick-tick of a bike in operation. An exaggerated comparison would be a Rolls Royce Silver Cloud without an exhaust system.

If you hear the scraping sounds of metal on metal as the pedals revolve, and you know the pedal isn't hitting the front changer or chain stays, figure that your chainwheel is bent.

Lift the bike onto a rack or the like which allows the rear wheel to rotate as the pedals are turned by hand. Look down at the chainwheel as you rotate the pedals and see if you can isolate the bend. You may have to examine it from different perspectives to be positive.

Once you have determined the bend site, remove the chainwheel from the crank or, if necessary, the entire crank/axle assembly. Lay the chainwheel on a flat surface like a workbench. Now, covering the bend site with a block of wood, blast once with a hammer. Check the bend now and give it a couple more doses as needs be. When straight, remount the components and you're off. If it can't be straightened, figure on buying another chainwheel.

A one-piece crank has the sprocket, axle and crank arms forged together as a single unit. When damaged or worn out, the entire assembly must be replaced. With the proper care, the crank will last as long as the bicycle.

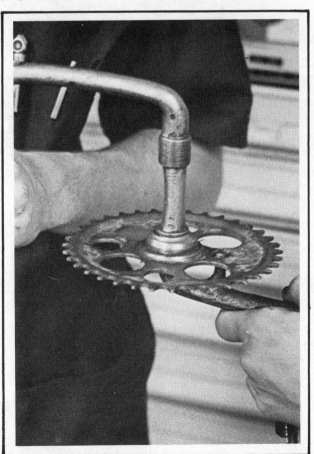

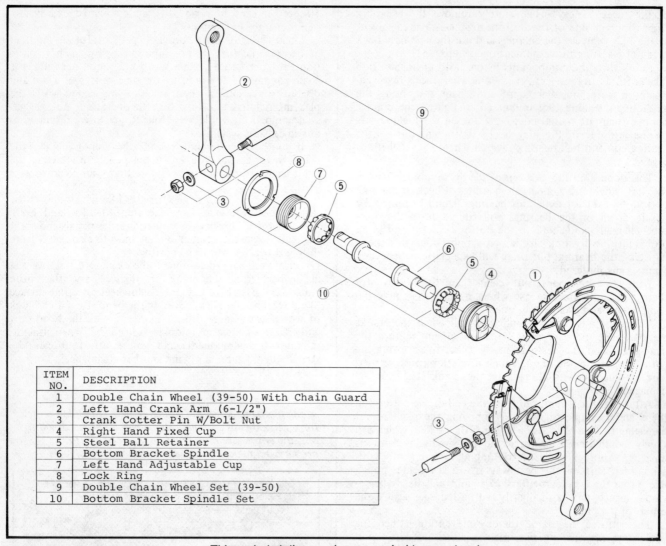

ITEM NO.	DESCRIPTION
1	Double Chain Wheel (39-50) With Chain Guard
2	Left Hand Crank Arm (6-1/2")
3	Crank Cotter Pin W/Bolt Nut
4	Right Hand Fixed Cup
5	Steel Ball Retainer
6	Bottom Bracket Spindle
7	Left Hand Adjustable Cup
8	Lock Ring
9	Double Chain Wheel Set (39-50)
10	Bottom Bracket Spindle Set

This exploded diagram shows a typical bottom bracket assembly, complete with axle, chainwheel, cottered cranks, bearings, et al. Learn the arrangement.

If you notice a clunk intermittently and know that the sound is not associated with a bent chainwheel, assume that you have a bent or badly worn tooth. Raise the bike so that the rear wheel revolves freely as the pedals are moved, and examine the chain as it passes over the teeth. It won't take long for the offending tooth to become apparent.

Taking a pair of heavy pliers, try bending the tooth back to its normal position. Strange as it seems, the tooth will bend easier if the chainwheel is of steel rather than an alloy. Once back to shape, run the chain over it several times. If no disconcerting clunk, you're in business. If it still gives off weird sounds, hustle down to the bike shop and buy a new one. The same applies for a tooth that is excessively worn.

Unfortunately for many 1 and 3-speed riders, if an excessively bent chainwheel or one with bad teeth is found, many times the entire crank/axle assembly will have to be replaced.

REAR SPROCKET/COGWHEELS

On 1 or 3-speed bikes, only one sprocket is utilized and not much can go wrong with them. However, when getting

into the area of the 5 or 10-speed models, with five sprockets or cogwheels of varying size located in one bristling mass, much can go wrong and/or made worse by the rider.

If for some reason you need replace one or more of the sprockets on your 5 or 10-speed bike, plan to go slowly and patiently about the repair procedure. The first thing you need do is slip the chain off, as well as the rear wheel. Pick up a freewheel remover of either the splined or two-pronged variety, depending upon the type your bike utilizes, and see if it will fit around the axle. If it won't fit, you may have to remove the spacer nut on the axle.

Now seat the freewheel remover firmly around the axle, making sure it is down as far as it will go and properly aligned. Put the axle nut or quick release nut that was removed earlier when the wheel came off back on the axle and tighten it down to the freewheel remover. Use as heavy a wrench as you have and try to back the freewheel off in counterclockwise fashion. They are stubborn and known to strip rather easily, so if something gives and it's not the freewheel loosening, stop and inspect. Most probably the freewheel has just been stripped. Take the whole assembly to the bike shop where they hopefully can salvage the damage.

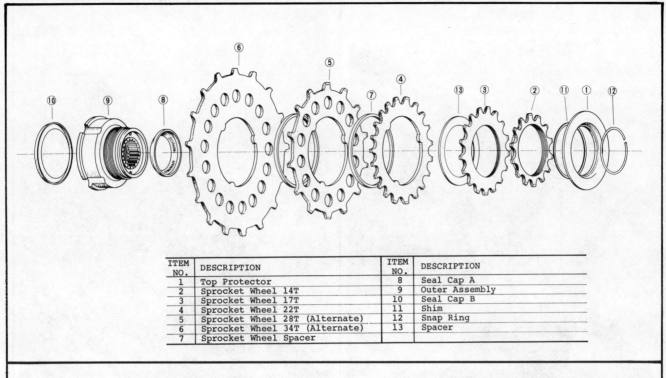

ITEM NO.	DESCRIPTION	ITEM NO.	DESCRIPTION
1	Top Protector	8	Seal Cap A
2	Sprocket Wheel 14T	9	Outer Assembly
3	Sprocket Wheel 17T	10	Seal Cap B
4	Sprocket Wheel 22T	11	Shim
5	Sprocket Wheel 28T (Alternate)	12	Snap Ring
6	Sprocket Wheel 34T (Alternate)	13	Spacer
7	Sprocket Wheel Spacer		

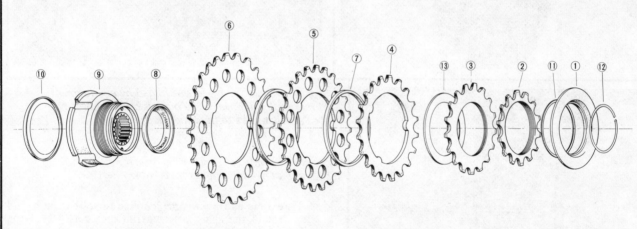

ITEM NO.	DESCRIPTION	ITEM NO.	DESCRIPTION
1	Top Protector	8	Seal Cap A
2	Sprocket Wheel 14T	9	Outer Assembly
3	Sprocket Wheel 17T	10	Seal Cap B
4	Sprocket Wheel 20T	11	Shim
5	Sprocket Wheel 24T	12	Snap Ring
6	Sprocket Wheel 28T	13	Spacer
7	Sprocket Wheel Spacer		

These two complicated drawings depict different sets of cogwheels and components found on 5 and 10-speed bikes.

If it comes off without undue hassle, replace the needed sprocket with the same amount of teeth. Clean and regrease the ensemble, then reassemble using no small amount of caution; remember how easily the freewheel can strip.

CHAIN

On bicycles of 1 or 3-speed design, a chain with a master link is employed, which enables the chain to be separated and subsequently removed with little fuss or bother. Chains for 5 and 10-speed bikes, however, have no master link and the chain only can be separated — on purpose — by the use of an inexpensive chain tool.

The master link is nothing more than one unit of the chain with a removable plate over it. By detaching the plate the chain separates. On chains without this link, a chain tool that drives rollers from the side plate is used.

The chain picks up all manner of foreign objects during its employment and must be cleaned and reoiled periodically. This can usually be done without removing the chain from the bike, providing it isn't rusted or really fouled with glotch.

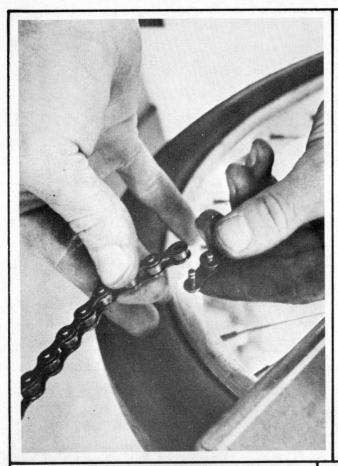

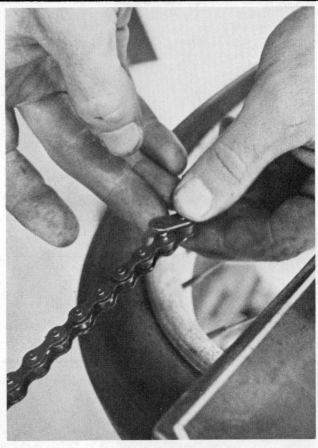

Separated chain (above left) is joined by employment of master link (above). The plate is clamped over two special roller links to hold the chain intact.

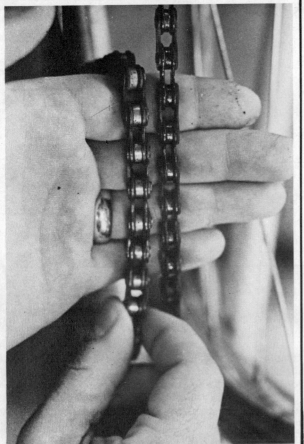

Difference in width of chain using master link (at left) and that needing chain tool is shown (left).

Take a rag and pour some gasoline or solvent on it, and wrap around the chain between the sprockets. Turn the pedals while holding the rag and the fouling material will come off. With the chain clean, crank the pedals slowly and place a drop of lightweight oil on the individual units. This completed, run the chain around both sprockets for a few moments, then wipe off any excess oil.

As the chain wears, it stretches and becomes loose. When this happens, the chain starts falling off the sprockets, which is extremely hazardous on a bicycle with a top tube. If the rider is pedaling while standing up, and the chain slips or detaches, his crotch comes crashing down on the top tube.

If the chain can be pressed farther than one-half inch down between the sprockets, it is too loose. In 1 and 3-speed bikes, all that needs be done is loosen the rear wheel and pull it back farther, then retighten the axle nuts.

On 10-speed bikes, there are a couple of other things that could really be the problem or contributing to it. One could be that the spring is shot in your rear derailleur. Put the chain on the two largest sprockets, which should pull the derailleur into a horizontal position. If it doesn't, remove one link from the chain with the chain tool and see if that does the trick. If not, take the bike to the shop and they'll replace the spring in the derailleur, which is a job too tough for the majority of bike riders.

If you're out in the middle of nowhere and the chain slips off the sprockets, you can remount and fix it when you get back to civilization. If your bike has a freewheel, simply start the chain on a couple of sprocket teeth at the bottom front and turn the pedals backwards. The chain will be pulled onto the sprocket and you're in business until it comes off again.

On 1 and 3-speed bikes, which don't have the freewheel capacity, you must start the chain on the top front teeth of the sprocket and revolve the pedals. It will pop back on, and then you can pull the rear wheel back to proper measurement.

GEARS

This is perhaps the most complicated area of a bicycle equipped with a multi-gear range, and much damage can be done by the individual attempting repair. The types and ranges of gears is so wide and varied that it is practically impossible to write a stock standard repair procedure for gear ills that would apply to all. For that reason, it is recommended that you take the bike into the shop when you feel the gears need adjusting. Watch what the repairman does to correct the problem. You then can complete further adjustments or repairs on your system at home.

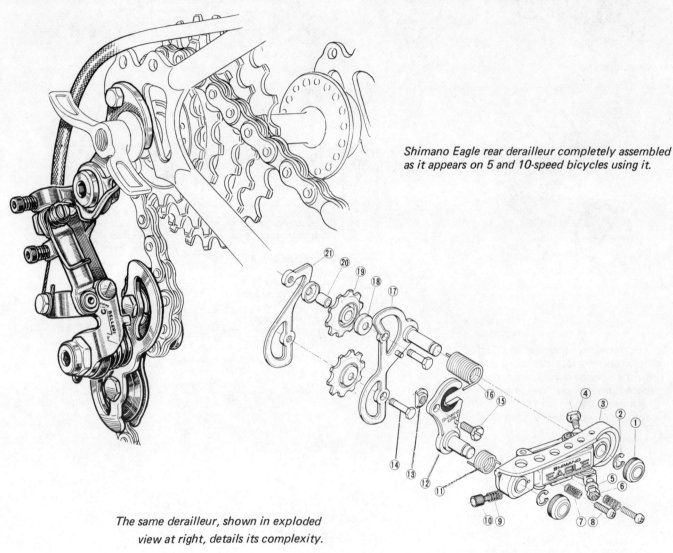

Shimano Eagle rear derailleur completely assembled as it appears on 5 and 10-speed bicycles using it.

The same derailleur, shown in exploded view at right, details its complexity.

ITEM NO.	DESCRIPTION	ITEM NO.	DESCRIPTION
1	Cap	12	Adapter With Mounting Shaft
2	Stop Ring (6 φ)	13	Adapter Nut
3	Mechanism Assembly (S.S. Type)	14	Pulley Bolt
4	Cable Fixing Bolt	15	Adapter Screw (M5 x 10)
5	Cable Fixing Washer	16	P-Tension Spring
6	Cable Fixing Nut	17	Inner Cage Plate W/Bolt
7	Adjusting Spring	18	Pulley Cap
8	Adjusting Screw	19	Pulley
9	Cable Adjusting Spring	20	Pulley Bushing
10	Cable Adjusting Barrel	21	Outer Cage Plate
11	B-Tension Spring		

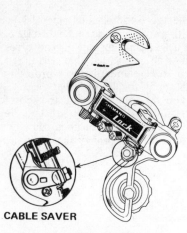

CABLE SAVER

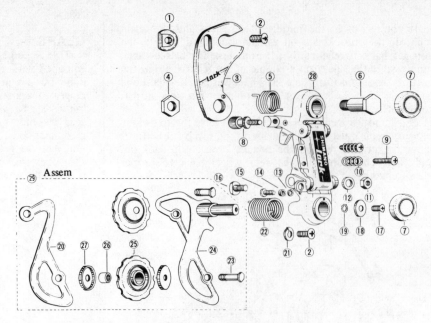

Assem

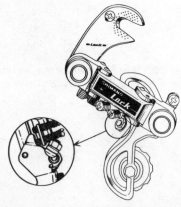

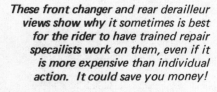

These front changer and rear derailleur views show why it sometimes is best for the rider to have trained repair specailists work on them, even if it is more expensive than individual action. It could save you money!

ITEM NO.	DESCRIPTION	ITEM NO.	DESCRIPTION
1	Adapter Nut	16	Wire Fixing Bolt
2	Adapter Screw	17	Cage Mounting Bolt
3	Adapter	18	Cage Mounting Washer
4	Lock Nut	19	Tooth Lock Washer
5	B-Tension Spring	20	Outer Cage Plate
6	Adapter Mounting Bolt	21	Spring Washer
7	Cap	22	P-Tension Spring
8	Wire Adjusting Bolt (Assem.)	23	Idler Wheel Bolt
9	Adjusting Screw	24	Inner Cage Plate
10	Adjusting Screw Spring	25	Idler Wheel
11	Wire Fixing Nut	26	Bushing for Idler Wheel
12	Wire Fixing Washer	27	Idler Wheel Cap
13	Spring Washer for Stopper	28	Link Assembly
14	Bushing for Stopper	29	Cage Plate Assem.
15	Stopper Screw		

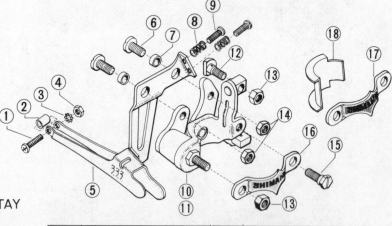

PARALLEL

CHAIN STAY

BRACKET INDICATOR LINE

SET BOLT

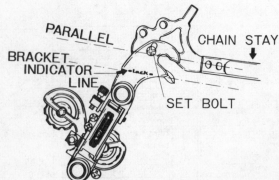

ITEM NO.	DESCRIPTION	ITEM NO.	DESCRIPTION
1	Bolt	11	Derailleur Member Assem. Upper Inlet Type
2	Bushing		
3	Toothed Lock Washer	12	Inner Cable Fixed Bolt
4	Nut	13	Inner Cable Fixed Nut
5	Chain Guide	14	Link Nut
6	Link Screw	15	Clamp Bolt
7	Collar	16	Clamp (1-1/8'')
8	Adjusting Spring	17	Clamp (1'')
9	Adjusting Bolt	18	Shim (1'' only)
10	Derailleur Member Assem. Lower Inlet Type		

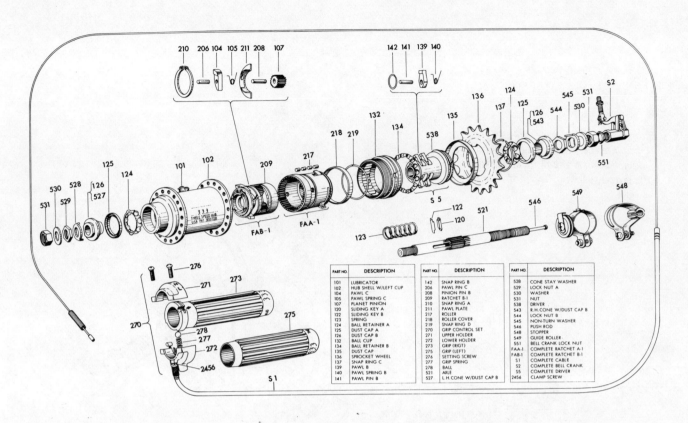

PART NO.	DESCRIPTION	PART NO.	DESCRIPTION	PART NO.	DESCRIPTION
101	LUBRICATOR	142	SNAP RING B	528	CONE STAY WASHER
102	HUB SHELL W/LEFT CUP			529	LOCK NUT A
104	PAWL C			530	WASHER
105	PAWL SPRING C			531	NUT
107	PLANET PINION			538	DRIVER
120	SLIDING KEY A			543	R.H. CONE W/DUST CAP B
122	SLIDING KEY B			544	LOCK NUT B
123	SPRING			545	NON-TURN WASHER
124	BALL RETAINER A			546	PUSH ROD
125	DUST CAP A			548	STOPPER
126	DUST CAP B			549	GUIDE ROLLER
132	BALL CUP			551	BELL CRANK LOCK NUT
134	BALL RETAINER B			FAA-1	COMPLETE RATCHET A-1
135	DUST CAP			FAB-1	COMPLETE RATCHET B-1
136	SPROCKET WHEEL			S1	COMPLETE CABLE
137	SNAP RING C			S2	COMPLETE BELL CRANK
139	PAWL B			S5	COMPLETE DRIVER
140	PAWL SPRING B			2456	CLAMP SCREW
141	PAWL PIN B				

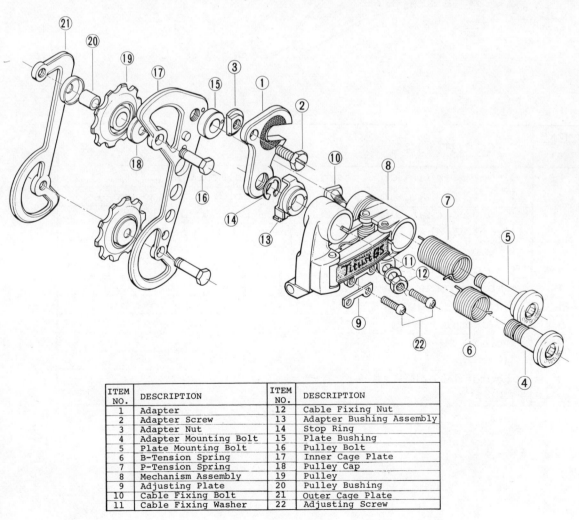

ITEM NO.	DESCRIPTION	ITEM NO.	DESCRIPTION
1	Adapter	12	Cable Fixing Nut
2	Adapter Screw	13	Adapter Bushing Assembly
3	Adapter Nut	14	Stop Ring
4	Adapter Mounting Bolt	15	Plate Bushing
5	Plate Mounting Bolt	16	Pulley Bolt
6	B-Tension Spring	17	Inner Cage Plate
7	P-Tension Spring	18	Pulley Cap
8	Mechanism Assembly	19	Pulley
9	Adjusting Plate	20	Pulley Bushing
10	Cable Fixing Bolt	21	Outer Cage Plate
11	Cable Fixing Washer	22	Adjusting Screw

213

Front changers are superbly designed to complete their assigned function. If a novice adjusts them, he could foul up the entire system. Learn how to do it.

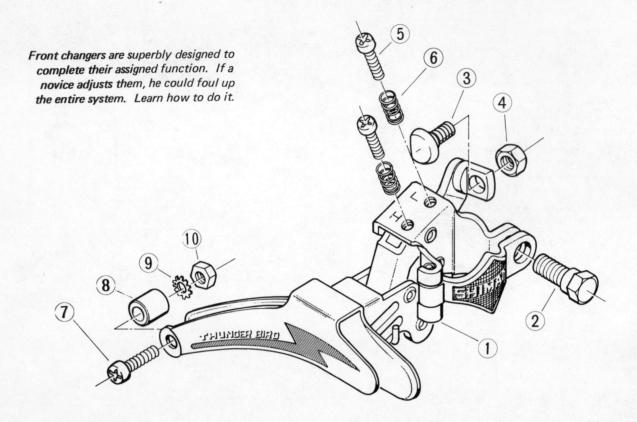

ITEM NO.	DESCRIPTION
1	Front Mechanism Assem. Lower Inlet Type (1")
	Front Mechanism Assem. Lower Inlet Type (1-1/8")
	Front Mechanism Assem. Upper Inlet Type (1")
	Front Mechanism Assem. Upper Inlet Type (1-1/8")
2	Clamp Bolt
3	Cable Fixing Bolt
4	Cable Fixing Nut
5	Adjusting Bolt (M4 x 14)
6	Adjusting Spring
7	Bolt
8	Bushing
9	Toothed Lock Washer
10	Nut

GEAR TROUBLESHOOTING

Conditions	Possible Causes	Corrections
Chain does not stay on larger sprocket	1. High gear adjusting bolt is out of adjustment 2. Wire has stretched or loosened	1. Readjust properly 2. Tighten wire to correct tension
Chain does not shift onto larger sprocket.	1. High gear adjusting bolt is out of adjustment 2. Wire has stretched or loosened	1. Readjust 2. Tighten wire to correct tension
Abnormal noise	1. Improper installation of chain and guide plate 2. Improper adjustment	1. Reinstall properly 2. Arrange the guide plate and gear in parallel. 3. Adjust the gear teeth and guide plate to the proper clearance 4. Readjust the adjusting bolt.

TROUBLES
(Front Derailleur)

Conditions	Possible Causes	Corrections
It is difficult to change from high gear to low gear.	1. Loose wire 2. Low gear adjusting bolt too far in.	1. Tighten wire to correct tension 2. Readjust properly
It is difficult to change from low gear to high gear	1. Wire too tight 2. High gear adjusting bolt too far in.	1. Tighten wire to correct tension 2. Readjust properly
Chain on high gear tends to slip off.	High gear adjusting bolt is too far out.	1. Readjust properly
Chain on low gear tends to slip off into spokes.	Low gear adjusting bolt is too far out.	1. Readjust properly
Chain jumps on gear teeth.	1. Wearing of chain or gear 2. Loose wire or improper lever operation 3. Damaged plate tension spring.	Replace with new one in case of 1 or 3. Adjust tension of wire, or set lever to proper position in the case of 2.
Chain has too much slack.	1. Length of chain 2. Damaged plate tension spring	1. Remove one or two links or replace chain As for 2, replace with new one.
When back pedaling chain slips off from front sprocket.	1. See from back side of frame and check whether guide pulley and tension pulley are vertical to the rear gear. 2. Units are improperly installed 3. Front derailleur or front sprocket is bent.	1. Adjust them properly. If caused by bicycle being toppled over, replace with new ones. 2. Disassemble and reassemble properly. 3. Adjust them properly. If caused by bicycle being laid down, replace with new ones.
Abnormal noise occurs on the rear derailleur mechanism.	1. Pulley plate is distorted	1. If caused by bicycle being laid down, replace with new one, or correct distortion.

TROUBLES
(Rear Derailleur)

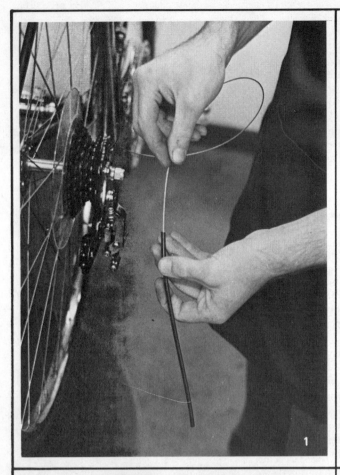

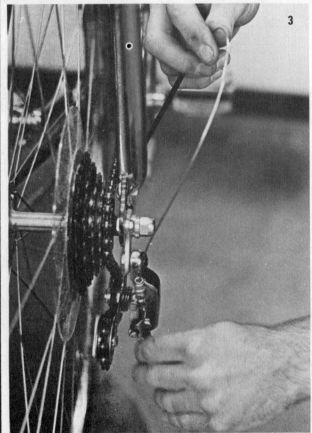

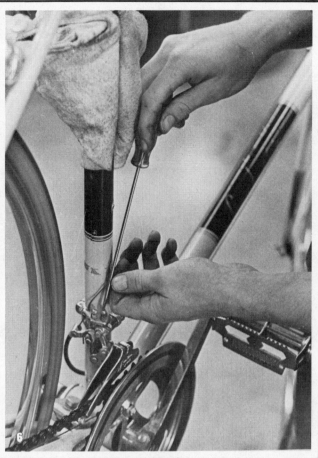

Cable replacement begins by threading cable through its housing (1) and into rear derailleur (2). It then is pulled through fitting (3) and adaptor mounting bolt (4) and tightened. Cable fixing nut is tightened around cable which then is clipped (5). Final adjustment is then made on the rear changer (6). Process takes 10 minutes.

Weinmann side pull caliper brake assembly, sans cable in this photo, applies force to one side of the brake.

BRAKES

As previously mentioned elsewhere in this book, brakes come in three varieties: Side pull caliper, center pull caliper and disc/coaster type. Each have their idiosyncrasies and need attention periodically.

In the case of caliper-type brakes, if the cables are lubricated with any degree of regularity, likelihood of problems is lessened. There isn't much that can be done with coaster brakes, except keep sand and water out of them as best you can.

If your caliper brakes tend to return open slowly after squeezing, the problem may be that the cable doesn't have enough lubrication. Grease it, work it several times and see if operation is easier. It should be.

If the brake shoe is not completely aligned on the rim, and tends to rub on the tire, simply loosen the nut holding it in position and adjust it until it is where it should be. Then retighten the nut and you're safe.

Many riders note a loud squeaking noise when they squeeze their brake levers, which is most embarrassing. Check to see if there is a coating of rubber worn from the braking block on the rim and, if so, clean it off to solve the problem. This also can be caused by old brake blocks which get hard with age, so replace them if this is the case. Clean them of grit and other foreign matter periodically to save wear.

THREE SPEED HUB WITH COASTER BRAKE

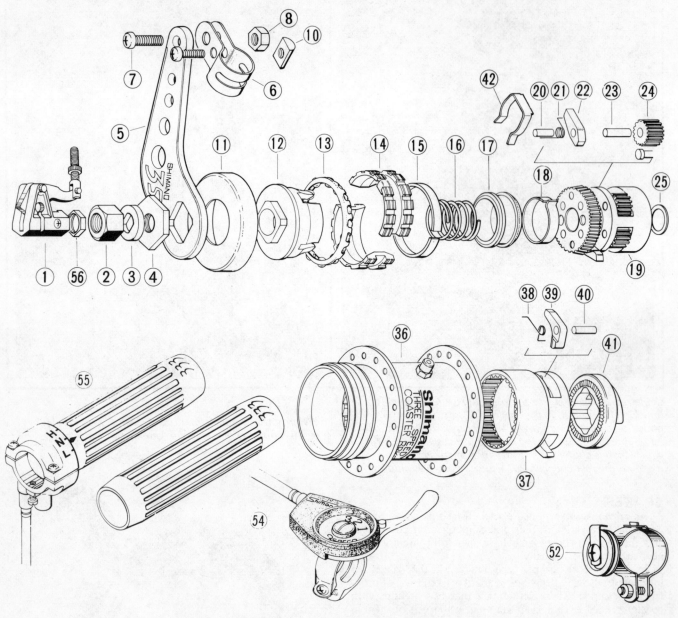

ITEM NO.	DESCRIPTION	ITEM NO.	DESCRIPTION
1	Bell Crank Complete	16	Return Spring
2	Axle Nut (3/8")	17	Spring Guide
3	Lock Washer	18	Slide Spring
4	L.H. Lock Nut	19	Carrier
5	Brake Arm	20	Pawl Pin D
6	Arm Clip (5/8")	21	Pawl Spring D
	Arm Clip (11/16")	22	Pawl D
	Arm Clip (3/4")	23	Pinion Pin
7	Arm Bolt (M6x15)	*24	Planet Pinion
8	Arm Nut	25	Thrust Washer
9	Arm Clip Bolt(ISO thread)	26	Stop Nut
10	Arm Clip Nut (ISO thread)	27	Non-turn Washer
11	Dust Cap L	28	Lock Nut B
12	Brake Cone	29	Clutch Spring B
*13	Ball Retainer B	*30	Push Rod (4-9/32")
14	Brake Shoe	31	Axle (6-5/8")
15	Brake Shoe Spring	32	Axle Key

* All parts asterisked are interchangeable in SHIMANO 3-speed hub.

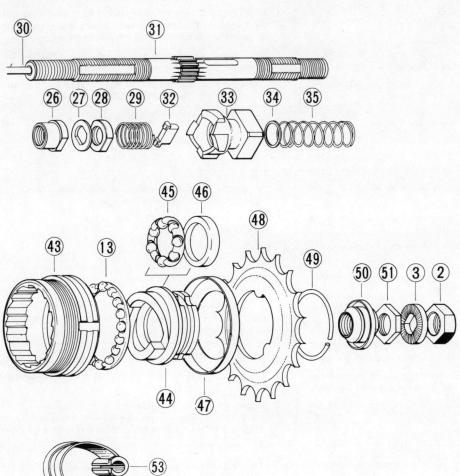

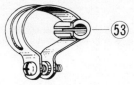

ITEM NO.	DESCRIPTION	ITEM NO.	DESCRIPTION
33	Sliding Clutch	*48	Sprocket Wheel 18T
34	Clutch Washer		Sprocket Wheel 19T
35	Clutch Spring A		Sprocket Wheel 20T
36	Hub Shell 28H	*49	Snap Ring C
	Hub Shell 36H	*50	R.H. Cone
37	Ring Gear	*51	R.H. Lock Nut
38	Pawl Spring E	52	Guide Roller Assem. 1"
39	Pawl E		Guide Roller Assem. 1-1/8"
*40	Pawl Pin C	53	Stopper Band Assem. 1"
41	Cam		Stopper Band Assem. 1-1/8"
42	Stop Ring		Stopper Band Assem. 5/8"
43	R.H. Ball Cup		Stopper Band Assem. 1/2"
44	Driver	54	Trigger Lever Assembly
*45	Ball Retainer A	55	Grip Control Assembly
*46	Dust Cap A	*56	Bell Crank Lock Nut
*47	Dust Cap		
*48	Sprocket Wheel 16T		

■ COASTER BRAKE TROUBLESHOOTING

Condition	What to check	How to correct
I Pedal idles when pressed during forward movement.	1. Loose cone	1. Adjust the cone on the sprocket side so that there is no play in the rim and it revolves smoothly.
	2. Bent axle	2. Roll the hub axle on a flat surface and check it. If it is bent, straighten it.
	3. Foreign matter caught between clutch cone and driver.	3. Clean off any foreign matter, mud, etc., from the threads of the driver or threads of the clutch cone.
	4. Insufficient pressure of clutch spring.	4. If the clutch spring is bent or stretched, spring pressure is weakened. In this case, exchange it for a new one. Be sure to assemble the spring facing the proper direction.
	5. Improper type of grease or oil has been used.	5. Grease and oil should not be of high viscosity. Disassemble, clean, and coat with proper grease and oil.
	6. Foreign matter caught between hub shell and clutch cone.	6. Clean the inner tapered part of the hub shell and the outer tapered part of the clutch cone.
II Braking angle is increased.	1. Brake shoe is worn.	1. Exchange the brake shoe.
	2. Same as items 1, 2, 3, 4, or 5 of number I.	
III Bicycle does not easily stop as quickly as desired.	1. Brake shoe is worn.	1. In case the brake shoe is worn so that there is no surface tread, replace it with a new brake shoe.
	2. Projecting parts of brake cone are broken.	2. If the projecting part of the brake cone is broken, exchange it for a new one.
	3. Same as item 5 of number I.	
IV Pedaling becomes heavy when pedal is pushed in forward direction after brake has been applied.	1. Insufficient pressure of the shoe spring.	1. If the pressure of shoe spring is insufficient, exchange it for a new one.
	2. Ball retainer C on the brake arm side is broken.	2. If the retainer C on the brake arm side is broken, it causes the brake to lock, so disassemble, clean, and replace it with a new one.
V Grinding noise is heard when brake is applied.	1. Balls of the retainer are damaged.	1. Disassemble, clean the inside and exchange the retainer.
	2. Damage to parts of the cone and hub shell that touch the balls.	2. Disassemble, clean the inside and exchange the damaged parts.
	3. Damage to internal part of the hub shell.	3. If damage to the inner surface of the hub shell is slight, polish it with emery paper or very fine whetstone. If this does not remove the damage, replace it with a new one.
VI Squeaking noise is heard when brake is applied.	1. Disassemble and clean internal parts.	1. This is usually caused by using oil and grease other than that specified. Be sure not to use gasoline, light oil or spindle oil.
VII Too much play between forward and reverse movements of pedal.	1. The brake shoe is worn.	1. Refer to item 1 of number III.
	2. The cone is loose.	2. Refer to item 1 of number I.
VIII Grinding noise is heard during forward movement.	1. Improper meshing of the chain and small sprocket.	1. This is caused by stretching of the chain or wear of the sprocket wheel. Exchange the part in question for a new one.
	2. Inner tapered part of shell is worn where it contacts the clutch cone.	2. Exchange the hub shell for a new one.
	3. Same as items 2 and 3 of number V.	
IX Pedal revolves backwards just before bicycle stops when brake is applied.	1. Brake arm clip is improperly assembled.	1. Long use in this condition causes the hub nut to loosen, causing play in the hub axle. Fasten the brake arm tightly to the chain stay, and fasten the hub nut tightly.

Cable housing should be clipped clean (below left) to avoid having burrs shorten cable life (below right).

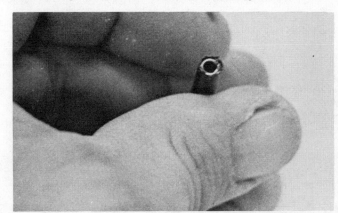

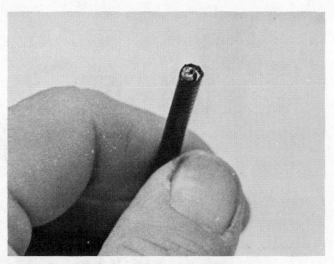

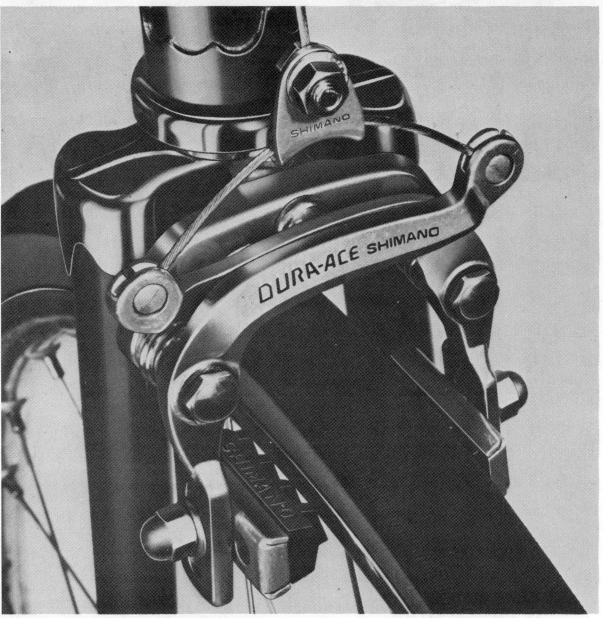

Center Pull Type

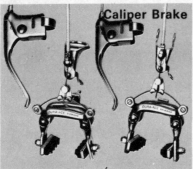

Caliper Brake

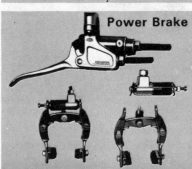

Power Brake

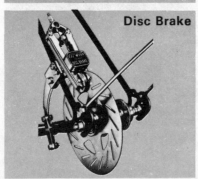

Disc Brake

Coaster Brake

3-Speed Hub with Coaster Brake

The five types of bicycle brakes are shown in the left column. Power and disc brakes are not used with the frequency of other types, mainly due to cost factor.

Seats come in a variety of styles and materials. While they do look uncomfortable, scientific technology says they function best of all seats, with no comfort loss.

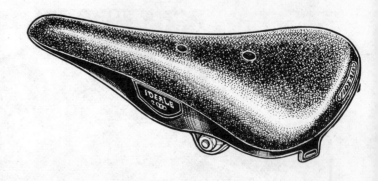

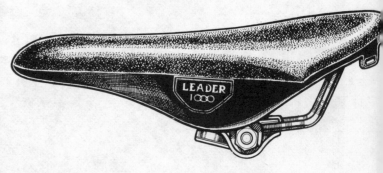

SEAT

Adjustment of the seat is a minor matter that most riders can resolve without reading this section. The seat angle is easily changed simply by loosening a binder bolt attached to the seat assembly, which then is retightened after the seat is positioned to the rider's desire.

Height of the seat is adjustable to a rider's growth or the like, simply by loosening a binder bolt at the spot where the seat post enters the frame. The seat post then can be extended to the desired height and the binder bolt retightened.

While this chapter does not cover every facet of the repair field, it should prove helpful in most instances. There are a couple of items that the repairman should have at all times, not found in tool kits or books: Patience and common sense. Armed with these two virtues, no problem is insurmountable. Add to them what you have read in this chapter and a couple of tools and you'll rarely find yourself walking instead of riding.

Chapter 17

Bicycle Review

**Here Are The Latest Offerings
From Domestic And
Foreign Foundries!**

CLAYTON-WILLARD SALES CORPORATION,
Box 3291, 1732 Danese Street, Jacksonville, Florida 32206

BOTTECCHIA PROFESSIONAL
FRAME: hand made Columbus tubing; COLORS: not specified; BRAKES: aluminum racing center pull; GEARS: 10-speed; FENDERS: none; RIMS: tubular, light alloy; TIRES: tubular; CHAINGUARD: not specified; HANDLEBARS: aluminum racing; PEDALS: Campagnola Record; SADDLE: professional racing; PRICE: not specified.

BOTTECCHIA GIRO D'ITALIA
FRAME: hand made Columbus tubing; COLORS: not speicified; BRAKES: aluminum sport center pull; GEARS: Campagnola Valentino Extra 10-speed; FENDERS: none; RIMS: aluminum racing; TIRES: tubular; CHAINGUARD: not specified; HANDLEBARS: aluminum racing with tape and plugs; PEDALS: not specified; SADDLE: racing, leather cover; PRICE: not specified.

BOTTECCHIA SPECIAL
FRAME: steel; COLORS: not specified; BRAKES: aluminum sport center pull; GEARS: Campagnolo Valentino Extra 10-speed; FENDERS: none; RIMS: chrome plated steel, 27 x 1.1/4 inch; TIRES: black hazel; CHAINGUARD: not specified; HANDLEBARS: aluminum racing with tape and plugs; PEDALS: metal, racing; SADDLE: racing, plastic cover; PRICE: not specified.

BOTTECCHIA DELUXE
FRAME: steel; COLOR: not specified; BRAKES: sport center pull; GEARS: Simplex 10-speed; FENDERS: none; RIMS: chrome plated 'steel, 27 x 1-1/4 inch; TIRES: black; CHAINGUARD: not specified; HANDLEBARS: aluminum racing with tape and plugs; PEDALS: metal racing; SADDLE: racing, plastic cover; PRICE: not specified.

BOTTECCHIA CLASSIC
FRAME: steel; COLOR: not specified; BRAKES: steel, sport lateral pull; GEARS: Campagnolo Valentino Extra 5-speed; FENDERS: none; RIMS: chrome plated steel, 27 x 1-1/4 inch; TIRES: black; CHAINGUARD: not specified; HANDLEBARS: aluminum with tape and plugs; PEDALS: metal racing; SADDLE: racing, plastic cover; PRICE: not specified.

BOTTECCHIA UNISEX
FRAME: steel; COLORS: not specified; BRAKES: sport, center pull; GEARS: Simplex, 10-speed; FENDERS: none; RIMS: chrome plated steel, 27 x 1-1/4 inch; TIRES: black; CHAINGUARD: not specified; HANDLEBARS: chrome steel, touring; PEDALS: metal racing; SADDLE: touring, soft padded cover; PRICE: not specified.

KALKHOFF
FRAME: special type, handmade 23 inch; COLOR: not specified; BRAKES: caliper, front & rear; GEARS: 5 and 10-speed; FENDERS: none; RIMS: 27 x 1-1/4 inch; TIRES: 27 x 1-1/4 inch; CHAINGUARD: not specified; HANDLEBARS: drop bar steel; PEDALS: sport; SADDLE: racing; PRICE: not specified.

UNITED IMPORT SALES, INC., 540 E. Alondra, Gardena, California 90247

PEUGEOT TOURING

FRAME: seamless lightweight tubing; COLORS: electric blue, moss green, bronze; BRAKES: MAFAC center pull; GEARS: 10-speed; FENDERS: none; RIMS: Rigida; TIRES: 27 x 1-1/4 inch white walls, butyl tubes; CHAINGUARD: not specified; HANDLEBARS: Ava bar and stem; PEDALS: rattrap; SADDLE: not specified; PRICE: not specified.

PEUGEOT TROPHEE DE FRANCE LADIES' RACER

FRAME: 21 and 23 inches, seamless lightweight tubing; COLORS: ultramarine blue, emerald green, white; BRAKES: MAFAC center pull; GEARS: 10-speed; FENDERS: none; RIMS: Rigida; TIRES: 27 x 1-1/4 inch gumwall, butyl tubes; CHAINGUARD: not specified; HANDLEBARS: Ava stem with special touring bars; PEDALS: rattrap; SADDLE: soft touring; PRICE: not specified.

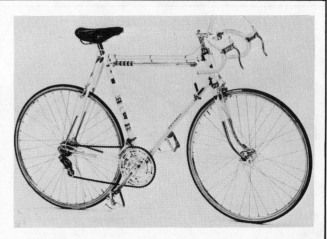

PEUGEOT TROPHEE DE FRANCE MEN'S RACER

FRAME: 21, 23, 24, 25 inches, seamless lightweight tubing; COLORS: ultramarine blue, emerald green, white; BRAKES: MAFAC center pull; GEARS: 10-speed; FENDERS: none; RIMS: Rigida; TIRES: 27 x 1-1/4 gumwall; CHAINGUARD: not specified; HANDLEBARS: Ava, Maes bend; PEDALS: rattrap; SADDLE: racing; PRICE: not specified.

PEUGEOT PROFESSIONAL

FRAME: Reynolds 531 tubing, 21, 23, 24, and 25 inches; COLOR: not specified; BRAKES: MAFAC center pull; GEARS: 10-speed; FENDERS: none; RIMS: MAVIC deluxe sew-up; TIRES: 700 C sew-up; CHAINGUARD: not specified; HANDLEBARS: Ava, Maes bend, dural; PEDALS: lyotard dural with toe clips and straps; SADDLE: Brooks professional; PRICE: $125 approx.

SHAKER VELO-SPORT,
18734 Chagrin Boulevard, Cleveland, Ohio 44122

MERCIAN — CAMPIONISSIMO
FRAME: alloy; COLORS: white, powder blue, yellow, orange; BRAKES: super alfa center pull; GEARS: Triplex Sport or Simplex Prestige, depending on ratios; FENDERS: none; RIMS: not specified; TIRES: 21-1/2, 22-1/2, 23-1/2 or 24-1/2 inches; CHAINGUARD: not specified; HANDLEBARS: Milremo sport alloy; PEDALS: Milremo Champion; SADDLE: Italian nylon; PRICE: $200 approx.

IVERSON CYCLE COMPANY,
33 W. Hawthorne Avenue, Valley Stream, New York

3-WHEEL FOLDING ADULT TRIKE
FRAME: 20 inch; COLOR: Flam blue; BRAKES: drum; GEARS: single; FENDERS: blue; RIMS: chrome; TIRES: not specified; CHAINGUARD: blue; HANDLEBARS: chrome; PEDALS: not specified; SADDLE: heavy duty; BASKET: heavy duty rear; PRICE: not specified.

IVERSON SIDEWALK CONVERTIBLE
FRAME: 16 inch; COLOR: hugger orange; BRAKES: coaster; GEARS: single; FENDERS: chrome; RIMS: chrome; TIRES: black pneumatic; CHAINGUARD: not specified; HANDLEBARS: junior hi-rise; PEDALS: not specified; SADDLE: bannana seat; Training wheels; PRICE: not specified.

IVERSON SIDEWALK CONVERTIBLE
FRAME: 16 inch; COLOR: plum; BRAKES: coaster; GEARS: single; FENDERS: chrome; RIMS: plated; TIRES: semi-pneumatic white striped; CHAINGUARD: plum; HANDLEBARS: junior space; PEDALS: not specified; SADDLE: banana seat, Training wheels; PRICE: not specified.

IVERSON TANK CONVERTIBLE
FRAME: 20 inch; COLOR: green; BRAKE: coaster; GEARS: single; FENDERS: flared chrome; RIMS: chrome; TIRES: whitewall; CHAINGUARD: green; HANDLEBARS: chrome bat-ray; PEDALS: not specified; SADDLE: banana with brace; Training wheels ; PRICE: not specified.

GROWING CONVERTIBLE
FRAME: 20 inch; COLORS: red, white and blue; BRAKE: coaster; GEARS: single; FENDERS: enamel; RIMS: enamel; TIRES: 20 x 1.75; CHAINGUARD: enamel; HANDLEBARS: chrome bat-ray; PEDALS: not specified; SADDLE: banana seat; Training wheels; PRICE: not specified.

BOY'S HI-RISE ROADRUNNER
FRAME: 20 inch; COLOR: international orange; BRAKE: coaster; GEARS: single; FENDERS: enamel; RIMS: enamel; TIRES: 20 x 1.75; CHAINGUARD: enamel; HANDLEBARS: hi-rise; PEDALS: not specified; SADDLE: banana with brace; PRICE: not specified.

GIRL'S HI-RISE ROADRUNNER
FRAME: 20 inch; COLOR: magenta; BRAKE: coaster; GEARS: single; FENDERS: enamel; RIMS: enamel; TIRES: 20 x 2.125; CHAINGUARD: enamel; HANDLEBARS: hi-rise; PEDALS: not specified; SADDLE: banana with brace; PRICE: not specified.

IVERSON BOY'S HI-RISE ROADRUNNER
FRAME: 20 inch; COLOR: yellow; BRAKES: caliper, coaster; GEARS: single; FENDERS: chrome; RIMS: chrome; TIRES: 20 x 1.75; CHAINGUARD: enamel; HANDLEBARS: hi-rise; PEDALS: not specified; SADDLE: banana racing stripe with brace; PRICE: not specified.

GIRL'S HI-RISE ROADRUNNER
FRAME: 20 inch; COLOR: lavender; BRAKE: coaster; GEARS: single; FENDERS: chrome; RIMS: chrome; TIRES: 20 x 1.75; CHAINGUARD: enamel; HANDLEBARS: hi-rise; PEDALS: not specified; SADDLE: floral banana with brace; BASKET: floral woven; PRICE: not specified.

BOY'S 3-SPEED ROADRUNNER
FRAME: 20 inch; COLOR: magenta; BRAKES: front and rear caliper; GEARS: 3-speed click stick; FENDERS: enamel; RIMS: chrome; TIRES: 20 x 1.75; CHAINGUARD: enamel; HANDLE-BARS: hi-rise; PEDALS: not specified; SADDLE: banana with brace; PRICE: not specified.

GIRL'S 3-SPEED ROADRUNNER
FRAME: 20 inch; COLOR: Flam Lime; BRAKES: front and rear caliper; GEARS: 3-speed twist grip; FENDERS: enamel; RIMS: chrome; TIRES: 20 x 1.75; CHAINGUARD: enamel; HANDLE-BARS: hi-rise; PEDALS: not specified; SADDLE: banana with brace; BASKET: floral woven; PRICE: not specified.

IVERSON BOY'S DRAG STRIPPER
FRAME: 20 inch; COLOR: Flam Lime; BRAKES: caliper, coaster; GEARS: single; FENDERS: chrome; RIMS: chrome; TIRES: 20 x 2.125; CHAINGUARD: enamel; HANDLEBARS: hi-rise; PEDALS: not specified; SADDLE: black banana with brace; PRICE: not specified.

GIRL'S MINI MISS DRAG STRIPPER
FRAME: 20 inch; COLOR: lavender; BRAKE: coaster; GEARS: single; FENDERS: chrome; RIMS: chrome; TIRES: 20 x 2.125; CHAINGUARD: enamel; HANDLEBARS: hi-rise; PEDALS: not specified; SADDLE: floral banana with brace; BASKET: flowered woven; PRICE: not specified.

BOY'S DELUXE CONSOLE
FRAME: 20 inch; COLOR: yellow; BRAKES: front and rear caliper; GEARS: 3-speed; FENDERS: chrome; RIMS: chrome; TIRES: 20 x 2.125; CHAINGUARD: enamel; HANDLEBARS: hi-rise; PEDALS: not specified; SADDLE: black banana with brace; PRICE: not specified.

GIRL'S TWIST GRIP
FRAME: 20 inch; COLOR: magenta; BRAKES: front and rear caliper; GEARS: 3-speed; FENDERS: chrome flared; RIMS: chrome; TIRES: 20 x 2.125; CHAINGUARD: enamel; HANDLEBARS: hi-rise; PEDALS: not specified; SADDLE: floral banana with brace; BASKET: flowered woven; PRICE: not specified.

IVERSON 5-SPEED DELUXE CONSOLE
FRAME: 20 inch; COLOR: orange; BRAKES: front and rear caliper; GEARS: 5-speed; FENDERS: chrome; RIMS: chrome; TIRES: 20 x 2.125; CHAINGUARD: enamel; HANDLEBARS: hi-rise; PEDALS: not specified; SADDLE: black banana with brace; PRICE: not specified.

BOY'S SPRINTER
FRAME: 20 inch; COLOR: silver; BRAKE: coaster; GEARS: single; FENDERS: chrome; RIMS: not specified; TIRES: 20 x 1.38; CHAINGUARD: chrome disc; HANDLEBARS: taped and plugged; PEDALS: not specified; SADDLE: black racing; PRICE: not specified.

GIRL'S SPRINTER
FRAME: 20 inch; COLOR: Kelly green; BRAKE: rear coaster; GEARS: single; FENDERS: chrome; RIMS: not specified; TIRES: 20 x 1.38; CHAINGUARD: chrome disc; HANDLEBARS: taped and plugged; PEDALS: not specified; SADDLE: flowered racing; PRICE: not specified.

BOY'S LIGHTWEIGHT SPRINTER
FRAME: 20 inch; COLOR: white; BRAKES: front and rear caliper; GEARS: 3-speed; FENDERS: chrome; RIMS: chrome; TIRES: not specified; CHAINGUARD: chrome disc; HANDLEBARS: dual cycle; PEDALS: not specified; SADDLE: racing; PRICE: not specified

IVERSON GIRL'S LIGHTWEIGHT SPRINTER
FRAME: 20 inch; COLOR: white; BRAKES: front and rear caliper; GEARS: 3-speed; FENDERS: chrome; RIMS: chrome; TIRES: not specified; CHAINGUARD: chrome disc; HANDLEBARS: dual cycle; PEDALS: not specified; SADDLE: racing; PRICE: not specified.

MEN'S GRAND TOURING
FRAME: 26 inch; COLOR: black; BRAKES: front and rear caliper; GEARS: 3-speed; FENDERS: enamel; RIMS: chrome; TIRES: 26 x 1.38; CHAINGUARD: not specified; HANDLEBARS: not specified; PEDALS: not specified; SADDLE: spring; PRICE: not specified.

GIRL'S GRAND TOURING
FRAME: 26 inch; COLOR: black; BRAKES: front and rear caliper; GEARS: 3-speed; FENDERS: enamel; RIMS: chrome; TIRES: 26 x 1.38; CHAINGUARD: not specified; HANDLEBARS: not specified; PEDALS: not specified; SADDLE: spring; PRICE: not specified.

MEN'S DELUXE 3-SPEED TRIGGER
FRAME: 26 inch; COLOR: lime; BRAKES; front and rear caliper; GEARS: 3-speed; FENDERS: chrome; RIMS: chrome; TIRES: 26 x 1.38 air; CHAINGUARD: chrome; HANDLEBARS: chrome touring; PEDALS: reflector; SADDLE: racing; Touring bag; PRICE: not specified.

IVERSON LADIES' 3-SPEED TRIGGER
FRAME: 26 inch; COLOR: lavender; BRAKES: front and rear caliper; GEARS: 3-speed twist grip; FENDERS: chrome; RIMS: chrome; TIRES: 26 x 1.38; CHAINGUARD: chrome; HANDLE-BARS: chrome touring; PEDALS: reflector; SADDLE: flower racing; Touring bag, Flower basket; PRICE: not specified.

MEN'S GRAND SPORT
FRAME: 26 inch; COLOR: white; BRAKES: front and rear caliper; GEARS: 10-speed; FENDERS: chrome; RIMS: chrome; TIRES: 26 x 1.38; CHAINGUARD: chrome disc; HANDLEBARS: taped and plugged racing; PEDALS: reflectors; SADDLE: padded racing; PRICE: not specified.

LADIES' GRAND SPORT
FRAME: 26 inch; COLOR: white; BRAKES: front and rear caliper; GEARS: 10-speed; FENDERS: chrome; RIMS: chrome; TIRES: 26 x 1.38; CHAINGUARD: chrome disc; HANDLEBARS: taped and plugged racing; PEDALS: reflector; SADDLE: padded racing; PRICE: not specified.

MEN'S GRAND TOURING
FRAME: 26 inch; COLOR: magenta; BRAKES: front and rear caliper; GEARS: 5-speed; FENDERS: chrome; RIMS: chrome; TIRES: 26 x 1.38; CHAINGUARD: chrome disc; HANDLEBARS: chrome touring; PEDALS: reflector; SADDLE: black racing; Touring bag; PRICE: not specified.

IVERSON LADIES' GRAND TOURING
FRAME: 26 inch; COLOR: magenta; BRAKES: front and rear caliper; GEARS: 5-speed; FENDERS: chrome; RIMS: chrome; TIRES: 26 x 1.38; CHAINGUARD: chrome disc; HANDLEBARS: chrome touring; PEDALS: reflector; SADDLE: racing; Flower basket; PRICE: not specified.

IVERSON UNICYCLE
FRAME: 18 inch; COLOR: Ruby Red; TIRE: semi-pneumatic; WHEEL: plated, riveted spoke; SADDLE: contour; PRICE: not specified.

PROFESSIONAL STYLE CYCLE
FRAME: 24 inch; COLOR: chrome plated; TIRE: whitewall; WHEEL: professional; SADDLE: not specified; PRICE: not specified.

DELUXE UNICYCLE
FRAME: 20 inch; COLOR: chrome; TIRE: 20 x 1.75 whitewall pneumatic; WHEEL: tangent spoke; SADDLE: deluxe ridged bucket; Adjustable seat post; PRICE: not specified.

THE MURRAY OHIO MANUFACTURING COMPANY,
Nashville, Tennessee 37204

CROSS COUNTRY
FRAME: 23 inch; COLOR: white with multi-color trim; BRAKE: center pull caliper; GEARS: 10-speed; FENDERS: none; RIMS: not specified; TIRES: 27 x 1-1/4 inch; CHAINGUARD: not specified; HANDLEBARS: plugged racer type; PEDALS: rattrap; SADDLE: racing style spring; PRICE: not specified.

MURRAY PHOENIX 27
FRAME: 21 inch; COLOR: metallic olive with white trim; BRAKES: side pull caliper; GEARS' 10-speed; FENDERS: none; RIMS: tubular; TIRES: 27 x 1-1/4 inch; CHAINGUARD: not specified; HANDLEBARS: racing; PEDALS: rattrap; SADDLE: racing; PRICE: not specified.

PHONEIX 26
FRAME: 26 inch; COLOR: silver-gray with red trim; BRAKES: hooded caliper; GEARS: 10-pseed; FENDERS: none; RIMS: tubular; TIRES: 26 x 1-3/8 inch; CHAINGUARD: not specified; HANDLEBARS: plugged racer style; PEDALS: rattrap; SADDLE: black racing with reflector; PRICE: not specified.

PHOENIX 24
FRAME: 24 inch; COLOR: silver-gray with red trim; GEARS: 10-speed; FENDERS: none; RIMS: tubular; TIRES: 24 x 1-3/8 inch; CHAINGUARD: not specified.; HANDLEBARS: plugged racing; BRAKES: hooded caliper; PEDALS: rattrap; SADDLE: black racing; PRICE: not specified.

FREEWHEELER
FRAME: 26 inch; COLOR: yellow with black trim; BRAKES: hooded caliper; GEARS: 10-speed; FENDERS: none; RIMS: not specified; TIRES: not specified; CHAINGUARD: chrome; HANDLEBARS: racing, plugged; PEDALS: rattrap; SADDLE: black channel top racing saddle; PRICE: not specified.

MURRAY MEN'S LEISURE TOUR
FRAME: 23 inch; COLOR: metallic light gold finish with multi-colored trim; BRAKES: caliper; GEARS: 10-speed; FENDERS: full length with rear reflector; RIMS: tubular; TIRES: 27 x 1-1/4 inch; CHAINGUARD: not specified; HANDLEBARS: tour comfort; PEDALS: ball bearing; SADDLE: not specified; PRICE: not specified.

LADIES' LEISURE TOUR
FRAME: 19 inch; COLOR: metallic gold with multi-colored decals; GEARS: 10-speed; BRAKES: caliper; FENDERS: full length with rear reflectors; RIMS: tubular; TIRES: 27 x 1-1/14 inch; CHAINGUARD: not specified; HANDLEBARS: tourist comfort; PEDALS: ball bearing; SADDLE: black comfort saddle; PRICE: not specified.

MEN'S ALPINE 5-SPEED
FRAME: 21 inch; COLOR: shamrock green with multi-colored decals; BRAKES: caliper; GEARS: 5-speed; FENDERS: full length chrome; RIMS: tubular; TIRES: 26 x 1-3/8 inch; CHAINGUARD: chrome; HANDLEBARS: tourist comfort; PEDALS: ball bearing; SADDLE: black comfort tourist; PRICE: not specified.

LADIES' ALPINE 5-SPEED
FRAME: 19 inch; COLOR: blue with multi-colored decals; BRAKES: caliper; GEARS: 5-speed; FENDERS: full length crome; RIMS: chrome tubular; TIRES: 26 x 1-3/8 inch; CHAINGUARD: chrome with red trim; HANDLEBARS: comfort; PEDALS: ball bearing; SADDLE: white; PRICE: not specified.

MURRAY MEN'S 3-SPEED
FRAME: 21 inch; COLOR: white; BRAKES: caliper; GEARS: 3-speed; FENDERS: black with white stripes; RIMS: not specified; TIRES: 26 x 1-3/8 inch; CHAINGUARD: not specified; HANDLE-BARS: touring; PEDALS: ball bearing; SADDLE: black quilted; PRICE: not specified.

MURRAY LADIES' 3-SPEED
FRAME: 19 inch; COLOR: white; BRAKES: caliper; GEARS: 3-speed; FENDRES: magenta with white stripes; RIMS: tubular; TIRES: 26 x 1-3/8 inch; CHAINGUARD: not specified; HANDLE-BARS: touring; PEDALS: ball bearing; SADDLE: quilted deluxe; PRICE: not specified.

MEN'S MONTEREY 3-SPEED
FRAME: 21 inch; COLOR: metallic olive finish with multi-colored decals; GEARS: 3-speed; BRAKES: caliper; FENDERS: full-length chrome with rear reflector; RIMS: chrome tubular; TIRES: 26 x 1-3/8 inch; CHAINGUARD: metallic olive; HANDLEBARS: tour-ing; PEDALS: ball bearing; SADDLE: black; PRICE: not specified.

LADIES' MONTEREY 3-SPEED
FRAME: 19 inch; COLOR: raspberry with multi-colored decals; BRAKES: caliper; GEARS: 3-speed; FENDERS: full length chrome with rear reflector; RIMS: chrome tubular; TIRES: 26 x 1-3/8 inch; CHAINGUARD: not specified; HANDLEBARS: touring com-fort; PEDALS: ball bearing; SADDLE: white vinyl; PRICE: not specified.

MURRAY BOY'S MINI-WEIGHT 3-SPEED
FRAME: 19 inch; COLOR: orange with multi-colored decals; BRAKES: caliper; GEARS: 3-speed; FENDERS: full length chrome with rear reflector; RIMS: tubular; TIRES: 24 x 1-3/8 inch; CHAINGUARD: circular chrome; HANDLEBARS: comfort design; PEDALS: ball bearing; SADDLE: black and white; PRICE: not specified.

GIRL'S MINI-WEIGHT 3-SPEED
FRAME: 17 inch; BRAKES: caliper; GEARS: 3-speed; FENDERS: full length chrome; RIMS: not specified; TIRES: 24 x 1-3/8 inch; CHAINGUARD: circular chrome; HANDLEBARS: comfort; PEDALS: ball bearing; SADDLE: leisure style; PRICE: not specified.

MEN'S LE MANS COASTER
FRAME: 21 inch; COLOR: black with multi-colored decals; BRAKE: coaster; GEARS: single; FENDERS: full length chrome; RIMS: not specified; TIRES: 26 x 1-3/8 inch; CHAINGUARD: black with white panel and red lettering; HANDLEBARS: comfort; PEDALS: ball bearing; SADDLE: black; PRICE: not specified.

LADIES' LE MANS COASTER
FRAME: 19 inch; COLOR: metallic ice-blue with multi-colored decals; BRAKES: coaster; GEARS: single; FENDERS: full length chrome; RIMS: not specified; TIRES: 26 x 1-3/8 inch; CHAINGUARD: ice-blue with white panel and red lettering; HANDLEBARS: comfort; PEDALS: ball bearing; SADDLE: white; PRICE: not specified.

MURRAY BOY'S FEATHERWEIGHT COASTER
FRAME: 16 inch; COLOR: red with multi-colored decals; BRAKES: coaster; GEARS: single; FENDERS: chrome; RIMS: chrome tubular; TIRES: 20 x 1-3/8 inch; CHAINGUARD: chrome circular with red trim; HANDLEBARS: comfort; PEDALS: ball bearing; SADDLE: black and white; PRICE: not specified.

GIRL'S FEATHERWEIGHT COASTER
FRAME: 16 inch; COLOR: competition blue with multi-colored decals; BRAKES: coaster; GEARS: single; FENDERS: full length chrome; RIMS: chrome tubular; TIRES: 20 x 1-3/8 inch; CHAIN-GUARD: circular chrome with blue trim; HANDLEBARS: comfort; PEDALS: ball bearing; SADDLE: white; PRICE: not specified.

BOY'S MARK FOUR ELIMINATOR
FRAME: 20 inch; COLOR: yellow with black trim and multi-colored decals; BRAKES: caliper; GEARS: 5-speed; FENDERS: chrome; RIMS: tubular; TIRES: 20 x 1-3/8 inch; CHAINGUARD: circular with two-color trim; HANDLEBARS: hi-rise; PEDALS: ball bearing; SADDLE: black bucket polo; PRICE: not specified.

BOY'S MARK FOUR ELIMINATOR
FRAME: 20 inch; COLOR: white with blue overspray and multi-colored decals; BRAKES: caliper; GEARS: 3-speed; FENDERS: blue fenders with white stripe; RIMS: tubular; TIRES: 20 x 1-3/8 inch; CHAINGUARD: chrome circular, with blue and white trim; HANDLEBARS: hi-rise; PEDALS: ball bearing; SADDLE: blue bucket polo; PRICE: not specified.

MURRAY BOY'S F-1 ELIMINATOR COASTER
FRAME: 20 inch twin bar; COLOR: blue with lemon-lime overspray; BRAKES: coaster; GEARS: single; FENDERS: chrome; RIMS: channel; TIRES: 20 x 2.125 inch; CHAINGUARD: chrome with yellow and blue panels; HANDLEBARS: hi-rise; PEDALS: ball bearing; SADDLE: yellow glitter polo; PRICE: not specified.

GIRL'S F-1 ELIMINATOR COASTER
FRAME: 20 inch twin bar; COLOR: raspberry with multi-colored decals; BRAKES: coaster; GEARS: single; FENDERS: chrome; RIMS: channel; TIRES: 20 x 1.75 inch; CHAINGUARD: chrome, orange and raspberry with multi-colored decals; HANDLEBARS: hi-rise; PEDALS: ball bearing; SADDLE: flower-power wet look polo; PRICE: not specified.

BOY'S WILDCAT 3
FRAME: 20 inch; COLOR: lemon-lime, with shamrock green overspray; BRAKES: caliper; GEARS: 3-speed; FENDERS: chrome; RIMS: channel; TIRES: 20 x 1.75 inch; CHAINGUARD: not specified; HANDLEBARS: hi-rise; PEDALS: ball bearing; SADDLE: green glitter bucket polo; PRICE: not specified.

GIRL'S BOBBI 3
FRAME: 20 inch; COLOR: light blue with blue overspray and multi-colored decals; BRAKES: caliper; GEARS: 3-speed; FENDERS: chrome; RIMS: channel; TIRES: 20 x 1.75 inch; CHAINGUARD: chrome with blue panel and white lettering; HANDLEBARS: hi-rise; PEDALS: ball bearing; SADDLE: flowered blue glitter; PRICE: not specified.

MURRAY BOY'S WILDCAT 1 COASTER
FRAME: 20 inch; COLOR: red with yellow overspray; BRAKES: front caliper coaster; GEARS: single; FENDERS: chrome; RIMS: channel; TIRES: 20 x 1.75 inch; CHAINGUARD: chrome with red and white trim; HANDLEBARS: hi-rise; PEDALS: ball bearing; SADDLE: red glitter polo; PRICE: not specified.

GIRL'S WILDCAT BOBBI 1 COASTER
FRAME: 20 inch; COLOR: spring green with yellow overspray; BRAKES: coaster; GEARS: single; FENDERS: chrome; RIMS: chrome; TIRES: 20 x 1.75 inch; CHAINGUARD: chrome with yellow and spring green trim; HANDLEBARS: hi-rise; PEDALS: ball bearing; SADDLE: bucket polo flowered wet look; PRICE: not specified.

BOY'S WILDCAT COASTER
FRAME: 20 inch; COLOR: orange; BRAKES: coaster; GEARS: single; FENDERS: chrome; RIMS: chrome; TIRES: 20 x 1.75 inch; CHAINGUARD: chrome; HANDLEBARS: hi-rise; PEDALS: ball bearing; SADDLE: black bucket polo with white rally stripes; PRICE: not specified.

GIRL'S WILDCAT BOBBI COASTER
FRAME: 20 inch; COLOR: metallic magenta; BRAKES: coaster; GEARS: single; FENDERS: chrome; RIMS: chrome; TIRES:20 x 1.75 inch: CHAINGUARD: chrome; HANDLEBARS: hi-rise chrome; PEDALS: ball bearing; SADDLE: white wet look bucket polo; PRICE: not specified.

MURRAY BOY'S COASTER
FRAME: 26 inch; COLOR: black and red with white trim; BRAKES: coaster; GEARS: single; FENDERS: full length chrome; RIMS: chrome; TIRES: 26 x 1.75 inch; CHAINGUARD: red with white trim; HANDLEBARS: comfort; PEDALS: ball bearing; SADDLE: black; PRICE: not specified.

GIRL'S COASTER
FRAME: 26 inch; COLOR: turquoise with white trim; GEARS: single; FENDERS: chrome full length; BRAKES: coaster; RIMS: chrome; TIRES: 26 x 1.75 inch; CHAINGUARD: turquoise with white trim; HANDLEBARS: chrome; PEDALS: ball bearing; SADDLE: white; PRICE: not specified.

BOY'S COASTER
FRAME: 26 inch; COLOR: red; BRAKES: coaster; GEARS: single; FENDERS: chrome; RIMS: chrome; TIRES: 26 x 1.75 inch; CHAINGUARD: not specified; HANDLEBARS: comfort; PEDALS: ball bearing; SADDLE: black and white; PRICE: not specified.

GIRL'S COASTER
FRAME: 26 inch; COLOR: metallic ice blue; BRAKES: coaster; GEARS: single; FENDERS: chrome; RIMS: chrome; TIRES: 26 x 1.75 inch: CHAINGUARD: not specified; HANDLEBARS: comfort; PEDALS: ball bearing; SADDLE: blue glitter; PRICE: not specified.

MURRAY SENIOR CYCLE
FRAME: tricycle; COLOR: blue with white trim and decals;
BRAKES: front caliper; GEARS: 3-speed; FENDERS: full length
chrome; RIMS: not specified; TIRES: 24 x 1.75 inch; CHAIN-
GUARD: blue with white lettering; HANDLEBARS: not specified;
PEDALS: ball bearing; SADDLE: black comfort with reflector;
PRICE: not specified.

SCHWINN BICYCLE COMPANY,
1856 N. Kostner Avenue,
Chicago, Illinois 60639

SCHWINN DELUXE TWINN
FRAME: tandem; COLOR: campus green, burgundy, kool lemon;
BRAKES: front caliper, expander rear; GEARS: 5-speed; FEND-
ERS: chrome; RIMS: not specified; TIRES: 26 x 1-3/8 inch;
CHAINGUARD: not specified; HANDLEBARS: not specified; PED-
ALS: not specified; SADDLE: not specified; PRICE: $150 approx.

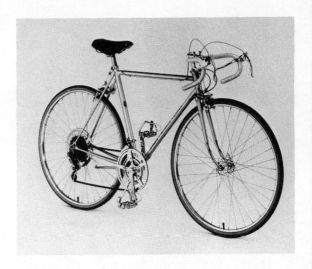

SPORTS TOURER
FRAME: 22 inch; COLOR: kool lemon, sierra brown, opaque green,
opaque blue; BRAKES: caliper; GEARS: 10-speed; FENDERS:
none; RIMS: not specified; TIRES: not specified; CHAINGUARD:
not specified; HANDLEBARS: drop style; PEDALS: not specified;
SADDLE: not specified; PRICE: $200 approx.

SCHWINN SUPER SPORT
FRAME: 22 inch; COLOR: kool lemon, opaque green, and opaque blue; BRAKES: caliper; GEARS: 10-speed; FENDERS: none; RIMS: not specified; TIRES: 27 x 1-1/4 inch; CHAINGUARD: not specified; HANDLEBARS: drop style; PEDALS: not specified; SADDLE: not specified; PRICE: $140 approx.

CONTINENTAL
FRAME: 22 inch; COLOR: kool lemon, sierra brown, burgundy; BRAKES: dual position caliper; GEARS: 10-speed; FENDERS: none; RIMS: steel; TIRES: 27 x 1-1/4 inch; CHAINGUARD: not specified; HANDLEBARS: drop style; PEDALS: not specified; SADDLE: not specified; PRICE: $108 approx.

COLLEGIATE SPORT
FRAME: 20 inch; COLOR: sierra brown, campus green, kool lemon; BRAKES: caliper; GEARS: 5-speed; FENDERS: not specified; RIMS: not specified; TIRES: 26 x 1-3/8 inch; CHAINGUARD: not specified; HANDLEBARS: not specified; PEDALS: not specified; SADDLE: not specified; PRICE: $86 approx.

SPEEDSTER 3-SPEED
FRAME: 17 inch; COLOR: campus green, burgundy; BRAKES: caliper; GEARS: 3-speed; FENDERS: not specified; RIMS: tubular; TIRES: 26 x 1-3/8 inch; CHAINGUARD: not specified; HANDLEBARS: not specified; PEDALS: not specified; SADDLE: cushioned; PRICE: $70 approx.

SCHWINN LADIES' SUPER SPORT
FRAME: 19 inch; COLOR: kool lemon, opaque green, opaque blue; BRAKES: hooded caliper; GEARS: 10-speed; FENDERS: not specified; RIMS: not specified; TIRES: 27 x 1-1/4 inch; CHAIN-GUARD: not specified; HANDLEBARS: drop style; PEDALS: rattrap; SADDLE: racing; PRICE: $140 approx.

VARSITY SPORT
FRAME: 19 inch; COLOR: sierra brown, campus green, kool lemon; BRAKES: dual position caliper; GEARS: 10-speed; FENDERS: none; RIMS: not specified; TIRES: 27 x 1-1/4 inch; CHAIN-GUARD: not specified; HANDLEBARS: drop style; PEDALS: not specified; SADDLE: not specified; PRICE: $93 approx.

LADIES' SUBURBAN
FRAME: 19 inch; COLOR: sierra brown, campus green, burgundy; BRAKES: caliper; GEARS: 10-speed; FENDERS: enameled; RIMS: not specified; TIRES: 27 x 1-1/4 inch; CHAINGUARD: not specified; HANDLEBARS: not specified; PEDALS: not specified; SADDLE: deluxe matress; PRICE: $98 approx.

LADIES' BREEZE
FRAME: 17 inch; COLOR: campus green, burgundy; BRAKES: caliper; GEARS: 3-speed; FENDERS: chrome; plated; RIMS: tubular; TIRES: not specified; CHAINGUARD: not specified; HANDLEBARS: not specified; PEDALS: not specified; SADDLE: two-tone padded; PRICE: $70 approx.

SCHWINN LADIES' COLLEGIATE
FRAME: 21 inch: COLOR: sierra brown, campus green, kool lemon; BRAKES: caliper; GEARS: 5-speed; FENDERS: chrome; RIMS: not specified; TIRES: not specified; CHAINGUARD: not specified; HANDLEBARS: not specified; PEDALS: not specified; SADDLE: foam cushioned; PRICE: $83 aprrox.

TOWN AND COUNTRY TRI-WHEELER
FRAME: tricycle; COLOR: sierra brown, campus green; BRAKES: caliper coaster; GEARS: single; FENDERS: chrome plated; RIMS: not specified; TIRES: not specified; CHAINGUARD: not specified; HANDLEBARS: not specified; PEDALS: not specified; SADDLE: contoured matress; PRICE: $153 approx.

MANTA-RAY
FRAME: 24 inch; COLOR: kool orange, kool lemon, campus green; BRAKES: disc; GEARS: 5- speed; FENDERS: not specified; RIMS: not specified; TIRES: not specified; CHAINGUARD: not specified; HANDLEBARS: not specified; PEDALS: not specified; SADDLE: Sting Ray style; PRICE: $105 approx.

KRATES
FRAME: 20 inch; COLOR: orange krate, lemon peeler, apple krate, pea picker green; BRAKES: front drum, rear disc; GEAR: 5-speed; FENDERS: not specified; RIMS: not specified; TIRES: not specified; CHAINGUARD: not specified; HANDLEBARS: not specified; PEDALS: not specified; SADDLE: bucket with shock absorber; PRICE: $117 approx.

SCHWINN STING-RAY DELUXE
FRAME: 20 inch; COLOR: campus green, kool lemon, flamboyant red; BRAKES: coaster; GEARS: single; FENDERS: chrome plated; RIMS: not specified; TIRES: 20 x 1-3/8 inch; CHAINGUARD: not specified; HANDLEBARS: hi-rise; PEDALS: not specified; SADDLE: bucket; PRICE: $70 approx.

FASTBACK
FRAME: 20 inch; COLOR: kool lemon, kool orange, campus green; BRAKES: caliper; GEARS: 5-speed; FENDERS: not specified; RIMS: not specified; TIRES: 20 x 1-3/8 inch; CHAINGUARD: not specified; HANDLEBARS: adjustable; PEDALS: not specified; SADDLE: adjustable; PRICE: $90 approx.

FAIR LADY
FRAME: 20 inch; COLOR: campus green, kool lemon, burgundy; BRAKES: coaster; GEARS: 3-speed; FENDERS: chrome plated; RIMS: not specified; TIRES: not specified; CHAINGUARD: not specified; HANDLEBARS: hi-rise; PEDALS: not specified; SADDLE: banana; PRICE: $79 approx.

STARDUST
FRAME: 20 inch; COLOR: campus green, kool lemon, burgundy; BRAKES: coaster; GEARS: 3-speed; FENDERS: chrome; RIMS: not specified; TIRES: not specified; CHAINGUARD: not specified; HANDLEBARS: hi-rise; PEDALS: not specified; SADDLE: Sting Ray; PRICE: $83 approx.

SCHWINN TYPHOON
FRAME: variable; COLOR: red or campus green; BRAKES: coaster; GEARS: single; FENDERS: chrome plated; RIMS: tubular; TIRES: 26 x 1-3/4 inch; CHAINGUARD: not specified; SADDLE: not specified; PEDALS: not specified; HANDLEBARS: not specified; PRICE: $60 approx.

HOLLYWOOD
FRAME: variable; COLORS: campus green or burgundy; BRAKES: coaster; GEARS: single; FENDERS: chrome plated; RIMS: tubular; TIRES: 26 inch; CHAINGUARD: not specified; HANDLEBARS: not specified; PEDALS: not specified; SADDLE: two-tone; PRICE: $60 approx.

PIXIE
FRAME: 16 inch; COLORS: campus green, flamboyant red; BRAKES: coaster; GEARS: single; FENDERS: chrome plated; RIMS: not specified; TIRES: 16 inch; CHAINGUARD: not specified; HANDLEBARS: not specified; PEDALS: not specified; SADDLE: not specified; PRICE: $40 approx.

STING-RAY PIXIE
FRAME: 16 inch; COLOR: campus green, kool lemon, flamboyant red; BRAKES: coaster; GEARS: single; FENDERS: not specified; RIMS: not specified; TIRES: 16 x 1-3/4 inch; CHAINGUARD: not specified; HANDLEBARS: Sting-Ray; PEDALS: not specified; SADDLE: adjustable; PRICE: $42 approx.

RALEIGH INDUSTRIES OF AMERICA, INC.,
1168 Commonwealth Avenue, Boston, Massachusetts 02134

PROFESSIONAL MARK 1V
FRAME: Reynolds 531 Tubing, 20½-25½ inch; COLOR: mink silver; GEARS: Campagnolo 10-speed; BRAKES: Campagnolo; FENDERS: none; RIMS: Winmann 293; TIRES: Hutchinson silk; CHAINGUARD: not specified; HANDLEBARS: G.B. Maes alloy embossed; PEDALS: Campagnolo Strada; SADDLE: Brooks professional team special; PRICE: not specified.

PROFESSIONAL TRACK
FRAME: Reynolds 531 tubing, 21, 22, 23, 24, inch; COLOR: team blue; BRAKES: none; GEARS: not specified; FENDERS: none; RIMS: Weinmann 293; TIRES: Hutchinson silk; CHAINGUARD: not specified; HANDLEBARS: Vantoux GB; PEDALS: Campagnolo Pista; SADDLE: Brooks professional team special; PRICE: not specified.

INTERNATIONAL
FRAME: Reynolds 531 tubing, 22½, 23½, 24½ inch; COLOR: champagne and chartruese; BRAKES: Weinmann 999 with quick release hand lever; GEARS: Campagnolo 10-speed; FENDERS: none; RIMS: Weinmann 294; TIRES: Hutchinson; CHAINGUARD: not specified; HANDLEBARS: Maes alloy; PEDALS: Campagnolo Strada; SADDLE: Brooks professional; PRICE: not specified.

GRAN SPORT
FRAME: Reynolds 531 tubing, 21½, 22½, 23½, 24½, 25½ inch; COLOR: white and blue; BRAKES: Weinmann 999 with quick release handlever; GEARS: Simplex 10-speed; FENDERS: none; TIRES: 27 x 1¼ inch; CHAINGUARD: not specified; HANDLEBARS: GB Raddoneur; PEDALS: Atom 700; SADDLE: Brooks B15; PRICE: not specified.

RALEIGH SUPER COURSE
FRAME: Reynolds 531 tubing, 21½, 23½, 25½ inch; COLOR: coffee, bronze-green; BRAKES: Weinmann 999 with quick release handlever; GEARS: Simplex 10-speed; FENDERS: none; RIMS: alloy; TIRES: 27¼ x 1¼; CHAINGUARD: not specified; HANDLEBARS: Maes; PEDALS: Atom 440; SADDLE: Brooks B15; PRICE: not specified.

GRAND PRIX
FRAME: 21½, 23½, 25½ inch; COLOR: white/black, blue/black, red/black, bronze-green/black; BRAKES: Weinmann 999; GEARS: Simplex 10-speed; FENDERS: none; RIMS: special lightweight; TIRES: 27 x 1¼ inch gumwall; CHAINGUARD: not specified; HANDLEBARS: Maes; PEDALS: Atom 440; SADDLE: Wrights W3N; PRICE: not specified.

RECORD
FRAME: 19½, 21½, 23½, 25½ inch; COLOR: blue/black, bronze-green/white, orange/white, yellow/black; BRAKES: Weinmann center pull; GEARS: Huret-Allvit 10-speed; FENDERS: none; RIMS: special lightweight; TIRES: 27 x 1¼ inch gumwall; CHAINGUARD: not specified; HANDLEBARS: Maes; PEDALS: rattrap; SADDLE: leather-racing (gent's) Mattress (ladies'); PRICE: not specified.

GRAND PRIX 24
FRAME: 18 inch; COLOR: red, blue; BRAKES: Weinmann; GEARS: Simplex 10-speed; FENDERS: none; RIMS: Steel; TIRES: 24 x 1-13/8 inch; CHAINGUARD: not specified; HANDLEBARS: GB Maes alloy; PEDALS: rattrap; SADDLE: Brooks; PRICE: not specified.

NEXUS INTERNATIONAL
5613 Main,
Buffalo, New York 14221

NEXUS EAGLE
FRAME: 20½ (ladies') 23 inch mens'; COLOR: not specified; BRAKES: caliper; GEARS: 5 or 10-speed; FENDERS: none; RIMS: not specified; TIRES: not specified; CHAINGUARD: not specified; HANDLEBARS: not specified; PEDALS: not specified; SADDLE: ultra soft; PRICE: $69 to $89 approx.

NEXUS SPIRIT, SABRE
FRAME: not specified; COLOR: not specified; BRAKES: caliper; GEARS: 5-speed; FENDERS: none; RIMS: not specified; TIRES: not specified; CHAINGUARD: not specified; HANDLEBARS: not specified; PEDALS: not specified; SADDLE: not specified; PRICE: $109 approx.

WESTERN AUTO SUPPLY COMPANY,
2107 Grand Avenue, Kansas City, Missouri 64108

BOY'S RACER
FRAME: 26 inch; COLOR: orange or blue; BRAKES: front and rear synchron caliper brakes with safety extension lever; GEARS: 10-speed; FENDERS: not specified; RIMS: not specified; TIRES: 26 x 1-3/8 inches; CHAINGUARD: not specified; HANDLEBARS: Maes; PEDALS: rattrap; SADDLE: racing style black; PRICE: not specified.

MEN'S RACER
FRAME: 23 inches lightweight; COLOR: brilliant yellow; BRAKES: center-pull caliper with safety extension levers; GEARS: 10-speed; FENDERS: not specified; RIMS: chrome; TIRES: 27 inches gum wall; CHAINGUARD: not specified; HANDLEBARS: Maes; PEDALS: rattrap; SADDLE: racing; PRICE: not specified.

DELUXE RACER
FRAME: 23 inches; COLOR: not specified; BRAKES: Center pull caliper; GEARS: 10-speed; FENDERS: not specified; RIMS: chrome; TIRES: 27 inches gum walls; CHAINGUARD: not specified; HANDLEBARS: Maes; PEDALS: rattrap; SADDLE: black racing; PRICE: not specified.

1 Speed

1 Speed Western

24 in. Mark 3 Racer

49^{95}

WESTERN AUTO BOY'S RACER
FRAME: 24 inch; COLOR: competition white; BRAKES: coaster; GEARS: single; FENDERS: splash guards; RIMS: chrome; TIRES: 24 x 1 3/8 inch; CHAINGUARD: not specified; HANDLEBARS: racing style; PEDALS: not specified; SADDLE: racing; PRICE: not specified.

MEN'S TOURIST
FRAME: 23 inch; COLOR: coffee brown; BRAKES: dual synchron caliper hand brakes; GEARS: 10-speed; FENDERS: full painted with white stripe; RIMS: chrome; TIRES: 27 inch gum walls; CHAINGUARD: not specified; HANDLEBARS: tourist; PEDALS: not specified; SADDLE: deluxe spring; PRICE: not specified.

Our Finest Women's Bike only 75^{95}

LADIES' TOURIST
FRAME: 21 inch; COLOR: beige with chrome trim; BRAKES: dual synchron safety caliper; GEARS: 10-speed; FENDERS: full painted with contrasting stripe; RIMS: chrome; TIRES: 27 x 1 1/4 inch; CHAINGUARD: not specified; HANDLEBARS: tourist; PEDALS: not specified; SADDLE: deluxe spring; PRICE: not specified.

MEN'S 5-SPEED TOURING
FRAME: 21 inch; COLOR: sierra green; BRAKES: front and rear Synchron caliper; GEARS: 5-speed; FENDERS: not specified; RIMS: chrome; TIRES: 26 x 1/8 inch; CHAINGUARD: not specified; HANDLEBARS: touring style; PEDALS: not specified; SADDLE: deluxe; PRICE: not specified.

WESTERN AUTO MEN'S 3-SPEED TOURING

FRAME: 26 inch; COLOR: yellow; BRAKES: Synchron caliper; GEARS: 3-speed; FENDERS: full painted; RIMS: not specified; TIRES: 26 x 1 3/8 inch; CHAINGUARD: not specified; HANDLEBARS: not specified; PEDALS: ball bearing; SADDLE: black; PRICE: not specified.

1 Speed

26 in. Tourister

$51⁹⁵

MEN'S 1-SPEED TOURING

FRAME: 21 inch; COLOR: flamboyant red; BRAKES: coaster; GEARS: single; FENDERS: full painted with white stripes; RIMS: chrome; TIRES: 26 x 1 3/8 inch; CHAIN-GUARD: not specified; HANDLEBARS: tourist style; PEDALS: ball bearings; SADDLE: deluxe; PRICE: not specified.

Remember Our Easy Gift Terms!

$70⁹⁵

LADIES' 5-SPEED

FRAME: 21 inch; COLOR: sierra green; BRAKES: dual Synchron; GEARS: 5-speed; FENDERS: full painted with gold stripes; RIMS: chrome; TIRES: 26 x 1 3/8 inch; CHAINGUARD: not specified; HANDLEBARS: touring; PEDALS: not specified; SADDLE: deluxe black; PRICE: not specified.

GIRLS' HI-RISE

FRAME: 24 inch; COLOR: lemon-lime; BRAKES: Bendix coaster; GEARS: single; FENDERS: chrome; RIMS: chrome; TIRES: 24 x 1 3/8 inch; CHAINGUARD:not specified; HANDLEBARS: chrome hi-rise; PEDALS: not specified; SADDLE: regular; PRICE: not specified.

WESTERN AUTO LADIES' 3-SPEED TOURING
FRAME: 21 inch; COLOR: blue; BRAKES: caliper on both wheels; GEARS: 3 speed; FENDERS: full painted; RIMS: full painted; TIRES: 26 x 1-3/8 inch; CHAINGUARD: not specified; HANDLEBARS: not specified; PEDALS: ball bearing; SADDLE: black; PRICE: not specified.

LADIES' 1-SPEED TOURING
FRAME: 21 inch; COLOR: flamboyant blue; BRAKES: coaster; GEARS: single; FENDERS: full painted with white stripes; RIMS: chrome; TIRES 26 inch; CHAINGUARD: not specified; HANDLEBARS: tourist; PEDALS: ball bearing; SADDLE: deluxe; PRICE: not specified.

65^{95}

GIRL'S LIGHTWEIGHT
FRAME: 24 inch; COLOR: flamboyant lilac mist; BRAKES: synchron caliper front and rear; GEARS: 3-speed; FENDERS: chrome; RIMS: chrome; TIRES: 24 x 1 3/8 inch; CHAINGUARD: chrome; HANDLEBARS: hi-rise; PEDALS: not specified; SADDLE: flowered; PRICE: not specified.

Deluxe Eliminator

53^{45}

BOY'S ELIMINATOR
FRAME: 20 inch; COLOR: flamboyant blue; BRAKES: caliper coaster; GEARS: single; FENDERS: chrome; RIMS: chrome; TIRES: front 20 x 1.75, rear 10 x 2.125 slick; CHAINGUARD: chrome; HANDLEBARS: hi-rise; PEDALS: not specified; SADDLE: deluxe; PRICE: not specified.

WESTERN AUTO BOY'S HI-RISE
FRAME: 20 inch; COLOR: shamrock green; BRAKES: caliper; GEARS: 3-speed; FENDERS: chrome; RIMS: chrome; TIRES: 20 x 1.75; CHAINGUARD: chrome; HANDLEBARS: hi-rise; PEDALS: not specified; SADDLE: vinyl; PRICE: not specified.

BOY'S BUZZ
FRAME: 20 inch; COLOR: magenta; BRAKES: coaster; GEARS: single; FENDERS: chrome; RIMS: chrome; TIRES: 20 x 1.75 front, 20 x 2.125 rear; CHAINGUARD: chrome; HANDLEBARS: hi-rise; PEDALS: not specified; SADDLE: two-tone vinyl; PRICE: not specified.

GIRL'S BUZZ
FRAME: 20 inch; COLOR: magenta; BRAKES: coaster; GEARS: single; FENDERS: chrome; RIMS: chrome; TIRES: 20 x 1.75; CHAINGUARD: chrome; HANDLE-BARS: hi-rise; PEDALS: not specified; SADDLE: vinyl; PRICE: not specified.

GIRL'S BUZZ
FRAME: 20 inch; COLOR: white enamel; BRAKES: coaster; GEARS: single; FENDERS: blue; RIMS: white; TIRES: 20 x 1.75; CHAINGUARD: blue; HANDLEBARS: hi-rise; PEDALS: not specified; SADDLE: vinyl; PRICE: Not specified.

GOBBY MANUFACTURING, INCORPORATED, P.O. Box 274, Glendale, Arizona

HEAVY DUTY INDUSTRIAL TRYKE
FRAME: 1 and 1 1/2 inch, 14 gauge welded steel tubing; COLOR: not specified; BRAKES: heavy duty front drum, caliper; GEARS: single; FENDERS: not specified; RIMS: heavy duty; TIRES: heavy duty with puncture resistant tubes; CHAINGUARD: not specified; HANDLEBARS: heavy duty; PEDALS: industrial; SADDLE: industrial; PRICE: $249 approx.

VILLAGER "3" ADULT TRYKE
FRAMES: 20, 24, and 26 inch middleweight; COLORS: red, blue, yellow, orange; BRAKES: front caliper; GEARS: single; FENDERS: not specified; RIMS: not specified; TIRES: 20, 24 and 26 inches; CHAINGUARD: not specified; HANDLEBARS: hi-rise; PEDALS: not specified; SADDLE: wide western. PRICE: $119 approx.

WESTERN AUTO GIRL'S ELIMINATOR
FRAME: 20 inch; COLOR: blue; BRAKES: coaster; GEARS: single; FENDERS: chrome; RIMS: chrome; TIRES: 20 x 1.75; CHAINGUARD: chrome; HANDLEBARS: hi-rise; PEDALS: ball bearing; SADDLE: vinyl; PRICE: Not specified.

ATLANTIC RICHFIELD CORPORATION, P. O. Box 73001, Atlanta, Georgia 30350

ARCO GRAND PRIX
FRAME: 21 or 23 inch; COLOR: lemon; BRAKES: dual-action; GEARS: 10-speed Hansen-X Derailleur; FENDERS: not specified; RIMS: not specified; TIRES: not specified; CHAINGUARD: lightweight chrome; HANDLEBARS: vinyl wrapped, drop-style; PEDALS: sure-grip; SADDLE: padded foam rubber; PRICE: not specified.

CYCLE PRODUCTS, INCORPORATED, 451 – 3rd Street, S.E., Largo, Florida 33540

ADULT 3-WHEELER EXPLORER
FRAME: 20, 24, 26 inch; COLOR: grabber blue, orange; BRAKES: caliper; GEARS: 3-speed; FENDERS: not specified; RIMS: not specified; TIRES: 24 inch; CHAINGUARD: not specified; HANDLEBARS: not specified; PEDALS: not specified; SADDLE: not specified; PRICE: $147 approx.

CHAIN BIKE CORPORATION,
350 Beach 79th Street, Rockaway Beach, New York 11693

ROSS CONVERTIBLE TANK
FRAME: 16 inch; COLOR: raspberry; BRAKE: coaster; GEARS: single; FENDERS: painted; RIMS: chrome plated; TIRES: 16 inch; CHAINGUARD: deluxe; HANDLEBARS: regulation; PEDALS: ball bearing; PRICE: not specified.

ROSS DELUXE CONVERTIBLE TANK
FRAME: 16 inch; COLOR: raspberry; BRAKE: coaster; GEARS: single; RIMS: chrome plated; TIRES: whiteline 16 x 1.75 inch tube; CHAINGUARD: deluxe; HANDLEBARS: regualtion; PEDALS: ball bearing reflectorized; SADDLE: two-tone spring; PRICE: not specified.

ROSS DELUXE FOUR BAR CANTILEVER
FRAME: 16 inch; COLOR: avocado; BRAKE: coaster; GEARS: single; RIMS: chrome plated; FENDERS: chrome plated; TIRES: 16 x 1.75 inch; CHAINGUARD: Barracuda Jr.; HANDLEBARS: Jr. hi-rise; PEDALS: ball bearing reflectorized; PRICE: not specified.

ROSS DELUXE
FRAME: 16 inch 3 bar frame; COLOR: raspberry; BRAKE: coaster; GEARS: single; FENDERS: chrome plated; RIMS: chrome plated; TIRES: 16 x 1.75 inch; CHAINGUARD: Barracuda Jr; PEDALS: ball bearing; PRICE: not specified.

ROSS CONVERTIBLE TANK
FRAME: 20 inch; COLOR: candy apple red; BRAKE: coaster; GEARS: single; FENDERS: painted; RIMS: chrome plated; TIRES: 20 x 1.75 inch; CHAINGUARD: deluxe; HANDLEBARS: regulation; PEDALS: ball bearing; PRICE: not specified.

ROSS POLOBIKE JR. CONVERTIBLE
FRAME: 20 inch; COLOR: avocado; BRAKE: coaster; GEARS: single; FENDERS: chrome plated; RIMS: chrome plated; TIRES: gran tour 20 x 1.75 inch; CHAINGUARD: polobike; PEDALS: ball bearing; PRICE: not specified.

ROSS DELUXE CONVERTIBLE TANK
FRAME: 20 inch; COLOR: blue; BRAKE: coaster; GEARS: single; FENDERS: chrome plated; RIMS: chrome plated; TIRES: 20 x 1.75 inch; CHAINGUARD: deluxe; HANDLEBARS: regulation; PEDALS: ball bearing; PRICE: not specified.

ROSS DELUXE CONVERTIBLE TANK
FRAME: 20 inch; COLOR: white, raspberry; BRAKE: coaster; GEARS: none; FENDERS: chrome plated; RIMS: chrome plated; TIRES: 20 x 1.75 inch; CHAINGUARD: delxue; PEDALS: ball bearing; SADDLE: daisy pattern, mattress; PRICE: not specified.

ROSS POLOBIKE
FRAME: 20 inch, three bar frame; COLOR: corn silk; BRAKE: coaster; GEARS: single; FENDERS: painted; RIMS: painted; TIRES: 20 x 1.75 inch; CHAINGUARD: polobike; HANDLE-BARS: hi-rise; PEDALS: ball bearing; SADDLE: contour; PRICE: not specified.

ROSS GIRL'S POLOBIKE
FRAME: 20 inch; COLOR: white, blue; BRAKE: coaster; GEARS: single; FENDERS: painted; RIMS: painted; TIRES: 20 x 1.75 inch; CHAINGUARD: polobike; HANDLEBARS: hi-rise; PEDALS: ball bearing; SADDLE: contour; PRICE: not specified.

ROSS BOY'S BARRACUDA
FRAME: 20 inch polobike; COLOR: gold; BRAKE: coaster; GEARS: single; FENDERS: chrome plated; RIMS: chrome plated; TIRES: 20 x 1.75 inch; CHAINGUARD: polobike; HANDLE-BARS: hi-rise; PEDALS: ball bearing; SADDLE: Fisher, silver glitter; PRICE: not specified.

ROSS GIRL'S POLOBIKE
FRAME: 20 inch three bar; COLOR: raspberry; BRAKE: coaster; GEARS: single; FENDERS: chrome plated; RIMS: chrome plated; TIRES: 20 x 1.75 inch; CHAINGUARD: polobike; HANDLEBARS: hi-rise; PEDALS: ball bearing; SADDLE: Fisher, flower pattern; PRICE: not specified.

ROSS GIRL'S CBC
FRAME: 20 inch three bar; COLOR: yellow; BRAKE: Bendix coaster; GEARS: single; FENDERS: chrome plated; RIMS: chrome plated; TIRES: front 20 x 1.75, rear 20 x 2.125 inch; CHAIN-GUARD: barracuda; HANDLBARS: hi-rise; PEDALS: ball bearing; SADDLE: Fisher, flower pattern; PRICE: not specified.

ROSS PACER
FRAME: 20 inch; COLOR: cognac; BRAKE: Bendix coaster; GEARS: single; FENDERS: chrome plated, flared; RIMS: chrome plated; TIRES: front, 20 x 1.75, rear 20 x 2.125 inch; CHAINGUARD: Apollo; HANDLEBARS: hi-rise; PEDALS: ball bearing; SADDLE: Apollo-White; PRICE: not spcified.

ROSS BOY'S APOLLO
FRAME: 20 inch; COLOR: cognac; BRAKES: front and rear caliper; GEARS: Shimano 3-speed with G.T. stick console; FENDERS: chrome plated, flared; RIMS: chrome plated; TIRES: front, gran tour 20 x 1.75, rear, 20 x 2.125 inch; CHAINGUARD: chrome disc; HANDLEBARS: hi-rise; PEDALS: ball bearing; SADDLE: white Apollo with rear safety reflector; PRICE: not specified.

ROSS GIRL'S CBC
FRAME: 20 inch three bar; COLOR: apple green; BRAKE: front and rear caliper; GEARS: Shimano 3-speed with twist grip; FENDERS: chrome plated, flared; RIMS: chrome plated; TIRES: front, 20 x 1.75, rear, 20 x 2.125 inch stud; CHAINGUARD: barracuda; HANDLEBARS: hi-rise; PEDALS: ball bearing; SADDLE: Fisher, flower pattern; PRICE: not specified.

ROSS APOLLO CBC 3-SPEED
FRAME: 20 inch; COLOR: yellow; BRAKE: front and rear caliper; GEARS: Shimano 3-speed stick control; FENDERS: chrome plated, flared; RIMS: chrome plated; TIRES: front, 20 x 1.75, rear, 20 x 2.125 inch; CHAINGUARD: chrome disc; HANDLEBARS: hi-rise; PEDALS: ball bearing; SADDLE: black Apollo with rear safety reflector; PRICE: not specified.

ROSS APOLLO CBC 5-SPEED
FRAME: 20 inch; COLOR: black; BRAKE: front and rear caliper; GEARS: Shimano 5-speed, stick control; FENDERS: chrome plated, flared; RIMS: chrome plated; TIRES: front, 20 x 1.75, rear, 20 x 2.125 inch; CHAINGUARD: chrome disc; HANDLEBARS: hi-rise; PEDALS: ball bearing; SADDLE: white Apollo; PRICE: not specified.

ROSS BARRACUDA
FRAME: 20 inch; COLOR: avocado; BRAKE: front and rear caliper; GEARS: Shimano 3-speed stick console; FENDERS: chrome plated; RIMS: chrome plated; TIRES: front, 20 x 1.75; rear, 20x 2.125"; CHAINGUARD: barracuda 3; HANDLEBARS: hi-rise; PEDALS: ball bearing; SADDLE: Fisher silver glitter; PRICE: not specified.

ROSS BOY'S BARRACUDA
FRAME: 20 inch full length; COLOR: gold; BRAKE: front and rear caliper; GEARS: Shimano 3-speed stick console; FENDERS: chrome plated, flared; RIMS: chrome plated; TIRES: front, 20 x 1.75, rear, 20 x 2.125 inch; CHAINGUARD: barracuda 3; HANDLEBARS: hi-rise; PEDALS: ball bearing; SADDLE: Fisher silver glitter; PRICE: not specified.

ROSS BOY'S PACER CBC
FRAME: 20 inch; COLOR: bronze, green; BRAKES: front and rear caliper; GEARS' Shimano 5-speed eagle derailleur stick console; FENDERS: chrome plated, flared; RIMS: chrome plated; TIRES: front, 20 x 1.75, rear, 20 x 2.125 inch; CHAINGUARD: chrome disc; HANDLEBAR: hi-rise; PEDALS: ball bearing; SADDLE: Fisher silver glitter; PRICE: not specified.

ROSS BOY'S CANTILEVER MIDDLEWEIGHT
FRAME: 20 inch four bar; COLOR: candy apple red; BRAKE: coaster; GEARS: single; FENDERS: painted; RIMS: chrome plated; TIRES: front black 26 x 1.75, rear, 26 x 1.75 inch; CHAINGUARD: deluxe; HANDLBARS: central park style; PEDALS: ball bearing; SADDLE: Mesinger; PRICE: not specified.

ROSS CENTRAL PARK
FRAME: 24 inch four bar; COLOR: avocado; BRAKE: coaster; GEARS: single; FENDERS: chrome plated, flared; RIMS: chrome plated; TIRES: 24 x 1-3/8 inch; CHAINGUARD chrome disc; HANDLEBARS: central park; PEDALS: ball bearing; SADDLE: lightweight; PRICE: not specified.

ROSS BOY'S CENTRAL PARK
FRAME: 24 inch four bar; COLOR: avocado; BRAKE: front and rear caliper; GEARS: Shimano 3-speed twist grip control; FENDERS: chrome plated, flared; RIMS: chrome plated; TIRES: 24 x 1-3/8 inch; CHAINGUARD: chrome disc; HANDLEBARS: new central park style; PEDALS: ball bearing; SADDLE: lightweight; PRICE: not specified.

ROSS GIRL'S CENTRAL PARK
FRAME: 24 inch three bar; COLOR: blue; BRAKE: coaster; GEARS: single; FENDERS: chrome plated; RIMS: chrome; TIRES: 24 x 1-3/8 inch; CHIANGUARD: chrome; HANDLEBARS: central park; PEDALS: ball bearing; SADDLE: lightweight; PRICE: not specified.

ROSS GIRL'S CENTRAL PARK
FRAME: 24 inch three bar; COLOR: yellow; BRAKE: front and rear caliper; GEARS' Shimano 3-speed twist grip control; FENDERS: chrome plated, flared; RIMS: chrome plated; TIRES: 24 x 1-3/8 inch; CHAINGUARD: chrome disc; HANDLEBARS: new central park style; PEDALS: ball bearing; SADDLE: lightweight; PRICE: not specified.

ROSS MEN'S DIAMOND FRAME
FRAME: 21 inch; COLOR: blue; BRAKE: coaster; GEARS: single; FENDERS: painted, lightweight, RIMS: chrome plated; TIRES: 26 x 1-3/8 inch; CHAINGUARD: lightweight, painted; HANDLEBARS: Wald, northroad style; PEDALS: ball bearing; SADDLE: lightweight; PRICE: not specified.

ROSS LADIES' DIAMOND FRAME
FRAME: 20 inch; COLOR: blue; BRAKE: coaster; GEARS: single; FENDERS: painted, lightweight; RIMS: chrome plated; TIRES: 26 x 1-3/8 inch; CHAINGUARD: lightweight, painted; HANDLEBARS: Wald, northroad style; PEDALS: ball bearing; SADDLE: lightweight; PRICE: not specified.

ROSS MEN'S DIAMOND FRAME
FRAME: 21 inch; COLOR: cognac; BRAKE: front and rear caliper; GEARS: Shimano 3-speed trigger control; FENDERS: painted; RIMS: chrome plated; TIRES: 26 x 1-3/8 inch; CHAINGUARD: lightweight, painted; HANDLEBARS: Wald, northroad style; PEDALS: ball bearing; SADDLE: lightweight; PRICE: not specified.

ROSS MEN'S DIAMOND
FRAME: 23 inch; COLOR: black; BRAKE: front and rear caliper; GEARS: Shimano 3-speed trigger control; FENDERS: painted, lightweight; RIMS: chrome plated; TIRES: 26 x 1-3/8; CHAINGUARD: lightweight, painted; HANDLEBARS: Wald, northroad style; PEDALS: ball bearing; SADDLE: lightweight; PRICE: not specified.

ROSS DIAMOND FRAME CBC
FRAME: 20 inch; COLOR: blue; BRAKE: front and rear caliper; GEARS: Shimano 3-speed trigger control; FENDERS: painted, lightweight; RIMS: chrome plated; TIRES: 26 x 1-3/8 inch; CHAINGUARD: lightweight, painted; HANDLEBARS: Wald, northroad style; PEDALS: ball bearing; SADDLE: lightweight; PRICE: not specified.

ROSS MEN'S DIAMOND
FRAME: 21 inch; COLOR: bronze, green; BRAKE: front and rear caliper; GEARS: Shimano 3-speed trigger control; FENDERS: chrome plated, lightweight; RIMS: chrome plated; TIRES: 26 x 1-3/8 inch; CHAINGUARD: lightweight, painted; HANDLEBAR: Wald, northroad style; PEDALS: ball bearing; SADDLE: lightweight; PRICE: not specified.

ROSS DIAMOND DELUXE
FRAME: 20 inch; COLOR: white; BRAKE: front and rear caliper; GEARS: Shimano 3-speed trigger control; RIMS: chrome plated; TIRES: 26 x 1-3/8 inch; CHAINGUARD: lightweight, painted; HANDLEBARS: Wald, northroad style; PEDALS: ball bearing; SADDLE: Mesinger lightweight; PRICE: not specified.

ROSS MEN'S DIAMOND 5-SPEED
FRAME: 21 inch; COLOR: yellow; BRAKE: front and rear caliper; GEARS: Shimano 5-speed eagle derailleur with stem shifter; FENDERS: chrome plated, lightweight; RIMS: chrome plated; TIRES: 26 x 1-3/8 inch; CHAINGUARD: chrome disc; HANDLEBARS: Wald, northroad style; PEDALS: ball bearing; SADDLE: Mesinger; PRICE: not specified.

ROSS LADIES' DIAMOND 5-SPEED
FRAME: 20 inch; COLOR: yellow; BRAKE: front and rear caliper; GEARS: Shimano 5-speed eagle derailleur with shifter; FENDERS: chrome plated, lightweight; RIMS: chrome plated; TIRES: 26 x 1-3/8 inch; CHAINGUARD: chrome disc; HANDLEBARS: Wald, northroad style; PEDALS: ball bearing; SADDLE: Mesinger, black; PRICE: not specified.

ROSS MEN'S SPEED RACER
FRAME: 21 inch; COLOR: gold; BRAKE: side pull caliper brakes with Yoshikawa hooded levers; GEARS: 10-speed; FENDERS: none; RIMS: chrome plated; TIRES: 26 x 1-3/8 inch; CHAINGUARD: chrome disc; HANDLEBARS: Maes bend; PEDALS: rattrap; SADDLE: Mesinger black, molded racing; PRICE: not specified.

ROSS MEN'S 10-SPEED RACER
FRAME: 21 inch; COLOR: cognac; BRAKE: side pull caliper with hooded levers; GEARS: Shimano 10-speed; FENDERS: none; RIMS: chrome; TIRES: 27 x 1-1/4 inch; CHAINGUARD: chrome disc; HANDLEBARS: Maes bend; PEDALS: rattrap; SADDLE: Mesinger black, molded racing; PRICE: not specified.

ROSS RACER
FRAME: 20 inch; COLOR: white; BRAKE: side pull caliper; GEARS: Shimano eagle 10-speed; FENDERS: none; RIMS: chrome plated; TIRES: 27 x 1-1/4 inch; CHAINGUARD: chrome disc; HANDLEBARS: Wald; PEDALS: rattrap; SADDLE: white, PRICE: not specified.

ROSS EUROSPORT
FRAME: 23 inch; COLOR: bronze, green; BRAKE: side pull caliper; GEARS: Shimano eagle 10-speed; FENDERS: none; RIMS: chrome; TIRES: 27 x 1-1/4 inch; CHAINGUARD: chrome disc; HANDLEBARS: Maes bend; PEDALS: rattrap; SADDLE: racing; PRICE: not specified.

ROSS EUROSPORT
FRAME: 21 inch; COLOR: cognac; BRAKE: diacompe center pull caliper; GEARS: 10-speed; FENDERS: none; RIMS: chrome plated; TIRES: 27 x 1-1/4 inch; CHAINGUARD: chrome disc; HANDLE-BARS: Maes bend; PEDALS: rattrap; SADDLE: deluxe racing; PRICE: not specified.

ROSS MEN'S EUPOSPORT X
FRAME: 23 inch; COLOR: white; BRAKE: diacompe center pull caliper; GEARS: Shimano eagle 10-speed; FENDERS: none; RIMS: chrome plated; TIRES: 27 x 1-1/4 inch; CHAINGUARD: chrome disc; HANDLEBARS: Maes bend; PEDALS: rattrap; SADDLE: Mesinger deluxe racing; PRICE: not specified.

LAWEE, INC.
531 W. 15th Street,
Long Beach, California

NOBLY
FRAME: Light steel tubing; COLOR: not specified; BRAKES: Weinmann side pull alloy; GEARS: 10-speed; FENDERS: not specified; RIMS: steel; TIRES: amber, 27 x 1¼ inch; CHAIN-GUARD: not specified; HANDLEBARS: all-rounder steel; PED-ALS: rubber with reflectors; SADDLE: spring mattress; PRICE: not specified.

LAWEE NOMADE
FRAME: light steel tubing; COLOR: not specified; BRAKES: Wienmann side pull alloy with twin levers; GEARS: 10-speed; FENDERS: none; RIMS: steels; TIRES: 27 x 1¼ inch amber; CHAINGUARD: not specified; HANDLEBARS: Maes bend; PEDALS: Lyotard steel with reflectors; SADDLE: racing; PRICE: not specified.

MIRAGE
FRAME: light steel tubing; COLOR: not specified; BRAKES: Weinmann or Dia-Compe center-pull, alloy with twin levers; GEARS: 10-speed; FENDERS: none; RIMS: steel; TIRES: 27 x 1¼ inch gumwall H.P.; CHAINGUARD: not specified; HANDLEBARS: Maes bend; PEDALS: Lyotard steel with reflectors; SADDLE: racing; PRICE: not specified.

GRAND TOURING
FRAME: light steel 1020 tubing; COLOR: not specified; BRAKES: Weinmann or MAFAC Lux center pull with quick release; GEARS: 10-speed; FENDERS: none; RIMS: alloy; TIRES: 27 x 1¼ gumwall H.P.; CHAINGUARD: not specified; HANDLEBARS: alloy Maes bend; PEDALS: Lyotard alloy; SADDLE: 80 leather with alloy seat post; PRICE: not specified.

GRAND RECORD
FRAME: Reynolds 531 double butted main tubes; COLOR: not specified; BRAKES: Universal 61 center pull with quick release; GEARS: 10-speed; FENDERS: none; RIMS: alloy; TIRES: 27 x 1¼ gumwall H.P.; CHAINGUARD: not specified; HANDLEBARS' alloy Maes bend; PEDALS: Atom 700 alloy; SADDLE: Brooks professional; PRICE: not specified.

THE COLUMBIA MANUFACTURING COMPANY, INC.,
Cycle Street, Westfield, Massachusetts 01085

WOMEN'S HURET TOURIST EXPERT
FRAME: 21 inch; COLORS: radiant mocha, surf white; BRAKES: side-pull caliper; GEARS: 10-speed; FENDERS: chrome; RIMS: 27 inch tubular straight side; TIRES: 27 x 1-1/4 inch. gum sidewall; CHAINGUARD: chrome; HANDLEBARS: touring; PEDALS: reflectors; SADDLE: mattress carriage; PRICE: not specified.

MEN'S HURET 5-SPEED
FRAME: 23 inch; COLORS: radiant blue, surf white; BRAKES: side-pull caliper; GEARS: 5-speed; FENDERS: chrome; RIMS: tubular straight side; TIRES: 27 x 1-1/4 inch gum sidewall; CHAINGUARD: conventional; HANDLEBARS: touring; PEDALS: reflector; SADDLE: mattress carriage; PRICE: not specified.

WOMEN'S HURET 5-SPEED
FRAME: 21 inch; COLORS: radiant blue, surf white, BRAKES: side-pull caliper; GEARS: 5-speed; FENDERS: chrome; RIMS: tubular straight side; TIRES: 27 x 1-1/4 inch gum sidewall; CHAINGUARD: conventional; HANDLEBARS: touring; PEDALS: reflector; SADDLE: mattress carriage; PRICE: not specified.

COLUMBIA MEN'S SA 3-SPEED
FRAME: 23 inch; COLORS: radiant green, surf white; BRAKES: side-pull caliper; GEARS: 3-speed; FENDERS: chrome; RIMS: tubular straight side; TIRES: 27 x 1-1/4 inch gum sidewall; CHAINGUARD: conventional; HANDLEBARS: touring; PEDALS: reflector; SADDLE: mattress carriage; PRICE: not specified.

WOMEN'S SA 3-SPEED
FRAME: 21 inch; COLORS: radiant green, surf white; BRAKES: side-pull caliper; GEARS: 3-speed; FENDERS: chrome; RIMS: tubular straight side; TIRES: 27 x 1-1/4 inch gum sidewall; CHAINGUARD: conventional; HANDLEBARS: touring; PEDALS: reflector; SADDLE: mattress carriage; PRICE not specified.

MEN'S SUPER TOURIST V
FRAME: 21 inch; COLORS: radiant turquoise, radiant copper, black; BRAKES: side-pull caliper; GEARS: 5-speed; FENDERS: chrome plated continental style; RIMS: straight side tubular; TIRES: 26 inch. twin-band white wall; CHAINGUARD: not specified; HANDLEBARS: light road; PEDALS: reflector; SADDLE: mattress carriage; LAMP: ball; CARRIER: spring; PRICE: not specified.

WOMEN'S SUPER TOURIST V
FRAME: 18 inch; COLORS: radiant turquoise, radiant copper, black; BRAKES: side-pull caliper; GEARS: 5-speed; FENDERS: chrome plated continental style; RIMS: straight side tubular; TIRES: 26 inch twin-band white wall; CHAINGUARD: not specified; HANDLEBARS: light road; PEDALS: reflector; SADDLE: mattress carriage; LAMP: ball; CARRIER: spring; PRICE: not specified.

COLUMBIA DELUXE CONVERTIBLE
FRAME: 13 inch tank-type convertibar; COLORS: radiant red, blue; BRAKES: junior coaster; GEARS: single; FENDERS: chrome; RIMS: flat chrome; TIRES: 20 x 1.75 inch black; CHAINGUARD: full length; HANDLEBARS: adjustable Scout; PEDALS: reflector; SADDLE: white, Training wheels; PRICE: not specified.

CRICKET CONVERTIBLE
FRAME: 12 inch tube-type convertibar; COLORS: radiant red, blue; BRAKES: coaster; GEARS: single; FENDERS: chrome; RIMS: flat chrome; TIRES: 16 inch mid-weight; CHAINGUARD: Junior II; HANDLEBARS: adjustable Scout; PEDALS: reflector; SADDLE: white ribbed, Training wheels; PRICE: not specified.

BENDIX SINGLE SPEED TANDEM
FRAME: tandem; COLORS: surf white, goldenrod; BRAKES: Bendix coaster; GEARS: single; FENDERS: chrome; RIMS: hook edge heavy duty; TIRES: 26 x 1.75 inch white sidewall; CHAINGUARD: full length; HANDLEBARS: not specified; PEDALS: reflector; SADDLE: black; PRICE: not specified.

DUOMATIC TWO-SPEED TANDEM
FRAME: tandem; COLORS: surf white, goldenrod; BRAKES: front caliper; GEARS: 2-speed duomatic; FENDERS: chrome; RIMS: hook edge heavy duty; TIRES: 26 x 1.75 inch white sidewall; CHAINGUARD: full length; HANDLEBARS: not specified; PEDALS: reflector; SADDLE: black; PRICE: not specified.

NEWSBOY SPECIAL
FRAME: 18 inch heavy duty; COLORS: radiant red, black trimmed with white; BRAKES: Bendix coaster; GEARS: single; FENDERS: not specified; RIMS: not specified; TIRES: 26 inch heavy duty Goodyear ballon; CHAINGUARD: extra long; HANDLEBARS: box-type; PEDALS: reflector; SADDLE: deluxe black padded; PRICE: not specified.

COLUMBIA UNICYCLE
FRAME: heavy duty; COLOR: radiant red; TIRE: 24 inch pneumatic; RIM: chrome; SADDLE: two-tone crescent-formed. Adjustable seat post, Chrome plated folding stand; PRICE: not specified.

GIRL'S SUPER COASTER
FRAME: 3-bar; COLORS: surf white, radiant cyclamen; BRAKES: coaster; GEARS: single; FENDERS: chrome; RIMS: flat chrome; TIRES: 1.75 inch, twin white band sidewalls, slick rear tead; CHAINGUARD: not specified; HANDLEBARS: hi-rise; PEDALS: reflectorized; SADDLE: flowered white; BASKET: flower decorated; PRICE: not specified.

COLUMBIA RACER X
FRAME: 21, 23 inches; COLORS: surf white, radiant copper; BRAKES: caliper; GEARS: Hyret Allvit 10-speed; FENDERS: not specified; RIMS: straight-side tubular chrome; TIRES: gum sidewall racing; CHAINGUARD: chrome; HANDLEBARS: Maes racing; PEDALS: rattrap all-steel reflector; SADDLE: black racing; PRICE: not specified.

MEN'S HURET TOURIST EXPERT
FRAME: 23 inch; COLORS: radiant mocha, surf white; BRAKES: side-pull caliper; GEARS: 10-speed; FENDERS: chrome; RIMS: 27 inch tubular straight side; TIRES: 27 x 1-1/4 inch. gum sidewall; CHAINGUARD: chrome; HANDLEBARS: touring; PEDALS: reflector; SADDLE: mattress carriage; PRICE: not specified.

COLUMBIA BOY'S DELUXE COASTER
FRAME: not specified; COLOR: radiant mocha; BRAKES: coaster; GEARS: single; FENDERS: chrome; RIMS: not specified; TIRES: 20 x 1.75 inch; CHAINGUARD: full length; HANDLEBARS: hi-rise; PEDALS: reflector; SADDLE: frame matching with 3 inch reflector; PRICE: not specified.

GIRL'S DELUXE SPECIAL COASTER
FRAME: not specified; COLOR: radiant green; BRAKES: coaster; GEARS: single; FENDERS: chrome; RIMS: not specified; TIRES: 20 x 1.75 inch; CHAINGUARD: full length; HANDLEBARS: Jr. hi-rise; PEDALS: reflector; SADDLE: frame matching with 3 inch reflector; PRICE: not specified.

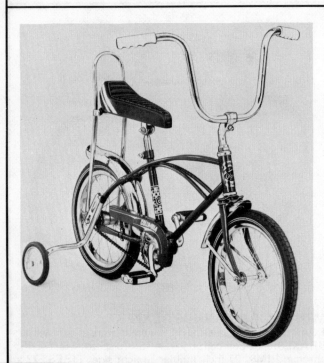

ADULT 3-WHEELER TAKE-APART
FRAME: 1-1/2 inch steel tubing; COLOR: tangerine; BRAKES: Bendix coaster; GEARS: single; FENDERS: chrome; RIMS: flat hook; TIRES: 20 x 1.75 inch; CHAINGUARD: chrome; HANDLEBARS: chrome; PEDALS: not specified; SADDLE: deluxe heavy duty with 2 inch reflector, Jumbo basket; PRICE: not specified.

BOY'S JUNIOR PLAYBIKE
FRAME: 12 inch four bar; COLOR: radiant green; BRAKES: coaster; GEARS: single; FENDERS: chrome; RIMS: chrome; TIRES: 16 x 1.75 inch twin white band; CHAINGUARD: not specified; HANDLEBARS: Jr. hi-rise; PEDALS: reflector; SADDLE: frame matching, Training wheels; PRICE: not specified.

COLUMBIA MIDDLEWEIGHT STERLING
FRAME: not specified; COLOR: radiant red; BRAKES: Bendix coaster; GEARS: single; FENDERS: enamel; RIMS: chrome; TIRES: 26 x 1.75 inch black; CHAINGUARD: decorated; HANDLEBARS: not specified; PEDALS: reflector; SADDLE: white; PRICE: not specified.

GIRL'S MIDDLEWEIGHT STERLING
FRAME: not specified; COLOR: radiant blue; BRAKES: Bendix coaster; GEARS: single; FENDERS: enamel; RIMS: chrome; TIRES: 26 x 1.75 inch black; CHAINGUARD: decorated; HANDLEBARS: not specified; PEDALS: reflector; SADDLE: white; PRICE: not specified.

BOY'S DELUXE RAMBLER
FRAME: 13 inch; COLOR: radiant red; BRAKES: junior coaster; GEARS: single; FENDERS: chrome; RIMS: flat chrome; TIRES: 20 x 1.75 inch black; CHAINGUARD: full length; HANDLEBARS: adjustable Scout; PEDALS: reflector; SADDLE: white; PRICE: not specified.

GIRL'S DELUXE RAMBLER
FRAME: 13 inch; COLOR: radiant turquoise; BRAKES: junior coaster; GEARS: single; FENDERS: chrome; RIMS: flat chrome; TIRES: 20 x 1.75 inch black; CHAINGUARD: full length; HANDLEBARS: adjustable Scout; PEDALS: reflector; SADDLE: white; PRICE: not specified.

COLUMBIA GIRL'S SPORT III
FRAME:15 inch; COLOR: radiant red; BRAKES: front caliper; GEARS: 3-speed Sturmey-Archer; FENDERS: not specified; RIMS: not specified; TIRES: 24 inch; CHAINGUARD: full formed; HANDLEBARS: not specified; PEDALS: reflector; SADDLE: not specified; PRICE: not specified.

ROADSTER JUNIOR
FRAME: 16 inch; COLOR: radiant blue; BRAKES: lightweight coaster; GEARS: single; FENDERS: not specified; RIMS: Not specified; TIRES: 20 inch; CHAINGUARD: full formed; HANDLE-BARS: not specified; PEDALS: reflector; SADDLE: Junior lightweight; PRICE: not specified.

SUPER 5-SPEED
FRAME: four-bar; COLORS: radiant dusty gold, surf white; BRAKES: front and rear caliper; GEARS: 5-speed; FENDERS: chrome; RIMS: not specified; TIRES: 20 x 2.125 inch dual band white sidewall rear, 20 x 1.75 inch middleweight front; CHAIN-GUARD: full length; HANDLEBARS: hi-rise; PEDALS: reflector; SADDLE: deluxe ribbed; PRICE: not specified.

SUPER 3-SPEED
FRAME: four-bar; COLORS: goldenrod, radiant blue; BRAKES: front and rear caliper; GEARS: 3-speed Sturmey-Archer; FEND-ERS: chrome; RIMS: not specified; TIRES: 20 x 2.125 inch dual band white sidewall rear, 20 x 1.75 inch middleweight front; CHAINGUARD: full length; HANDLEBARS: hi-rise; PEDALS: reflector; SADDLE: deluxe ribbed; PRICE: not specified.

COLUMBIA SUPER COASTER BRAKE
FRAME: four-bar; COLORS: tangerine, surf white; BRAKES: coaster; GEARS: single; FENDERS: chrome; RIMS: not specified; TIRES: 20 x 2.125 inch dual band white sidewall rear, 10 x 1.75 inch middleweight front; CHAINGUARD: full length; HANDLE-BARS: hi-rise; PEDALS: reflector; SADDLE: deluxe ribbed; PRICE: not specified.

GIRL'S SUPER 3-SPEED
FRAME: three-bar; COLORS: goldenrod, mod blue; BRAKES: front and rear caliper; GEARS: 3-speed Sturmey-Archer; FEND-ERS: chrome; RIMS: flat chrome; TIRES: 1.75 inch twin band sidewalls; CHAINGUARD: full length; HANDLEBARS: Jr. hi-rise; PEDALS: reflector; SADDLE: white flowered; BASKET: white decorated; PRICE: not specified.

BOY'S DELUXE SPECIAL
FRAME: not specified; COLOR: radiant mocha; BRAKES: front and rear caliper; GEARS: 3- speed; FENDERS: chrome; RIMS: not specified; TIRES: 20 x 1.75 inch; CHAINGUARD: full length; HANDLEBARS: hi-rise; PEDALS: reflector; SADDLE: frame matching with 3 inch reflector; PRICE: not specified.

GIRL'S DELUXE SPECIAL
FRAME: not speicified; COLOR: radiant green; BRAKES: front and rear caliper; GEARS: 3-speed; FENDERS: chrome; RIMS: not specified; TIRES: 20 x 1.75 inch; CHAINGUARD: full length; HANDLEBARS: Jr. hi-rise; PEDALS: reflector; SADDLE: frame matching with 3 inch reflector; PRICE: not specified.

COLUMBIA MODEL 3618 3-SPEED - 26" WHEEL, 21" FRAME

COLUMBIA MODEL 4618 - 3-SPEED - 26" WHEEL, 18" FRAME

COLUMBIA MEN'S DELUXE TOURIST

FRAME: 21 inch; COLORS: radiant mocha, goldenrod, black; BRAKES: side-pull caliper; GEARS: 3-speed; FENDERS: chrome, continental; RIMS: straight side tubular; TIRES: 26 inch, duo-band white widewall; CHAINGUARD: full formed; HANDLEBARS: light road; PEDALS: reflector; SADDLE: black, deluxe padded mattress; LAMP: ball; CARRIER: spring; PRICE: not specified.

WOMEN'S DELUXE TOURIST

FRAME' 18 inch; COLORS: radiant mocha, goldenrod, black; BRAKES: side-pull caliper; GEARS: 3-speed; FENDERS: chrome, continental; RIMS:straight side tubular; TIRES: 26 inch, duo-band white sidewall; CHAINGUARD: full formed; HANDLEBARS: light road; PEDALS: reflector; SADDLE: black, deluxe padded mattress; LAMP: ball; CARRIER: spring; PRICE: not specified.

MEN'S SPORTS TOURIST

FRAME: 21 inch; COLORS: radiant blue, surf white, black; BRAKES: side-pull caliper; GEARS: 3-speed; FENDERS: enamel; RIMS: straight side tubular; TIRES: 26 inch balckwall; CHAINGUARD: full formed; HANDLEBARS: light road; PEDALS: reflector; SADDLE: standard lightweight; PRICE: not specified.

MEN'S TCW SPORTS TOURIST COASTER

FRAME: 21 inch; COLORS: radiant mocha, dusty gold; BRAKES: front caliper; GEARS: 3-speed Sturmey-Archer; FENDERS: not specified; RIMS: not specified; TIRES: 26 inch; CHAINGUARD: full formed; HANDLEBARS: light road; PEDALS: reflector; SADDLE: not specified; PRICE: not specified.

COLUMBIA WOMEN'S TCW SPORTS TOURIST
FRAME: 18 inch; COLORS: radiant mocha, dusty gold; BRAKES: front caliper; GEARS: 3-speed Sturmey-Archer; FENDERS: not specified; RIMS: not specified; RIMS: not specified; TIRES: 26 inch; CHAINGUARD: full formed; HANDLEBARS: light road; PEDALS: reflector; SADDLE: not specified; PRICE: not specified.

MEN'S ROADSTER COASTER
FRAME: 21 inch; COLOR: radiant blue; BRAKES: Bendix coaster; GEARS: single; FENDERS: not specified; RIMS: not specified; TIRES: 26 inch; CHAINGUARD: full formed; HANDLEBARS: not specified; PEDALS: reflector; SADDLE: not specified; PRICE: not specified.

WOMEN'S ROADSTER COASTER
FRAME: 18 inch; COLOR: radiant blue; BRAKES: Bendix coaster; GEARS: single; FENDERS: not specified; RIMS: not specified; TIRES: 26 inch; CHAINGUARD: full formed; HANDLEBARS: not specified; PEDALS: reflector; SADDLE: not specified; PRICE: not specified.

BOY'S SPORTS III
FRAME: 17 inch; COLOR: radiant red; BRAKES: front caliper; GEARS: 3-speed Sturmey-Archer; FENDERS: not specified; RIMS: not specified; TIRES: 24 inch; CHAINGUARD: full formed; HANDLEBARS: not specified; PEDALS: reflector; SADDLE: not specified; PRICE: not specified.

accessories

tHERE CAN, AND HAVE BEEN, entire volumes directed toward accessories available to the bicyclist. Most major bicycle companies have lists of accessories they have developed included in the catalogs; others, like Shimano American, have catalogs specifically filled with items they procure and market from many Japanese corporations affiliated with them.

What follows is basically a sampling from some of the corporations that responded to a request for information and photographs of accessories they are known to market. Unfortunately for the reader of this and other bicycle-related books, the showing is far from complete or even adequate. Most manufacturers are riding the high tide of big item sales caused by the bicycle boom, and perhaps for this reason felt no need for the free advertising space.

I regret that this feeling is prevalent in the industry, and that this accessory section is somewhat limited. However, shown is a sampling of some items available to bicycle riders, and information can be obtained from writing the manufacturers listed at its conclusion.

An electric power assist for bicycles provides power when pedaling gets rough. Plans include detailed drawings and a list of suppliers for the major parts. Plans from F. J. Kielian.

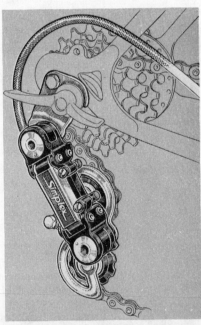

Simplex Prestige derailleur has a 37-tooth capacity, operates on three to six speed freewheels. Rear mechanism fits standard fork end.

Goodyear Double Eagle is designed for quick stops and starts. It has contoured shoulders for tight cornering. Available in 26, 24 or 20 inch sizes.

Goodyear's Grasshopper Slick is specifically for rear wheel stamina, takes the hard braking and fast starts of a hard-digging rider. Comes in 20 inch only.

Goodyear's hook bead rib tire is made of 3-T nylon cord and forms a flexible cushion with minimum bulk. Tufsyn rubber in the tread makes the hook bead rib strong and durable. Blackwall, 26 and 24 inch sizes.

TOTE-A-TOT molded plastic, one-piece unit lets little one ride in security and comfort. Restraining strap and foot rest permit relaxed riding. Seat mounts close to handlebars or saddle for ease in handling. From Wall Mfg. Co.

Goodyear straight side rib tire provides swift rolling, easy pedaling and long-lasting protection against cuts and impact bruises. Fits most American and British lightweight bicycles. Five sizes in blackwall, 27 and 26 inch in whitewall.

Goodyear lightweight rib tire, with sporty tan sidewalls, is made with nylon cord fabric and natural rubber tread for jackrabbit starts and low-friction roll. 27x1-1/4 and 26x1-3/8 inches.

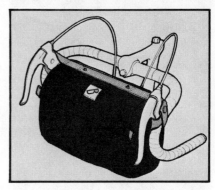

Cannondale Corp. — Handlebar Pack is of waterproof nylon, contains map case, liner, internal pockets and zipper. Mounts easily between handlebars, does not impede brake levers or rider comfort. Colors are international orange and Cal blue.

accessories

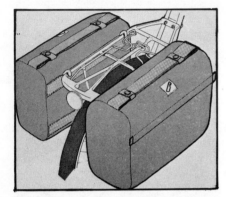

Cannondale Corp. — Waterproofed nylon Rack Pack has capacity and convenience, does not restrict use of rack as carrier. Plastic-covered hooks protect painted surfaces and offset mounting provides pedal clearance. Carrying handle opens into full shoulder strap as off-bike pack. In international orange and Cal blue.

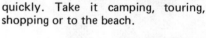

Cannondale Corporation's Bugger is designed to carry your gear with ease. It attaches to any lightweight bicycle quickly. Take it camping, touring, shopping or to the beach.

Troxel's new deluxe baby carrier mounts to rear frame of any 26 or 27-inch bicycle. Thick foam padding and soft vinyl covering insures comfort.

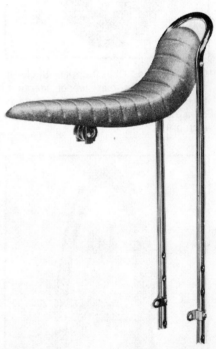

Troxel Hi-Back seat has dragster appeal. Upsweep back is a full 6 inches above seating area and sweeps down to a long, lean nose. Comes in glitter colors, black, white or flower power design.

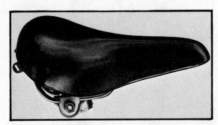

Troxel models 375 and 378 have chrome wire truss with molded leather-grain top, plus adjustable clamp. Fit all foreign and domestic bikes.

BIKE SAFE flag is an 8x18-inch triangular fluorescent flag, is light and inexpensive, easily installed, rides high above bicycle and signals of rider's presence even when hidden by traffic, dips and obstructions.

accessories

Troxel model 32 is contoured for comfort for the adult market. Fits foreign and domestic designs. Extra-wide seating area, quality spring assembly and foam padded. Comes in white and black or standard two-tone.

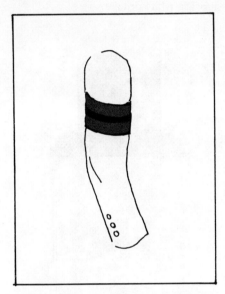

Fluorescent armbands provide visibility protection for cyclists, from Safety Flag Co. of America.

This solid-color fluorescent Day-Glo blaze orange vest offers excellent daytime visibility protection. From Safety Flag Co. of America.

SOUNDLOCK alarm system helps eliminate theft. It is lightweight, compact, weather resistant, of solid state construction has adjustable sensitivity, automatic silence/reset. From Paul W. Beggs & Son, Incorporated.

Goodyear tubes are made of finest butyl compounds, precision molded for perfect fit and have durable Lock-Flange valve.

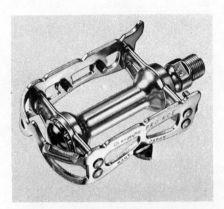

KYOKUTO PRO ACE (ROAD) professional racing pedal made of strong forged light alloy body, special steel alloy steel side plates. Spinning parts highly resistant to friction, long service life. Toe clip and strap attachable. From Shimano American.

KYOKUTO TOE CLIP comes in small, medium, large and extra large, is made of special steel C.P. and weighs 100 grains. From Shimano American.

THREE ARROWS all steel double chainwheel and crank with alternate teeth sprockets. Size outer chainwheel, 52 (26T) or 50 (25T) teeth only, inner chainwheel 40, 39 or 36 teeth. From Shimano American.

accessories

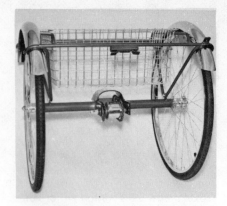

THREE ARROWS chain guards are chome plated finish for 48 or 50 teeth chain sprocket: From Shimano American.

Thunder Bird front derailleur made of steel is upper and lower inlet type and has pantograph mechanism. Crane G.S. rear derailleur has a capacity up to 38 teeth with Servo pantograph mechanism, weighs 9.5 ounces. From Shimano American.

New Gobby model 500 conversion kit easily installs on bicycle. Wheels are always in line and come with chrome fenders, rims, basket, coaster or 3-speed brakes, two wheels, tires and tubes in white or blue.

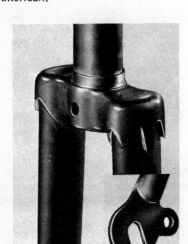

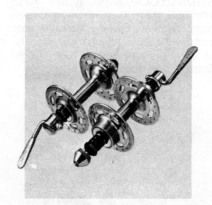

Quick release hub has large flange, spokes for 36 x 36 holes. From Shimano American.

FRONT FORKS for sports bikes have butted column and oval blades with solid ends. From Shimano American.

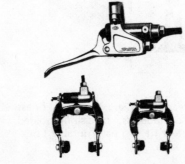
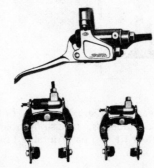

World champion Randnner handlebars, made of steel with 15½-inch width, 4½-inch curve and a diameter of 15/16-inch. From Shimano American.

Shimano power brake is oil pressure braking system using pressure from master cylinder through fluid lines to front and rear wheel cylinders. Comes complete with pressed steel arms, specially shaped solid levers and tubes.

HALT! dog repellent comes in 3/4 or 1-1/2-ounce sizes, both with adjustable clip cap. Used by U.S. Postal Service HALT! is not injurious to dog, shoots a stream up to 12 feet, safe for humans. From Animal Repellents, Incorporated.

RADIO RACK holds all standard transistors, fits all style handlebars and adjusts to any position. Constructed of high impact plastic, with rust-proof steel mounting bracket. From Bright Star Industries, Incorporated.

SAFETY ZONE KIT combines bike light and giant relfector. Has wide track beam, snaps out for flashlight use, unbreakable, won't dent or corrode. Complete with clamp to fit all bike handlebars. From Bright Star Industries, Incorporated.

Hoop hangers store bikes off the floor in apartments and homes; can be used as repair stand for minor adjustments.

Bicycles can be locked to Hoop Hanger. From Good Earth Associates.

Hoop rack solves transportation problem, adapts to any rear bumper, easily detached, adds beauty in gold, chip-proof epoxy finish. From Good Earth Associates.

accessories

JCI Bicycle Exerciser Kit is easy to assemble and mount. Constructed of one-inch chrome plated steel tubing. Converts bicycles to exercisers in just a few minutes. Compact, lightweight, ideal for home or office.

JCI Roof-top Bicycle Carrier is designed to carry up to four bicycles. Sturdy steel construction, zinc plated for corrosion resistance. Will carry all types of bicycles. Easy to assemble and install, fits all vehicles with rain gutters. Kit includes supertuf chain and fittings to secure carrier and bicycles to car.

JCI Cycle Lugger is versatile, dual purpose utility rack. Will carry two bicycles or luggage. Made from one-inch chrome plated steel tubing, kit is easy to assemble and install. May be permanently mounted.

JCI Cycle Caddies are designed to carry two bicycles in complete safety, easy to assemble. Fits most cars with adaptive fittings supplied free for hard-to-fit bumpers. Available in 29 or 36-inch heights, choice of chrome or vinyl finish.

accessories

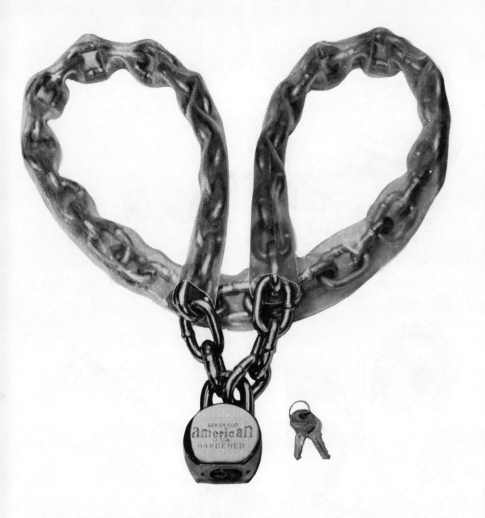

CYC-L-LOC has many locking positions: wheel to wheel, wheel to frame, bike to pole, bike to rack and others. Eliminates heavy chains and padlocks. Telescoping slide action, hardened steel, vinyl coated, lightweight, easily transported. From Engineering Graphics Corporation.

American Lock Company — Vinyl sleeve covers this extra heavy duty alloy steel Hercules chain. Five-pin tumbler padlock, case and shackle constructed of hardened, chrome plated steel. Includes two keys.

Oxford Pop-Art basket of woven plastic comes 14x8½x8.

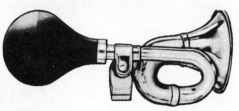

Oxford Bugle Horns in chrome or brass have two tones. Sizes, 8-5/8x2-7/8 inches.

American Lock Company — Hercules Jr., a 3/16-inch hardened alloy steel chain has heavy vinyl sleeve to prevent scratching. Available in three, four and six-foot lengths.

SWING-A-WAY bike racks have flush wall mount, pivots for display examination, designed for safety from rolling or falling over. Doubles floor space. Handy for home storage unit. Accommodates all lightweight bicycles 24-inch wheel size and larger. From Alco Cycle Products, Incorporated.

accessories

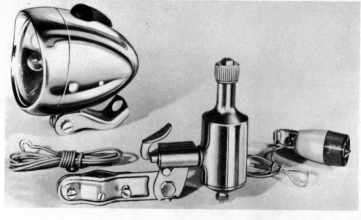

Oxford one-cell taillight with red lens has universal swivel bracket. Made of high polish anodized aluminum.

Oxford generator set is two-bulb set complete with generator, headlight with hi-low beam and taillight. Made in Japan.

Three inch diameter swivel mirror by Oxford has ball joint and jewel reflector set in back. True-Vision glass.

Oxford English pump comes complete with frame clamps. Chrome plated, 15 inch length. Valve depressor pin included.

Oxford Pop-Art 3-1/2-inch flowers come three per package, one each of blue, yellow, pink. Individual mounting wires. For baskets, wheels, other decorative uses.

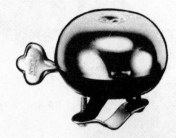

Oxford chrome plated deluxe bell is 2-1/4-inch diameter, with universal bracket.

Oxford cyclometer has accurate front wheel mileage meter. Comes in three sizes, 20, 26 and 27 inch.

accessories

The Oxford giant touring bag is of black vinyl with side pockets, in size 13x7x-1/2 inch.

Oxford Waterproof plastic material storage cover is specially designed to cover bicycles and small motorcycles with tie-down wheel strings. Made in Hong Kong.

Chrome top handle bar mounting electric horn. Operates from one "C" flashlight battery. Direct "top-touch" button. Loud warning sound. Pack-Poly bag with header. 10 per inner ctn. 100 per shipping ctn. Weight 47 lbs.

Chrome plated tail light with remote control handlebar switch. Use as constant tail light or directional turn signal. Operates from two "C" flashlight batteries.

accessory manufacturers index

Derailleur Le Simplex, Cycle Division,
75 rue General-Fauconnet,
Dijon 21, France

Goodyear Tire & Rubber Company,
Cycle Tire Department, Box C-801,
New Bedford, Massachusetts 02741

Wall Manufacturing Company,
1912 East Catalpa,
Springfield, Missouri 65804

American Lock Company,
Crete, Illinois 60417

Cannondale Corporation,
35 Pulaski Street,
Stamford, Connecticut 06902

Bike Safe,
P.O. Box 1005,
Marion, Indiana 46952

Troxel Manufacturing Company,
Moscow, Tennessee 38057

Safety Flag Company of America,
390 Pine Street,
Pawtucket, Rhode Island 02862

Paul W. Beggs & Son, Incorporated,
P.O. Box 5508,
San Mateo, California 94402

Goodyear Tire & Rubber Company,
Akron, Ohio 44316

Shimano American,
1133 Avenue of the Americas,
New York, New York 10036

Gobby Manufacturing, Incorporated,
P.O. Box 274,
Glendale, Arizona 85301

Animal Repellents, Incorporated,
P.O. Box 168,
Griffin, Georgia 30223

Bright Star Industries, Incorporated,
600 Getty Avenue,
Clifton, New Jersey 07015

Good Earth Associates,
17221 South Western Avenue,
Gardena, California 90247

JCI,
904 South Nogales Street,
City of Industry, California 91744

ALCO Cycle Products, Incorporated,
451 3d Street S.E.,
Largo, Florida 33540

Engineering Graphic Corporation,
82 Aero Camino,
Goleta, California 93017

Oxford International Corporation,
777 Central Avenue,
Highland Park, Illinois 60035

F. J. Kielian
Specialty Merchandising
130 Drake Avenue
So. San Francisco, CA 94080

287